UNDERSTANDING

TERRORISM

UNDERSTANDING TERRORISM

Groups, Strategies, and Responses

JAMES M. POLAND
California State University
Sacramento

Prentice Hall
Englewood Cliffs, N.J. 07632

LIBRARY OF CONGRESS
Library of Congress Cataloging-in-Publication Data

Poland, James M., 1937–
    Understanding terrorism : groups, strategies, and responses / by
James M. Poland.
        p. cm.
    Bibliography: p.
    Includes index.
    ISBN 0–13–936113–8
    1. Terrorism. 2. Terrorism—Prevention. I. Title.
HV6431.P6 1988
303.6′25—dc19

Editorial/production supervision and
  interior design: Margaret Lepera
Cover design: Ben Santora
Manufacturing buyer: Peter Havens

 © 1988 by Prentice-Hall, Inc.
A Division of Simon & Schuster
Englewood Cliffs, New Jersey 07632

Printed in the United States of America
10 9 8 7 6

ISBN   0-13-936113-8

Prentice-Hall International (UK) Limited, *London*
Prentice-Hall of Australia Pty. Limited, *Sydney*
Prentice-Hall Canada Inc., *Toronto*
Prentice-Hall Hispanoamericana, S.A., *Mexico*
Prentice-Hall of India Private Limited, *New Delhi*
Prentice-Hall of Japan, Inc., *Tokyo*
Simon & Schuster Asia Pte. Ltd., *Singapore*
Editora Prentice-Hall do Brasil, Ltda., *Rio de Janeiro*

To Barbara, Amanda, and Michael

CONTENTS

PREFACE   ix

ACKNOWLEDGMENTS   xiii

CHAPTER 1   **CONCEPTS OF TERROR AND TERRORISM**   1

Introduction, 1
Definitional Problems and Terrorism, 2
Morality of Terrorism, 5
Definitions of Terrorism, 9
Terrorist Typologies, 11
Terrorist Atrocities, 16
Purpose of Terrorism, 18
Conclusions, 19
Review Questions, 21

CHAPTER 2   **HISTORICAL ANTECEDENTS OF VIOLENCE
AND TERRORISM**   22

Introduction, 22
Sicarii and Zealots, 23
The Assassins and Other Secret Societies, 25
Narodnaya Volya, 29
The Anarchist Tradition, 33

Terrorism and Violence in the United States, 36
Conclusions, 42
Review Questions, 43

**CHAPTER 3   VIOLENCE AND TERORRISM:
THE ROLE OF THE MASS MEDIA   44**

Introduction, 44
Contagion Theory, or The Copycat Syndrome, 45
Propaganda Value and the "Deed," 50
Law Enforcement and the Media, 61
Censorship and Terrorism, 64
Conclusions, 67
Review Questions, 68

**CHAPTER 4   THE U.S. EXPERIENCE:
DOMESTIC TERRORIST GROUPS   69**

Introduction, 69
Puerto Rican Independence, 72
Armenian Nationalism, 76
Croatian Separatists, 81
Anti-Castro Cubans, 85
Jewish Defense League (JDL), 88
Revolutionary Armed Task Force (RATF):
    The Ideological Left, 89
The Ideological Right, 93
Conclusions, 96
Review Questions, 96

**CHAPTER 5   INTERNATIONAL TERRORISM:
THE MIDEAST AND WESTERN EUROPE   98**

Introduction, 98
Palestine Resistance Movement, 99
Historical Antecedents, 99
Palestine Liberation Organization (PLO), 102
Palestinian Extremism and the 1973 War, 103
Rejectionist Front, 105
Invasion of Lebanon, 106
The Irish Republican Army (IRA), 109
Historical Tradition of Insurrection, 110
Northern Ireland After Partition, 113
IRA Gunman Take Over, 114

Protestant Paramilitary Groups, 115
Western Europe, 118
Conclusions, 119
Review Questions, 122

**CHAPTER 6   THE DYNAMICS OF HOSTAGE-TAKING
AND NEGOTIATION   123**

Introduction, 123
Early History of Hostage-Taking, 124
Typologies of Hostage-Takers, 126
Time, Trust, and the Stockholm Syndrome, 129
Guidelines for Hostage Events, 132
Kidnapping and Terrorism, 135
Surviving Hostage Situations, 138
Conclusions, 141
Review Questions, 142

CHAPTER 7   CONTEMPORARY TERRORISM AND BOMBING   143

Introduction, 143
Historical Perspective, 145
Effects of an Explosion, 147
Velocity and Explosives, 151
Vehicle Bombs, 153
Letter Bombs, 158
Bombings Aboard Aircraft, 160
Conclusions, 163
Review Questions, 164

CHAPTER 8   ASSASSINATION AND POLITICAL MURDER   165

Introduction, 165
What is Assassination?, 167
Types of Assassination, 168
Assassination in the Middle East, 172
Assassination in the United States, 178
Conclusions, 189
Review Questions, 190

**CHAPTER 9   COUNTERTERRORIST MEASURES:
THE RESPONSE   191**

Introduction, 191
Security Measures, 193

Intelligence Function, 195
Counterterrorist Operations, Retaliation,
    and Preemption, 199
Covert Military Operations: Proactive
    Measures, 203
Counterterrorist Operations: Reactive
    Measures, 205
Legal Framework: Apprehension, Prosecution,
    and Punishment, 210
Conclusions, 216
Review Questions, 217

CHAPTER 10   **FUTURE OF TERRORISM**   **218**

Introduction, 218
Israel versus Palestinian Resistance Movement, 220
Islamic Extremism, 223
Low-Intensity Warfare, 227
Super Terrorism, 231
Influence of Terrorism on Democracy, 238
Conclusions, 241
Review Questions, 242

BIBLIOGRAPHY   **243**

INDEX   **256**

1) Definition of teasrism
Terrorism & media/USA

PREFACE

Understanding Terrorism: Groups, Strategies, and Responses presents the essential lessons contained in the books, articles, and terrorist literature that have had the greatest impact upon the analysis of the terrorist strategy. The text is a synthesis in the respect that it brings together the divergent theories and methods that make up this dynamic field of scholarly inquiry. The book offers the various analytical approaches to the study of terrorism that identifies terrorist groups, reviews terrorist tactics, and examines police and governmental responses to reduce or eliminate the incidence of terrorism.

The text is written for all those who will have to deal with future terrorist events and who today are struggling to understand the motivation of contemporary terrorist groups. This list includes criminal justice students, professionals in the criminal justice system, and any student wishing to gain more information on the phenomenon of "terrorism." To be well informed about terrorism, students and professionals in the field must be familiar with the concepts, techniques, and theories drawn from political science, social psychology, and sociology as well as from the traditional criminal justice literature. The scholars who have assembled the knowledge on terrorism are obliged to relate their concepts of terrorism to the solution of the terrorist problem. The students and professionals in the field who must eventually confront the problem of terrorism are expected to keep up with new developments in terrorist theory and strategies, and to possess special training, knowledge, and skills. Future trends indicate the necessity of increasing personal and scholarly awareness of the threat of terrorism to democratic states. Thus, it is hoped that this book provides the information and knowledge to understand better the concept of terrorism.

However, terrorism must be kept in perspective. The terrorist threat is in reality a multiplicity of real and imagined threats, each originating from a different source and each presenting a separate set of tactical and political problems. For example, the military retaliatory bombing raid against Libya for allegedly assisting in terrorist attacks against American targets in Europe was viewed as deterrent retaliation. At the same time, few policymakers would suggest that the U.S. military send F-111 bombers to attack the headquarters of the KKK, the Order, or PLO base camps in Lebanon. In addition, the number of people killed and injured every year by terrorists must be kept in perspective. In the United States, for instance, the State Department has recorded the deaths of 26 terrorist victims between 1979 and 1986. Compare these figures with the approximately 160,000 recorded homicides during the same period. The fact is that most terrorists are not career criminals, insane fanatics, or government surrogates, but ordinary individuals driven to violence by what they see as unacceptable social conditions or by radical political beliefs.

Clearly, the most confounding problem in the study of terrorism is arriving at a definition acceptable to all. Few people want to be called terrorists; terrorism is essentially what the other side has done. This is why there is no satisfactory political definition and no common academic consensus as to the essence of terrorism. For example, were the bombers of the Marine Compound in Beirut "terrorist criminals" or heroic "freedom fighters?" Which terms best describe the Nicaraguan contras or Afghan rebels? Where there is political consensus, problems of definition are moot. Where there is no political consensus, definitions have a tendency to polarize differences. Ours are freedom fighters and commandos; yours are terrorist fanatics. So numerous are the definitions of terrorism proposed by scholars and policymakers that recently the focus has shifted to the intimidation of "soft" civilian targets as an "unbiased" technique for defining terrorism. This textbook presents and compares several of the more popular definitions in the belief that each contributes to the growth of new knowledge.

The plan of the book is presented in the following manner. The fundamental concepts and theories of terrorism are summarized in Chapter 1. Chapter 2 briefly outlines the historical antecedents of "terrorism." In Chapter 3 the role of the media in contributing to the increase in terrorism is examined. Terrorist groups active in the United States are reviewed in Chapter 4, and Chapter 5 outlines two important case studies. The Palestine question and the Northern Ireland troubles are analyzed to provide knowledge on terrorist motivation, structural organization of extremist or terrorist groups, and terrorist strategies. Chapter 6 provides an overview of hostage-taking and negotiation. In Chapter 7 the reader is introduced to the techniques of explosive materials. The terrorist tactic of assassination is explored in Chapter 8. Chapter 9 explains the analytic, political, legal, scientific, and behavioral responses that government policymakers have used to attack and solve the problem of terrorism. Finally, Chapter 10 attempts to look into the future and delineate potential areas of terrorism, such as nuclear terrorism and Islamic extremism. The influence of terrorism on democratic states is also analyzed in terms of changes that might be anticipated as a result of a prolonged campaign of terrorism in a democracy.

As with most controversial subjects, the author must wrestle with his own bias and prejudice. I have done my utmost to present an unbiased, balanced view of contemporary terrorism in the modern world. This project was undertaken at the request of criminal justice students who continually complained that the literature on terrorism was overwhelming and confusing. I only hope that I have not added to that confusion. So we begin, as have previous scholars, with a systematic probe into the uncertain world of contemporary terrorism.

JP
Sacramento

ACKNOWLEDGMENTS

I want to thank my family: my wife, Barbara, who typed the entire manuscript from a tangle of handwritten pages, encouraging and criticizing as she reviewed each page, and my children, who contributed indispensable encouragement along with some penetrating critiques.

I am also indebted for general analytical comments to the students of "Violence and Terrorism," Criminal Justice Division, California State University, Sacramento.

UNDERSTANDING

TERRORISM

■ONE

CONCEPTS OF TERROR
AND TERRORISM

CHAPTER OBJECTIVES

The study of this chapter will enable you to:
■ Explore several definitions of terrorism
■ Review several typologies of terrorism
■ Discuss the purposes of terrorism
■ Construct a basic typology of terrorism
■ Appreciate the difficulty of law enforcement in dealing with terrorism
■ Reflect on the moral justification of terrorism

INTRODUCTION

In recent years, small groups labeled as insurgents, rebels, social revolutionaries, armies of national liberation, guerrillas, commandos, and freedom fighters have demonstrated repeatedly that certain tactics of random violence can achieve effects on democratic societies that often produce overwhelming fear. Such violent tactics attract the media, which ensures immediate worldwide publicity and often can cause democratic governments to overreact by "tightening security." The result of this tactical violence has been the gradual erosion of human rights and civil liberties in many parts of the world. For example, according to Sterling, the Tupamaros "deliberately killed democracy" by engaging in acts of indiscriminate terrorism that swept through Uruguay in the late 1960s and early 1970s.[1] As a result of this "terrorism," the military seized power and established their own reign of state "terror" in 1973. Uruguay is a remarkable example of a democratic government being replaced by totalitarian rule. Political parties were banned, all citizens were required to register with the military regime, the press was tightly controlled, and thousands of people became "political" prisoners. This reign of terror lasted for 12 years. By April 1985 Uruguay finally returned to democracy.

Other examples of civil and human rights violations can be found in Northern Ireland. The continued escalation of terrorism in Northern Ireland forced the British Parliament to abolish the government of Northern Ireland and to impose direct rule and implement emergency powers.[2] Along with direct rule and emergency powers came warrantless searches, seizures and arrests, the abolishment of jury trials, and internment.[3] In Canada, terrorism caused the government to invoke the War Measures Act of 1970, which temporarily abolished many civil liberties including warrantless searches and arrests.[4] The Canadian government took these extreme measures in response to a double political kidnapping and a campaign of indiscriminate bombing by the Front for the Liberation of Quebec (FLQ). In Turkey, Syria, Iraq, Bolivia, Peru, Chile, and Argentina, brutal military dictatorships have replaced parliamentary government after organized terrorist groups conducted a campaign of indiscriminate random terrorism. In many countries, terrorism by insurgent minorities has been replaced by governmental "terror." The cycle of terrorist violence, military repressions, and vengeance is now quite commonplace. Thus, these facts alone create a need for a vigorous academic analysis of the use of terrorism and terror to achieve a political objective. The function of the criminal justice system is to maintain the balance between liberty and law enforcement. This paradox is crucial to the effective management of law and order in our future society.

Definitional Problems and Terrorism

The first analytical task facing scholars on terrorism is to define the term. At first glance the definition of terrorism appears straightforward. Being held

---

[1]Claire Sterling, *The Terror Network: The Secret War of International Terrorism* (New York: Holt, Rinehart, and Winston, 1980), pp. 18-23.

[2]Alfred L. McClung, *Terrorism in Northern Ireland* (New York: General Hall, 1983), pp. 224-27.

[3]Ibid., pp. 59-74.

[4]Jan Schreiber, *The Ultimate Weapon: Terrorists and World Order* (New York: Morrow, 1978), p. 19.

hostage for some vague political reasons, the assassination of military and diplomatic personnel, or the suicidal car bombing of an embassy are considered acts of terrorism. Yet as soon as one goes beyond these obvious examples, problems arise. The term *terrorism* can produce extreme emotions, partly as a reaction to the indiscriminate nature of the violence and fear associated with it and partly because of its philosophical substance. The search for a definition that is both concise enough to provide an intelligent analytical premise yet general enough to obtain agreement by all parties in the debate is laden with complexity. As a result of this problem, many observers and analysts get around the definitional problem by referring to one of several peremptory phrases, such as "one person's terrorist is another person's freedom fighter," "terrorism to some is heroism to others," "today's terrorist is tomorrow's freedom fighter," and so on. These phrases, aphoristic though they may seem, outline the problem facing scholars who have attempted to define the limits of terrorism either for the purpose of developing some type of international agreement or to conduct scholarly research.

The problem of definition is further exacerbated by observers who frequently engage in the familiar rhetorical tactic of answering a question or a charge by leveling a countercharge. The key to this tactic is the speed and facility that the "but what about" phrase can be used; that is, "but what about . . . " followed by some act of terrorism or violence allegedly committed by the opposition. Some examples are:

> The Soviet Union and the KGB are supporting world terrorism.
> BUT WHAT ABOUT the United States and the CIA?
> The car bombing of the Marine compound in Beirut was an act of senseless, wanton terrorism.
> BUT WHAT ABOUT the naval shelling of Lebanese villages?
> The Palestine Liberation Organization is a terrorist group.
> BUT WHAT ABOUT the Zionist terrorism of the Israeli Mossad?

The purpose of such a tactic, according to Wilson, is to avoid the discussion of a specific issue by changing the subject in such a manner that implies the moral inferiority of your opponent. Moreover, the "but what about" response infers that the countercharge is precisely analogous to the original statement and therefore, no distinctions among statements can be made. Thus, no distinction can be made between the KGB and the CIA, the PLO and the Israeli Mossad, suicidal car bombings and naval bombardment of enemy positions, or for that matter, the Hell's Angels and the Los Angeles Police Department. The result is that the "but what about" strategy renders discussion virtually impossible, since analytical arguments are based on a willingness to make useful distinctions.[5]

---

[5]James Q. Wilson, "Thinking about Terrorism," *Commentary* 72 (July 1981), pp. 34–39.

The "but what about" tactic is also a clever and very old propaganda technique called *guilt transfer.* Tugwell describes guilt transfer as the switching of public attention away from the originator of the act toward the act of the adversary. For example, when the Soviet Union deliberately shot down a South Korean commercial jetliner with 269 people aboard after it inadvertently wandered into Soviet airspace, the Soviet government responded by claiming the plane was on a spy mission for the United States. This claim was designed to erode both confidence in and the legitimacy of the United States acting through its surrogate South Korea. It was used to justify the shooting down of an unarmed civilian plane, diverting attention away from the original act while simultaneously stripping the United States and South Korea of any moral righteousness.[6]

The tactic of guilt transfer has been widely criticized as one method for spreading disinformation. Obviously, many governments practice disinformation campaigns. Disinformation, however, is the anglicization of the Soviet term *desinformatsiya.* Disinformation is the spread of false, misleading, or incomplete information that is fed, passed, or confirmed to be from a targeted country, group, or individual.

Contemporary society appears to be particularly vulnerable to such tactics since a strong moral reference point for terror and violence is often lacking. In this same way the Palestinians justify random bombings and hostage-taking by claiming the perfidy of the Zionist state. The IRA justifies the ambush murder of British soldiers by affirming that the British Army is an army of occupation on foreign soil and therefore takes its chances in Northern Ireland. The Armenian Secret Army for the Liberation of Armenia (ASALA) justifies the murder of the Turkish diplomatic corps by claiming the Turkish genocide of Armenians in 1915. The list goes on.

Furthermore, such terms as international terrorism, transnational terrorism, or national terrorism complicate the search for a working definition of terrorism. International terrorism most often refers to terrorist acts committed by offenders who represent the interests of a sovereign nation, for example, Islamic Jihad. Transnational terrorists, such as Fatah, operate across national borders, where the act of terrorism may affect more than one ethnic group. National terrorists—such as Basque separatists—seek to achieve political power within a single nation.

Reference to such statements and rhetoric should not convince the student that the search for a working definition of terrorism is fruitless. Wardlaw maintains that without a basic definition it is impossible to say whether the phenomenon we call terrorism is a real threat to the stability of democratic nations or whether it is just another crime problem that eventually must be

---

[6]Maurice A. J. Tugwell, "Guilt Transfer," in *The Morality of Terrorism: Religious and Secular Justifications,* eds. David C. Rapoport and Yonah Alexander (New York: Pergamon, 1983), pp. 275–90.

dealt with by the criminal justice system.[7] The fundamental problem in arriving at a definition acceptable to all is the moral issue associated with terrorism. As the reading of the literature should show, there are indeed many ambiguities about the morality of terrorism and about the meaning of related terms such as terror, coercion, force, and violence.

Morality of Terrorism

The scholarly analysis of the morality of terrorism has produced a wide range of observations. For example, Walter describes terror as an emotional state caused by specific acts or threats of violence, and terrorism as a compound of three elements: the act or threat of violence, the emotional reaction, and the social effects. In 1934 Hardman referred to terrorism as activities involving a "systematic use of violence" but somehow sought to distinguish between mass violence and the "terrorist method."[9] Moore described violence and terrorism as "negative compulsions" and stated there is an analogous relationship between violence and terrorism.[10] Rapoport, on the other hand, views terrorists and terrorism as involving individuals and acts of violence designed to cause extreme injury and unconstrained by "moral limits."[11] Rapoport argues that a moral distinction can be made between acts of political violence and indiscriminate random terrorism. Laqueur admits that terrorism has a wider meaning than violence and entitles his recent text *The Age of Terrorism*. According to Laqueur, the "study of terrorism is with movements that use systematic terrorism" to achieve political goals.[12]

Another scholarly analysis of terrorism is presented by Bell. Bell calls attention to the great diversity of motivation of terrorists, distinguishing between psychotic, criminal, and self-dramatizing terrorists. Bell further acclaims that state terror has always been with us and that "attention has usually focused on the lone assassin or the tiny band of conspirators." Bell's primary concern is with transnational terrorism, which he defines as terrorists who operate across national borders and whose action and political aspirations may affect individuals of more than one nationality.[13]

Other writers have been concerned with the responses to rebel or insur-

[7]Grant Wardlaw, *Political Terrorism: Theory, Tactics and Countermeasures* (Cambridge: Cambridge University Press, 1982), pp. 4–10.

[8]Eugene V. Walter, *Terror and Resistance: A Study of Political Violence* (New York: Oxford, 1969), p. 5.

[9]J. B. S. Hardman, "Terrorism," in *Encyclopedia of the Social Sciences,* eds. E. R. A. Seligman and A. Johnson (New York: MacMillan, 1934), pp. 14, 575–76.

[10]Barrington Moore, Jr., *Terror and Progress—U.S.S.R.* (New York: Harper, 1954), p. 11.

[11]David C. Rapoport, "The Politics of Atrocity," in *Terrorism: Interdisciplinary Perspectives,* eds. Yonah Alexander and S. M. Finger (New York: John Jay, 1977), p. 47.

[12]Walter Laqueur, *The Age of Terrorism* (Boston: Little, Brown, 1987), p. 7.

[13]Bowyer Bell, *Transnational Terror* (Washington, D.C.: American Enterprise Institute, 1975), p. 3–10.

gent terrorism and the protection of individual rights. For example, Gerstein observes that the terrorist is not a criminal but more of an outlaw. He argues that the purpose of terrorism is to cause feelings of fear, dread, and insecurity in the community. Gerstein maintains that individuals involved in terrorist violence forfeit their right to have rights.[14] Rapoport counters by arguing that some basic civil and legal rights may be forfeited; however, there still remains a vital core of human and civil rights that should be protected no matter what the terrorist has done.[15] Rapoport believes that democratic governments often engage in torture, internment, and trials that do not accord full or normal due process when dealing with serious terrorist problems. For example, Northern Ireland and Israel have been accused by investigative journalists and Amnesty International of establishing a planned program of torture, internment, and violations of due process in their efforts to prevent outrageous acts of indiscriminate terrorism.

While Gerstein and Rapoport dispute the relationship of moral principles and legal dogma, the noted political scientist Wilkinson is concerned with whether the domestic or international legal system should have jurisdiction over the apprehension and prosecution of suspected terrorists.[16] This is a very important question, since most captured terrorists claim they are freedom fighters or rebels and as such should be treated in accordance with the rules of war since they claim a moral justification for using terrorist tactics. The claim has troubled many thoughtful writers who, for the most part, attempt to provide a careful distinction between the political, criminal, and common lawbreaker.[17] According to Dugard, international agreements are difficult to achieve because some governments protect escaping terrorists and actively support terrorist activity.[18] For example, the U.S. State Department has identified Iran, Libya, Cuba, North Korea, and South Yemen as governments of state-supported terrorism. Former director of the CIA Casey called governmental-sponsored terrorism "a weapons' system that obliterates the distinction between peace and war."[19] The U.S. State Department has identified 50 major terrorist groups for hire in the world today. With training bases to improve

---

[14]Robert S. Gerstein, "Do Terrorists Have Rights," in *The Morality of Terrorism: Religious and Secular Justifications,* eds. David C. Rapoport and Yonah Alexander (New York: Pergamon, 1983), p. 6.

[15]David C. Rapoport, "The Politics of Atrocity," in *Terrorism,* p. 47.

[16]Paul Wilkinson, *Political Terrorism* (London: MacMillan, 1976), pp. 136–42.

[17]For example, Stephen Schafer, *The Political Criminal* (New York: Free Press, 1974); Tom Bowden, *The Breakdown of Public Security* (Beverly Hills: Sage, 1977); Barton L. Ingraham, *Political Crime in Europe* (Berkeley: University of California Press, 1979); Austin T. Turk, *Political Criminality* (Beverly Hills: Sage, 1982).

[18]John Dugard, "International Terrorism and the Just War," *Stanford Journal of International Studies,* 12 (1977), 21.

[19]Central Intelligence Agency, *International and Transnational Terrorism: Diagnosis and Prognosis* (Washington, D.C.: U.S. Government Printing Office, 1976).

terrorist skills located in Iran, Syria, Libya, South Yemen, and the Soviet Union.

Beginning about 1979 and climaxing with the publication of Sterling's text *The Terror Network,* there has been mounting evidence that the Soviet Union has provided substantial supplies of weapons and training facilities to a variety of terrorist organizations.[20] This Soviet complicity may range from simply allowing suspected terrorists the freedom to move about in its satellite states to directing skyjackings, assassinations, and bombings from some central location. Sterling asserts, however, that the Soviet Union is not the mastermind behind the phenomenon called terrorism, but that the Soviets do provide weapons, training, sanctuaries, and the right introductions to a widely fragmented and interconnected set of terrorist groups.[21] In other words, there is no global organization of terrorist groups, but there certainly are international ties that are exploited by the Soviets. It must be made clear, however, that we do not know the extent of Soviet involvement in global terrorism although the Soviets seem to have a great deal of influence over such groups as the Popular Front for the Liberation of Palestine (PFLP) and the Provisional Wing of the IRA (PIRA, or Provos). The financial backing for many terrorist groups probably comes not from the Soviet Union but from wealthy Arab nations and from criminal activities. Sterling's timely text suggests that we should take the claims of Soviet participation in international terrorism more seriously. To this end a U.S. Senate subcommittee has been conducting hearings on both domestic and international terrorism since 1974.[22]

Even so, the allegations made by Sterling have been widely criticized. The preeminent opponent of Sterling's work has been Herman in *The Real Terror Network.* Herman maintains that Sterling very carefully ignores official state or governmental terror and focuses on the terror of selected individuals and small groups on the left. Herman rejects the central thesis of the Sterling book, i.e., that the Soviet Union has been involved in terrorist activities, by stating that she presents no documentation to support the charge and ignores the historical context of terrorism. Herman declares that we should not forget the Soviet charges of American sponsorship of right-wing terrorism in the more than ten U.S. client states in Latin America that he refers to as the National Security States. Herman makes a careful distinction between "retail" terrorism that is employed by isolated individuals or small groups and "wholesale" terror that is used by governments. Thus, retail terror is usually on a much smaller scale than pervasive wholesale terror.

Herman not only describes the techniques and extent of wholesale terror

---

[20]Sterling, *The Terror Network,* pp. 256–297.

[21]Ibid.

[22]United States Congress, House, Committee on Internal Security, *Terrorism,* 93rd Congress (Washington, D.C.: Government Printing Office, 1974), Part 3 & Part 4.

by regimes supported by the United States but explores the financial interest of U.S. corporations in the Third World. He argues that U.S.-supported repression and terror results in the perpetuation of poverty and growing inequality, especially in Latin America. In quantitative terms, Herman affirms that U.S.-sponsored state or wholesale terrorism has victimized nearly a million people.[23]

However, Herman does not clearly differentiate the strategies of the two types of terror. In Herman's view the semantics of the morality of terrorism has a dualistic meaning. The term morality is used when applying moral values to our enemies, while moralistic refers to the morality of friends or ourselves.

More than a half-century ago the principal ideologue of fascism, Panunzio, attempted to make a moral distinction between terror, terrorism, force, and violence. In Panunzio's analysis, terror represents the use of force to maintain the present social and political system, while terrorism is the application of violence to bring about the downfall of the existing social and political system.[24] Although force and violence seek to alter individual and collective behavior through coercion, intimidation, and fear, the distinction between terror/force and terrorism/violence apparently lies in the selection of victims. The distinction can be clearly discerned:

> . . . between the torture of an editor of an opposition newspaper (terror) and the death of the housewife in the commission of a terrorist bombing (terrorism). For the terrorist anyone who is a member of society and not a member of his "revolutionary committee" is guilty of "complicity" with the "establishment" and hence exposed to violence.[25]

In other words, official state terror is used to attack and intimidate specific individuals or groups who threaten the existence of the state, while unpredictable, indiscriminate terrorism is directed at all members of society. Terrorism, then, is a strategy that exposes innocents to unpredictable attacks. The trait of this extraordinary violence is the indiscriminate, random nature of the violent act. There is every difference between the planned assassination of a leader of an oppressive regime and the shooting of innocent hostages who just happen to be available to the political terrorist. In sum, then, terror is the manufacture and spread of fear by legitimate authority or its official agent, the police or military, while terrorism is the execution and spread of fear by

---

[23]Edward S. Herman, *The Real Terror Network: Terrorism in Fact and Propaganda* (Boston: South End, 1983), pp. 4–16.

[24]William Ebenstein, *Today's isms: Communism, Fascism, Capitalism, Socialism* (Englewood Cliffs, N.J.: Prentice Hall, 1985), pp. 111–41; A. James Gregor, *The Ideology of Fascism: The Rationale of Totalitarianism* (New York: Free Press, 1969), pp. 170–75.

[25]A. James Gregor, "Fascism's Philosophy of Violence and the Concept of Terror," in *The Morality of Terrorism: Religious and Secular Justifications,* eds. David C. Rapoport and Yonah Alexander (New York: Pergamon, 1983), p. 164.

rebels, revolutionaries, insurgents, and freedom fighters or agents labeled "terrorists."

Definitions of Terrorism

Let us examine some of the more popular definitions of terrorism proposed by the criminal justice system and scholars of related disciplines. Then we will attempt to clear away the rhetoric and formulate a more precise definition of terrorism appropriate for the criminal justice system. The lack of a precise definition causes three problems for criminal justice agencies:

1. Ambiguity over the distinction between common crime and political crime.
2. Lack of a comprehensive statistical base which may make it impossible to use statistical surveys.
3. Difficulty in planning for terrorist activity since philosophical definitions of terrorism differ.

However, once a working definition is established, statistical data can be organized into meaningful forms for policy-making and planning purposes. Some popular definitions of terrorism follow:

1. An organized pattern of violent behavior designed to influence government policy or intimidate the population for the purpose of influencing government policy.[26]
2. Terror: violence committed by groups in order to intimidate a population or government into granting their demands.[27]
3. Terror is symbolic action designed to influence political behavior by extranormal means entailing the use or threat of violence.[28]
4. Terrorism may be defined as violent, criminal behavior designed primarily to generate fear in the community, or a substantial segment of it, for political purposes.[29]
5. Terrorism is the culturally unacceptable use or threat of violence directed toward symbolic targets to influence political behavior either directly through fear, intimidation, or coercion, or indirectly by affecting attitudes, emotions, or opinions.[30]

[26]James Lodge, ed., *Terrorism: A Challenge to the State* (Oxford: Martin Robertson, 1981), p. 5.

[27]"Terror," *Webster's Ninth New Collegiate Dictionary* (Springfield, Mass.: Merriam and Webster, Inc., 1983), p. 1218.

[28]Thomas P. Thornton, "Terror as a Weapon of Political Agitation," in *Internal War,* ed. H. Eckstein (New York: Free Press, 1964), pp. 71–99.

[29]National Advisory Committee on Criminal Justice Standards and Goals, Law Enforcement Assistance Agency, *Disorders and Terrorism* (Washington, D.C.: U.S. Government Printing Office, 1976), p. 3.

[30]*U.S. Air Force Special Operations School,* Hurlburt Field, Mary Estes, (Florida: July, 1985).

6. Terrorism is nongovernmental public violence or its threat performed by an individual or small group and aimed at achieving social or political goals that may be subnational, national, or international.[31]
7. Terrorism is the use of force, violence, or threats thereof to attain political goals through fear, intimidation, or coercion.[32]
8. In general, the word terrorism is used today to define almost all illegal acts of violence committed for political purposes by clandestine groups.[33]

Two common features are characteristic of all definitions of terror and terrorism. First, terrorism is a technique for inducing *fear.* Terrorists attempt, by the nature of indiscriminate acts of violence, to manipulate fear to achieve a variety of tactical and political objections. Wilkinson addresses this point and notes that the key issue in defining terrorism lies in the ambiguous nature of fear.[34] We all have different thresholds of fear based on our personal and cultural backgrounds. Certain images and experiences are more terrifying than others, and it appears that those engaged in the business of terrorism know the right *fear* buttons to push. Wardlaw maintains that owing to the complex relationship between the subjective force of fear and the frequently irrational, individual response to fear, it becomes difficult to define terrorism accurately and to study it scientifically.[35] For this reason behavioral scientists have tended to disagree on a definition of terrorism that accurately reflects the subjective nature of fear and the methods used to arouse both individual and collective fear.

The second common denominator found in most definitions of terrorism is the achievement of some vague political objective. The political content of the act of terrorism distinguishes it from such ordinary criminal activities as murder, robbery, kidnapping, extortion, and hijacking, all of which are committed with far greater frequency by "nonterrorists" for motives of simple profit or passion. However, it is obvious that terror and terrorism need not be politically motivated. For example, criminals frequently resort to terrorist-type tactics for personal gain. Fleeing felons, upon encountering the police, will often take hostages and attempt to negotiate their escape. In fact, over 60 percent of all hostage-taking incidents in the United States involve criminal hostage-takers, not political terrorists. Mentally disturbed persons may also terrorize others because of their condition. For example, it is very common in the United States for a mentally deranged person to hold his or her family members hostage. Likewise, political assassinations in the United States have

[31]David M. Krieger, "What Happens If? Terrorists, Revolutionaries, and Nuclear Weapons," *The Annals of the American Academy of Political and Social Sciences,* 430 (March, 1977), pp. 44–57.
[32]Robert A. Friedlander, *Terrorism and The Law: What Price Safety?* (Gaithersburg, Md: IACP, 1981), p. 3.
[33]Lester A. Sobel, ed., *Political Terrorism* (New York: Facts on File, Inc., 1975), pp. 3–12.
[34]Wilkinson, *Political Terrorism,* p. 10.
[35]Wardlaw, *Political Terrorism: Theory, Tactics and Countermeasures,* pp. 10–14.

been motivated not by political conspiracy, but by the mentally distraught, gunwielder acting most often as an "agent of God." Some individuals may terrorize others because they are bored, sadistic, or angry, which causes them to engage in some type of violent act of protest against society. The distinctions between various forms of terrorism then are unclear, since criminals or psychopaths may use terror tactics and seek legitimacy by adopting political slogans and claiming to be political activists. In addition, terrorist organizations often recruit and collaborate with criminals and psychopaths.

These confusions, together with the pejorative usage of the word terrorism, make the problem of definition nearly insolvable. The problem is further complicated by writers who refuse to recognize that terrorism is not only a tactic of insurgents or political extremists but also a strategy of the state. All the same, in order to discuss the subject of terrorism in a meaningful way, it is necessary to accept some basic definition. For our purposes then, "Terrorism is the premeditated, deliberate, systematic murder, mayhem, and threatening of the innocent to create fear and intimidation in order to gain a political or tactical advantage, usually to influence an audience." Obviously this definition has limitations, but it attempts to distinguish between random murder and guerrilla warfare directed at the state. Moreover, this definition can be applied to terrorism from the left or right as well as terror practiced by a government, or terrorism used by common criminals. Simply put, the purpose of terrorism is to terrorize. The contemporary terrorist uses terrorism as a preferred strategy rather than as a last resort. The terrorist prefers violence over other forms of political dissent. The routine nature of terrorist violence makes it difficult to distinguish completely betweeen the political fanatic or the bloodthirsty killer. As pointed out earlier, the escalation of terrorism contributes to the spread of the totalitarian state. This next section will explore several popular typologies of terrorism.

Terrorist Typologies

For years political scientists have attempted to construct a consistent typology of terrorism, and many ingenious classifications have emerged. (See Table 1-1, p. 17.) Probably the clearest framework for analyzing terrorism is provided by Wilkinson. Wilkinson categorizes four types of terrorism: (1) criminal, (2) psychic, (3) war, and (4) political. Criminal terrorism is defined as the planned use of terror for financial and material gain. Psychic terrorism is related to magical beliefs, myths, and superstitions induced by fanatical religious beliefs. War terrorism is the annihilation of the enemy through whatever means possible. Political terrorism is defined as the systematic use of violence and fear to achieve a political objective. Wilkinson lists seven specific characteristics of political terrorism:

1. The systematic use of murder, injury, or threats to realize a political objective such as revolution or repression;

2. An atmosphere of fear, coercion, and intimidation;
3. The inherent indiscriminateness: indiscriminate attacks are made on noncombatants (soft targets)—no one in particular is the target, no one is safe;
4. Its unpredictability: the individual is unable to avoid injury or death;
5. Its abidance by no rules or conventions of war;
6. The savage methods of destruction used, such as car bombs, nail bombs, double bombs, and mass murder;
7. The moral justification for acts of terrorism, found in the group's political philosophy.[36]

Wilkinson further divides political terrorism into three types: revolutionary, subrevolutionary, and repressive. Revolutionary terrorism represents the "systematic tactics of terroristic violence with the objective of bringing about political revolution."[37] This type of terrorism is characterized by four major points:

1. It is always a group activity rather than an individual act of violence.
2. The moral justification for the use of terror is always found in the revolutionary ideology.
3. Terroristic leadership is an important element in recruiting people for terrorism.
4. The revolutionary movement must develop its own policy-making board, infrastructure, and code of conduct.[38]

The second category in Wilkinson's classification of political terrorism is subrevolutionary terrorism. This is defined as terror used for "political motives other than revolution or governmental repression." Subrevolutionary terrorism is directed at forcing the state to change its policy on a controversial political issue, warning state officials, or retaliating against the state for some act seen as reprehensible by the terrorist group.[39] For example, a clandestine antiabortion group, calling itself the "Army of God," has planted bombs in several abortion clinics in the United States to protest what it sees as liberal abortion laws.

Wilkinson's third category, repressive terrorism, is defined as "the systematic use of terroristic acts of violence for the purposes of suppressing, putting down, quelling, or restraining certain groups, individuals, or forms of behavior deemed to be undesirable by the oppressor."[40] Repressive terrorism relies heavily on the apparatus of the state security police who are usually set apart from the rest of society. In fact, various aspects of contemporary terror-

[36]Paul Wilkinson, *Terrorism and the Liberal State* (London: MacMillan, 1977), pp. 47–64.
[37]Wilkinson, *Political Terrorism,* p. 56.
[38]Ibid., pp. 32–45.
[39]Wilkinson, *Political Terrorism,* p. 38.
[40]Ibid., p. 40.

ism were introduced to international affairs by a state rather than an independent terrorist organization. Hitler's SS and Gestapo used a variety of terrorist methods against the Jews. The final solution, or mass extermination, of the Jews of Europe represents the last phase of Hitler's terror campaign against them. This type of terrorism is also exemplified by the Black Hand operating in the Balkans prior to World War I, by the Red Hand in Algeria during and after political emancipation from France in the 1950s, by the White Hand terrorizing El Salvadorans, by the Ulster Defense Association in Northern Ireland, and by the Syrian Saiqa.[41] Wilkinson writes that initially this type of terror/terrorism is direct against specific opposition groups, but frequently is shifted to a much broader audience, for example, ethnic or religious minorities.[42] Consequently, repressive terrorism by the state may be the most potentially dangerous form of present-day terrorism.

Hacker attempted to classify terrorists according to motives: crusaders, criminals, crazies. According to Hacker, the emotionally disturbed (crazy) are driven by reasons of their own that often do not make sense to anybody else. The motives of criminal terrorists are simply personal gain through illegitimate criminal behavior. Crusading terrorists are idealistic aspired, seeking no personal gain but prestige and power for a collective political goal, while acting for the interests of the "common good." Hacker further delineates his classification into crazy terrorists from above (governmental terror) and crazy terrorists from below (psychotic terrorism). The latter category is very similar to the "motiveless" murder, which can offer no moral justification for the act of terroristic violence other than individual recognition. Likewise, Hacker outlines the difference between criminal terrorists from above, or individuals who consolidate governmental power through criminal activity and eventually adopt a strategy of terror to hold that power, and criminal terrorists from below, such as D. B. Cooper and members of crime syndicates. But to Hacker, the "real terrorists" are the crusaders out to save the world, or at least part of it. Similar to crazy and criminal terrorists, crusading terrorists can be from above or below. However, Hacker perceives the crusading terrorists from below as posing the greatest threat to global security and individual freedom since a common objective is the attempt to cause democratic governments to overreact and become repressive. Hacker's portrayal of terrorists is interesting, but most authors prefer a classification based on behavioral, political, historical, or sociological characteristics such as those we have listed by Wilkinson.[43]

Thornton identifies two broad classifications of the use of terrorism.[44]

[41]Caroline Holland, "The Black, the Red and the Orange: System Terrorism Versus Regime Terror" (unpublished manuscript, 1982), pp. 3–10.

[42]Wilkinson, *Political Terrorism,* pp. 42–44.

[43]Frederick J. Hacker, *Crusaders, Criminals, Crazies: Terror and Terrorism in Our Time* (New York: Bantam, 1978), pp. 3–38.

[44]Thornton, "Terror as a Weapon," in *Internal War,* pp. 71–99.

The first is enforcement terror, which is used by governments to extinguish threats to their power and authority. The second is agitational terror, which specifies the terrorist activities of an organized group attempting to disrupt the existing political establishment and take political control. In a sense, Thornton discusses terrorism from above and terrorism from below.

A similar argument is acknowledged by May, who categorizes terrorism as "regime of terror" and "siege of terror."[45] Regime of terror refers to the use of terrorism by the established political system, while siege of terror pertains to terrorism used by revolutionary movements. According to May, the regime of terror is the most insidious type of terrorism, but public attention is focused on the siege of terror due to the sensationalism of media reporting.

Gregor recognizes that terroristic violence has as its purpose not coercive sanction but some proximate end. He classifies terror into four distinctive groups:

> Instrumental terror is employed to impair the functioning of some system or institution.
> Demonstrative terror is used to bend entire populations to the purpose of others.
> Prophylactic terror is employed in anticipation of resistance or rebellion.
> Incidental terror involves those criminal acts—assaults, armed robbery, kidnapping—that impact upon innocent victims in the service of the perpetrator's pathology, profit, or advantage.[46]

Gregor observes that the most salient trait of terrorism is its indiscriminate nature. In a sense terrorist acts are like natural catastrophes: everyone is a potential victim. To Gregor the distinction is based on the selection of victims.

More recently Schmid and de Graaf have presented an interesting classification of political terrorism distinguished by three principal types: (1) insurgent terrorism directed against the state, (2) state or repressive terrorism directed against less powerful segments of society, and (3) vigilante terrorism directed neither at the state nor on behalf of the state. Insurgent terrorism is further subdivided into three categories: (1) social revolutionary terrorism which aims at causing worldwide revolution, (2) separatist, nationalist, or ethnical terrorism, which is concerned with radical changes in one part of society and not the entire political structure, and (3) single issue terrorism, which is concerned with the granting of some privilege to a specific group.[47] Schmid and de Graaf recognize that this typology concerns itself only

---

[45]W. F. May, "Terrorism as Strategy and Ecstasy," *Social Research* 41 (1974) p. 277.

[46]Gregor, *The Morality of Terrorism,* p. 159.

[47]Alex P. Schmid and Janny de Graaf, *Violence as Communication: Insurgent Terrorism and the Western News Media* (Beverly Hills: Sage, 1982), pp. 59–60.

with domestic and national terrorism while omitting international and transnational terrorism:

> . . . there is also so-called international terrorism. Its targets are sometimes foreign states and at other times foreign nonstates. Its perpetrators are often nonstate actors, but states also sometimes engage in it. Quite often, however, there is a mix of state and nonstate actors who ally with each other. This allows for a multitude of combinations. If only states are involved as actors and targets, we might speak of interstate terrorism. In all other cases one might speak of transnational terrorism. Yet in fact there are so many variations possible.[48]

Complicated as this picture may appear, in reality it is less complex than the actual cases of reported international terrorism. For example, it has been reported that Palestinian terrorist groups have been associated with at least 14 state and nonstate terrorist actors. In truth, most acts of political terrorism are less international or transnational than it would seem at first analysis. Even the Palestinians have a major target of political terrorism in their frequent attempts to disrupt the Israeli state. Further study of the international aspects of terroristic violence seems likely to be fruitful.

From these general statements that have been made on the types of terrorism, we now seek to provide a reasonably comprehensive typology of terrorism. The focus of this typology is on the indiscriminate nature of terrorist violence. Again, the problem of definition is recognized, but we must not overlook the fact that the victim is someone to be manipulated for purposes of creating intense fear.

Figure 1-1 outlines five distinct categories of terrorism: political, criminal, pathological, labor, and war.

The political nature of the purpose and origin of terrorism is the most important characteristic shared by such disparate groups as repressive state regimes or insurgent revolutionaries (for example, Sendero Luminoso, Red Brigades, al Fatah, Sikh extremists, and a variety of neo-fascist groups).

Criminal "terrorists" are motivated by simple profit. Prison gangs, juvenile street gangs, and organized criminal cartels use fear to protect their turf and control criminal activity, especially drug traffic.

The pathological "terrorist" may be motivated by greed, passion, pleasure, pain, or some undefined psychological aberration. The serial killer or mass murderer can certainly create an atmosphere of fear that easily paralyzes a large community.

The history of labor violence is one of constant confrontations between striking workers and company-supported strikebreakers. The industrialists of the nineteenth and twentieth centuries and their enforcers indiscriminately attacked striking workers, ruthlessly putting down labor strife. Workers often

[48]Ibid.

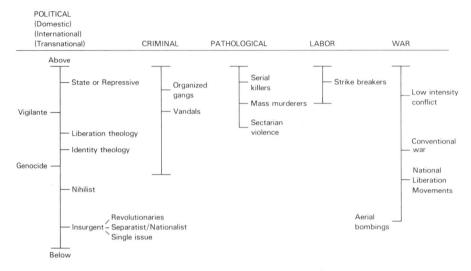

FIGURE 1-1   A Typology of Terrorism and Violence

retaliated against company bosses with assassination and mayhem. (Chapter 2 contains more on labor violence.)

Finally, the best example of terrorism during a declared war is the indiscriminate aerial bombing of civilian targets. The purpose of aerial bombing is to spread panic and fear in civilian populations. The first concentrated aerial bombardment of a civilian target in modern warfare occurred at Guernica, Spain, on April 26, 1937, when Nazi German planes dropped 10,000 tons of explosives in support of Franco's rebel nationalist forces. Guernica was obliterated and thousands of civilians were killed.

In conclusion, the collected evidence for a consistent classification of terrorism is scarce and unreliable. The several studies explored here confirm the fact that diagnosis remains a matter for the individual ability of the researcher. This negative summation does not exclude the importance of a careful and comprehensive assessment of the negative factors associated with the term terrorism. The choice of typologies remains a problem to be solved in relation to the purpose of the definition. In general, however, classification of terrorism could be improved by better research designs and by awareness of political, social and psychological determinants of terrorist and violence behavior.

Terrorist Atrocities

Following the initial taxonomic efforts of Wilkinson, Shultz and Ivanesky discuss the varying degrees of extranormal violence used by terrorist

TABLE 1-1   Summary of Typologies of Terrorism

AUTHOR	TYPES
Wilkinson	Criminal, psychic, war, political
Hacker	Crusaders, criminals, crazies
Thornton	Enforcement, agitational
May	Regime, siege
Gregor	Instrumental, demonstrative, prophylactic, incidental
Schmid and de Graaf	Insurgent, state, vigilante, social revolutionary, separatist

guerrillas or revolutionaries.[49] In recent years, considerable attention has been paid to those terrorist instances where surface-to-air missiles or the indiscriminate bombing and shooting of large numbers of innocent civilians were used to terrorize the general population. Law enforcement authorities are concerned that terrorists will go "nuclear." The mystery and threat surrounding anything nuclear makes it an effective source of terrorists fear and manipulation. This extranormal dimension can also be illustrated in other acts of violence such as shooting innocent travelers, shooting a teacher in the presence of the teacher's students, cutting off an ear or finger to dramatize the extortionist/kidnapper's demands, "kneecapping" or shooting the legs of the victims to cause a permanent disability. A possible explanation for the cruel nature of terrorist atrocity is offered by Neale:

> Terroristic violence must be totally ruthless, for moral scruples and terror do not mix and one or the other must be rejected. There can be no such thing as a weak dose of terror. The hand that controls the whip must be firm and implacable.[50]

Thus, terroristic atrocities serve several essential objectives for the terrorist. First and foremost, they can produce pure terror or paralyzing fear. They are most effective when directed against specific critical groups. For example, in the popular revolutionary film, *Battle of Algiers,*[51] the systematic assassination of police officers is portrayed in order to dramatize how to effectively paralyze the law enforcement community. More recently, the indiscriminate killing of police officers from ambush has been tried by the Provisional Irish Republican Army (PIRA) in Northern Ireland and the Black Liberation Army (BLA) in the United States.

A second major purpose of terrorist atrocities is to attract attention and

---

[49]Richard Shultz, "Conceptualizing Political Terrorism: A Typology," *Journal of International Affairs,* 32 (1978), p. 7; Ze'ev Iviansky, "Individual Terror: Concept and Typology," *Journal of Cont. History,* 12 (1977), p. 43.

[50]William D. Neale, "Terror: Oldest Weapon in the Arsenal," *Army* (August 1973), pp. 10–17.

[51]Gillo Pontecorro, *Battle of Algiers,* film written by Franco Solivar (New York: Scribner, 1973).

gain sympathy through publicity. The nature of an atrocity is to attract widespread attention; thus, the more spectacular the act of terroristic violence the most interest it arouses in the general population. Rapoport observes that reaction to the violence varies depending on the audience. Viewing the atrocity may lead one audience to supply recruits, another to supply material aid, and yet another to offer encouragement.[52] Additionally, the terrorist atrocity may increase the prestige of the terrorist group and strengthen its acceptability and influence among other terrorist groups. The boldness of the act of terrorism may also strengthen the terrorist groups' claim that they are the only legitimate representatives of the "people." In sum, the terrorist atrocity of today is similar to the type of terror so effectively used by nineteenth-century Russian anarchists known as the "propaganda by the deed."

The third purpose of terrorist atrocities is to provoke the existing political establishment to commit counteratrocities. If the government is seen as employing the same tactics as the terrorist group, then potential sympathizers become allies and the strength of the terrorist group grows. The aim of the terrorist group is to *enrage* the establishment. Frequently, as Merari pointed out in his classification of terrorist groups, the target selected for the terrorist atrocity may enrage not only political bureaucrats but also rival ethnic and religious groups.[53] For example, the targets and victims of the Provisional wing of the Irish Republican Army (Provos) are both foreigners (British soldiers) and fellow countrypeople (Ulster Protestants). There is no doubt that terrorist atrocities will continue since they produce outrage and fear, which is the purpose of terrorism.

Purpose of Terrorism

The purpose, direction, and focus of terrorism is *fear*. Terrorism is a technique for inducing fear. However, contrary to popular belief, terrorism is not senseless, wantonless destruction of life and property. There are many reasons for acts of terrorism besides fear. Crenshaw believes that terrorism serves several functions: (1) to seize political power, (2) to affect public opinion and seize the media, (3) to maintain discipline within the terrorist organization and enforce obedience and conformity, (4) to discredit and disrupt the everyday operations of government, (5) to win new recruits, and (6) to project an image of strength that far exceeds their numbers.[54] Likewise, Jenkins of the Rand Corporation expands on the following purposes of terrorism:

---

[52]David C. Rapoport, "Terror and the Messiah: An Ancient Experience and Some Modern Parallels," in *The Morality of Terrorism: Religious and Secular Justifications,* eds. David C. Rapoport and Yonah Alexander (New York: Pergamon, 1983), pp. 15–17.

[53]Ariel Merari, "Classification of Terrorist Groups," *Terrorism* 1 (1978), p. 331.

[54]Martha Crenshaw, "The Causes of Terrorism," *Comparative Politics* 13 (1981), p. 374.

1. To provoke government overreaction, especially indiscriminate reaction;
2. To overthrow oppressive regimes;
3. To cause isolation and demoralization of individuals, creating an atmosphere of anxiety and insecurity;
4. To release prisoners and publish manifestos;
5. To immobilize security forces; and
6. To obtain financial resources in order to purchase weapons and explosives.[55]

On the other hand, Herman argues that terrorism is a tactic to maintain power and to destroy and eradicate internal threats to that political power.[56] At least one writer believes that terrorism is an all-powerful and all-purpose method of action, the "ultimate weapon."[57]

Therefore, while the principal effect of terrorism is fear and insecurity, terrorism may be used to achieve a variety of objectives: widespread publicity for the terrorists' cause, specific concessions, the provocation of repression, the dissolution of social norms, the enforcement of internal obedience, and the holding of hostages. A single terrorist incident may be aimed at accomplishing several of these objectives simultaneously.

CONCLUSIONS

Mencken said it best: "There's always an easy solution to every human problem—neat, plausible, and wrong."[58] So, too, with terrorism. In this chapter we have surveyed many definitions and types of political and domestic terrorism. Some are scholarly, such as Wilkinson's observations. Others are chic, such as Hacker's crusaders, criminals, and crazies. Still others argue that the real terror network is the state. The only common denominator seems to be that victims of terrorist acts are killed, injured, and threatened, and the acts are for the most part illegal.

Some recurring patterns were noted in the types of terrorist behavior and other violent offenses. However, no one terrorist group has an exclusive franchise on terrorism and the causes of terrorism are as varied as the human condition itself. One of the objectives of this chapter was to introduce the student to the complexity of terrorism and to beware of easy, neat, and plausible explanations of terrorism.

Another major objective of this chapter was to set forth a conceptual framework for the study of terrorism and the later evaluation of terrorist orga-

---

[55]Brian Jenkins, *International Terrorism: A New Mode of Conflict* (Los Angeles: Crescent, 1975), pp. 4–7.

[56]Herman, *The Real Terror Network*, pp. 83–87.

[57]Schreiber, *The Ultimate Weapon*, p. 1.

[58]Laurence J. Peter, *Peter's Quotations* (New York: Morrow, 1977), p. 410.

nizations. It is hoped that this chapter reflects the complexity of the phenomenon and encompasses the wide variety of terrorist types who engage in various forms of violent behavior. This chapter is probably best suited for exploring the theoretical rationale of terrorism rather than predicting what will occur in the future. If terrorism is a growth industry, then we can anticipate a steady escalation in the amount of terrorism in the years to come. As such, criminal justice students must be cognizant of the insidious nature of terrorism, both from the state and from "insurgent rebels." This problem is reflected in a major deficiency in the study of terrorism, which is, of course, the difficulty of operationally defining the term.

However, it must be emphasized that terrorism is neither wanton nor irrational. Terrorism is not mindless violence. It is a deliberate strategy with proximate ends. Terrorism has objectives, although they are often obscured by the fact that terrorist acts appear random and indiscriminate. The killing and terrorizing of seemingly innocent people who can be of no value to the terrorist cause may be very perplexing to criminal justice students. Terrorism, then, may be characterized as discriminate indiscriminate violence. Terrorism is discriminate since it has a definite purpose, but indiscriminate in that the terrorist has neither sympathy nor hate for the randomly selected victim. In order to understand this difficult paradox, we will examine the historical antecedents of modern terrorism to outline historical trends and future prospects.

One of the intriguing aspects of the study of terrorism is the volume of historical literature associated with terrorism from below (rebels, insurgents, revolutionaries) as opposed to official state terror. There are several explanations. First, acts of terrorism by insurgents are dramatic, news-making events. The impact of the media cannot be overstated, as will be discussed in Chapter 3. Government by terror simply does not generate the news coverage that a suicide truck bombing does. Second, many people may see state terrorists as rational political beings trying to hold on to their power, whereas insurgent terrorism is viewed as a last desperate act by the lunatic fringe. Third, even though state terrorism may be unjust and brutal, most citizens know what behavior or activities not to engage in to arouse the state security services. By contrast, rebellious terrorism seems random and thus presents a greater danger to the individual. The impression, therefore, is one of society plagued by dangerous antisocial extremists threatening to destroy our way of life while disregarding the more outrageous abuses of official government. Also, it is safer for the media to focus on small groups or individuals rather than government bureaucracies. Nevertheless, the immediate threat to the criminal justice system and the law enforcement community in the United States is not governmental terror but terrorism carried out by small groups dedicated to some vague political objective. The focus of this text, therefore, will concern itself with terrorism from below, or insurgent terrorism.

REVIEW QUESTIONS

1. Define terrorism, force, and violence.
2. Compare and contrast the observations of Sterling and Herman. Cite examples.
3. Identify at least six purposes of terrorism.
4. Should police organizations be overly concerned with a precise definition of terrorism? Explain.
5. Discuss three current examples of guilt transfer. Review current media references of disinformation campaigns.
6. Outline Wilkinson's typology of terrorism. Construct your own typology.
7. Is terrorism ever morally justified? Explain fully.
8. Describe the difference between terror and terrorism. Do you agree or disagree with this distinction? Be specific!
9. What distinguishes terrorism from other forms of violence?
10. How does criminal terror differ from political terror? Cite examples.
11. Give a contemporary example of:
    a. separatist/nationalist terrorism
    b. social revolutionary terrorism
    c. state or governmental terrorism
    d. pathological terrorism
    e. criminal terrorism
12. Why are democratic nations vulnerable to terrorism? Be specific.
13. List three reasons for terrorist atrocities.
14. Identify the following groups:
    a. FLQ
    b. PIRA
    c. ASALA
    d. PFLP
    e. BLA

TWO

HISTORICAL ANTECEDENTS OF TERRORISM AND VIOLENCE

CHAPTER OBJECTIVES

The study of this chapter will enable you to:
- Identify historical trends of violence and terrorism.
- Trace the relationship between ancient and modern terrorist groups.
- Explore the difference between anarchism and terrorism.
- Survey the historical evidence of violence and terrorism in the United States.
- Develop an insight into the relationship between American value orientation and pervasive violence.

INTRODUCTION

Although this is not a history of terrorism and our analysis does not emphasize terrorist groups of antiquity, some appreciation of their violent past is essential. The history of terrorism constitutes a major undertaking in its own right. That is not our intention here. However, it is important that we not ignore certain historical antecedents of terrorism and violence in order to appreciate the relationship between ancient and contemporary terrorist movements. War and revolution in general and the terrorist strategy in particular have a rich heritage.

The terms terrorism and terrorist have their roots in the French Revolution. Since that time terrorism has been widely used to describe almost every form of violent behavior. Even though the term is relatively recent, the terrorist strategy is not. Criminal justice practitioners and students of the terrorist method sometimes ignore this important history or feel that terrorism is a contemporary phenomenon and thus new and unprecedented. The purpose of this chapter is to review some of the important attributes in the practice of terrorism as a political strategy. Particular attention is given to histrionic terrorism, or the *fear*-inducing aspect of terrorism and violent behavior.

Sicarii and Zealots

Terrorism as a strategy to produce panic or paralyzing fear for the purpose of accomplishing premeditated political objectives was first introduced by the Jewish Sicarii and Zealot movements of ancient Palestine. The Sicarii and the Zealots, through acts of histrionic terror, successfully influenced a massive revolt against their colonial Roman rulers. However, the revolt ended after the Romans had encircled the Sicarii at Masada. Fearing retaliation by the Romans in the form of torture and death, the Sicarii refused to surrender and ended the siege of Masada by engaging in a dramatic mass suicide. Nearly a thousand Sicarii, including women and children, committed suicide rather than become Roman prisoners.[1]

The Sicarii were Jewish religious zealots who fomented popular uprising in Palestine between A.D. 66 and 70. Like many popular uprisings, both historical and contemporary, the tactic of passive resistance was used as a first strategy to influence the apathetic. The Romans had abolished the Jewish monarchy and imposed direct rule over the Jewish community of Palestine. This action, along with the desecration of Jewish religious symbols and the arrest of important religious leaders, led to an escalation of the conflict. Roman soldiers began to use excessive force to break up demonstrations. This led to unorganized Jewish retaliation. At first a more moderate faction attempted to induce the Jewish community to reject the use of retaliatory violence. But several atrocities were committed by Roman soldiers that resulted in the more radical Sicarii emerging as the dominant influence in the Jewish community. The Sicarii quickly went into action against the oppressive rule of the Romans, adopting a strategy of "pure terror." Rapoport notes that the Sicarii struck in broad daylight when the victim, either a Jewish moderate or a Roman soldier or a government official, was usually surrounded by witnesses and support-

[1]E. M. Smallwood, *The Jews Under Roman Rule* (Leiden, Netherlands: Brill, 1976), pp. 133–38.

ers.[2] The intention of such high-risk assaults was to demonstrate that no circumstance could provide immunity from attack; and if the soldiers could not protect themselves, how could they provide security for citizens or government officials? This tactic, therefore, caused a situation of total uncertainty for the potential victim and certainly caused a sense of profound fear. No religious terrorist movement has ever been so successful. The Sicarii used a wide range of tactics designed to influence the Jewish community and to provoke, escalate, and inspire hatred between Jews and Romans. All efforts to find an acceptable political solution were frustrated by the terror tactics of the Sicarii. The primary purpose of Sicarii terrorist strategy, like so many terrorist groups today, seems to be the provocation of indiscriminate countermeasures by the established political system and to deliberately provoke repression, reprisals and counterterrorism. To this end the Sicarii were successful. Not only did a mass suicide occur at Masada, but the Jewish community in Judea was decimated by Roman soldiers; and with a vengeance the Second Temple was destroyed in Jerusalem and the Jews were scattered to the four corners of the earth. The Diaspora had begun and would continue for 2000 years, ending with the creation of Israel and the fulfillment of an ancient biblical prophecy.[3]

Parallels between the Sicarii and contemporary terrorism can be found in Northern Ireland and Palestine. For example, the tactic of passive resistance has a tendency to draw large numbers of participants into the conflict and dramatically raises the consciousness level of potential participants. In Northern Ireland, for instance, the current troubles began when the Northern Ireland Civil Rights Association protested peacefully against the Protestant majority and the British government. However, the peaceful marches soon escalated when police and British Security Forces overreacted. In one confrontation between Catholics and Protestants, British forces fired into the crowd, killing eight Catholics. Then on January 30, 1972, the Northern Ireland Civil Rights Association held an illegal protest march in reaction to the new British policy of internment. The march came to an abrupt end when British Security Forces fired into the marchers, killing 13 and wounding at least 12. The significant conclusion reached by a government investigation stated that "those who organized the illegal march created a highly dangerous situation in which a clash between demonstrators and security forces was inevitable."[4] The result was the deliberate provocation and the forthcoming retaliation and escalation by the newly formed Provisional Wing of the Irish Republican Army.

In Palestine, the contemporary counterpart of the Sicarii/Zealot movement was the Irgun Zvai Leumi-be-Israel (National Military Organization of

[2]David C. Rapoport and Yonah Alexander, eds., *The Morality of Terrorism: Religious and Secular Justifications* (New York: Pergamon, 1983), pp. 16–23.

[3]Samuel G. Brandon, *Jesus and The Zealots: A Study of the Political Factor in Primitive Christianity* (New York: Scribner, 1967).

[4]Lord Widgery, *Report of the Tribunal Appointed to Enquire into the Events on Sunday, 30th January, 1972 in Londonderry* (London: HMSO, 1972), p. 6.

Israel) and their leader, Menachem Begin. The Irgun directed its terrorist attacks against the British military government of Palestine between 1942 and 1947. They carried out numerous bombings and assassinations that eventually forced the British to abandon Palestine and turn the problem over to the newly formed United Nations. The frequent manifestos of the Irgun reiterated their slogan, "No Masada." In fact, Begin describes in his book, *The Revolt,* the determination of the Irgun to avoid a second Masada.[5] In the eyes of the British, however, the Irgun was considered the most violent and unrestrained terrorist organization of the modern era. For the British there seemed to be no way out of the cycle of terror and counterterror. Begin and the Irgun were driven by history and despair to take on the mighty British empire, mirroring the terror campaign of the Sicarii and the Roman Empire.

The Assassins and Other Secret Societies

A similar mixture of religious zeal and political extremism was the feature of a better-known religious sect called the Assassins.[6] The Assassins were a division of the Shi'ite Ismaili Muslim sect that appeared in the eleventh century and were finally extinguished in the thirteenth century by conquering Mongols. A religious despot referred to as the "Old Man of the Mountains" was the acknowledged leader and founder of the Assassins. The Assassins gained widespread notoriety when the crusaders returned to Europe with stories of the murderers who killed their victims with golden daggers while under the influence of hashish. The hashish was to induce visions of paradise before the terrorists set out on their missions of assassination and terror. The name Assassin is derived from the Arabic *hashashin,* or "hashish-eaters." The Assassins practiced the secret murder of their enemies from bases in Persia, Iraq, and Syria, where a corps of devoted followers directed the activities of dedicated terrorists. The Assassins realized that the success of their organization depended on secrecy and a small number of dedicated followers to prevent detection from rival religious and political groups. So, they planned a long-term campaign of terror, often striking their victims at night while they slept. This program of terror by a small religious sect to maintain its religious autonomy succeeded in terrorizing the Mideast for two centuries. The legends about the Old Man of the Mountains and the Assassins have no doubt deeply inspired subsequent generations and apparently have motivated a campaign of suicidal truck bombings in the 1980s by a Shi'ite fundamentalist group calling itself the Islamic Jihad.

At this time little information is available on the newest group of Islamic

---

[5]Menachem Begin, *The Revolt: Story of the Irgun* (rev. ed.) (New York: Nash, 1977), p. 47.

[6]For example, see M. G. S. Hodgson, *The Order of Assassins* (The Hague: Morton, 1955); Bernard Lewis, *The Assassins: A Radical Sect in Islam* (New York: Basic Books, 1968), Chapter 2; Enno Franzius, *History of the Order of Assassins* (New York: Funk and Wagnalls, 1969).

assassins who promise to drive all foreigners out of Lebanon and have taken numerous Westerners hostage. The group is believed to be a clandestine coalition of Iranian-influenced Shi'ite Muslim fanatics. They have taken credit for several spectacular terrorist suicide truck bombings, including the U.S. Embassy in Lebanon (twice), the U.S. Marine compound in Lebanon, and the Israeli military and the French military compounds in Lebanon.

Other secret societies have existed for centuries in India and the Far East. The Thugs were a well-organized society of professional assassins who terrorized India for over 300 years. Unlike the Sicarii and the Assassins who killed their victims with daggers, the Thugs strangled their victims with a silk handkerchief. The choice of victims was random and indiscriminate; as a result they were feared throughout India, especially in the provinces of Punjab and Hindustan. They traced their origin to the religious dogma and practices of Kali, the Hindu goddess of destruction. The Thugs had complete contempt for death. Their political goals were not easily understandable and seldom did they terrorize members of the British Raj or Indian Rajah. Sporadic efforts were made to suppress the Thugs, but it was not until about 1837, through the cooperative efforts of the British military and various princely states, that the Thugs were driven underground. By 1852 the Thug religious cult had become extinct.[7]

The Thug phenomenon is yet another historical footnote to religious and secular terrorism. The same applies to the more fearsome secret societies in China that terrorized the countryside and urban areas for centuries.[8] Their political objectives were for the most part vague or nonexistent. Many secret societies engage in the criminal activities of gambling, smuggling, extortion and murder, hiring themselves out to the highest bidder. However, most secret Chinese societies despised foreigners. For that reason the Boxer Rebellion was encouraged by the union of several secret societies to rid China of all foreign influence. Even so, their political ambitions were limited to the control of criminal activities. In this respect they were more like the Mafia rather than a well-organized political terrorist movement.

The interest of the Fenian Brotherhood in revolutionary politics was probably more obvious, but it was still not a serious threat to the security of the United States or Ireland. The Fenians were an Irish-American nationalist revolutionary secret society active during the 1860s. They derived their name from a legendary band of warriors in Ireland led by Finn MacCumhaill. Fenianism had as its major political objective the starting of a popular uprising in Ireland against colonial British rule. Irish communities in the United States as well as Australia, Canada and South America supported the Fenians and

---

[7]For example, see George Bruse, *The Stranglers: The Cult of Thuggee and Its Overthrow in British India* (New York: Harcourt, Brace and World, 1969).

[8]For example, see Jean Chesneaux, ed., *Popular Movements and Secret Societies in China, 1840–1950,* (Stanford: Stanford University Press, 1972).

revolution in Ireland. Their greatest opportunity came at the close of the U.S. Civil War when the Irish who fought for both the Union and the Confederacy were influenced by the Fenians to return to Ireland and prepare for the uprising that would finally defeat the British. The Fenians began a campaign of terror and assassination against the ruling British administration and Irish collaborators who supported the British. The British reacted quickly and suspended many civil liberties, including the enactment of the Habeas Corpus Act. A considerable number of rebels and potential rebels were arrested, thus destroying the planned uprising. The movement came to an end in both the United States and Ireland with the death of its founder, John O'Mahony, in 1877.[9]

According to Irish historian O'Farrell, the Fenian movement was a primitive attempt at revolution since it had no political program other than violent revolution based more on emotions and random terrorism than revolutionary discipline.[10] However, the emotional nature of Fenian rhetoric did awaken the latent revolutionary spirit of the Irish. The nationalist fervor of the Fenians eventually led to the formation of the Irish Republican Brotherhood, which has evolved into the oldest guerrilla army in the world today and probably the best known, the Irish Republican Army (IRA).

The Ku Klux Klan may not have been organized like an army, but its rhetoric has incited many Americans to join the most nefarious secret society in the United States. Its origin is somewhat sketchy, but historians seem to agree that the original Klan was organized by southern Civil War veterans in Pulaski, Tennessee, in 1865. The name aparently is derived from the Greek word *kyklos,* from which comes the English *circle.* Klan was added for the sake of versification, and the Ku Klux Klan emerged. Laqueur reminds us that there are three Klans.[11] The first, a product of the Reconstruction period (1865–1876), was a secret, violent society organized to intimidate and spread fear among blacks and carpetbaggers. It was set up as the "Invisible Empire of the South" with a definable organizational structure. It was divided into state Realms, county Provinces, and individual Dens. The empire was presided over by a Grand Wizard with a descending hierarchy of Grand Dragons, Grand Titans, and Grand Cyclopses. There were also some minor functionaries known as giants, genii, hydras, furies, goblins, and nighthawks. They adopted intimidating symbols: wearing white hoods and robes, and burning crosses. Symbolic threats gave substance to the power of terrorism and elevated the level of fear created by indiscriminate acts of violence. The more

---

[9]For example, see Wilfried Neldhardt, *Fenianism in North America* (University Park: Pennsylvania State University, 1975); William D'Arcy, *The Fenian Movement in the U.S.: 1858–1886* (Washington: Catholic University Press, 1947).

[10]Patrick O'Farrell, *Ireland's English Question* (New York: Schocken, 1972), pp. 138–43.

[11]Walter Laqueur, *Terrorism* (Boston: Little, Brown, 1977), p. 10.

violent members escalated their level of fear through harassing, beating, and terrorizing blacks and white sympathizers, who were called scalawags.[12]

The second Klan (1915–1944), like the first, also stood for white supremacy; but in addition it campaigned for many other causes, such as American patriotism and attacks on bootleggers and other law violators. This new Ku Klux Klan was organized at Stone Mountain, Georgia, in 1915 and proclaimed the protection and supremacy of white Protestants. The new Klan added Catholics, Jews, foreigners, and organized labor to its hate list. By the mid-1920s membership had increased to between 4 and 5 million. The Klan controlled local politicians, judges, governors, and at least two U.S. senators. In 1928 the Democrats nominated Al Smith, a Catholic, for president. This action produced a hate campaign against all Catholics, using the slogan "Keep the Pope out of the White House." The Klan was no longer a small secret society; instead it was a formidable political threat to freedom and democracy. This threat further manifested itself in the late 1930s when it was discovered that the Klan had a close association with members of the Nazi party. Finally, the U.S. government began to arrest Klan members for a variety of civil rights violations and for unpaid back taxes. The Klan fell into disrepute and for the next 20 years was quiescent; but in the mid-1960s the civil rights movement renewed interest in the Klan, and once again Klan membership began to grow.[13]

The emergence of the third Klan (1960–1975) began with accounts of beatings, shootings, and bombings in southern communities carried out by Klansmen attempting to terrorize blacks and civil rights workers. Birmingham, Alabama, became Bombingham, Alabama, since more than 100 bombs were detonated by apparent Klan members to intimidate blacks and civil rights workers. In fact, 50 bombings that occurred in the sixties in Birmingham are to this day unsolved. Crosses were burned at Klan meetings and night riders roamed the countryside. By 1966 the random, indiscriminate violence of the Klan had escalated and overwhelmed local law enforcement. The federal government stepped in and prepared an agenda to arrest and prosecute the top leadership of the Klan for the slaying of civil rights workers. President Johnson even appealed to all Klan members to withdraw from the organization "before it is too late." Nevertheless, the Klan energetically participated in the hate campaign directed toward the civil rights movement. In the end Klan members received little profit for their efforts. The Klan once again has fallen into disrepute and membership today consists of a small number of malcontents who have aligned themselves with the American Nazi party and the White

---

[12]For example, see David M. Chalmers, *Hooded Americanism: The First Century of the Ku Klux Klan 1865–1965* (Garden City, N.J.: Doubleday, 1965).

[13]William P. Randel, *The Ku Klux Klan: A Century of Infamy* (Philadelphia: Chilton, 1965); David M. Chalmers, *Hood Americanism: The History of the Ku Klux Klan* (New York: Franklin Watts, 1981), pp. 190–325.

Peoples Supreme party. These three groups have apparently formed a secret society of hate, calling the group the United Racist Front.[14]

Narodnaya Volya

Compared to the Sicarii, Assassins, Thugs, Fenians, Chinese secret societies and Ku Klux Klan, the Narodnaya Volya was historically the most successful terrorist organization, even though its struggle with tsarist Russia lasted only from January, 1878, to March, 1881. The Narodnaya Volya (People's Will), organized as a socialist movement in Russia in the 1870s, was based on the concept that an overt campaign of political propaganda would excite the peasantry and workers and influence reforms in the regime. The movement first arose, like so many revolutionary movements, among intellectual and professional people. The writings of Herbert Spenser, August Comte, and John Stuart Mill encouraged the intellectuals; the teachings of Karl Marx dominated much of ther ideology. The Narodnaya Volya was also enhanced by the failure of the ruling elite to recognize the legitimate grievances of the workers. The failure of tsarist Russia to respond to these grievances led to a split in Narodnaya Volya on how to react to the regime.[15]

The moderates believed that a concentrated propaganda campaign would incite the workers and undermine the authority of the tsar's regime. Another faction, led by the anarchist Bakunin, was convinced that the use of force and violence through a popular uprising would effect political changes.[16] Opposed to both approaches, Tkachev preached a doctrine of the forcible overthrow of the regime by dedicated revolutionaries, followed by a general education of the populace in communist teachings.[17] At first the extremists were rejected in favor of a strategy of peaceful reforms, but the tsar's regime overreacted and began to arrest and imprison many moderate members of Narodnaya Volya. The most famous political trial was the "trial of the 193" in 1878.[18] Some defendants were sentenced to death, others to prison and still others were exiled. This action by the regime did not destroy Narodnoya Volya but widened the difference between moderates and extremists on the use of violence to overthrow the tsar. The radicals won the "debate" and immediately began a campaign of violent retaliation against the tsar's regime. The switch had been

[14]Jerry Thompson, *My Life in the Klan* (New York: Putnam, 1982).

[15]For example, see Astrid Von Borcke, "Violence and Terror in Russian Revolutionary Populism, The Norodnaya Volya, 1879–1883," in *Social Protest, Violence, and Terrorism in 19th and 20th Century Europe* (London: MacMillan, 1982), pp. 48–62; Ronald Seth, *The Russian Terrorists: The Story of Narodniki* (London: Barrie and Rockliff, 1967).

[16]James Joll, "Anarchism: A Living Tradition," in *Anarchism Today,* eds. David E. Apter and James Joll (New York: Anchor, 1972), pp. 245–61.

[17]Franco Venturi, *Roots of Revolution: A History of the Populist and Socialist Movements in 19th Century Russia* (New York: Knopf, 1960), pp. 389–428.

[18]William E. Mosse, *Alesander II and the Modernization of Russia* (New York: MacMillan, 1958), p. 159.

made from peaceful propaganda to the terrorist method. Narodnaya Volya set out to change the regime by acts of random terrorism directed toward the tsar's family and government officials.

This terrorism frequently involved the tactic of planned, selective assassinations. The key targets represented minor government officials as well as the most visible symbols of the tsar's power—police and military personnel. However, their favorite target was, of course, the tsar. There were at least six recorded attempts on the life of Tsar Alexander II by Narodnaya Volya before he was finally killed by an exploding bomb. The tactic of assassination was also used to intimidate and coerce government bureaucrats who abused the power of their position. For example, several prominent police officials were assassinated for their brutal treatment of political prisoners.

Moreover, many members of Narodnaya Volya were realistic and recognized that a strategy of selective assassination could not topple the tsar's regime. Narodnaya Volya reasoned that a campaign of selective assassination would cause government officials to become overly security-conscious, thus weakening their ability to cope with rising political dissatisfaction in the general society. One of the more articulate members of Narodnaya Volya explains:

> In a struggle against an invisible, impalpable, omnipresent enemy, the strong is vanquished not by arms of his own kind, but by the continuous exhaustion of his own strength, which ultimately exhausts him, more than he would be exhausted by defeat. . . . The terrorists cannot overthrow the government, cannot drive it from St. Petersburg and Russia, but having compelled it, for many years running, to neglect everything and do nothing but struggle with them, they will render its position untenable.[19]

At this stage in the struggle, the acts of terrorism were sporadic and often unsuccessful. But terrorist technology was in its early, evolutionary phase: the pistol, dagger, and crude explosive devices were being replaced by a new discovery, dynamite. Narodnaya Volya was the first terrorist organization to use dynamite on a wide scale. Crude bombs were fashioned that were both highly effective and very dangerous. The successful assassination of Alexander II was accomplished by the assassin approaching the tsar's carriage with a quantity of dynamite and blowing himself up along with the tsar. This act of terrorism caused the government to finally round up the leaders of Narodnaya Volya. Once the leadership was gone, the popularity of Narodnaya Volya began to decline. The attack that killed the tsar also doomed the Narodnaya Volya.

It is the terrorist ideology that distinguishes the "People's Will" from today's terrorist organizations. The Russian terrorists maintained that they had been forced to use murder since the tsarist government was corrupt and closed all possibilities of peaceful reform. They even promised to discontinue

---

[19]T. Stepniak, *Underground Russia: Revolutionary Profiles and Sketches from Life* (New York: Scribner, 1892), p. 32.

their terrorist activity once the government demonstrated its commitment to reforming the "system." Ivianski argues that Narodnoya Volya was desperately concerned about the concept of morality and terrorism.[20] Unlike terrorists today, the Narodnaya Volya would meticulously plan their assassinations to avoid the killing of innocent people. A favorite quote of the Russian terrorists is that we will not shed "one drop of unnecessary blood." The victim was always a person seen guilty of specific acts of brutality or corruption against the "people." The political goal was the thirst for basic freedoms embodied in the U.S. Bill of Rights. They had complete contempt for the anarchist element or pathological person who committed indiscriminate assassinations to overthrow a democracy. Where people were free to express their ideas through elected officials, Narodnaya Volya condemned the use of assassination and terrorism as a means of changing the system.

Though Narodnaya Volya did not completely understand the moral dilemma of the terrorist strategy, adherents did pay the moral price—one that established their reputations as noble, tragic, historical figures found in the novels of Dostoyevski and Turgenev. They had to accept death and even seek it in order to justify and recognize the aura of evil that surrounds an act of premeditated murder. Laqueur writes that the moral and intellectual distance between Narodnaya Volya and contemporary terrorists "is to be measured in light years."[21]

Even so, it must be pointed out that Russian terrorists of the period, including Narodnaya Volya, admired the rhetoric of Nechayev, encompassed in his *Revolutionary Catechism*. The portrait of the ideal terrorist and the terrorist method are dramatized in this document. This ideal type was distinguished by inhumanity and a lack of moral sensitivity. The Terrorist was to denounce present-day social morality, be suspicious of friends, and have only one mission in life—the merciless destruction of the system. The *Revolutionary Catechism* is generally acknowledged to be the most cold-blooded manual of instruction in terrorist literature. It proposes a plan that has become familiar to all political terrorists. The function of the terrorist, who represents the vanguard of the revolution, must be to provoke governmental repression that would set the stage for a popular uprising. The *Catechism* glorified assassination as the tactic of political change. Nechayev advised that moderate political leaders should be the first targets of assassination since those remaining would represent the hardliners and would, therefore, be more useful in stimulating a popular revolution. Nechayev eventually became entangled in an internal struggle that resulted in the ritual murder of an innocent comrade. After the details of the murder became known to the Narodnaya Volya, Nechayev was discredited and his influence in the Russian revolutionary movement declined.

---

[20]Ze'ev Ivianski, "The Moral Issue: Some Aspects of Individual Terror," in *The Morality of Terrorism: Religious and Secular Justifications,* eds. David C. Rapoport and Yonah Alexander (New York: Pergamon, 1983), pp. 229–57.

[21]Laqueur, *Terrorism,* p. 4.

He was imprisoned for the murder of his comrade, and he later died of tuberculosis.[22]

However, the writings of Nechayev, particularly the *Revolutionary Catechism,* have inspired contemporary revolutionary theorists such as Debray[23] and "Che" Guevara.[24] Both writers outline the means of revolution by engaging in a campaign of indiscriminate terroristic violence designed to produce a situation of intense fear. For example, Guevara was unable to influence the peasants of Bolivia to support his revolution so he attempted to neutralize them by terrorizing village leaders and elders in a planned program of assassination and mutilation. Probably the best-known manual of terrorist strategy is presented in the *Mini-Manual of Urban Guerrilla Warfare.*[25] Its author, Carlos Marighella, was a dedicated Brazilian revolutionary who advocated terrorist action to destroy the existing democratic political system. The more radical and destructive, the better for the revolution. Marighella approved of the poisoning of food and water supplies, the sabotage of transport systems and oil pipelines, and a general strategy of the scorched-earth policy used by the military. He assumed that the populace would blame the government for resulting disasters. Typically for Marighella, the terrorist tactic of assassination was preferred over other violent acts. There is nothing intellectual in Marighella's dissertation, and the moral ambiguity in the use of the terrorist method is of no major concern. The *Mini-Manual* is nothing more than a rehash of some of the original ideas of Nechayev. Its irrational and anti-intellectual approach is an elitist and mechanistic view of the way in which terrorism and revolution could be successful.

The *Document on Terror*[26] is yet another frightening review of the terrorist method. It offers a two-stage approach: (1) *general* terrorism, which is directed at the entire population, and (2) *enlightened* terrorism, which is motivated by selective attacks on specific groups. The author of this *Document* is unknown, although it is believed the manuscript was initially found on a dead KGB agent in the Soviet Union. Eventually the *Document* made its way into Western Europe, appearing for the first time in 1948. It is not unreasonable to assume that the author was greatly influenced by Nechayev since much of

---

[22]For example, see Sergei Nechaev, "Catechism of the Revolutionist," *Daughter of a Revolutionist,* ed. M. Confino (London: Alcove, 1982); Robert Payne, *The Life and Death of Lenin* (New York: Simon and Schuster, 1964), pp. 24–29.

[23]Regis Debray, *Revolution in the Revolution: Armed Struggle and Political Struggle in Latin America* (New York: Grove, 1967).

[24]Ernesto (Che) Guevara, *Episodes of the Revolutionary War* (New York: International, 1968).

[25]For example, see Carlos Marighella, "The Mini-Manual of Urban Guerrilla Warfare," in *Urban Guerrilla Warfare,* ed. Robert Moss (London: Institute for Strategic Studies, 1971); Carlos Marighella, *The Terrorist Classic: Manual of the Urban Guerrilla,* trans. Gene Hanrahan (North Carolina: Documentary Pub., 1985).

[26]"Document on Terror," *The Morality of Terrorism: Religious and Secular Justifications,* eds., David C. Rapoport and Yonah Alexander (New York: Pergamon, 1983), pp. 186–216.

the *Document* is a replication of the *Revolutionary Catechism*. It is also entirely possible that the sudden emergence of the *Document* was a propaganda ploy by the West. In any event the suggested tactics of terrorism and the specific practices of terrorism are familiar elsewhere.

In sum, Narodnaya Volya has passed into the pages of history. Other terrorists and revolutionaries sprang up in Russia. In 1905 uprisings and the well-documented Russian revolution of 1917 proved to be the final death blow to tsarist Russia. The moral issue of the use of terrorist tactics so hotly debated by Narodnaya Volya posed no problem to the newly emerged Soviet state. State terror replaced insurgent terrorism with a savage brutality that the Narodnaya Volya would not have recognized.

The Anarchist Tradition

Another political ideology closely linked to terrorism is the anarchist tradition of assassination. Anarchism has frequently been associated with terrorism. The equation *anarchism = terrorism* is well documented and persistent in the literature.[27] This relationship is based on the political assassination of kings, heads of state and other symbols of government in the nineteenth century. For example, King Humbert of Italy; William McKinley, president of the United States; George I, king of Greece; Sadi Carnot, president of France; and Elizabeth, empress of Austria, were all assassinated by anarchists, thus supporting the popular opinion of anarchy.[28] However, most anarchists have not supported the terrorist method, so this association with terrorism may be unjustly deserved. In order to fully understand the doctrine of anarchism, Schmid suggests it is necessary to distinguish between three distinctive types: anarchism as a political ideology, anarchism as a movement, and the ambitions of individual anarchists.[29]

Three distinct principles form the basic analytical framework of anarchist dogma. First, anarchism is opposed to all forms of government that apply political, economic, and social coercion. In place of organized governmental systems, anarchists foresee voluntary arrangements of mature and independent human beings. Anarchists are uniformly anti-institution; thus, the repudiation of state, political party, associations, unions, churches and all forms of institutionalized law. Second, anarchists believe that all political and religious ideologies are manifestations of the domination of institutional life and the ultimate submission of man to a formalized system of rules and laws. Anarchism is not only international in its approach but anational. Thus, territorial boundaries cease to exist and man belongs to one human community. Third, the objective of anarchism is a domination-free society, or total anarchy. An-

---

[27]George Woodcock, *Anarchism: A History of Libertarian Ideas and Movements* (New York: World Publishing, 1962). David Miller, *Anarchism* (London: J. M. Dent and Sons, 1984).

[28]James Joll, *The Anarchists* (Cambridge: Harvard University Press, 1980).

[29]Alex Schmid, *Political Terrorism* (New Brunswick: Transaction, 1983), p. 52.

archy would replace institutional law with the self-organization of individual personalities who were committed to the "good" of society. Each individual would be left *absolutely* free. However, two exceptions applied. If any person attempted to injure another, all well-meaning persons would have the right to protect the aggrieved person; and law-abiding citizens could suppress the criminal element, but only through voluntary cooperation, not institutionalized legal rules.

The substance of philosophic anarchism is based on the creation of a "good" society that would exclude authority, repudiate violent methods of control, and strive toward anarchic organization. In order to achieve this blissful existence, dedicated and enlightened anarchists would set an example of their goodness by practicing the anarchist method in their isolated utopias. These islands of "freedom" would then be imitated by others seeking a more libertarian existence and the creation of a new organization of human relationships.

Anarchism as a political movement gained prominence in the nineteenth century when it became associated with socialist doctrine and the influence of Bakunin.[30] But this relationship was short-lived. Led by the radical Russian revolutionary Bakunin, the anarchists were expelled from the first Socialist International because of a dispute over their reliance on organized violence and the use of the terrorist fear tactic of "propaganda by the deed." As a movement, anarchism survived until World War I in Russia and until the beginning of World War II in Spain. But in the United States the anarchists attained their greatest success by relying on labor unions as the main instrument of revolutionary struggle.

The anarcho-syndicalists, or syndicates, favored a syndicate of workers and professionals working (in both private industry and public service) to take over the workplace from the bosses and manage the means of production. In towns, villages, and cities, representatives of the local syndicates would agree on economic policies; a national syndicate would formulate policy at the national level. It was believed that syndicates controlling a vital industry or service would not attempt to take advantage of their position and abuse their power since all people were working for the good of society. There were, however, anarchists who rejected this approach, maintaining that social cooperation of this magnitude can never be wholly voluntary. Thus, some constraints were necessary; as such, the individual would not be absolutely free. Despite internal problems and opposition from the bosses, an anarcho-syndicalist labor union, known as the Industrial Workers of the World (IWW), was formed. They were supportive of numerous strikes that impacted on the industrial worker. Wages and benefits increased and working conditions improved, but employers were not about to turn the management of their enterprises over

---

[30]For example, see Richard B. Saltman, *The Social and Political Thought of Michael Bakunin* (Westport, Conn.: Greenwood, 1983).

to the employees. By the end of World War I the IWW had lost its importance. Joe Hill, organizer and leader of the IWW, had been convicted and executed on a disputed murder charge that greatly divided the movement.[31]

In 1903 the U.S. Congress passed a law to bar foreign anarchists from entering the United States and to deport foreign nationals who supported the anarchist doctrine. More stringent legislation was enacted in 1918, sparked by the activities of the IWW. During the anticommunist excitement of 1919–20 several foreign-born anarchists were deported to the Soviet Union. But the most celebrated case of the period involved the robbery and murder of a mail clerk by two admitted Italian anarchists, Nicola Sacco and Bartolomeo Vanzetti.[32] After a long-delayed trial and worldwide protests that the evidence was not conclusive, the two were executed in August 23, 1927. Popular opinion held that the two were executed not for the murder and robbery but for their extreme, anarchist political ideas. The case is still angrily debated in law schools and criminal justice classes today. In 1952 earlier legislation was superceded, and the language was changed to allow native Americans to freely express their political opinions. Anarchism has declined steadily both as a political ideology and an organized movement during the last quarter-century.

There are, however, several attributes of anarchist philosophy that may be directly related to terrorism. The original anarchists believed that they were at the forefront of world revolutionary movements. Hence, they had to be inciters of action in order to inspire the masses. Anarchist theory placed great emphasis on individual initiative and freedom. Rather than wait for the revolution to change society, anarchists supported the position of demonstration by example. This demonstration took the position that the state is extremely vulnerable, asserting that prominent political figures are easy targets. The basic tenet of "propaganda by the deed" became the guiding principle of dedicated anarchists. This tenet, together with the individual character of anarchistic violence, caused a chain reaction of revenge and conspiratorial assassinations of kings, queens, judges, police, and other authority figures. Anarchist publications of the time applauded successful assassinations of high-ranking political personalities. This led to the belief that perhaps an anarchist conspiracy existed to terrorize world leaders, although some writers have argued that the assassinations were not related in any way, that the "lone wolf," or individual assassin, seeking to free the masses was responsible for the killings.[33] While all anarchists deny authority, history concludes that only a few resorted to the

[31]John G. Brooks, *American Syndicalism: The IWW* (New York: MacMillan, 1913); Bertrand Russell, *Roads to Freedom: Socialism, Anarchism, and Syndicalism* (London: Allen and Unwin, 1919).

[32]For example, see Brian Jackson, *The Black Flag: A Look Back at the Strange Case of Nicola Sacco and Bartolomeo Vanzetti* (Boston: Routledge and Kegan Paul, 1981); Francis Russell, *Sacco and Vanzetti: The Case Resolved* (New York: Harper and Row, 1986).

[33]Ze'ev Iviansky, "Individual Terror: Concept and Typology," *Journal of Contemporary History* 12 (1977), p. 50.

use of violence and terrorism. The individualist nature of anarchism, its penchant for revolutionary ideals, and the propaganda by deed lend some credibility to the notion that *anarchism = terrorism;* beyond this the relationship is superficial.

Terrorism and Violence in the United States

On November 7, 1983, a powerful pipe bomb ripped through the Senate chambers of the U.S. Capitol, causing extensive property damage in the 183-year-old structure. In a communiqué issued by a little-known group, the Armed Resistance United/United Freedom Front claimed credit for the attack, announcing that their action was taken in retaliation for the U.S. government's policies in Central America and Lebanon. This act of violence and terrorism represents the action of the most recent clandestine terrorist group to openly confront the U.S. government. However, there have been literally hundreds of groups and individuals who have used the terrorist method in an effort to intimidate the federal government as well as to create fear among specific population categories in the United States. Let's return briefly to those violent days of yesteryear and trace the main trends of violence and terrorism that have become part of American folklore. (In Chapter 4 contemporary domestic terrorist groups active in the United States will be reviewed.)

Many unique aspects of our cultural and political life have contributed to the collective and individual violence that has historically troubled the United States. These include the Revolutionary War, the Civil War, the issue of slavery and the Indian Wars, labor strife, the violence of racial, ethnic and religious prejudice, criminal gang violence, indiscriminate lynchings, vigilante groups, urban riots, and the serial killers that roam urban America. Violence in our culture also stems from the frontier tradition and our long love affair with firearms, especially handguns. Violence has been used repeatedly as a means to an end and has been widely encouraged and accepted. Using our earlier definition of terrorism, the deliberate use of murder and threats to induce fear in order to gain a political or tactical advantage, it is possible to classify as terrorism much of our violent past.

Our nation was founded on the use of violence. Before the actual beginning of the Revolutionary War, the Sons of Liberty engaged in acts of sporadic violence and terrorism in an effort to provoke the British and stir patriotic feelings among the colonists. One such incident was the Boston Massacre of 1770, where five unarmed Americans were killed by British soldiers firing into a crowd of patriotic demonstrators. The Boston Tea Party is yet another example. A group of responsible citizens, protesting an unjust tax, boarded British ships in Boston harbor and in an orderly fashion began to throw tea into the bay. The British viewed this as a premeditated act of open defiance against British sovereignty; they had to react. The Boston port was closed, thus ruining trade and causing economic chaos, and more British troops were dispatched to control the defiant rebels. These measures only served to promote open revolt in the Bay colony.[34]

The Bostonians formed a small military organization called the Minutemen, which was prepared to muster on the shortest possible notice. The actions of the Minutemen so inspired the remaining 12 colonies that open rebellion was imminent. With the decision by the rebels to resist militarily, it was necessary to have the full support of all colonists. However, there were a substantial number of colonists who supported the cause of the British crown. These Tories, as they were called, were intimidated, threatened, and exposed by the rebels for their support of the British.[35] Many were tarred and feathered; others were beaten and lynched by the patriots. The tactics of intimidation, coercion, and fear were successful since many Tories began to denounce the British crown and support open rebellion.

The tactics of guerrilla warfare were also an intricate part of rebel strategy. The rebels recognized that they were, at first, numerically inferior to the British and so they emphasized the need to be highly politically motivated. This political determination to carry on a long, protracted military campaign began to wear down the most dedicated and committed British soldier. Hit-and-run forays of pillage and mayhem destroyed British morale and Tory support. Unpredictable, random violence and terrorism was widespread in the colonies as the British and the Revolutionaries competed for popular support.

Thus, two important aspects of the Revolution emerge. First, it has been glorified in our tradition and history. Second, it set the tone that justifies the use of violence in any cause that is identified as good by Americans.

The manifestation of violence and terrorism in the Revolution resulted in the creation of the American nation. In the same way, that manifestation became the instrument of the nation's preservation in the era of the Civil War. The Civil War itself was one of pervasive violence and terror. One of the most violent periods in American history followed the Civil War. It was a decades-long struggle with Ku Kluxers, lynch mobs, night riders, outlaws, and racial strife. Outlaws such as Quantrell, and the James and Younger boys, roamed the border states of Kansas, Missouri and Kentucky looting, pillaging, and murdering. Outbreaks of feuding erupted that continue to this day in Texas, Kentucky, Missouri and West Virginia. Racial strife and the intimidation of blacks became routine in the old Confederate States. Possibly no single event contributed more to the escalation of criminal violence and terrorism in the United States than the Civil War.

Unmistakably the longest and most revengeful war in American history

[34]For example, see Henry B. Dawson, *The Sons of Liberty in New York* (New York: Arno, 1969); Hiller B. Zobel, *The Boston Massacre* (New York: Norton, 1970); Wesley S. Griswold, *The Night the Revolution Began: The Boston Tea Party* (Vermont: S. Greene, 1972).

[35]For example, see Wallace Brown, *Victorious in Defeat: The American Loyalists in Exile* (New York: Facts on File, 1984); Daniel W. Howe, *The Political Culture of American Whigs* (Chicago: University of Chicago, 1979).

was the one between white settlers and native Americans. This was continued with only infrequent truces for nearly 300 years, culminating in the final massacre at Wounded Knee, South Dakota, in 1890.[36] Racial prejudice and greed encouraged many white settlers to appropriate Native American land either through trickery or violence. Inevitably the Native Americans would retaliate, thus ensuring the escalation of a cycle of terror and counterterror. To whites the norms of Native American warfare seemed savage and barbaric, but they learned quickly and adopted some practices for their own. The taking of scalps, for instance, was customary among experienced white settlers and fighters as well as Native Americans. Unkept promises, broken treaties, the massacre of defenseless women and children by both whites and Native Americans characterized a relationship between the two groups that is evident even today. This unremitting war has done much to shape our propensity for violence and terrorism. But wars represent only one aspect of violence in America. The labor movement also has a rich heritage of violence and has done much to shape labor-management relations in our past and present.

The United States has had the most violent and murderous labor history of any industrial nation of the world. This violence was not confined to particular industries, geographical locations, or specific labor organizations. However, it has been more frequent in the "smokestack" industries of coal, steel, railroads, and auto manufacturing. The coming of the Industrial Revolution to America also brought violence to the coalfields, steel mills, and railroad yards. Labor organizations proliferated, and the strike became a major weapon for advancing the well-being of the work force. Violent attempts to suppress union activity and break up strikes only served to incite workers and escalate violence. In Pittsburgh a railroad strike in 1877 reached the level of insurrection and federal troops had to restore order. Not far away in the coalfields of eastern Pennsylvania the Molly Maguires, a secret organization of Irish miners, was engaged in a terrorist campaign of assassination and mayhem against coal operators.[37] In Homestead, across the river from Pittsburgh, the steel mill strike of 1892 resulted in several deaths and the destruction of the union that is still evident in Homestead today.[38] The silver miners of Coeur d'Alene, Idaho, organized a strike that resulted in a lockout and every mine in the area was closed.[39] The strikers at Coeur d'Alene went on the offensive and when all the dust cleared at least eight strikers were killed and several

[36]Dee Brown, *Bury my Heart at Wounded Knee: An Indian History of the American West* (New York: Bantam, 1972), pp. 3–7.

[37]David Brohle, *The Molly Maguires* (London: Oxford University, 1964), pp. 237–39.

[38]Arthur G. Burgoyne, *The Homestead Strike of 1892* (Pittsburgh: University of Pittsburgh, 1979), pp. 12–22.

[39]Philip Taft, *History of Labor in the U.S.* (New York: MacMillan, 1935); Robert W. Smith, *The Coeur d'Alene Mining War of 1882: A Case Study of an Industrial Dispute* (Corvallis: Oregon State College, 1961).

wounded. The National Guard finally restored order by arresting all union men and charging thirty strikers with conspiracy.

Without a doubt, the most violent spasm of labor violence occurred in Colorado from 1884 to 1915. Strikes and violence were typical during this 30-year period but culminated with the most devastating violence in American labor history. The coal miners struck the Colorado Fuel and Iron Company in 1913–14; during the first 5 weeks of the strike 18 persons were killed. But the final atrocity took place on April 20, 1914, at Ludlow, Colorado. Strikers and state militia had been engaged in a 15-hour pitched battle on the defensive. The strikers retreated to their tent city where they were immediately surrounded by the militia. After a brief period of unsuccessful negotiation, the militia attacked the tent city with heavy weapons, firing indiscriminately into the tents that were occupied by women and children as well as strikers. The flimsy tents burst into flames. Among the dead were 2 women and 11 children who suffocated to death in the inferno that later became known as the "Black Hole of Ludlow." The enraged miners erupted in an orgy of violence and bloodletting that lasted for ten days, creating havoc and disorder over a 250-mile area of southern Colorado. The entrance of federal troops finally ended the violence and order was restored.[40]

Labor violence and "terrorism" reached its peak in the 1930s when successful strike actions were used to organize the automobile industry and other great mass-production industries. Labor violence has subsided considerably over the last decades. Flare-ups in the coal industry of Kentucky and copper mines of Arizona have been the most recent examples of labor violence. By comparison today's labor violence is moderate, with few deaths and personal injuries. Today labor violence is directed more toward the destruction of property. Closely related to labor violence have been our numerous, convulsive eruptions of racial, ethnic, and religious violence.

In fact, labor violence of the nineteenth century and early twentieth century was in reality ethnic conflicts between upper-class capitalists, their managers, and the unskilled immigrant labor force of Irish, Italians, Slavs, Jews, and others of eastern and southern European stock.[41] For example, the victims of the Ludlow massacre were mostly Italians, Greeks, and Irish immigrants. In 1891, 11 Italian anglers were the victims of a lynch mob in New Orleans.[42] The lynching was the outgrowth of a labor dispute over fishing rights in Louisiana. By 1900 the coal fields of Pennsylvania were dominated by eastern and southern European miners, and violence began to escalate between the immigrants and English-speaking miners and coal operators. This violence culmi-

---

[40]Zeese Papanikolas, *Buried Unsung: Louis Tikas and the Ludlow Massacre* (Salt Lake City: University of Utah, 1982).

[41]David Brody, *Steelworkers in America* (Cambridge: Harvard University Press, 1960), pp. 96–111.

[42]John E. Coxe, "The New Orleans Mafia Incident," *La Hist. Q.* 20 (1937), p. 1067.

nated when a group of striking Pennsylvania miners of mostly eastern and southern European origin marched from Hazelton to Latimer.[43] The peaceful marchers were met by sheriff's deputies who ordered them to disperse. When they failed to comply, the deputies were ordered to fire on the unarmed and unresisting marchers. Eighteen were killed and over 40 seriously wounded. Later a federal grand jury determined that most of those killed were shot in the back as they fled the indiscriminate firing of the deputies.

One of the most persistent factors in American violence has been the racial conflict between whites and blacks that can be traced back to the eighteenth century. The frequent uprisings of black slaves in American are well documented. For example, an alleged slave conspiracy in New York in 1712 caused white men to go on a hysterical rampage of lynching and burning black slaves.[44] There were literally hundreds of slave insurrections in the nineteenth century. The best-documented and the greatest of all slave rebellions is described in Styron's novel, *The Confessions of Nat Turner*.[45] Even so, Nat Turner's uprising was quickly suppressed by the retaliatory violence of white slaveowners.

As the institution of slavery ended, white men of the South developed a more specialized organization for dealing with blacks—the Ku Klux Klan (discussed earlier). Lynchings, whippings, torture, and murder were indiscriminately applied against blacks, Catholics, and Jews. Often the only criteria for becoming a victim of such extranormal violence were racial characteristics or religious preference. Other religious and racial instances of violence can be found in the anti-Catholic riots that were commonplace throughout the East before the Civil War. In California anti-Chinese sentiments often burst into violence and lynchings as the nineteenth century came to a close. However, one of the most resolute strands of violence in America has been our long history of urban riots and disorders.

At times it has appeared that urban racial and ethnic riots would bring about the total destruction of American cities. In essence urban riots have continued from colonial times, when the predominately Irish North End and South End mobs were active in Boston, to the more recent, spontaneous black Liberty City riots in Miami. In fact, the modern urban police system was created in reaction to the spontaneous urban riots of the 1840s and 1850s.[46] The whole purpose of creating a formalized police force was to maintain order in large metropolitan communities. Additionally, the present National Guard system was formalized to respond to urban uprisings that escalated beyond the control of the local police.

[43]For example, see Edward Pinkowski, *The Latimer Massacre* (Philadelphia: Sunshine, 1950).

[44]Winthrop D. Jordan, *White over Black: American Attitudes Toward the Negro* (Chapel Hill: University of North Carolina, 1968), pp. 115–17.

[45]William Styron, *The Confessions of Nat Turner* (New York: Random House, 1967).

[46]Edward Fogelson, *Big City Police* (Cambridge: Harvard University Press, 1978), p. 14.

The modern era of urban race riots began around the turn of the present century. From 1900 to 1949, there were 33 major interracial riots recorded in the United States. The peak period of interracial violence was from 1915 to 1919, when 22 of the 33 riots occurred. In these riots whites emerged as the main aggressors, attacking black urban centers and indiscriminately assaulting blacks. This period of racial unrest is comparable to the racial disorders that occurred between 1964 and 1969, but with one exception. Blacks now took the initiative and primarily attacked white businesses and stranded whites. The most shocking and frightful riots occurred in Detroit and Los Angeles where numerous blacks were killed or injured in pitched battles with the police. Most black rioting since 1964, however, has concentrated on property destruction and attacks on white-dominated police forces rather than assaults on the white community.[47]

Today urban riots are generally precipitated by violent action the police have taken while arresting a suspected felon. This usually takes the form of the white police officer using deadly force while attempting to apprehend a suspected black felon. The black offender is killed by the white police officer. Then, the police officer's judgment is questioned on the application of deadly force. The black neighborhood or entire black community erupts into spontaneous violence, destroying property and attacking police officers. Since 1980 this scenario has been repeated in Liberty City, Miami, Philadelphia, Washington, D.C., Orlando, Boston, and Los Angeles. Certainly, it is now possible to predict and anticipate future urban disruptions based on an analysis of historical precedents.

Another category of violence that can produce paralyzing fear is the multiple murderer and serial killer, a recent emergence in American society. According to English criminologist Dickson, the serial killer and multiple murderer have become quite commonplace in contemporary Western society.[48] In fact, the Federal Bureau of Investigation estimates that 35 serial murderers were committing heinous crimes across the United States in 1987. Psychiatric and legal literature sometimes make a distinction between multiple (mass) murder and serial murder. Mass murder refers to the killing of two or more victims, usually by one person in a single episode. For example, James Huberty killed 22 people and injured 12 others in a shooting spree at a McDonald's restaurant that lasted approximately 90 minutes. The reason for Huberty's outburst is still unknown. However, there is little doubt that a great deal of fear will be felt in the San Ysidro area for many years to come.

Serial murder refers to a number of murders usually committed by a single offender over a period of weeks, months, or years. Each murder is generally a discrete episode with a common motive, method, and type of victim.

---

[47]Otto Kerner, *Report of the National Advisory Commission on Civil Disorders* (New York: Bantam Books, 1968), pp. 85–105.

[48]Grierson Dickson, *Murder by Numbers* (London: Robert Hall, 1958), p. 8.

For instance, several recent examples of serial murder can be found in California: the Zebra killings, the Skid Row and Trash Bag murders, the Hillside strangler, and the trailside and freeway killers. While example after example can be identified, such questions as the actual number of serial murderers and their relationship to the creation of fear and terror still await serious study by the criminologist.

The obvious conclusion from this brief survey of violence and terrorism in the United States is that there has been a great deal of it. Violence and terrorism have also been used to support the highest ideals of American values: the birth of the nation, the preservation of the union and the end of slavery, the occupation of land, the improvement of the common worker, the stability of the city, and the preservation of law and order.

The most significant fact, however, has been the introduction of a formalized police system to maintain the peace. The fundamental role of the police in our democratic system has evolved into one of order maintenance. Closely related to the development of police organizations has been the expanded role of the military, both National Guards and federal troops to quell domestic urban violence. It seems incredible that so many examples exist of military personnel firing indiscriminately into unarmed crowds or marchers. The latest occurred, of course, at Kent State and Londonderry. Later we will review the role of the military in counterterrorist operations.

CONCLUSIONS

There is little doubt that the understanding of terrorism is enhanced by reviewing historical perspectives and stimulating an interest in the complexities of terrorist causes and doctrines. Many commentators believe that the terrorist phenomenon had no significant impact on society until the 1960s. Beginning in the sixties, the full impact of terrorism, supported by modern technology, was felt throughout the world. Specifically, terrorist groups today pose a much greater threat than before because of advanced weapons technology. Today's weapons are not only much easier to conceal, but readily available, and more destructive. Transportation systems and mass communication now allow terrorists to coordinate attacks with deadly efficiency. The availability of potential targets is unlimited. The tightening of security systems cannot hope to protect *all* potential targets.

However, those who subscribe to this thesis fail to understand the historical significance of terrorism. The historical record reveals the use of histrionic terrorism as a strategy to influence religious, political, social, and economic changes. From the ancient Sicarii to the more contemporary al Fatah, terrorism has proven to be a "successful" strategy to capture popular support and media attention. Writers often have difficulty identifying this historical tradition of terrorism since terrorist activity erupts only periodically throughout history at uneven intervals.

The fact is that we know very little about how deeply rooted terrorism is in our traditional cultural systems, and even less is known about the interaction of historical terrorist groups and their contemporary counterparts. Perhaps not until we develop a better understanding of the history of terrorism can we appreciate the impact of terrorism today.

In short, violence, and to a lesser extent, certain forms of "terrorism," have become a part of the human value system. In the next chapter we will explore the role of media and its relationship to violence and terrorism. The media has been widely criticized as being the principal factor in the growth of worldwide terrorism and in the general increase of violence in the world today. In later chapters political assassination and vigilante activity in the United States will be reviewed.

REVIEW QUESTIONS

1. Describe the terror tactics used by the Sicarii.
2. Outline the difference between the first, second, and third Klans.
3. What major attribute distinguishes Narodnaya Volya from modern terrorist groups?
4. Discuss the following "terrorist" publications:
   a. *Revolutionary Catechism*
   b. *Mini-Manual of Urban Guerrilla Warfare*
   c. *Document on Terror*
5. Who were the Assassins? Do terrorist actions of the Islamic Jihad resemble those used by the Assassins?
6. Identify three distinct types of anarchism. Define anarchism.
7. What is propaganda by the deed?
8. Compare and contrast the violence associated with the Revolutionary War, the Civil War, and the Indian Wars.
9. Identify the following:
   a. Masada
   b. Irgun Zvai Leumi
   c. Fenian Brotherhood
   d. anarcho-syndicalists
   e. Sons of Liberty
   f. Sacco and Vanzetti
   g. Bakunin
   h. Nat Turner
10. What has been identified as the main cause for urban disturbance in American cities?

THREE

VIOLENCE AND TERRORISM: THE ROLE OF THE MASS MEDIA

CHAPTER OBJECTIVES

The study of this chapter will enable you to:
- Explore the relationship between television and the escalation of violence in American society.
- Analyze the nature of contagion theory.
- Outline historical trends of skyjacking.
- Detail the uses of propaganda by terrorist groups.
- Interpret the use of a hunger strike as a media attention strategy.
- Recognize the insidious nature of censorship.
- Evaluate law enforcement and media relations.

INTRODUCTION

Modern terrorist groups make extensive use of the mass media, particularly the electronic media. One of the major purposes of a terrorist act is to inform the world. We are reminded by Crenshaw that "the most basic reason for terrorism is to gain recognition or attention."[1] Advertising the aims of the terrorist groups and the specific act of terrorism is extremely important to the success of the terrorist incident. In fact, publicity and attention are the only objectives in many cases.

For example, on September 10, 1976, five members of the Croatian National Resistance, or Fighters for Free Croatia (CFF) hijacked a Boeing 727 with 63 passengers and the flight crew aboard. The odyssey began in New York and ended some 30 hours later in Paris. The hijackers made stops in Montreal, Newfoundland, London, and Paris. The demands of the Croatians included the publication of their manifesto in its entirety in the *New York Times, Chicago Tribune, Los Angeles Times,* and the *International Herald Tribune.* This manifesto outlined Croation grievances against the Yugoslav government and the Tito regime. Furthermore, the Croatians demanded that pamphlets be scattered over New York, Chicago, Montreal, London, and Paris. These pamphlets proclaimed that the world would not have peace until Croatia had the same freedoms that other nations enjoy. On board the hijacked plane, the Croatians had planted a fake bomb and threatened to injure the passengers. The plane was forced to land in Newfoundland where 35 passengers were unexpectedly released. The hijackers then continued on to Paris where they finally surrendered to the police and were returned to the United States. After dismantling his fake bomb and being taken into custody by the FBI, one of the hijackers announced, "Well, that's show biz"! So for the price of 5 one-way tickets to Chicago, the printing of some pamphlets, the ingredients for at least two bombs, all worth approximately $400 taken together, the Croatians received media attention worth millions of dollars in terms of free advertisement, and they captured the attention of millions of people for some 30 hours. Certainly the purpose of this act of air piracy was to gain publicity for a political cause. To this end the Croatians were successful. However, they were not the first terrorist group to use this attention-getting strategy.[2]

Contagion Theory, or The Copycat Syndrome

In the last 40 years our days and nights have been illuminated by the electronic media. Television has transformed our time at a rate unmatched by any past technology or social idea, including the printing press. In fact, television viewing is preferred to the reading of books, journals, and magazines. Many of our earliest memories represent images transmitted by television; our heroes (the police-action dramas), symbols (the prevalent use of firearms and drugs), shared values (the use of force, coercion, and intimidation), and behavior (the effect of product advertising) are influenced by prolonged television viewing. The images projected on the television screen flood into our

---

[1]Martha Crenshaw, "The Causes of Terrorism," *Comparative Politics* 13 (1981), p. 396.

[2]J. Bowyer Bell, *A Time of Terror: How Democratic Societies Respond to Revolutionary Violence* (New York: Basic Books, 1978), pp. 11–23.

homes seven days a week, and many of these images reinforce the violence theme. This daily barrage of television violence is perceived as "entertainment" by the television networks. During the years since the introduction of television into our lives, real-life violence has risen to epidemic proportions, and acts of political violence and terrorism have become pandemic. Has television brought on this explosion of domestic violence and international terrorism, or does it merely reflect a dangerous social trend? Jenkins of the Rand Institute thinks television has stimulated the growth of terrorism and violence from insurgent terrorist groups, or terrorism from "below."

Jenkins argues that terrorism is theater; therefore, terrorists do not want a lot of people dead. They want a lot of people watching and listening.[3] The world has hardly noticed the struggle of emerging Third World countries in Africa, Latin America, and the Mideast where the tactics of terrorism and guerrilla warfare are widespread. But a handful of Palestinian "freedom fighters" have demonstrated the importance of media attention. In September, 1970, the theatrical introduction of the *new* terrorism, the holding of completely innocent hostages and the making of outrageous political demands, began with the carefully staged skyjacking of three airliners. A total of 276 persons were held hostage and brought to an abandoned World War II airfield in Jordan. Another much larger jumbo jet that had been too big to land in Jordan was wired with explosives and blown up in Cairo. This action served as a prelude to a six-day spectacular played out on the desert sands of Jordan. The Popular Front for the Liberation of Palestine (PFLP) proudly claimed credit for the incident. The initial demands of the PFLP involved a complicated exchange of hostages and Palestinians imprisoned in Israel, West Germany, France, and England, but these demands most certainly were secondary. The primary purpose of the terrorist action was later explained in a *news conference* by Bassam Abu Sherif: "It was a direct assault on the consciousness of international opinion. What mattered most to us was that one pays attention to us."[4] Television crews and news reporters from around the world converged on the scene, and regular press conferences were held with hostages and the spokesman of the PFLP. These scenes were broadcast to millions of viewers. The Palestinian issue had finally erupted onto the world scene. Eventually the hostages were bussed to Amman, and the planes worth $30 million were wired with explosives and blown up. Negotiations began to break down and Jordanian troops attacked the PFLP and civil war broke out in Jordan. The Palestinians referred to that month as Black September. After several days of intense fighting, the hostages were freed by the Jordanian army, and the PFLP was driven out of Jordan.

Film of the entire incident—the exploding planes, the hostage negotia-

[3]Brian Jenkins, *International Terrorism: A New Mode of Conflict* (Los Angeles: Crescent, 1975), p. 4.

[4]Peter Jennings, *Hostage: An Endless Terror* (ABC Documentary Film, 1978).

tion, the civil war, and finally the release of the hostages—was immediately prepared to inform the entire world. The reporter who put together the film, David Phillips, was honored at the Cannes Television Festival for his exclusive coverage of the affair. He had unwittingly provided the Palestinian Resistance Movement and the PFLP with the publicity the Palestinians so desperately wanted. The full meaning of this terrorist tactic was realized when other Palestinian groups and "rebels" around the world emulated the new terrorist strategy of taking hostages and making political demands.

There is no doubt that the copycat, or contagion effect, is motivated by the media. The basis for contagion theory is that any time someone does something new and novel and is successful, others will attempt to imitate that success. This is particularly evident in the case of skyjacking. The chronicles of air piracy, or skyjacking, reveal four distinct trends. First, a series of skyjackings occurred in the early 1950s when individuals as well as small groups attempted to escape the tyranny of Eastern Bloc countries. Most of the aircraft were diverted to airfields in West Germany and France. The passengers of these skyjacked aircraft were merely innocent captives, not pawns used in a deadly game of blackmail. The second trend also involved the attempted escape of some rather desperate skyjackers from Cuba to the United States in the late 1950s and the early 1960s. Several skyjackings originated in the United States where aircraft were forced to land in Cuba. For the most part, the skyjackers just wanted to return home or flee Cuba. A new trend began in 1968 that was to encompass the entire world. This new form of skyjacking was introduced by the PFLP when an Israeli El Al airliner was seized.[5] The status of innocent passengers quickly changed to that of political hostages; a new category of victims had been created. The phenomenon began to spread when other political terrorist groups as well as criminals hijacked aircraft for the purposes of making political demands or extortion. The role of the media seems to have significantly influenced this type of skyjacking.

The eminent psychiatrist Hubbard, who has interviewed hundreds of skyjackers, writes that skyjackers often kept scrapbooks and detailed notes of skyjacking incidents in order to understand how to carry out a skyjacking.[6] The parachute hijackings provide an excellent example of media influence. On November 12, 1971, a young Scotsman living in Canada hijacked a DC-8. He carried his own parachute and threatened to blow up the aircraft if he was not given $50,000. The hijacker was eventually overpowered by the crew and turned over to the police. However, the incident received considerable publicity in U.S. news reports.[7] On November 24, 1971, a successful parachute sky-

[5]David Phillips, *Skyjack* (London: Hairap, 1973), p. 72.

[6]David Hubbard, *The Skyjacker: His Flights of Fancy* (New York: Macmillan, 1973), p. 16–30.

[7]James Avery, *The Sky Pirates* (London: Ian Allan, 1973), p. 75.

jacking was accomplished by a hijacker using the name of D. B. Cooper.[8] Cooper's extortion demands included $200,000 and four parachutes. D. B. Cooper left the aircraft somewhere between Portland and Reno, never to be seen again. This skyjacking received enormous media attention, and D. B. Cooper became a folk hero of sorts with the pop media contributing songs, poems, and short stories glorifying this success. If D. B. Cooper imitated the young Scotsman, then media reporting provided the impetus for a whole series of parachute hijackings following D. B. Cooper's "success." Subsequently, 27 such hijackings were attempted in the United States, Europe, Japan, Latin America, and Australia.

The media played a decisive role in fostering the parachute hijackings that followed the Cooper episode. For example, precise details were reported on the type and proper use of the parachute. Therefore, it is reasonable to conclude that if these details had not been printed and described by the media, imitations would have been rare. In fact, in two cases the hijacker demanded $200,000 and four parachutes, identical to the D. B. Cooper ultimatum. Yet another indication of media-fostered contagion is that 20 of the 27 hijackings occurred in the United States and Canada and 7 cases were separated from each other by 8 days or less.[9] Of the 27 parachute skyjackers, only D. B. Cooper is still a fugitive. Other hijackers either were killed by the police, committed suicide, or were arrested after making the parachute jump. The case histories for media-induced contagion seem incontestable when applied to parachute hijackings.

The fourth skyjacking episode is more recent and involves two specific groups of people.

After the Mariel boatlifts from Cuba, thousands of Cubans made their way to the United States. Many eventually became disillusioned with life in the United States and longed for their native Cuba. So, the quickest and most inexpensive way to return to Cuba was to hijack an airliner. In 1982, there were ten such hijackings that originated in the United States. The airline policy requiring that all passengers and carry-on luggage be screened through metal detectors caused the Cuban skyjackers to use carry-on explosive devices that were undetected by metal security devices. Gasoline bombs, dynamite and improvised explosive devices were used in order to intimidate crews and passengers. Security, however, was further tightened, especially in Florida, and the skyjackings were discontinued by early 1983. In the summer of 1984 Iranian dissidents protesting the cruelty of the Khomeni regime hijacked airliners in Iraq, Egypt, Cyprus, and Italy. Like the Cuban hijackers, the Iranians possessed "liquid explosives" and threatened to blow up the airliners. The moti-

---

[8]Marcia M. Trick, "Chronology of Incidents of Terroristic, Quasi-Terroristic and Political Violence in the U.S.: January 1965 to March 1976," in *Disorders and Terrorism* (Washington, D.C: U.S. Government Printing Office, 1977), p. 563.

[9]Ibid., pp. 563–83.

vation for the Iranian skyjackings was twofold: to seek political asylum in the democratic West and to gain publicity for their counterrevolution in Iran. In sum, the media spread the idea of the "gasoline bomb" hijackings as well as the know-how and techniques on how to do it. It is surprising that a "how-to" text on air hijackings has not been mass-marketed. All the same, other poignant examples of contagion theory and imitation are evident in the media.

The wave of cases involving product tampering spread terror and fear throughout the United States in the early 1980s. The discovery of cyanide-laced Tylenol in several pharmacies in the Midwest created a serious epidemic of product-tampering incidents. The media widely reported tactics used in the Tylenol incident. Soon other products, including patent medicines, beverages, and food products, were found to have been tampered with by imitators of the Tylenol strategy. This type of extortionist tactic eventually made its way to Japan. In October, 1984, an extortionist gang threatened to place 100 packets of cyanide-laced candy onto grocery shelves. The Japanese extortionists demanded $410,000 in ransom from the candy manufacturer, who refused to pay and subsequently lost over $25 million in sales. The candy caper has been emulated throughout Japan by other extortionist gangs who threaten to place poisoned candy in stores that are frequented by large numbers of children. This product tampering emerged again in March 1986 in the United States. Again, Tylenol was the unfortunate victim. This incident was followed by the tampering of three products, Teldrin, Contac, and Diatec.

Films that are seen in theaters and in reruns on television are also an influential medium through which acts of violence and terrorism are encouraged and emulated. In 1979 the gang warfare films *Boulevard Nights* and *The Warriors* so aroused teenage audiences around the country that during several showings they started shooting in the theaters. Eight people were killed at these films and five wounded. Security guards eventually were provided at every showing, and juvenile gang members were advised to remain outside the line of fire during the performance. In San Francisco where the violence was particularly brutal, the mayor was loudly criticized by the "media" and theater managers for suggesting that these films not be shown. The Academy Award-winning film *The Deerhunter* provides yet another example of emulation by people repeating the Russian roulette scene. Several suicides and accidental deaths due to imitation of the film were reported to the police. Nevertheless, television network executives and film producers maintain that media presentations affect all kinds of human behavior, from helping, sharing, and altruism to decisions about what products to buy, and, of course, aggression. On the other hand, social science investigations reveal that exposure to media violence and terrorism leads to the creation of fear, anxiety, insensitivity, and emulation. If the social scientists are correct, then perhaps media distributors should concentrate more on the themes of sharing, altruism, and helping rather than the brutality, violence, and terrorism that presently dominate television and film airtime.

Several additional factors have contributed to the contagion/imitation model of terrorism and violence.

Clearly, certain acts of terrorist violence often make abnormal behavior seem justified. Several examples are evident. First, seldom are the perpetrators of terrorist acts ever punished. This fact is not lost on potential terrorists. Second, the terrorist act is often portrayed as justified. The Irish Republican Army, South Moluccans, and Palestinian freedom fighters all feel justified in using terrorist violence to gain media attention. Third, terroristic violence is often characterized by an intent not to inflict injury on unwitting victims. In other words, the terrorist group is forced to use extranormal violence because of alienation, frustration, and a lack of political power. Fourth, the extraordinary coverage of terrorist incidents encourages an identification with the group by other irresponsible "rebels." Fifth, the terrorist group is often portrayed as having great strength, power, and support. In reality terrorist groups are impotent without the media, which impulsively concentrate on the violence or potential for violence. Sixth, the act of violence is overdramatized in an entertainment way, where a disproportionate amount of time is spent photographing victims, scenes of violence, and interviewing terrorists. The causes, issues, and viewpoints that produced the act of violence are overlooked for the dramatic value of the violence. Thus, an unrealistic and exaggerated image which both invokes and stimulates acts of terrorism by others is presented.

Finally, the frivolousness in the news coverage of terroristic violence involving car bombs, assassinations, and hostage-taking where groups and individuals are often referred to as freedom fighters, commandos, guerrillas, protesters, dissidents, or rioters may cause confusion among people. This confusion may be interpreted by organized terrorist groups as a justification for acts of violence. The distinction between freedom fighter or guerrilla and terrorist is significant. The connotation implies that if one is fighting for his freedom, then conventional rules of warfare need not apply. The present media trend apparently favors the legitimization and the reporting of all methods of violence or terrorism as pursuit of "freedom." This may set a dangerous precedent since freedom fighter and terrorist are concepts that defy precise definition. Hence, groups that specialize in acts of terrorism against the "oppressor" now become freedom fighters. The revival of the concept of freedom fighter presents serious implications for the protection of human rights. If the most brutal acts of terrorism directed at innocent civilian targets are justified in the name of freedom, human rights will suffer a severe setback. Today hundreds of freedom fighters exist in the world, evidence that contagion and imitation are perpetrated by news media interpretation of acts of political violence. In the same view, the growth of terrorism must not be defined simply in terms of contagion and imitation but also in terms of propaganda.

Propaganda Value and The "Deed"

Propaganda is the dissemination of facts, arguments, half-truths, or lies in order to influence public opinion. The making of propaganda involves a systematic effort to persuade a mass audience by deliberately presenting one-sided statements. One-sided presentations often spread and convey unrealistic images by concentrating only on the good points of one position and the bad points of another. In a colloquial sense, then, propaganda is used to refer to someone else's efforts as persuasion while one's own are described as informational or educational. The communication is clearly propaganda when it appeals to the emotions and sentiments of the target audience. In analyzing any specific political-terrorist propaganda campaign in either a historical or contemporary sense, several questions arise:

1. Who are the groups that initiate the propaganda campaign?
2. What objectives are they trying to accomplish?
3. By what strategies are objectives sought?
4. What political resources and assets does the group begin with?
5. What outcomes are desired by the group?
6. How extensive is media coverage of specific incidents?

In modern totalitarian states the means of communication is monopolized by government officials. At the other extreme are democratic pluralistic states where freedom of the press is considered an important, fundamental civil right. In a free society, the media compete for audiences, and circulation is often stimulated by the reporting of violent events. In some respects the media has replaced government as an authority figure. In political-terrorist incidents, it has become evident to the leaders of terroristic/revolutionary movements that they can greatly enhance the chances of success by using propaganda to win popular support and to recruit new members. The eagerness of the media to respond to terroristic violence is a perverse incentive to organized terrorist groups as well as the criminally unstable and fanatical individual. Terrorist propaganda depends on accessible networks of communication. The violence and terrorism in Northern Ireland provide an example of competing political ideologies, all desperately trying to influence public opinion.

In Northern Ireland there are several competing political philosophies. These include the British military, a British-supported government, Protestant paramilitary groups Ulster Volunteer Force (UVF); Ulster Defense Association (UDA); Ulster Freedom Fighters (UFF); Red Hand Commandos (RHC), the Catholic left (Free Ireland Saor Eire); People's Liberation Army (PLA), and the Irish Republican Army (IRA). But the most prominent and "newsworthy" group is the Provisional wing of the IRA (PIRA, or Provos). The objective of PIRA is to influence the British to withdraw support from the dominant Protestant community of Northern Ireland who control the economy and to provoke the British military into open warfare that eventually would bring about the withdrawal of Britain's 20,000 combat troops.

In this propaganda war PIRA has been holding clandestine press conferences with exclusive television interviews on the British Broadcasting Corporation (BBC), Independent Television (ITV), and the American Broadcasting Company (ABC). In one of these interviews David O'Connell, PIRA chief of staff, proclaimed that the Provos would conduct a bombing campaign in Great Britain. One week later several bombs were detonated in Birmingham with the loss of 21 innocent lives. In another interview conducted by ABC, O'Connell described the tactics and moral justification for PIRA's indiscriminate attacks against the British military and the Royal Ulster Constabulary (RUC). This interview was part of a documentary titled *To Die For Ireland* that was widely distributed in the United States.[10] In yet another interview PIRA invited an American-TV film crew to accompany a terrorist squad on an actual terrorist mission. The TV crew filmed the Provos loading a car with explosives and then driving it to a city street where it was blown up, injuring several people and causing extensive property damage.[11] Certainly the impact of such deeds is heightened by the willingness of the media to participate in the propaganda aims. In one respect PIRA has bombed their way into the hearts and minds of the "people."

The bombing strategy of PIRA is also used to influence the coverage of other events in Northern Ireland and Great Britian. According to PIRA chief of staff O'Connell, the first car bombs were placed in London to *bomb* the election in Northern Ireland from the front pages.[12] The strategy was successful and taught the Provisionals a very valuable lesson. As one PIRA source stated, "Last year taught us that in publicity terms one bomb in Oxford Street is worth ten in Belfast. It is not a lesson we are likely to forget."[13]

They did not forget for on October 11, 1984, PIRA tried unsuccessfully to wipe out the entire British government in a savage hotel bombing. About nine hours after the blast the Provisional IRA claimed responsibility asserting that it had set off a 100-pound gelignite bomb in an attempt to kill the "British Cabinet and Tory warmongers." The British prime minister, Margaret Thatcher, 13 of her 20-member Cabinet, and many of her senior advisors were staying at the Grand Hotel in Brighton when at about 3 a.m. a thundering explosion ripped out a 500-square-foot section of the hotel's facade. The prime minister escaped injury, but others were not so fortunate. Four government officials were killed and 40 were seriously injured. To date it is the boldest and most outrageous terrorist attack against British government officials in Great Britian or Northern Ireland. A spokesman for the Provos promised more terrorist strikes in the future:

[10]*To Die For Ireland* (ABC Documentary Film, 1980).

[11]U.S. Congress, Senate, Committee on the Judiciary, Subcommittee to Investigate the Administration of the Internal Security Act and Other Internal Security Laws, *Part 5: Hostage Defense Measures,* Hearings, 94th Congress, July 25, 1975, (Washington, D.C.: Government Printing Office, 1975), pp. 275–76.

[12]J. Bowyer Bell, *IPI Report* 25 (June 1976), p. 4.

[13]Michael Moodie, "The Patriot Game: The Politics of Violence in Northern Ireland," In *International Terrorism in the Contemporary World,* ed. Marius H. Livingston (Connecticut: Greenwood, 1978), p. 98.

Thatcher will now realize that Britian cannot occupy our country, torture our prisoners and shoot our people in their own streets and get away with it. Today we were unlucky. But remember, we have only to be lucky once. You will have to be lucky always.[14]

The attack triggered a wave of anger, revulsion, and a strong condemnation of the PIRA by prominent world political leaders. In fact the attack seemed to provide a rallying point for the British prime minister and the British public, who could easily identify with such a tragedy. Nevertheless, the Provos accomplished their propaganda aims of putting the British government on the defensive and dominating media coverage. For two consecutive weeks the media published details of the bombing, the status of victims, the political position of the IRA and the tightening of security measures to protect British government officials.

The PIRA strategy of concentrating on spectacular acts of terrorist bombing is not the only tactic to attract the media. Perhaps the most effective propaganda tactics have been the well-publicized hunger strikes by the PIRA and the INLA (Irish National Liberation Army) in 1980–81. On October 27, 1980, seven Provos began a hunger strike in Maze Prison, Belfast. The strike lasted for 53 days with no deaths. At the same time 3 women members of the PIRA and 23 men who supported the Nationalist cause joined in the strike. The hunger strikers wanted segregation from "common criminals" and to be granted "political prisoner status." They also wanted an independent investigation of prison brutality and torture. The strike was eventually stopped through clergy and family pressure, when prison officials agreed to review the strikers' request. But by the beginning of 1981 the Provos concluded that British prison officials had no intention of granting political prisoner status to members of PIRA or INLA, and the mistreatment of inmates continued. Plans to renew the hunger strike were developing, and Bobby Sands began the new strike on March 1, 1981. All terrorist activity of PIRA and INLA was discontinued so that world attention might be focused on the hunger strike of Bobby Sands. At about the same time an opportunity for Sands to run for political office arose when the representative from his district suddenly died. Sands won the election on April 9 and then died on May 5. Another hunger striker, Owen Carron, succeeded Sands and was elected to the Irish Parliament. Like Sands, Carron also died after a prolonged hunger strike. Nonetheless, the deaths of Sands and Carron demonstrated to the British government that the hunger strikes target audience had been reached. Until the deaths of the hunger-strikers, there appeared to be little support for PIRA's political program. Now world media attention was attracted to Northern Ireland and the hunger strike.

The propaganda impact of Sands' protest, election, and death equaled or exceeded that of any other terrorist incident carried out by the PIRA. There

---

[14]*Time,* October 22, 1984, p. 50.

were massive parades in Belfast, Londonderry, Dublin, and several British cities. The British Parliament spent countless hours debating the issue of political prisoner status and how to react to international pressures to free the prisoners. Riots, shootings, and bombings escalated in Northern Ireland against the British military and the police. The media coverage of Sands' funeral involved no less than 164 TV crews. The event received international recognition and no doubt greatly enhanced the political image and prestige of the Provos. Needless to say, the British were distressed by the PIRA's propaganda victory, especially in Europe and America, and at least a few members of Parliament recommended that the government take steps to stop the procession of dying hunger-strikers. By October 3, 1981, ten PIRA and INLA hunger-strikers had died. But it was not British capitulation to the hunger-strikers' demands that stopped this retinue of death.

Like previous hunger strikes, clergy and family members urged PIRA and INLA to discontinue the protest. The Provos rejected this appeal and announced the hunger strike would continue until the British granted political prisoner status to all Irish Nationalists in British and Irish jails. In spite of the Provos' adamant position, as Irish prisoners lapsed into unconsciousness toward the end of their hunger strikes, family members were permitted to take control; and most consented to the forced feedings of the strikers. Thus, the eight-month-long hunger strike was called off, and a very effective propaganda campaign came to an end. The entire world was now aware of the "troubles" in Northern Ireland.

Three days after the strike ended one of the strikers' demands was conceded to by prison officials. The Irish nationalists (PIRA and INLA) now had the right to wear their own clothes, but they would not be granted the status of political prisoners.

The hunger strike proved to be a dramatic event and touched the lives of everyone in Northern Ireland, the Republic of Ireland, and the United Kingdom. Television news coverage of the event vividly described the pain and agony associated with death due to starvation. The history of propaganda makes it clear that in order for propaganda to be effective it must be in devoted hands. The most important factor is certainly the emotional involvement of the participants. In terms of propaganda value, the Irish nationalist hunger strike represents the ultimate act of propaganda—the willingness to sacrifice one's life for political or religious beliefs. However, the Irish hunger-strikers claimed they were murdered by the British, and that their protest was not an act of suicide.

Unlike the Irish hunger-strikers, German terrorists of the notorious Baader-Meinhoff gang did use their bodies as an ultimate propaganda weapon. On October 18, 1977, four members of the Baader-Meinhoff gang committed suicide while incarcerated in Stammheim prison, a maximum security institution. It was later determined that handguns were smuggled into the prison by attorneys for the gang. The plan was to commit suicide by shooting themselves in the back of the head, execution style. The method was intended to suggest that they had been murdered or executed by the West German "fascist" state. Many people believed this account, and the media were full of speculation that prison guards had murdered the members of the gang. An independent commission of forensic pathologists reconstructed the scene of the mass suicide and concluded that the victims had indeed committed suicide. The evidence was conclusive, but by then the propaganda value generated by the suicides indicated that few people believed the findings of the commission. This form of terrorism and propaganda-making, therefore, selects its victims from its own ranks with the intention of having the guilt attributed to the "enemy."[15]

In yet another act of terrorism designed for its propaganda value, five members of the little-known Armenian Revolutionary Army shot their way into the Turkish ambassador's residence in Lisbon, Portugal, on July 24, 1983, and vowed to blow it up. Shortly after the Armenian terrorists seized the residence, negotiations appeared fruitless, and the police planned to assault the building and free several Turkish hostages. However, the residence had been wired with explosives by the terrorists; as the police approached, the explosives were detonated, killing all inside the building including the five Armenian terrorists. A typewritten message signed by the Armenian Revolutionary Army was later found in the residence; it stated, "We have decided to blow up this building and remain under the collapse. This is not suicide nor an expression of insanity, but rather our sacrifice to the altar of freedom." Ostensibly, Armenian terrorist groups want the world to believe that this "self-sacrifice" is necessary because the Turkish government refuses to acknowledge the realities of the Armenian genocide that systematically killed thousands of Armenians between 1894 and 1915.[16] This incident was widely publicized by the news media.

The tactical objective of the Armenians as well as the IRA and the Baader-Meinhoff gang was to propagandize politics as a drama in which the forces of good and evil stand opposed to one another. The strategy of self-sacrifice was no doubt intended to induce a sense of guilt among Turkish government officials and dramatize the self-righteousness of the Armenian cause to the entire world, i.e., the acknowledgment of the Armenian genocide. The marked success of this tactic was designed to capture media attention and influence the Armenian community. On September 10, 1984, the U.S. Congress agreed to set aside a day of remembrance for the 1.5 million Armenians killed in this century's first recorded act of genocide. Thus, April 24 has been set aside to remember the Armenian dead. The Congress was careful to state that

[15]Alex P. Schmid, and Janny de Graaf, *Violence as Communication* (London and Beverly Hills: Sage, 1982), p. 5.

[16]Michael M. Gunter, "The Armenian Terrorist Campaign Against Turkey," *Orbis* 27 (1983), pp. 447–77.

this action was not an endorsement of Armenian terrorism or an acknowledgment of Turkish complicity in the Armenian genocide.

An alternative to this self-destructive type of terrorism is another popular propaganda strategy that does not create a news event but instead intrudes on other newsworthy events to maximize propaganda. The most successful of such events was the decision to take Israeli athletes hostage during the 1972 Munich Olympic Games. The popularity of the Olympic games ensured Palestinian extremists that millions of people were already watching the Olympics on television. On September 5, 1972, 8 Palestinian terrorists of the Black September group took 11 Israeli athletes hostage and captured the attention of 800 million spectators. The terrorists demanded the release of 200 Arab prisoners being held in Israel. However, as the tense drama unfolded, it became apparent that the release of prisoners was secondary to the propagandistic nature of the event. A Palestinian explained it like this:

> We recognize that sport is the modern religion of the Western world. We knew that the people of England and America would switch their television sets from any programme about the plight of the Palestinians if there was a sporting event on another channel. So we decided to use their Olympics, the most sacred ceremony of this religion, to make the world pay attention to us. We offered up human sacrifices to your gods of sport and television. And they answered our prayers.[17]

After Munich, nobody could ignore the Palestinians or their cause. The media did not hesitate to cooperate and broadcast the bloody spectacle via satellites to all continents. In the Arab world the Black September were widely applauded, and thousands of Palestinians joined various Palestinian extremist groups in the wake of this public-relations success.[18] However, the operation, which began with military precision, ended in failure. Five Palestinian terrorists were killed, all eleven Israeli athletes were killed, and one police officer was killed in a firefight that took place at the Furstenfeldbruck airport. But the military failure of the terrorist incident did not detract from the propaganda triumph. On the contrary, the spectacular nature of the attack reinforced its emotional appeal. The Palestinian cause once more exploded onto the international political scene. Part of the world condemned the attack as a savage, barbaric act of wantonless murder; others defended the Palestinan terrorists as dedicated nationalists willing to sacrifice their lives for a viable political cause. The Palestinians were not advocating world revolution; instead they wanted the creation of a Palestinian state and recognition of the Palestinian

[17]Christopher Dobson and Ronald Paine, *The Carlos Complex: A Pattern of Violence* (London: Hodder and Stroughton, 1977), p. 15.

[18]Frederick Hacker, *Crusaders, Criminals, Crazies: Terror and Terrorism in our Time* (New York: Bantam, 1978), p. 223.

people. Certainly other patriots in the world saw this as a plausible goal, and a compromise with Israel was not altogether impossible.

The breakthrough came two years later, in November 17, 1974, when the chairman of the PLO, Yasir Arafat, addressed the United Nations General Assembly. The event was widely televised and Arafat received a standing ovation. The idea that a compromise was feasible on the Palestinian-Israeli issue had become a widely shared opinion in international politics. The PLO was later granted observer status at the United Nations. Apparently the consciousness of the world and the media had been aroused by several sensational, Palestinian terrorist acts. The taking of hostages, skyjacking, and the throwing of bombs can be very effective communication strategies. Nevertheless, the propaganda war between the Palestinians and Israelis continues. We will have more on this conflict in Chapter 5.

The skill of propaganda-making and communication manipulation was most clearly evident in the kidnapping of Aldo Moro by the Italian Red Brigades (RB). Aldo Moro, one of Italy's leading political figures, was held captive for 55 days. During this period the Red Brigades were able to manipulate the media by spreading false information, lies, and rumors concerning the condition of Aldo Moro. For example, the Red Brigades claimed that Moro had been "executed by suicide," that he had been tried by a people's court and confessed to crimes against society, that he divulged state secrets about corruption, graft, and bribery in Italian politics. The whole nation was held in a state of tension waiting for the next communiqué by the Red Brigades. In fact, rival newspapers, magazines and television newscasts competed for the communiqué, and circulation more than doubled for the printed media. The government tried unsuccessfully to stop the communiqués from being published, and Italy began to look like a nation under seige. Ordinary civil and human rights were suspended while the Italian police and military searched the country trying to locate Moro and the Red Brigades.[19]

Since the Red Brigades indirectly controlled the Italian media, they were able to create a situation of terror, fear, and anxiety as well as to provoke the Italian government to overreact by suspending normal legal procedures.[20] The Italian media overwhelmingly condemned the kidnapping and the eventual murder of Aldo Moro. But by merely reporting only what the Red Brigades wanted, the media were easily manipulated and the incident which normally would have become a matter of police investigation and one family's tragedy instead became another chapter in international terrorism and the political instability of Italian politics. The media defended their publication of Red Brigades' communiqués by rationalizing that it was the public's right to know. However, the various Italian publics became polarized over the affair and

---

[19]*Time,* March 28, 1977, p. 13; *Newsweek,* May 22, 1978, p. 35.
[20]E. Fiorillo, "Terrorism in Italy: Analysis of a Problem," *Terrorism,* 2, (1979), pp. 261-70.

identified with a variety of positions. Most, of course, identified with the victim, sharing his sense of desperation and impotence. Others identified and supported the Red Brigades, sharing their sense of revenge against a corrupt political system.

Still others identified with the police, sharing their moral dilemma of balancing liberty, freedom, and individual rights. The Red Brigades very skillfully used the media to translate an isolated act of physical violence into one of "psychic terror" that affected millions of Italians. Of all terrorist propaganda strategies, media concentration on one isolated terrorist incident is probably the most insidious. The media grant modern terrorism much of its power, for without media cooperation it is doubtful that the Red Brigades would have eluded the police for so many years. Today more than 4,000 terrorists—Red Brigade and others—are incarcerated in Italian jails. The Red Brigades have been terrorizing Italy for over a decade.

The United States has also experienced the manipulation of the mass media by political extremists. Probably the most daring act of media exploitation was carried out by the then little-known Black Panther Party (BPP). The Black Panthers had been trying to mobilize the mass of lower-class blacks for several years without much success. The group owed its popularity almost entirely to clever manipulation of the mass media. They first gained national attention by their massed entry into the California Legislature, wearing paramilitary uniforms and carrying "unloaded" rifles. The Legislature, in session, was debating a proposed bill to make it unlawful to carry loaded guns in California. The Black Panthers invited the media to witness this scene of armed extremists on the floor of the California State Legislature. The incident made the headlines and newscasts across the United States. The Panthers were suddenly catapulted onto the national scene. They were invited to participate in speaking engagements and were eagerly sought by the national media, both print and electronic, to tell their story. The Black Panther newspaper was established and became an immediate success with circulation rising to 200,000 copies by 1971. In this paper the Black Panthers advocated armed resistance, urban guerrilla warfare methods, and the indiscriminate terrorist tactic of murdering the uniformed police officer. Even though the Black Panthers were capable of issuing their own propaganda statements, they still relied heavily on the national media to spread their exaggerated rhetoric about violence and revolution. The strategy of the Black Panthers was to use the media to introduce a technique of "liberation" through propaganda by deed that would "awaken all oppressed people of the world."[21]

Perhaps the most adroit manipulation of the media by terrorists in the United States was the terrorism of the Symbionese Liberation Army (SLA). This California army consisting of less than a dozen soldiers managed to influ-

[21]Charles E. Silberman, *Criminal Violence Criminal Justice* (New York: Random House, 1978), pp. 157–59.

ence media attention for two years by kidnapping Patricia Hearst on February 4, 1974. The SLA held not only Patty Hearst hostage but also her father, Randolph Hearst, ruler of the media empire that included the *San Francisco Examiner*. After the abduction of Patty Hearst, the SLA demanded that the entire text of all communications be published in Hearst-owned newspapers. Randolph Hearst was warned that a failure to do so would endanger the safety of his daughter Patricia. The SLA–Patty Hearst saga became one of the most publicized stories in media history. For example, in the years 1974–1976, Patty Hearst, who was taken hostage and who allegedly turned terrorist, made the cover of *Newsweek* seven times.[22]

The public was treated to a variety of taped and printed communiqués from the SLA and their hostage. In one message on February 12, 1974, the SLA announced their demands for the release of Patty Hearst. They demanded that a food distribution program be initiated by Randolph Hearst. The program was to distribute $70 worth of "quality food" to each and every person in need in California. It was estimated that 5 million people in California were living below the poverty level. Such a program would have cost Randolph Hearst approximately $400 million. Unable to accommodate such an outrageous demand, Randolph Hearst set up a $2 million food distribution program. Thousands of people in Oakland and San Francisco showed up at four announced locations to receive the free food. The plan to distribute the food was ill conceived, and soon fighting broke out for the free food. The scenes of unruly mobs fighting for food were broadcast by the three major television networks to over 80 million viewers. The Robin Hood image projected by the program of taking from the rich and giving to the poor turned into a circus. Thus, a second food giveaway program was demanded by the SLA with the stipulation that media coverage of the giveaway be suspended. This second free food program was successful in the sense that the orderly distribution of the food was achieved. The Robin Hood image of the SLA began to grow. In fact one reporter noted that the "tone of the press in the Bay area is subdued and even sympathetic toward the SLA."[23] Even so, the only convert to the preposterous rhetoric of the SLA was Patty Hearst, who now became Tanya (named after a female companion of Che Guevara). Tanya eventually became an ardent supporter of the political aims of the SLA. The initial skill the SLA had demonstrated in manipulating the media ultimately was overshadowed by the entertainment value of the exploits of the SLA.[24] To date 3 movies and 12 books have capitalized on the story, not to mention hundreds of dramatic embellishments by journalists who covered the story and produced countless articles.

[22]Vin McLellan, and Paul Avery, *The Voices of Guns* (New York: Putnam, 1977), p. 22.

[23]Desmond Smith, *The Nation*, March 30, 1974, pp. 392–94.

[24]James Monaco, *Celebrity: The Media as Image Maker* (New York: Delta, 1978), pp. 65–78.

Another expressive case of media manipulation and propaganda-making involved an obscure Hanafi Moslem sect. Led by Hamaas Abdul Khaalis and 12 followers, the sect seized 134 hostages in 3 buildings in Washington, D.C., on March 9, 1977. During the takeover, one hostage was shot and 16 were subsequently injured. Unlike most hostage-takers, Khaalis was seeking revenge. He demanded the release from prison of three members of a rival Muslim sect who had been convicted for the murders of his family, including three children. Khaalis wanted to administer his personal interpretation of Islamic justice. A secondary demand was that a movie released that day, *Mohammed, Messenger of God,* be banned from American theaters because Khaalis regarded it as heretical.[25] The first demand was out of the question and could not be negotiated, but the second was met when producers of the film agreed to remove it from distribution. This represented a clear victory for the terrorists for they temporarily had the power to censor the film media. Even so, the movie was later shown in various United States cities.

The incident lasted for some 39 hours, and involved the media in other ways as well. Khaalis called local reporters to discuss his demands and even more often news reporters called Khaalis. This greatly complicated the process of negotiation since the negotiators began to lose control of the situation. One reporter disclosed to Khaalis that several people were hiding on the top floor of one of the buildings where hostages were being held. Yet another report insulted and infuriated Khaalis by referring to him as a Black Muslim. Khaalis' family had been slain by Black Muslims, and he demanded an immediate apology from the newscaster or a hostage would be killed in retaliation for the remark. On the advice of police negotiators, the reporter publicly apologized for the blunder. Nevertheless, the episode did nothing to ingratiate the media to the hostages. As one of the hostages later responded:

> As hostages, many of us felt that the Hanafi takeover was a happening, a guerrilla theater, a high-impact propaganda exercise programmed for the TV screen, and secondarily for the front pages of newspapers around the world. . . . the resentment and anger of my fellow hostages toward the press is . . . that the news media and terrorism feed on each other, that the news media, particularly TV, create a thirst for fame and recognition. Reporters do not simply report the news. They help create it. They are not objective observers, but subjective participants—actors, scriptwriters, and idea men.[26]

The Hanafi incident finally ended when Khaalis agreed to negotiate with Islamic intermediaries. There is no doubt that media interference prolonged this incident and endangered the lives of the hostages.

In sum, the preceding section has attempted to describe some contemporary propagandist uses of the news media by terrorist groups. This is, of

---

[25]Askia Muhammed, The Nation 224 (June 1977), p. 721.

[26]Charles Fenyvesi, *The Media and Terrorism* (Chicago: Field Enterprises, 1977), p. 28.

TABLE 3-1   Propagandist Uses of Mass Media by Modern Terrorist Groups

1. Instill fear in a mass audience
2. Polarize public opinion
3. Gain publicity by agreeing to clandestine interviews
4. Demand publication of a manifesto
5. Provoke government overreaction
6. Spread false and misleading information
7. Bring about the release of prisoners
8. Attract converts and support to a cause
9. Coerce the media by assaulting journalists
10. Profit from "free advertising"
11. Discredit public officials while being held hostage
12. Divert public attention by bombing their way onto front page
13. Use the media to send messages to comrades in another country
14. Excite public against the legitimate government
15. Bolster the terrorist group's morale
16. Gain the Robin Hood image by fighting "injustice"
17. Obtain information on counterterrorist strategies
18. Identify future victims
19. Acquire information about popular support for the terrorist group
20. Exploit the exaggerated media image of a powerful, omnipotent group

Source: Schmid and de Graff. *Violence as Communication* (London and Beverly Hills, Sage, 1982), pp. 53–54.

course, only a limited survey of examples. However, it is possible to summarize the main points. Table 3-1 represents a list of propagandist uses of the media by contemporary terrorist groups.

This propagandist use of the media by modern terrorist groups has resulted in yet another conflict involving the law enforcement community. The different roles of law enforcement and the media are certain to result in conflict since each sees the other as interfering with its functions and community responsibilities.

Law Enforcement and the Media

In an attempt to acquire news, the media at times interfere with police operations. Similarly, the police often ignore the needs and potential contribution to be gained from having the media disseminate factual information and dispel rumors. This is particularly true in situations involving hostages and barricades. However, this is by no means the only area of conflict. Police management personnel have voiced loud criticism over the manner in which the terrorists or their operations are portrayed by the media. Consider, for example, the following interactions of police, media, and terrorist:

1. In 1974 a group of convicted felons in Washington, D.C. attempted to escape from the District of Columbia courthouse by seizing several hostages in the

courthouse cellblock. Unknown at the time to the hostage-takers, the police were able to observe their actions through a one-way mirror. Furthermore, police sharpshooters were able to direct fire through the one-way mirror if the hostages' lives were at any time endangered. Somehow the local media discovered the information about the one-way mirror that they immediately made public. It did not take long for the hostage-takers to realize the significance of the one-way mirror. The hostage-takers demanded masking tape and thus covered the mirror. The advantage was, therefore, taken away from the police negotiators.

In addition, a young, aggressive, overachieving reporter was able to conduct lengthy telephone interviews with the hostage-takers and attempted unsuccessfully to gain admittance to the cellblock so that "on the spot" interviews could be conducted. In a later conversation with the police negotiator, the reporter was asked if he had considered the lives of the hostages while interviewing the hostage-takers. He responded that it had been the furthest thing from his mind. This reporter was concerned solely with a story worthy of the front page and the personal recognition that results in journalistic awards and prizes. Clearly the actions of the media complicated the process of negotiation.

2. As previously cited, in 1977 a group of Hanafi Muslims seized hostages at three locations in Washington, D.C. During the course of negotiations, arrangements were made for food to be brought in to the hostages being held in the B'nai B'rith building. As a truck pulled up and local police began to deliver the food to the hostages, a reporter on the scene broadcast that the alleged food boxes contained weapons for a special police assault team that was preparing to attack the building. The Hanafi hostage-takers received the false information on the evening newscast. It took several hours for police negotiators to persuade the Hanafis that the news report was false and to regain the trust of the hostage-takers.

3. In November, 1974, a British Airways plane was hijacked in Dubai for an exchange of 13 terrorists being held in Egyptian jails. After the complicated negotiations were completed, arrangements were made to transport the freed terrorists from Cairo to Cuba. As the exchange of hostages and freed terrorists was about to take place, a reporter announced that the exchange was a trap and the freed terrorists from Egypt were not aboard the aircraft. In retaliation, the hostage-takers selected a West German banker for execution. The premature broadcast by the reporter prolonged the incident and resulted in several unnecessary injuries and deaths.

4. A similar episode took place in October 1977, when a Lufthansa airplane was hijacked to Mogadishu, Somalia. The plane's captain was executed by the terrorists after it was discovered that he had passed information to the negotiating team through normal radio transmissions. The media broadcast the story of the captain's clever manipulation of the hostage-takers through the use of his radio. The media's action undoubtedly cost the captain his life.

Almost every major police department in the world can recall its own experiences where hostage negotiation teams have been obstructed by the media for the sake of a story. Media representatives seem willing to put the lives of hostages at risk to gain an exclusive story. For this reason the police often discuss the need to restrict the access of the media to in-progress hostage-taking incidents and terrorist operations.

However, the media have not been totally unresponsive to these important issues. The National News Council has called for a reexamination of live coverage of violent and terroristic incidents.[27] Of particular concern is the practice of obtaining live interviews with terrorists during an ongoing terrorist event as well as the development and refinement of guidelines to ensure ethical and responsible conduct during the coverage of in-progress terrorist situations. These guidelines are directed at the coverage of in-progress terrorist events and at keeping the media from either jeopardizing the police rescue efforts of hostages or overly dramatizing the terrorist event. Even so, media critics argue that the major concern of reporters still is getting a story. How that story is obtained becomes secondary to getting it. For example, after a careful analysis of the Iranian hostage crisis, Friedlander concluded that:

> . . . throughout the Iranian captivity these guidelines were ignored to a far greater extent than they were observed. All three television networks taking advantage of the Iranian drama developed a blind eye to professional, ethical considerations in a fervent competitive quest for audiences.[28]

Guidelines and cooperation between the law enforcement community and the news media are undoubtedly necessary for the safe resolution of terrorist incidents. Law enforcement and the news media both share a desire to serve the public by providing a free flow of information to satisfy the public's constitutional right to know. To this end the California Peace Officers Association has developed a set of written guidelines, delineated into several major topics.[29] The most important of these topics is the establishment of a written law enforcement-media policy. The importance of written policy guidelines cannot be overestimated since it influences the relationship that the law enforcement community enjoys with the news media and the public. These relationships often determine the effectiveness of law enforcement. It is proposed, then, that joint policy guidelines be established rather than a set of individual media guidelines. The news media must work closely with the police since the dangerous question of censorship and freedom of the press arises. Many governments have in the past imposed censorship on terroristic news, especially terrorist hostage-taking episodes.

[27]The National News Council, "Paper on Terrorism," in *Terrorism, The Media and Law Enforcement,* ed. A.H. Miller (Washington, D.C.: Government Printing Office, 1983), pp. 117–33.

[28]Robert A. Friedlander, "Iran: The Hostage Seizure, the Media and International Law," in *Terrorism, the Media and Law Enforcement,* ed. Miller, p. 5.

[29]California Peace Officers Association, *Law Enforcement Media Relations: Model Policy Manual* (Sacramento: California Peace Officers Association, 1983).

Censorship and Terrorism

The concept of a free press presently is not held in very high esteem by many governments of the world. It has been recorded by the United Nations that in 1974 only 30 out of the then 138-member countries had a free press.[30] In fact, in some Third World countries governmental leaders sarcastically state that a free press is irrelevant in a country when the general population represents an illiteracy rate of over 90 percent. Nevertheless, countries exist where an escalation of terrorist activity has led to media censorship. For example, in 1967 the government of Uruguay closed a local newspaper for publishing a communiqué of the Tupamaros.[31] By 1973 the military government of Uruguay had passed legislation which prohibited:

> the publication by means of oral, written, or televised media all information, commentaries, or impressions which directly or indirectly mention or refer to those persons who conspire against the nation or against antisubversive operations, excluding official communication.[32]

Furthermore, the news media was prohibited from any criticism of government measures to combat and repress the terrorism of the Tupamaros.

Likewise, in Argentina the government suspended media publication of the names of two popular terrorist groups: the Montoneros and the Ejercito Revolucionario del Pueblo (ERP). In April, 1976, a governmental proclamation prohibited the Argentinian media from reporting, commenting, or mentioning politically related acts of violence. In addition, the political viewpoints of groups considered in opposition to the ruling elite cannot be printed without first being reviewed by a government censor. Hundreds of journalists have been arrested, kidnapped, and interned in prison without regard to individual rights because they violated the restrictions of Argentinian government censorship.[33]

To some degree what has occurred in Uruguay and Argentina has been true for other countries experiencing escalating terrorism. For example, in Sri Lanka the government has prohibited any reporting of terrorist activities by the news media.[34] In Lebanon reports of political violence are closely censored within the country.[35] In Rhodesia-Zimbabwe media censorship was imposed

---

[30]Peter M. Sandman and others, *Media* (Englewood Cliffs, N.J.: Prentice-Hall, 1976), p. 165.

[31]James Kohl and John Litt, eds., *Urban Guerrilla Warfare in Latin America* (Cambridge: MIT, 1974), p. 186.

[32]Jordon J. Paust, "International Law and Control of the Media: Terror, Repression and the Alternatives," *Ind. Law Journal,* 53 (1978), pp. 644–45.

[33]United States, Congress, House Committee on Internal Security, *Terrorism,* Hearing, 93rd Congress, 2nd Session (Washington, D. C.: Government Printing Office, 1974).

[34]Paust, *Indiana Law Journal,* p. 661.

[35]Ibid.

to prevent the spread of political violence and terrorism throughout the country. An examination of the South African media illustrates a self-imposed censorship since only governmental responses toward combating terrorism are reported, not the acts of terrorism. The Republic of Ireland censors all interviews with representatives of the IRA, the Sinn Fein and the Ulster Defense Association (UDA).[36] The Israeli government requires that all news material relating to incidents of in-progress terrorist acts be routed through a military censor who then decides if the information is aiding the terrorists or hampering the operations of the police or Defense Forces. Reportage is not the only part of freedom of the press that has experienced governmental censorship. The well-known "bible" of leftist guerrilla and terrorist groups, the *Mini-Manual of Urban Guerrilla Warfare,* is outlawed in Latin America and several Western European countries.[37]

In sum, censorship may reduce the value of the terrorist strategy by hampering the spread of fear, but it cannot prevent terrorists from engaging in other forms of political violence. The grievances and political aspirations of terrorist groups will remain whether censored or not. In some countries, such as Uruguay and Argentina, terrorist incidents increased after the imposition of censorship. It could well be that pro-government forces will feel freer to engage in terrorist acts against those who oppose the government knowing they will not be exposed or criticized by the media. For example, the mass terrorism and executions carried out by Hitler and Stalin were possible only because the victims were not aware of what was going on since Hitler and Stalin each had complete control of the media. Therefore, if censorship is considered, one should first ask, "whose best interests does the introduction of censorship serve?" There are, of course, arguments both pro and con for censorship. In Table 3-2, a review of the literature on the arguments for and against censorship is presented by Schmid and de Graaf.[38]

In conclusion, some forms of guidelines on media coverage of terrorism are desirable and defensible. The question is, who should promulgate such guidelines? If the media formulate the guidelines, then they may be seen as self-serving. Acts of violence, particularly spectacular acts of terrorist hostage-taking, serve to heighten viewer interest and increase circulation. The challenge for the media is to maintain interest while at the same time not allowing the media to be manipulated by terrorists. If the government formulates the guidelines, those guidelines will support and protect the government's position first. In the long run that could be detrimental to public relations. What is recommended then is a joint governmental/police/media commission that would best serve the interests of the two competing parties, law enforcement and

---

[36]Alfred McClung Lee, *Terrorism In Northern Ireland* (New York: General Hall, 1983), p. 48.

[37]Francis M. Watson, *Political Terrorism* (Washington, D.C.: R. B. Luce, 1976), p. 93.

[38]Schmid and de Graaf, *Violence as Communication,* p. 172.

TABLE 3-2   Censorship and Terrorism

ARGUMENTS FOR CENSORSHIP	ARGUMENTS AGAINST CENSORSHIP
1. Insurgent terrorists use the media as a platform for political propaganda which also helps them to recruit new members to their movement	1. If the media would keep quiet on terrorist atrocities, the violent men might be judged less negatively by sections of the public
2. Since publicity is a major and in some cases the unique reward sought by terrorists, censorship would make terrorism a less desirable strategy	2. With psychotic terrorists, publicity can be a substitute for violence. Without media attention their threats might be translated into acts
3. Detailed coverage of incidents by the media provides potential terrorists with a model that increases their success chance in their own acts	3. Political terrorists boycotted by the media might step up their level of violence until the media have to cover their deeds
4. Information broadcast during incidents can be useful to terrorists	4. If the media did not report on terrorism, rumours would spread, which might be worse than the worst media reporting
5. Media presence during acts of hostage-taking can endanger hostages	5. During siege situations, media presence can prevent the police from engaging in indefensible tactics, causing unnecessary loss of lives among hostages and terrorists
6. Reporting on acts of terrorism can produce imitative acts	6. If terrorism would be treated with silence, governments could label all sort of quasi- or non-terroristic activities by political dissenters terroristic; uncontrolled government actions might be the result
7. In cases of kidnapping, media reports can cause panic with the kidnapper so that he kills the victim	7. If the media would censor terrorism, the public would suspect that other things are censored as well; credibility in the media will decline
8. People who have so little respect for other people's lives as terrorists do, should not be enabled to command public attention only because they use violence	8. Suppression of news on terrorism might leave the public with a false sense of security. People would be unprepared to deal with terrorism when directly faced with it
9. Sadism in the public might be activated by reporting terrorist acts	9. The lack of public awareness of certain terroristic activities would keep the public from fully understanding the political situation
10. Media reports on terrorist outrages might lead to vigilantism and uncontrolled revenge acts against the group the terrorists claim to speak for	10. The feeling of being deprived of vital information might create a public distrust in the political authorities
11. Negative news demoralizes the public while 'good news makes us good'	11. The assertion of insurgent terrorists that democratic states are not really free would gain added credibility if the freedom of the press were suspended

media. If the United States is going to find a solution that will decrease the probability of media intrusion into ongoing terrorist events and make the media more aware of the consequences of some of their dramatic and romantic portrayals of terrorist acts, that solution is going to have to come through an informed dialogue by both parties. The greatest ally law enforcement has in its struggle with terrorism is the media. Differences between law enforcement and the media are bound to exist, but these differences should not obscure their mutual interest in saving the lives of hostages and in the preservation of an orderly society.

CONCLUSIONS

Laqueur notes that the terrorist's act by itself is nothing, "publicity is all."[39] Since terrorists need to advertise their acts of violence on the world stage, one would anticipate that they would be masters of the communication process. Certainly terrorist groups have failed to fully manipulate the means of communication. The present-day terrorist scenario is to let the media communicate the terrorist act to the viewing public. Given the increased sophistication of terrorists and the need of the electronic media to provide "good" pictures, it can only be a matter of time before the level of violence is escalated to produce nightly news. Thus, instead of channels of communication reporting news-making events, terrorist groups actually create the news by amplifying the level of violence.

Terrorist groups that simply distribute manifestos and other printed material to the media detailing grievances or political demands quickly learn that there is little chance their views will be published by the national or international media. Therefore, terrorists rely on spectacular acts of violence. Experience has demonstrated that the media will report all the details of a terrorist attack, including specific details of the group responsible for the attack. The more blood that is shed, the greater the news coverage. Terrorist groups want to communicate this message to the world. What better tactic than through the use of outrageous acts of indiscriminate violence.

Guerrilla wars have been waged for 20 years by ethnic and religious minorities in Angola, Morocco, and Uganda with little effect or recognition by a large viewing audience. However, when a small number of Palestinians moved their armed struggle from Israel to Western Europe, their grievances quickly became news-making events around the world. The Palestinians understood that access to the media magnified their voice and eventually put pressure on Western governments to seek a resolution to the Palestinian question.

[39]Walter Laqueur, "The Futility of Terrorism," *Harpers* (March 1976), p. 104.

Terrorism is a dynamic process, and the media represent an important asset to the success of terroristic events. Thus, the media should regularly evaluate the changing strategies used by terrorists, the increasing threats posed to society by incompetent reporting of terrorist attacks, and the responsibility of accurately reporting on terrorist attacks. Unfortunately there is no foolproof way for the media to avoid being used by terrorist groups in the future.

The next chapter will explore terrorism in the United States with a special emphasis on current terrorist groups identified by the Federal Bureau of Investigation.

REVIEW QUESTIONS

1. Describe the origins of Black September.
2. Why is contagion theory, or the copycat syndrome, such a difficult problem for the printed and electronic media?
3. What precautions can commercial airlines take to protect themselves from the threat of skyjacking?
4. Identify the following:
   a. CFF
   b. PFLP
   c. PIRA
   d. UDA
   e. RB
   f. BPP
5. Develop a set of policy guidelines for law enforcement and media relations.
6. Discuss the "propaganda value" of "self-sacrifice." Cite examples.
7. Present an argument for the introduction of government censorship in ongoing terrorist events.
8. How did the Black Panther Party generate media attention?
9. Why is the 1972 Munich Olympics considered a turning point for international terrorist groups?
10. Describe the Hanafi Muslim siege in Washington, D. C.
11. Argue for or against censorship of terrorist events in the United States.
12. Defend the role of the media in terrorist incidents.

FOUR

THE U.S. EXPERIENCE: DOMESTIC TERRORIST GROUPS

CHAPTER OBJECTIVES

The study of this chapter will enable you to:
- Specify the reasons for the lack of widespread political terrorism in the United States.
- Explain the "internal colonialism" hypothesis.
- Explain the political objectives of Puerto Rican independence.
- Describe the historical origins of contemporary Armenian, Croatian, and Cuban extremism in the United States.
- Outline the relationship of U.S. extremist groups of the late 1960s.
- Increase a general awareness of political terrorism in the United States.

INTRODUCTION

To most Americans terrorism is a bomb that kills people in a far-off land, or an assassin's bullet aimed at a foreign head of state. However, today terrorism is becoming a matter of grave concern in the United States. Witness the unprecedented use of barricades and metal detectors in the nation's capital, the growth and refinement of a special U.S. counterterrorist team—Delta Force—and the U.S. government's retaliatory air strikes against suspected terrorist bases in Libya. How great is the threat? From where is the threat coming? What are its causes? How can the United States cope with this perceived or real terrorist threat?

The purpose of this chapter is to identify terrorist groups active in the United States. Fears that major terrorist campaigns could be launched in the United States are well founded. Terror in the United States tends to come from foreign groups conducting operations in the country: the ideological left, insurgent nationals, criminal gangs, and the ideological right. Most terrorist groups currently active in the United States are either transnational or strongly identified with separatist or leftist movements. For example, Puerto Rican independence, Armenian nationalism, Croatian separatism, anti-Castro groups, the Jewish Defense League, the Revolutionary Armed Task Force, and the United Freedom Fighters/Armed Resistance Unit are "dissident" groups this chapter will explore. The growth of right-wing extremism, which was relatively quiet in the 1970s, is also a continuing source of major concern for the criminal justice system. Groups such as the Order, Posse Comitatus, American Nazi party, the Aryan Nations, and the Covenant, the Sword and the Arm of the Lord (CSA) still pose a serious threat to the values of constitutional liberty in the U.S. This chapter will examine the rebirth of right-wing militancy.

Thus far, the use of political violence and terrorism in the United States has not been sufficiently serious to warrant much attention from either academic analysts or governmental policymakers. In fact, the United States has been relatively free from the kind of political terrorism that dominates in other parts of the world. Even the terroristic or guerrilla-like movements of the 1960s, namely, the Weathermen[1] and Black Panther Party[2], were mild when compared to terrorist or guerrilla movements elsewhere in the world. The political radicals of the 1960s were certainly responsible for many riots, some bombings, and a few assassinations. But at no time did their violent terroristic actions reach the level of guerrilla activity achieved by such groups as the Tupamaros, the Irish Republican Army (IRA), or the various Palestinian extremist groups. Several reasons may explain the absence of widespread terrorism in the United States.

First, it has been argued that terrorism and political violence are endemic

---

[1]Harold Jacobs, ed., *Weathermen* (Berkeley: Ramparts, 1970); John Castellucci, *The Big Dance: The Untold Story of Kathy Boudin and the Terrorist Family That Committed the Brink's Robbery Murders* (New York: Dodd, Mead, 1986); Ellen Frankfort, *Kathy Boudin and The Dance of Death* (New York: Stein and Day, 1983).

[2]Philip S. Foner, ed., *Black Panthers Speak* (Philadelphia: J. B. Lippincott, 1970); G. Louis Heath, ed., *Off the Pigs!: The History and Literature of the Black Panther Party* (New Jersey: Scarecrow Press, 1973).

to certain cultures. This seems so particularly in Latin America.[3] Displays of personal courage and fearlessness, the devotion to the image of folk heroes, and the pursuit of a "macho" lifestyle are important elements in Latin American culture. The strength of this argument is based on the fact that many urban terrorist groups in Latin America do not seek total power but only the demonstration of power through outrageous acts of terrorism. Physical aggression is often viewed as a demonstration of masculinity and toughness. Therefore, rates of violence and terrorism are high in cultures that retain notions of *machismo* and continue to equate maleness with overt physical violence.[4] In the United States, this machismo can be found in juvenile gangs who repeatedly have been involved in territorial fights, feuds, and the use of overt violence to acquire or maintain a reputation of toughness. This suggests then that the juvenile, macho image of toughness associated with violence dissipates as juveniles grow into adulthood. However, the notion of machismo has been widely criticized in the scholarly literature, and little hard evidence has been uncovered that validates the theory based on it. Nonetheless, crime and violence are essentially a juvenile activity where criminal gain is equated with male toughness.

Second, the criminal justice system in the United States has often overreacted to the slightest provocation to our democratic ideals. Thus, groups like the Weathermen, Black Panthers, Yippies,[5] and Students for a Democratic Society (SDS)[6] had to do little in the way of violent or terroristic activity to provoke the criminal justice system, especially the law enforcement community. Often their violent rhetoric was enough.

Third, the philosophical framework of many of the self-styled revolutionary factions in the United States was basically "love" oriented. The popular Yippie movement exemplified their ideology of self-love and, to a lesser extent, the love of others in the popular 1960s' saying "make love, not war." This made it extremely difficult to practice the terrorist method of indiscriminate random violence and terrorism. In fact, most self-styled, U.S. revolutionaries avoided the indiscriminate killing of innocent victims.[7] Instead they proposed an ideology of "we" versus "the pigs." The pigs represented the political establishment, especially the police and military. However, at least one group, the Black Liberation Army (BLA), did indiscriminately attack uni-

---

[3]Marvin Wolfgang and Franco Ferracuti, *The Subculture of Violence* (Beverly Hills: Sage, 1982), pp. 273–79.

[4]Ibid., pp. 155–56.

[5]David L. Stein, *Living the Revolution: Yippies in Chicago* (Indianapolis: Bobbs-Merrill, 1969), p. 1–4.

[6]Kirkpatrick Sale, *S.D.S.* (New York: Random House, 1973); G. Louis Heath, *Vandals in the Bomb Factory: The History and Literature of the Students for a Democratic Society* (New Jersey: Scarecrow, 1976).

[7]Robert Ridenour, "Where Are the Terrorists and What Do they Want?" *Skeptic*, 11 (1976), pp. 18–23.

formed police officers. Patrol cars were attacked with submachine-gun fire, patrol officers were shot down while on patrol, and a desk sergeant was shot point-blank with a shotgun.[8] In time the BLA disappeared, reemerging only briefly in 1981. Attack on the most visible symbols of government (police and military) is, in fact, the initial step towards systematic terrorism. But the campaign of violence of the BLA, Yippies, Weathermen, and SDS can hardly be interpreted as a systematic campaign of terrorism.

Finally, probably the most valid explanation for the growth of terrorism in the world today is the presence of a subculture that is ethnically, religiously, or racially segregated as a minority and has a long history of economic deprivation or exploitation, whether real or imagined. The result has been the use of violence to secure either complete separation from, or a degree of autonomy for, the ethnic, religious, or racial subcultures within the ruling nation. Examples can be found in Northern Ireland, France, Spain, Iran, Israel, and many other countries. The "internal colonialism" thesis argues that economically deprived regions of a nation-state may be kept in a condition of dependence by systematic exploitation for the benefit of the ruling elite.[9] An excellent example of this thesis can be found in Northern Ireland, where ethnic and religious differences and economic exploitation have a long and violent tradition. However, there are many ethnic, religious, and racial "subcultures" that respond to oppression in nonviolent ways. In the United States, for example, the civil rights movement of the 1960s was a nonviolent protest that eventually resulted in the Civil Rights Act of 1964. This act profoundly changed the social, political, and economic institutions in the United States. The democratic nature of the U.S. governmental system, which constitutionally supports the redress of grievances and conflicts involving ethnic, religious, or racial minorities, has effectively prevented the escalation of political terrorism. Outside the United States, however, many ethnic, religious, or racial minorities are prohibited from challenging governmental policies that oppress or deprive specific groups.

The most serious terrorist attacks committed in the United States have been linked to nondomestic issues. The most active and firmly implanted terrorist group in the United States in fact, is motivated by a desire for Puerto Rican independence.

Puerto Rican Independence

The most active terrorist groups in the United States have historically been groups seeking Puerto Rican independence. After the Spanish-American War, Puerto Rico was ceded to the United States by the Treaty of Paris, De-

---

[8]J. Bowyer Bell, *Assassin: The Theory and Practice of Political Violence* (New York: St. Martin's Press, 1979), p. 75.

[9]W. R. Beer, *The Unexpected Rebellion* (New York: New York University, 1980), pp. 55–81.

cember 19, 1898. By 1900 the U.S. Congress had established a civil government on Puerto Rico, and American citizenship was granted to its residents. In 1948 the first native governor was elected and steps were taken by the United States to proclaim the Commonwealth of Puerto Rico. But Puerto Rican nationalists wanted total independence from the United States, not the proposed commonwealth status.[10]

In October 1950, the Puerto Rican nationalists conducted an uprising that was quickly suppressed by loyal government troops. As part of the uprising, two Puerto Rican extremists dramatized their desire for independence by attempting to assassinate President Truman.[11] On November 1, 1950, while Truman was in residence at the Blair House, located across the street from the White House, the Puerto Rican nationalists fired several shots, killing a District of Columbia police officer who engaged the Puerto Rican assassins in a brief gun battle. Truman escaped unharmed, but the nationalists were successful in attracting widespread attention in the United States to their cause of independence. They attracted international attention on March 1, 1954, when several Puerto Rican nationalists invaded the House of Representatives in the U.S. Capitol while Congress was in session and shot and wounded five Congressmen.[12] Puerto Rico is currently a self-governing political entity associated voluntarily with the United States and is no longer considered a United States colonial territory. But this concept of ''independence'' has been challenged by several Puerto Rican nationalist/separatist groups.

Formed in 1974, the most active Puerto Rican terrorist group is Fuerzas Armadas de Liberation Nacional, the Armed Forces for National Liberation (FALN).[13] The FALN is apparently the merger of two nationalist movements, the Armed Commandos of Liberation and the Armed Independence Revolutionary Movement of the 1960s. The introduction of the FALN occurred on October 16, 1974, with the bombing of five banks in New York City.[14] Since its formation, the FALN has claimed responsibility for over 200 bombings on the United States mainland and in Puerto Rico. Their most deadly attack occurred on January 20, 1975, when a powerful pipe bomb destroyed the Fraunes Tavern in New York, killing 4 persons and injuring 63 others.[15] Even though the ideological underpinning of the FALN is the belief in Puerto Rican independence, many of its communiqués concern themselves with the rhetoric of the far left. The bombings of the New York banks and Fraunes Tavern were

---

[10]Robert W. Anderson, *Party Politics in Puerto Rico* (Stanford: Stanford University Press, 1965).

[11]National Commission on Causes and Prevention of Violence, *Assassination and Political Violence* (Washington, D.C.: U. S. Government Printing Office, 1968), pp. 58–59.

[12]Ibid., p. 29.

[13]Patricia Atthowe, ''Terrorism: The FALN's Undeclared War,'' *Defense and Foreign Affairs Digest* (1978), p. 48.

[14]*New York Times,* October 27, 1974, pp. 1, 64.

[15]*New York Times,* January 25, 1975, pp. 1, 10.

carried out to denounce American imperialism, the exploitation of the working class by bankers and stockbrokers, and the U.S. military presence in Puerto Rico.

The FALN is not the only Puerto Rican terrorist group. Too often Puerto Rican terrorist groups are seen as a single entity, but in reality they consist of several competing factions which often cooperate with each other.

All the groups have been active since 1974, concentrating primarily on the destruction of property, especially American corporations with interests in Puerto Rico, the U.S. military based in Puerto Rico, and the federal government. However, the FALN and Macheteros have no apparent feelings of remorse for the indiscriminate taking of lives. On the contrary, it is often their intent to inflict maximum injury and death. Their most spectacular operation was the ambush on December 3, 1979, of a navy bus carrying unarmed U.S. sailors to their daily assignments.[16] Two sailors were killed and ten others were seriously wounded. This ambush involved the classic terrorist tactic of the stalled vehicle blocking the road, then the emergence of the terrorists firing automatic weapons indiscriminately into the crowded bus. This ambush maneuver has been used satisfactorily by the Red Brigades, PFLP, IRA, Red Army Faction, and Basque separatists. After the bus attack three ROTC officers were ambushed as they left the campus of the University of Puerto Rico. One was seriously wounded, the other two escaped unharmed. Like the victims on the bus, the ROTC officers were unarmed.

One incident stands out as a clear indication of the indiscriminate nature of attacks on U.S. military personnel in Puerto Rico by the Macheteros. Four U.S. sailors on shore leave in San Juan were just leaving a popular night club when a car drove alongside and cut them down with automatic weapons. One sailor died and three were seriously wounded. Additional attacks on U.S. military personnel were recorded in Illinois and New York. Possibly the most dramatic and theatrical attack on the U.S. military occurred on January 12, 1981, when the Macheteros entered the Puerto Rican National Guard headquarters at Muniz Air Base and destroyed approximately $60 million in jet aircraft.[17] Later investigation revealed that they entered the base by penetrating a security fence, evaded armed guards by wearing military uniforms, and planted 21 bombs in the intake manifolds and wheel wells of "11" jet fighters. The attack on the air base was carried out by "11" Macheteros terrorists to dramatize their solidarity with "11" members of the FALN who were then on trial in Evanston, Illinois.

The symbolic nature of the attack on Muniz Air Base may be a subtle cue to the "expressive symbolism" of Puerto Rican culture. Jarger and Selznick pursue this hypothesis and stress the degree of attachment or intensity of

---

[16]*New York Times,* December 4, 1979, pp. 1, A10.
[17]*New York Times,* January 13, 1981, pp. 1, A12.

meaning in the expressive symbolism of a culture.[18] They argue that culture consists of sharing symbolic experiences and that shared experiences eventually become part of normative behavior. If this hypothesis is valid, then agents of the criminal justice system may have missed some important cues sent by Puerto Rican terrorist groups. By analyzing past terrorist actions of Puerto Rican nationalists and terrorist groups, it may be possible to predict with some degree of accuracy the date, time, and target of subsequent attacks.

Another example of the expressive symbolism theory took place at midnight March 1, 1982, when four explosions tore through the financial district of New York City.[19] The explosions were timed to commemorate the March 1, 1954, assault on the U.S. Congress. The FALN claimed credit for the bombings, stating that it was a strike against U.S. imperialist forces that are suppressing the Puerto Rican people.

In addition to bombings the FALN has also taken over buildings and held hostages as a selective propaganda tactic. On March 15, 1980, armed terrorists of the FALN seized the Bush and Carter-Mondale election headquarters in Chicago and New York.[20] The terrorists threatened and terrorized campaign workers and ransacked the offices, seizing the records of campaign contributors. Law enforcement officials speculated that the lists of contributors contained the names of possible victims of assassination or kidnapping. Shortly after this assault, on April 4, 1980, eleven members of FALN were arrested in Evanston, Illinois, during the planning of an apparent robbery and kidnapping.[21] Consequently, the 11 FALN members, including the acknowledged leader, Carlos Alberto Torres, were tried and convicted for a variety of offenses and sentenced to long prison terms. The FBI proclaimed, "We have decapitated their leadership." But FALN terrorists never stopped the bombing campaign initiated in 1974; they were merely slowed until new recruits could be found. By December 30, 1981, the sentencing procedure had been completed for the 11 FALN members arrested earlier. On New Year's Eve, 1982, to protest the long prison terms for dedicated "freedom fighters," the FALN placed four bombs at federal and local government buildings in New York City.[22] The four bombs were timed to explode at approximately 30-minute intervals. An FALN communiqué stated: "This is the FALN, we are responsible for the bombings in New York City today. Free Puerto Rico. Free all political prisoners and prisoners of war." The bombing campaign continued through 1983 and 1984 with continued attacks on federal facilities and U.S. corporations doing business in Puerto Rico.

[18]Gertrude Jaeger and Phillip Selznick, "A Normative Theory of Culture," *American Sociological Review* 29 (1964), pp. 653–69.

[19]*New York Times,* March 1, 1982, pp. 1, D11.

[20]*New York Times,* March 16, 1980, pp. 1, 45.

[21]*New York Times,* April 15, 1980. pp. 1, 7.

[22]*New York Times,* January 1, 1983, pp. 1, 23.

In sum, Puerto Rican terrorist groups are generally organized along the following lines:

1. *Groups*
   Armed Forces for National Liberation (FALN)
   National Liberation Movement (MLN)
   Revolutionary Commandos of the People (CRP)
   Organization of Volunteers for the Puerto Rican Resolution (OVRP)
   Armed Forces of Popular Resistance (FARP)
   The Machete Wielders, or Puerto Rican Popular Army (Macheteros)

2. *Political Ideology*
   FALN is a group of "neoricans," or Puerto Ricans born or raised in the United States who are aligned with left-wing groups in the United States as well as in Puerto Rico.
   The Macheteros are ideologically motivated by Marxist-Leninist rhetoric.
   Other groups support political ideologies from Socialism to Marxism.

3. *Membership*
   Membership is small; thus, it is difficult for the police to penetrate and develop intelligence.

4. *Tactics*
   Bombings, assassinations, armed takeovers, ambushes and specific booby trap targets. Several police officers in New York have been killed or injured by antipersonnel devices.

5. *Specific Operations*
   February 29, 1982—four explosions in New York City financial district.
   December 31, 1982—bombs detonated in Manhattan and Brooklyn, injuring three police officers.
   May 29, 1983—shootout with Mexican police in Puebla, Mexico, during recapture of William Morales, FALN explosive expert.
   November 7, 1985—two men from OVRP shoot and seriously wound Army major on way to Fort Buchanan, San Juan, Puerto Rico.
   October 28, 1986—two U.S. military recruiting centers bombed in San Juan by Macheteros.

6. *Goal*
   Stated goal is Puerto Rican independence.

7. *Training*
   Law enforcement officials believe they receive training in Cuba, and also learn through trial and error.

The Puerto Rican terrorists will no doubt continue their quest for Puerto Rican independence. Considering their past performance, there is little doubt that the terror tactics of bombing and assassination will be abandoned in the future.

Armenian Nationalism

Infuriated by the alleged planned genocide of approximately 1.5 million Armenians during World War I by the Ottoman Turks and the loss of their ancestral homeland, contemporary Armenian terrorists have gone on a rampage of bombing, assassination, and hostage-taking of Turkish diplomats or members of their immediate families.[23] Armenian terrorists claim the attacks against the present Turkish state are justified because Turkey refuses to acknowledge the Armenian genocide of 1915. The present Turkish government denies that the Ottoman Empire systematically killed Armenians in a program of planned genocide. The Turks insist that they were fighting a five-front war during World War I and that Armenian nationalists were aligned with Western powers and therefore, posed an immediate threat to their internal security.[24] Hence, the Ottoman Turks were ''forced'' to deport Armenians from Turkey to the Syrian desert to avert partisan warfare. In the process thousands of Armenians were killed and displaced.

Who to blame for this century's first recorded instance of genocide is unclear. European Christians charged the ''Unspeakable Turk,'' the Sultan Abdul-Hamid II, with the massacre of thousands of innocent Christian Armenians.[25] Others maintain that the Turks were justified in their response since Armenian nationals at the turn of the century used indiscriminate terrorism to provoke Turkish reprisals and massacres.[26] The purpose of this early Armenian terrorism was apparently to cause cycles of massacre and countermassacre that would end only with European intervention. (A similar situation has existed in Lebanon between Christians and Moslems.) The cycle of violence and terrorism came to an abrupt end during World War I with what Armenians refer to as the twentieth-century's first genocide. To understand what motivates today's Armenian terrorists, a brief review of the events of World War I is necessary.

The Armenian contention asserts that the Ottoman government meticulously planned and then executed a systematic genocide of 1.5 million Armenian citizens. The Turkish strategy involved outright massacres of innocent civilians and the forced relocation of Armenians into the Syrian deserts, which resulted in attacks by nomadic tribesmen along the way and death due to starvation for those who survived the trek. Armenian sources argue that the Turks were motivated by a desire to unite all Turkish peoples and the Armenians blocked their path.[27] Thus, under the cover of World War I and charges of Armenian collaboration with the invading Russian army, the Ottoman Turks

[23]Andrew Corsun, ''Armenian Terrorism: A Profile,'' *U. S. Department of State Bulletin* (August 1982), pp. 31–35.

[24]''Setting the Record Straight on Armenian Propaganda Against Turkey'', *ATA-USA: Bulletin of the Assembly of American Turkish Associations,* Washington, D. C., Fall, 1982, pp. 4–9.

[25]Lord J. P. Kinross, *The Ottoman Centuries: The Rise and Fall of the Turkish Empire* (New York: Morrow, 1977), pp. 24–46.

[26]William Langer, *The Diplomacy of Imperialism: 1890–1902* (Boston: Knopf, 1951), p. 157.

[27]Aram Audonian, ed., *The Memoirs of Naim Bey: Turkish Official Documents Relating to the Deportation and Massacres of Armenians* (Pennsylvania: American Historical Review Association, 1964).

devastated the Armenian community. The noted British statesman Bryce-Toynbee, after extensive interviews, stated that the Turks attempted "to exterminate a whole nation without distinction of age or sex."[28] An equally unsavory account was recorded by Henry Morgenthau, then U.S. ambassador to Turkey. Morgenthau wrote that:

> It is absurd for the Turkish government to assert it ever seriously intended to deport Armenians to new homes . . . extermination was the real purpose.[29]

The Turks adamantly deny that they committed genocide. They point to the fact that after the war the British detained several hundred Ottoman government officials and ranking military personnel suspected of war crimes, but despite British enthusiasm to find proof of guilt, no evidence existed to substantiate the Armenian allegations of planned genocide.[30] Given the understandable passion on both sides, Armenians seeking revenge and Turks protecting ethnic integrity, it is doubtful that the two positions can be reconciled. Each has its own interpretation of historical events.

In sum, the roots of modern Armenian terrorism can be found in the events of 1915. Idealistic and fanatical young Armenian nationalists form the nucleus of the various terrorist groups associated with Armenian terrorism. The organized campaign of terror against primarily Turkish targets began in 1975 when the Armenian Secret Army for the Liberation of Armenia (ASALA) claimed credit for the bombing of the office of the World Council of Churches in Beirut for promoting emigration of Armenians to the United States. Why, after 60 years, has this wave of Armenian terrorism begun? Precise analysis is, of course, difficult since it has been virtually impossible for law enforcement officials to penetrate the terrorist cells of Armenian terrorist groups. Nevertheless, ASALA apparently emerged when the Lebanese Civil War began in 1975. ASALA's rhetoric indicates that they have been influenced by the Palestinian Resistance Movement, particularly the Palestinian tactics of terrorist atrocities to gain attention and recognition. Like the Palestinian Left, ASALA began by supporting the Marxist ideology of a war of national liberation. By the late 1970s, however, this ideology caused a split in the ranks of ASALA when a rival anti-Marxist/communist group surfaced, calling itself the Justice Commandos for the Armenian Genocide (JCAG). The goals of both groups are the same, and they cooperate and work together. However, they are also distinguished by their selection of victims. ASALA claims credit for attacks both on Turkish targets and organizations that have commercial

---

[28]Great Britain Parliamentary Papers, *The Treatment of Armenians in the Ottoman Empire, 1915–16* (London: Cavston, 1916), No. 31.

[29]Henry Morgenthau, *Ambassador Morgenthau's Story* (New York: Doubleday, 1918), pp. 309–12.

[30]"Armenian Allegations and Some Facts," *ATA-USA: Bulletin of the Assembly of American Turkish Associations,* April, 1980, p. 4.

relations with Turkey, while JCAG states they undertake actions against only Turkish targets.[31]

The stated goals of ASALA and JCAG have been defined as the three Armenian *r*'s:

1. Recognition by Turkey of the crimes committed against the Armenians
2. Reparations for the Armenians in terms of money and territory
3. Return of the land expropriated during World War I.[32]

Despite the fact that the Ottoman Empire no longer exists, the nationalists insist the present Turkish state must pay for the crimes of the past. The fact their political goals seem unrealistic does not dim their determination. Armenians cite the creation of Israel, the influence of the Zionist movement, and the struggle for the recovery of Palestine as comparable examples. They also cite the reparations paid to the Jews by West Germany after the Holocaust. The returned Turkish Armenia would be united with Soviet Armenia, thus ending the Armenian diaspora. Armenians would finally have their own homeland.

The conduct of Armenian terrorists demonstrates they are prepared to go on suicide missions to accomplish these goals. The previously cited seige at the Turkish embassy in Lisbon, where Armenian terrorists blew themselves up, demonstrates this commitment. Geographically, Armenian terrorist operations have occurred on four different continents, with the majority being in Western Europe. The United States recorded 16 incidents between 1975 and 1984. Several Armenian terrorists were convicted in the United States for murder, arson, bombing, and conspiracy in 1984.[33] The worst year for worldwide Armenian terrorism was recorded in 1981, with 56 incidents.[34]

1. *Groups*
   Armenian Secret Army for the Liberation of Armenia (ASALA)
   Justice Commandos for the Armenian Genocide (JCAG)
   Armenian Revolutionary Army (ARA)
   Avengers of the Armenian Genocide (AAG)
2. *Political Ideology*
   Moderate conservative to Marxist.
3. *Membership*
   Estimates range from 300 to 1000.

[31]Paul Wilkinson, "Armenian Terrorism," *The World Today* 39 (September 1983): 336–44.

[32]Michael M. Gunter, "The Armenian Terrorist Campaign Against Turkey," *Orbis* 27 (Summer 1983): 460.

[33]*New York Times,* February 19, 1984, and October 10, 1984.

[34]Gunter, "Armenian Terrorist Campaign," *Orbis,* p. 468.

4. *Tactics*

   Bombings, assassinations, ambushes, and hostage-taking, including 50 murders of Turkish diplomatic personnel and 100 attacks on Turkish targets.

5. *Specific Operations*

   January 28, 1982—assassinated Turkish consul general in Los Angeles.

   August 7, 1982—indiscriminately killed 9 and wounded 72 in a bombing at tack at the Ankara International Airport, Turkey.

   July 16, 1983—indiscriminate bombing attack at Orly Airport in Paris; 5 killed and 56 wounded.

6. *Goal*

   Turkish recognition of the Armenian genocide; reparations and recovery of Armenian homeland.

7. *Training*

   Believed to be trained by the PLO and Syrian military.

Until the recent ASALA terrorist campaign, few people knew much about Armenian grievances against the Turks. The young, fanatical Armenian idealists who affirm the necessity to go on suicide missions in order to demonstrate Turkish perfidy have a close relationship with the Palestinian fedayeen. Like the Palestinians, the Armenian terrorists of ASALA and JCAG believe that terrorism is the only weapon at their disposal and that the propaganda of atrocity will bring international recognition to them and pressure to the Turkish government. However, the aspirations of the Armenians seem impossible, given the current realities of the Turkish state and international politics. The international community can ill afford to tolerate an orgy of vendetta violence by every ethnic or national group that alleges to have suffered at the hands of another state. This would be a recipe for a decline into anarchy, where international relationships would be based on revenge and retaliation.[35]

Even so, the political and moral cause of the Armenians deserves reexamination by the international body politic. According to Kuper, the Turkish genocide against the Armenian people "disappeared down the United Nation's memory hole" when the UN Convention on Genocide failed to consider the case of the Armenians.[36] Attempts to raise the issue by Armenian supporters have been blocked by Turkish supporters of the UN Commission on Human Rights. If this committee persists in its efforts to block debate on Armenian grievances, then the world may witness an increase in Armenian terrorism. When Adolf Hitler was asked whether Germany's genocidal campaign to eliminate the Jews of Europe might one day bring down retribution on Germany, he stated, "Who speaks today of the Armenians?" This sense of Armenian identity and nationalism has been reawakened by terrorism and violence. The voice of terrorism, the bomb and the gun, speak for the Armenians.

---

[35]Wilkinson, "Armenian Terrorism," *The World Today,* pp. 349–50.

[36]Leo Kuper, *Genocide* (New Haven, Conn.: Yale, 1981), p. 219.

Croatian Separatists

Another example of the use of the terrorist method may be found in the strategy of Croatian separatists, or Fighters for Free Croatia. Like the Armenians, few people of the world were aware that a small number of Croatians harbored strong feelings of animosity toward the Yugoslavian government of President Tito. This hatred led the Fighters for Free Croatia to embark on the first successful skyjacking in years in the United States. The skyjacking, staged for the media, informed the world of Croatian grievances, and their cause became a subject of avid media interest. A 3500-word manifesto issued by the "Headquarters of Croatian National Liberation Forces" during this spectacular skyjacking outlined Croatian discontent. It was a mixture of historic grievance and rhetoric advocating Croatian liberation:

> National self-determination is a basic human right, universal and fundamental, recognized by all members of the UN, a right which may not be denied or withheld any nation regardless of its territorial size or number of inhabitants. . . . We fight for Croatia which will be, for all people, either a cherished presence or a beloved homeland.[37]

While the identity and size of the Croatian Liberation Movement still remains uncertain, the ideological background is readily available for historical analysis. A brief review of the antecedents of Croatian "liberation" is, therefore, necessary to fully understand the motivation for Croatian terrorism.

Croatia is the second largest of six Republics that make up present-day Yugoslavia. After World War I the Treaty of Versailles established the Kingdom of Serbs, Croats, and Slovenes. However, by 1929 deep dissatisfaction had developed within the Croatian people since the new kingdom was dominated by Serbs. Not only was the king a Serb, but 90 percent of all governmental and military officers were from the Serbian ethnic group, which represented only 41 percent of the "Yugoslav" population. Because of gerrymandering and election fraud, this domination extended into the parliament. As a result of the Serbian domination, many Croatian leaders advocated an independent or semi-autonomous Croatian state as had existed for approximately 1000 years prior to the creation of the multinational state of Yugoslavia. Croat leaders continued to argue for independence before the "Yugoslav" Parliament. In one such heated debate, a Serbian minister calmly assassinated three Croat representatives. Fearing Croatian reprisals, King Alexander suspended the new Yugoslavian Constitution, declared a royal dictatorship, and banned all political parties. As Serbian troops moved into the province of Croatia to maintain order, leaders of all Croatian political parties went into exile. One of these

---

[37]*New York Times,* September 12, 1976.

leaders was Ante Pavelic, the founder of the notorious and much feared Croatian Ustasa movement.[38]

Pavelic, along with approximately 500 members of Ustasa (insurgents), found sanctuary and support under direct Italian sponsorship. All followers of Ustasa were required to take an oath of obedience to achieve a "free and independent Croat state" and to accept a fascist political ideology. Under the protection of Italy, Ustasa began to conduct raids into "Yugoslavia," adopting a strategy of indiscriminate bombing in which innocent travelers became the major victims. The purpose of the indiscriminate bombing campaign was to draw international attention to their cause and demonstrate that Yugoslavia was incapable of maintaining law and order and, therefore, should be dissolved. Their most successful terrorist operation was the assassination of King Alexander and the French foreign minister in 1934. After the assassination of Alexander, Yugoslavia rapidly descended into civil war. To forestall the inevitable war, an agreement was reached whereby Croatia became a semi-autonomous state, as it had been in the old Austro-Hungarian Empire. Although the Croats now controlled education, criminal justice, industry, and commerce within their state, they still demanded complete independence.[39]

Then on April 6, 1941, German, Italian, Hungarian, and Bulgarian troops invaded Yugoslavia and quickly destroyed the impotent Yugoslav army and proceeded to partition the South Slavs. Croatia thus became a German wartime puppet state under the leadership of Pavelic and Ustasa.[40] The dreams of the separatists had been realized. Sadly, one of the first acts of the new state and Ustasa was to purge the Serbian minority who lived in Croatia. Ustasa went so far as to establish Nazi-style concentration camps for the elimination of Serbs, Jews, Gypsies, and Croat democrats. It is estimated that about one-third of the Serbs were physically exterminated or rounded up and deported. However, by the end of 1941 several guerrilla forces emerged, attacking Ustasa and the armies of occupation. The Communist-inspired Partisans, the Serbian Nationalists, the Cetniks, the Montenegrin Federalists, the Slovenian White and Blue Guards, and the Domobrans, or Croatian Regular Army, represented virtually every ethnic, political, and religious group in Yugoslavia.[41] During the war these groups frequently switched allegiance, and it was very difficult to determine who was on what side. In effect there was a civil war raging within the larger context of World War II.

Nonetheless, as the war dragged on, the Partisans were emerging as the most powerful and dominant guerrilla group. By 1945 the Nazi Germans be-

---

[38]C. Michael McAdams, "White paper on Dr. Andrija Artukovic," *California: Croatian Information Series* 4 (July 1975), pp. 4–11.

[39]Stephen Clissold, *Croat Separatism: Nationalism, Dissidence, and Terrorism* (London: Institute for the Study of Conflict, 1979), pp. 3–4.

[40]Ibid., p. 5.

[41]McAdams, *White Paper,* p. 14.

gan to pull their support forces from Croatia, and Ustasa was left alone to face the Partisans. Then on May 6, 1945, Ustasa leaders and followers fled to Austria and surrendered to the Allies. The Allies refused their surrender and returned them to the Partisans, who promised to treat them as war criminals. But once under Partisan control massive and ruthless reprisals were taken, which brought an end to Croatian independence. However, Pavelic and other top leaders of Ustasa escaped and vowed to continue the fight for an independent Croatia.

With the end of the war, members of Ustasa were hunted down and returned to Yugoslavia to stand trial for war crimes. In fact, the Yugoslavian government was pressuring the Allies to round up all Ustasa members and treat them as war criminals. Few were returned; many escaped to the United States, Canada, and Argentina. In one case, after a lengthy legal battle lasting 30 years, the United States arraigned Dr. Andrija Artukovic on an extradition warrant. Artukovic, who was known as the "butcher of the Balkans," is accused of the mass murder of over 700,000 people.[42]

Still the separatists yearned for Croatia. By 1956 the movement was given new life. The Croatian Liberation Movement was organized by Anton Pavelic, but it remained under the control of old-line Ustasa leaders. At first the movement had little support, but by the late 1960s there was a resurgence of Croatian nationalism, and Croats began once again to participate actively in the Yugoslav government and military. Then, in the spring of 1971, students at Zagreb University in the Province of Croatia went on strike. Instead of putting down the student strike, the Croat military and government officials supported it.

This action, especially by the military, caused the Tito regime to overreact and purge the "rebellion." Many Croatian students and members of the military were given long prison terms or sentenced to death. Apparently this governmental overreaction was what the separatists were waiting for and anticipating. Acts of terrorism both abroad and in Yugoslavia began to increase, and the ranks of the Croatian Liberation Movement began to grow. Bombings, assassinations, and attacks on Yugoslav institutions and representatives increased. In Chicago the German consul was held hostage. The Yugoslav mission to the United Nations was attacked and bombed several times between 1977 and 1987. But the most outrageous incident was the skyjacking of TWA flight 355 in 1976, which catapulted the Croatian cause onto the international scene.[43]

During this escalation of terrorism the Yugoslav government took its own countermeasures, apparently in the form of "state terror." The government has been accused of using the Yugoslav Security Service (UDBA) to track

---

[42]*San Francisco Chronicle,* "War Crimes Extradition Hearing Begins," February 28, 1985, p. 7.

[43]J. Bowyer Bell, *A Time of Terror* (New York: Basic, 1978), pp. 6–35.

down and kill Croatian separatists. The separatists maintain that 20 of their members have been killed by the UDBA in the United States. These counter-measures have been condemned by the United States and other democratic nations as police-state tactics.[44]

Today, of the many rival Croatian separatist groups that exist, only a small minority are committed to violence and terrorism. All share the same goal: the creation of an independent Croatia. Despite the denials, the old organization of Ustasa still seems to exist, controlled by the Croatian Liberation Movement.

But there are several factors working against the successful achievement of Croatian separatism:

1. A lack of unity is prevalent. No umbrella group provides a general organizational framework for all Croatian separatist groups.
2. No special political program exists other than the reclaiming of Croatia and the destruction of Yugoslavia. But a sovereign Croat nation may cause more problems than it solves. What would become of their historical, traditional enemy, the Serbian minority? How would territorial boundaries be determined?
3. They lack the cooperation and support of other international terrorists or "freedom fighters."
4. The separatists suffer from the legacy and the reputation of brutality earned by Ustasa before and during World War II.
5. Ustasa still brings to mind images of fascism and Nazi collaboration.

The theatrical and exhibitionist-style terrorism of Croatian separatists has transformed the name of an obscure Balkan province into an international issue. For Croatian separatists, terrorism has worked. However, it is unlikely that even the most dedicated efforts of Croatian separatists can be achieved as long as a Communist government controls Yugoslavia.

In sum, Croatian terrorist groups can be outlined as follows:

1. *Groups*
    Croatian Revolutionary Brotherhood (HRB)
    Croatian National Resistance (Spain)
    United Croats of West Germany
    Croatian Liberation Movement
    Fighters for Free Croatia (United States)
2. *Political Ideology*
    Nationalist, anti-communist with fascist tendencies.
3. *Membership*
    Police estimates are unreliable, although the number of those engaged in terrorist operations is small, approximately 50. However, the Croatian diaspora is sympathetic with the goal of the terrorists.

---

[44]Clissold, *Croat Separatism*, pp. 12–15.

4. *Tactics*
   Bombing, skyjacking, and assassination directed at the Yugoslav government at home and abroad.
5. *Specific Operations*
   September 10, 1976—hijacked TWA and subsequently informed the world of their cause.
   January 23, 1981—bombed Supreme Court, Lower Manhattan, New York.
6. *Goal*
   To establish a free and independent Croatia.
7. *Training*
   Believed neo-Fascists in Western Europe provided training.

Anti-Castro Cubans

Opponents of Fidel Castro have been active in the United States since the early 1960s in a variety of organizations. The anti-Castro groups were originally founded by the CIA and U.S. military, which trained Cuban exiles in the tactics of guerrilla warfare to destabilize the pro-Soviet Castro regime in the early 1960s. The covert-action program of destabilization was authorized by the Kennedy administration following the failure of the Bay of Pigs.[45] This U.S.-government sponsorship of Cuban guerrillas, or freedom fighters, was similar to the support given to the contras in Nicaragua by the Reagan administration to fight the Marxist Sandinistas. However, armed covert action against Cuba was terminated after President Johnson entered office. But Cuban exile groups continued to train and expand their influence in the Cuban community in the United States, eventually forming an uncontrolled terrorist network of anti-Castro groups.

The oldest of these anti-Castro groups is Alpha 66, still led by members of the Cuban militia that attempted the landing at the Bay of Pigs. Although Alpha 66 continues to stage raids into Cuba, it rarely engages in terrorist activities in the United States. The origins of Alpha 66 are vague. But apparently the name was chosen by a group of Cuban seamen who were loyal to Fulgencio Batista, the Cuban dictator overthrown by Fidel Castro. Alpha, the first letter of the Greek alphabet, represents the first group of Cuban exiles to oppose the pro-Soviet government of Castro. The number 66 refers to the year 1966, the year of its formation and the beginning of its effort to reclaim Cuba. Thus, Alpha 66 was the first group of Cuban exiles to actively oppose Fidel Castro through the use of a planned program of terrorism and political violence.

However, the most active anti-Castro group, and the one which poses a serious urban terrorist threat to the United States as well as Latin American

---

[45]Peter Wyden, *Bay of Pigs: The Untold Story* (New York: Simon and Schuster, 1980); Lloyd S. Etheredge, *Can Governments Learn: American Foreign Policy and Central American Revolutions* (New York: Pergamon Press, 1985).

states that support Fidel Castro, is Omega 7. In fact, the FBI declared that Omega 7 is "the most dangerous terrorist organization in the U.S."[46] Further, the apprehension of its members was said to be a matter of the highest priority for the federal government. After an intense investigation of Omega 7 by the FBI, several leaders of the group were arrested and convicted for terrorist activities. On September 23, 1984, Eduardo Arocena, reputed leader of Omega 7, was convicted of first-degree murder and involvement in 14 bombings in New York City and Miami.[47] Several other members and leaders of Omega 7 have also been indicted on federal charges of murder and bombing. The FBI expects these indictments and convictions to reduce the terrorist acts of Omega 7 for some time to come.

The main targets of Omega 7 have been Cuban and Soviet diplomats and commercial interests. But recently Omega 7 has expanded its target list to include any country that does business with the Castro government. Omega 7 has also been accused of bombing, murder, and intimidation in the Cuban exile community, especially in the Miami area. Police officials in Dade County, Florida, estimate that Omega 7 may have been responsible for 30 bombings in 1975 alone in the Cuban exile community.[48] This bombing blitz is continuing. On September 2, 1982, Omega 7 bombed the Venezuelan Consulate to protest the treatment of Orlando Bosch. Bosch, a reputed Omega 7 leader, is incarcerated in Venezuela for the 1976 bombing of a Cuban airliner flying between Havana and Guyana; 73 lives were lost. Between January and February, 1983, Omega 7 exploded a series of bombs, targeting industries involved in business transactions with Cuba. A travel agency, a Spanish-language magazine, a freight company, and a cigar factory were all attacked by Omega 7 for doing business with Cuba.

But bombing is not the only terrorist activity of Omega 7. It has also been involved in the selective assassination of Cuban diplomats in Lisbon, Mexico, and New York City. Omega 7 members claimed responsibility for the assassination of leftist exile Orlando Letelier in Washington, D. C., in 1977. On July 11, 1981, *Gramma,* the official Cuban Communist party newspaper, announced that a combined force of members of Alpha 66 and Omega 7 landed on the northern coast of Cuba with explosives, weapons, and propaganda. Their objective was the attempted assassination of Fidel Castro. *Gramma* further claims that the groups have been responsible for 85 bombings, 1 bazooka attack, and 94 murders since 1973.[49]

---

[46]*New York Times,* March 3, 1980, p. 2.

[47]*New York Times,* September 23, 1984, p. 2.

[48]Jeff Stern, "An Army in Exile: Cuban Nationalist Movement in Union City, N.J.: *New Yorker* 12 (September 10, 1979), pp. 42–46.

[49]William Schapp, "New Spate of Terrorism: Key Leaders Unleashed," *Covert Action Information Bulletin,* December, 1980, pp. 7–9.

The Cuban government publishes lists of terrorist acts carried out against its employees. The lists contain specific details of time, place, methods, damage inflicted, and number of participants. These terrorist acts are often verifiable and Cuban exile groups frequently claim responsibility. However, Omega 7 and other Cuban exile groups assert that these figures are inflated and that members of the DGI (Cuban intelligence) are in fact responsible for many of the acts of reported terrorism.

U.S. intelligence reports indicate that the exodus of refugees from Cuba in the "Mariel boatlift" included a number of Cuban intelligence operatives of the DGI. The confusion created by the 125,000 refugees who left Cuba on the "freedom flotilla" bound for the United States was easily exploited by Fidel Castro. More than 2,000 hard-core criminals, 24,000 refugees with prison records for political or minor crimes, trained Communist revolutionaries, and Cuban intelligence agents were among the refugees. In April 1983, a former Cuban intelligence agent testified at a New York State hearing that Cuban agents directed drug traffic in the United States. Antiterrorist specialists in the United States believe that Cuban intelligence agents have been assigned specific missions including: (1) drug trafficking, (2) disruption of civil order by perpetrating robberies, (3) indiscriminate terrorism, (4) sabotage of critical U.S. defense industries, and (5) the disruption of U.S. prisons when incarcerated.[50] Fidel Castro just may be retaliating against the United States. If Cuban exiles can be trained to destabilize Cuba, then why not Cuban agents to infiltrate and destabilize the United States?

Nevertheless, the recent arrests and convictions of Omega 7 and Alpha 66 leaders have weakened their operation, especially in New York and New Jersey. But to eliminate their support in Miami, the largest Cuban community in the United States, is probably impossible. Additionally, the increased penetration of the United States by Cuban DGI agents could develop into underground warfare between Omega 7 and Cuban-supported leftist groups. In sum, the Cuban exiles of Omega 7 and Alpha 66 claim they are freedom fighters fighting the spread of world communism, not an out-of-control terrorist organization attacking random indiscriminate targets.

Cuban terrorist groups are organized as follows:

1. *Groups*
   Omega 7
   Alpha 66
   Variety of paramilitary groups in Florida, New York, and New Jersey.
2. *Political Ideology*
   Anti-communist with no specific political program for change other than the overthrow of Fidel Castro.

---

[50]*Wall Street Journal* (New York), April 30, 1984, p. 1.

3. *Membership*
   Estimates are unreliable although those engaged in actual terrorist operations number approximately 35. However, much of the Cuban exile community is supportive of their anti-communist philosophy.
4. *Tactics*
   Bombing and selective assassination of Cuban targets and any country or business sympathetic to the Castro regime.
5. *Specific Operations*
   September, 1976—assassination of Letelier and Mouffet in Washington, D. C.
   September 2, 1982—bombed Venezuelan Consulate in New York City.
   January-February, 1983—Miami bombing blitz.
6. *Goal*
   To harass and destabilize the Castro government.
7. *Training*
   Southern Florida has been the home of several anti-Castro training centers.

The Jewish Defense League (JDL)

The Jewish Defense League was founded in 1968 by Rabbi Meir Kahane in New York City to protest the Soviet treatment of Jews, to support the Jewish State of Israel, and to protect elderly Jewish citizens.[51] Members of the JDL, whom Kahane called the *Jewish Panthers,* are trained in the use of weapons and karate to defend themselves against the threat of anti-Semitism. The motto of the JDL is "Never Again," a reminder of the Jewish Holocaust. Despite the fact that terrorist activity of the JDL appears to be declining, acts of anti-Semitism by the KKK and newly formed neo-Nazi groups have sparked renewed interest in the JDL. During the early 1980s the terrorist activities of the American Nazi Party (ANP) were primarily directed at Jewish targets. Several incidents occurred in California—for example, arson attacks on Jewish businesses, the desecration of Jewish cemeteries, and an assault on the Center for Jewish Studies in Los Angeles.

Initially the JDL made headlines by marching with baseball bats through black neighborhoods of New York City, where attacks on elderly Jews had occurred, and by planting bombs in Soviet United Nations' offices to protest the treatment of Russian Jews.[52] But in 1971, Kahane emigrated to Israel where he has become equally infamous as the leader of an even more militant Zionist organization, Kach (Hebrew for "thus"). Kahane is supported by a small group of Zionist extremists who advocate the total expulsion of all Arabs from Israel. Kahane has been arrested more than 100 times while in Israel for incit-

---

[51]"Meir Kahane: A Candid Conversation With the Military Leader of the Jewish Defense League," *Playboy* (October, 1972), p. 69.

[52]"Anti-Soviet Zionist Terrorism in the U.S.," *Current Digest of the Soviet Press* 23 (1971): pp. 6–8.

ing violence. He is the only Jew ever to be held in Israel under administrative detention or imprisoned without trial for alleged security offenses.[53] In New York he was sentenced to five years' probation for conspiracy to manufacture explosives. Kahane frequently returns to the United States on fund-raising expeditions; he maintains offices in New York City and Washington, D.C.

The extremist rhetoric of Kahane and Kach has apparently affected the target selection of the JDL in the United States. According to reports, a faction within the JDL is attacking targets it believes is conspiring against the Jewish race. This faction has bombed the French, Lebanese, and Egyptian diplomatic delegations in New York City. It also bombed the West German airline offices of Lufthansa in New York City. The extremist element of the JDL apparently views Mideast peace initiatives with the Palestinian Arabs as threatening to the principles of Zionism.

In sum, Kahane and the JDL represent the most vengeful, extreme, and confrontational views of the Jewish people.

1. *Groups*
   Jewish Defense League (JDL)
   Jewish Defenders (JD)
   Thunder of Zion
2. *Political Ideology*
   Anti-Soviet and anti-Arab; religious zealots who totally support the principles of militant Zionism.
3. *Membership*
   Estimates are unreliable although it is believed that 50 members are active terrorists.
4. *Tactics*
   Bombings and harassment of Soviet and Arab targets.
5. *Specific Operations*
   December 24, 1981—bombing of Soviet Mission in New York City.
   January 26, 1981—bombing of Bank Melli Iran in San Francisco.
   October 25, 1981—Molotov cocktail caused extensive damage to Egyptian government tourist office.
   March-August, 1986—New York bombing campaign.
6. *Goal*
   To harass Soviet and Arab government officials and to remind Jews and non-Jews of the anti-Semitism of right-wing groups in the United States.
7. *Training*
   Unknown if organized training bases exist.

Revolutionary Armed Task Force (RATF): The Ideological Left

The Revolutionary Armed Task Force first emerged after an unsuccessful attempt to ambush a Brinks' armored bank truck in New York on October 20,

[53] *Time*, August 13, 1984, p. 26.

1981.[54] After the abortive holdup attempt, law enforcement officials arrested 11 people. Later investigation revealed that the individuals were members of an unknown guerrilla group calling itself the Revolutionary Armed Task Force.[55] As investigators began to reconstruct the holdup attempt, they discovered and arrested several fugitives from violence-prone revolutionary groups of the late 1960s and early 1970s, including the Weather Underground, the Black Liberation Army, the Republic of New Africa, and the May 19 Communist Organization. This new relationship between fugitives from the sixties and seventies was unique. Law enforcement officials believe it is the first time that black dissident groups joined with predominately white middle-class groups to use crime and terror in order to overthrow the established power in the United States.

In effect, the formation of the RATF suggests that political differences which kept black and white radical groups from cooperating a decade ago may have been overcome. During the late sixties, radical, white university students who eventually formed the Weather Underground Organization (WUO) tried in vain to form an alliance with violent members of the growing black power movement.[56] The advocates of black power, however, tended to abhor the affluent white middle-class status and backgrounds of the Weatherman, often expressing contempt for the lack of total commitment to revolutionary ideals by white militants. Eventually internecine disputes about who should lead the revolution developed within both the black power movement and the white revolutionary groups. That subsequently led to radical organizational splits in both groups. The failure to encourage support among racial minorities, for example, resulted in the East Coast branch of the WUO breaking away and forming the May 19 Communist Organization (CO).[57] The May 19 CO derived its name from the birthdays of Malcolm X, Ho Chi Minh, and Che Guevarra. The group devoted itself entirely to strengthening and developing links with elements of the radical black, Hispanic, and women's movements. Communication channels were established with members of the Black Liberation Army (BLA), many of whom were in prison. In turn, the members of the BLA would recruit hardened black criminals by convincing them that American society was racist and unjust. Marighella's *Mini-Manual of Urban Guerrilla Warfare* stated that revolution can only be successful in the United States when it combines elements of black prison inmates and radical white college students. The May 19 CO also made contact with the Republic of New Africa (RNA), another black extremist group.

[54]*New York Times,* October 20, 1981, p. 1.

[55]Ibid.

[56]Stuart Daniels, "The Weathermen," *Government and Opposition* 9 (Autumn 1974), pp. 430–59.

[57]*The Split of the Weather Underground Organization* (Seattle: John Brown Book Club, 1977).

The Republic of New Africa was formed in March, 1968, as part of the Black Government Conference which was sponsored by the Malcolm X Society. The purpose of the conference was to establish a national black movement to be known as the Republic of New Africa. The stated goal of the RNA was to establish a separate black nation by annexing the states of Georgia, Louisiana, Alabama, Mississippi, and South Carolina. The FBI reports that over 400 members were recruited between 1968 and 1972. The recruits were organized into a group known as the Black Legion (BL), which was to support and defend the principles of the newly formed "African republic." Between 1969 and 1972, the RNA became involved in several shootouts with police and FBI agents. Following the shootouts, RNA activity began to decline. By 1976 the RNA was considered to be a loosely knit organization which generated little financial or popular support. In fact, the FBI discontinued investigation of RNA activities on July 9, 1976. However, documents seized by the FBI after the attempted Brinks' robbery on October 20, 1981, disclosed that active RNA membership was approximately 300, with close ties to the WUO and the Black Liberation Army (BLA).[58]

The Black Liberation Army appeared in February 1971, when the Black Panther Party split into the Newton faction and the Cleaver faction.[59] Eldridge Cleaver called for the overthrow of the U.S. government by creating a climate of paralyzing fear. The BLA campaign of fear was to begin with the indiscriminate killing of uniformed police officers. Members of the BLA murdered uniformed police officers in New York, New Jersey, and San Francisco. They were also involved in numerous bank robberies, bombings, and prison escapes. Today most members of the BLA have either been killed in shootouts with the police or incarcerated in U.S. prisons. The FBI estimates their current strength at approximately 30 to 40 members.

The oldest and most active of the revolutionary groups affiliated with the RATF is the Weatherman Underground Organization, a revolutionary group dedicated to the violent overthrow of the U.S. government. The WUO began as a paramilitary support group of Students for a Democratic Society (SDS). The SDS, founded in 1960, called for an alliance of blacks, students, peace groups, and liberal organizations and publications to influence the "liberal" policies of the Democratic Party. By 1965 the SDS had organized the first "anti-Vietnam War" march in Washington, D. C. The "March on Washington" stimulated interest in the SDS, and the number of local chapters grew to 100 in six months. As the SDS gained in popularity among students, draft resistance became its top priority. After the escalation of the Vietnam War,

[58]U. S. Congress, Senate, Committee on the Judiciary, Subcommittee on Security and Terrorism, *Committee on the Judiciary, U. S. Senate,* 97th Congress, February 4, 1982 (Washington, D. C.: Government Printing Office, 1982), pp. 41–43.

[59]Ibid., p. 44.

the SDS split into several competing factions, each advocating violence and terrorism. The most vocal and prominent was the WUO.[60]

At the Chicago national convention of the SDS in June 1969, the Weatherman faction surfaced with a position paper titled "You Don't Need a Weatherman to Know Which Way the Wind Blows." (The phrase is contained in the Bob Dylan song "Subterranean Homesick Blues.") The paper attempts to define a political ideology based on aggressive and prolonged guerrilla tactics that would overthrow the U.S. economic system and its "military industrial complex" and replace it with a classless society: world communism. The Weatherman style evolved over the summer of 1969. Members began to seriously study revolutionary doctrine, especially the writings of Mao. By 1970 the WUO changed its tactics and came into the open, claiming responsibility for several bombings, including the bombing of the U. S. Capitol on March 1, 1971.[61] With the end of the Vietnam War, interest in the WUO declined, and internal battles split the original organizational structure.

In 1976, internal dissension split the WUO: the heavily feminist faction, the "Revolutionary Committee" (RC), broke away from what it called the "Central Committee" (CC).[62] After 1977 nothing was heard from the WUO, either under its own name or under the RC or CC names. However, no evidence suggested that the WUO ceased to exist. Then, during 1978 and 1979, several WUO members surfaced and came "above ground" but would not reveal the status of the group. Ultimately the FBI closed its domestic security case against WUO since it could not be substantiated that the group was involved in criminal or "revolutionary" activities. The WUO has not claimed credit for any criminal activities since late 1977.

Nonetheless, the FBI believes that the RATF is composed of a group of "survivors" from the WUO, BLA, RNA, and May 19 CO who have been responsible for a series of bombings directed at U.S. government and corporate facilities. The bombings have been carried out by revolutionary cells of the RATF using a variety of names. The most active names are the United Freedom Front and the Armed Resistance Unit, which clearly are cells of the RATF. The United Freedom Front (UFF) and Armed Resistance Unit (ARU) are believed to be directly linked to the RATF through the WUO and May 19 CO. The practice of claiming terrorist attacks under different group names may be a clever attempt used by RATF to bypass federal laws which provide for the prosecution of members of an organization involved in illegal activity. Therefore, members linked to any RATF revolutionary cells cannot be indicted for a bombing committed by the United Freedom Front unless they can be directly tied to that group, which most likely exists only on paper.[63]

[60]G. Louis Heath, *Students For a Democratic Society* (Metuchen New Jersey: Scarecrow, 1976).

[61]*New York Times,* March 1, 1971.

[62]*The Split of the Weather Underground Organization* (Seattle, Wash.: John Brown Book Club, 1977).

[63]U. S. Congress, Subcommittee on Security and Terrorism, pp. 52–81.

The FBI maintains that the UFF and ARU are one and the same. They arrived at this conclusion by citing the similar language used in communiqués issued after each bombing, the consistency in target selection, and the materials used in bomb construction. It is important to recognize that terrorist groups use a variety of aliases to frustrate counterterrorist efforts and to persuade the police and mass media that a variety of formidable "radicals" are active and prepared to attack the "system" of "American imperialism."

The future of homegrown terrorist groups is evident while members of the WUO, BLA, RNA and May 19 CO remain fugitives. Political terrorism in the United States is bound to escalate in the coming years. In sum, U.S. terrorist groups of the ideological left are organized as follows:

1. *Groups*
   Weather Underground Organization (WUO)
   Republic of New Africa (RNA)
   Black Liberation Army (BLA)
   May 19 Communist Organization (May 19 CO)
   Revolutionary Armed Task Force (RATF)
   United Freedom Front (UFF)
   Armed Resistance Unit (ARU)
2. *Political Ideology*
   Violent overthrow of American imperialism replaced with leftist/Maoist-style system.
3. *Membership*
   Survivors of 1960s-style radical groups with an estimated strength of 40 to 50 members.
4. *Tactics*
   Bombing and criminal activities, especially armed robbery, to raise funds.
5. *Specific Operations*
   October 20, 1980—Brinks armored car holdup.
   November 7, 1983—Bombing at Senate Chambers of U.S. Capitol in Washington, D.C.
   January 29, 1984—Bombing of offices of Motorola, Inc., in New York.
   August 22, 1984—Bombing of General Electric Co. in New York.
6. *Goal*
   Violent overthrow of U.S. government.
7. *Training*
   Reports by FBI indicate training received from leftist political groups, such as the PFLP.

Even though the ideological left frequently emerges, the greatest current threat to the United States remains the ideological right.

The Ideological Right

Right-wing extremism has waged a continuous assault against the values supported by the U.S. Constitution since the KKK emerged after the Civil War. The terrorist activities of the KKK succeeded in "liberating" the old Confederacy from white Republicans, expelling Union soldiers from the South and dominating the lives of southern blacks for many years. The early Klan terrorism was based primarily on the principles of patriotism and nationalism. The success of Klan extremism can be traced to four important conditions needed for the terrorists' strategy to be effective: (1) post-war disruption and economic chaos; (2) solidarity based on nationalist pride; (3) terrorist objectives limited to destabilization of the "system"; and (4) the established governmental system lacking the resources to conduct an effective counterterrorist campaign. These conditions certainly existed after the Civil War, World War I, and the Vietnam War—historical periods when Klan violence reached its greatest peak.

The Klan has evolved into a variety of "right-wing" extremist groups that vary greatly in the use of the terrorist strategy. For example, the Sheriff's Posse Comitatus (SPC) has murdered police officers from ambush, and the group calling itself the Order is responsible for a series of bank and armored car robberies. The Covenant, the Sword and the Arm of the Lord (CSA) consists largely of young idealists who embrace religious revival, spiritual regeneration, patriotism and nationalism. The CSA, although founded on Christian fundamentalist religious principles, believed that "society" was going to collapse. So they began to arm and train their members for the coming racial and religious "war."

The legacy of right-wing extremism introduced by the KKK has taken on a new dimension. Not only is the old patriotism and nationalism heard to suppress the threat of social revolution, but fundamentalist religious ideas supported by a growing number of identity churches has provided a rallying point for right-wing extremism. (Identity churches support a religious belief based on racism and anti-semiticism, proclaiming the supremacy of whites and non-Jews.) Who are these right-wing groups? What do they hope to achieve by engaging in acts of "political" terrorism? More importantly, how much of a threat does right-wing extremism pose to the criminal justice system?

1. *Groups*
   Arizona Patriots
   Sheriff's Posse Comitatus (SPC)
   The Aryan Nations
   The Convenant, the Sword and the Arm of the Lord (CSA)
   The Order or Bruder Schweigen
   United Klans of America
   White Patriot Party
   Ku Klux Klan (KKK)
2. *Political Ideology*
   All groups support romantic nationalism since the U.S. government is weak and discredited. Only by restoring national independence and destroying the existing social structure can the U.S. be free of "left-wing" influences.
3. *Membership*
   Membership in such groups varies with economic conditions. Estimates range from 400 members in the Aryan Nations to 50 members of the CSA.

4. *Tactics*

   Tactics are very similar to that used by left-wing groups. Bank and armored car robberies, ambush murders of police officers, bombings and specific booby trap assassinations are preferred.

5. *Specific Operations*

   August 23, 1984—armored car robbery in Seattle; $500,000 reported taken.

   July 19, 1984—armored car robbery in Ukiah, California; $3.6 million reported taken.

   April 29, 1984—bombed Jewish synagogue.

   September, 1986—several bombings in Coeur d'Alene, Idaho.

6. *Goal*

   Stated goal is the revolutionary overthrow of the U.S. government, replaced by a neo-facist government that would revive allegiance to the nation and the white race.

7. *Training*

   Federal law enforcement officials believe right-wing groups provide their own training programs. Right-wing groups are largely made up of ex-military personnel who have the skills needed to carry out a variety of criminal actions and training programs.

In sum, there are, of course, certain similarities in practice between terrorist groups that support the ideological right and the ideological left. For example, their targets in many cases are identical; they prefer violent action rather than a nonviolent approach; and on occasion they have trained together. The similarity is further strengthened when ideologically opposed terrorist groups take credit for the same terrorist event. Viewed from the center, then, all extremist groups, whether right or left, appear identical; however, we would be making a serious error if we took this literally for there are significant differences between the ideological right and left.

First of all, they occupy specifically different positions in relation to the governmental power structure. Even though both right and left may plan to overthrow the existing political structure, right-wing extremists often have allies and supporters in the police, armed services, and among wealthy, conservative corporate executives and business people. Ordinarily, groups on the left do not have such sponsors. For example, the overlap between the Klan and local police agencies throughout the South is well documented, although admittedly this relationship between the Klan and local police forces is often exaggerated. Consider, for example, the campaign undertaken by the FBI and local law enforcement agencies against members of the Aryan Nations and the Order.

The most recent confrontation between right and left extremist groups occurred in Greensboro, North Carolina, in November, 1979. During an anti-Klan rally, five members of the Communist Workers Party (CWP) were slain by the KKK and the American Nazi Party. In the subsequent trial, the Klansmen and Nazis were found not guilty of both murder and conspiracy. However, in a later civil suit brought against Klansmen, Nazis, and three police officers, the court found them liable for the wrongful death of one of the

CWP victims and ordered them to pay $355,100 in damages. The Greensboro police were accused of complicity and support for Klan actions against the CWP victims.

Right-wing extremists generally attack "alien" targets. Targets are carefully chosen on the basis of race, religion, ethnic origin, or ideology. In the case of the Greensboro incident, ideology and race provoked the Klan assault. The targets are quite frequently "out groups" competing for scarce economic resources. Right-wing terrorists would prefer to arouse the support of the masses as an ethnic (Aryan race) or religious (identity church) nation to attack Communists, aliens, and nonbelievers. Today, religious fundamentalism provides the medium by which right-wing groups express their political views. Right-wing groups inspiring nationalist pride can be highly effective when an entire community or nation defines itself on the basis of race, nationality, or religion. Terrorism can be an effective strategy for exciting communal violence. In short, right-wing terrorist groups are inspired by the political principles of fascism.

CONCLUSIONS

There is sufficient cause to suspect that terrorism will intensify in the United States. The numerous groups that this chapter has identified illustrate that extremists could find justification in their perceived grievances against the United States or governments sympathetic to the United States. Additionally, controversial issues such as abortion and nuclear disarmament or even the liberation of animals could escalate and include acts of indiscriminate terror. International issues could also excite campaigns of domestic terrorism. For example, U.S. military intervention in Central America or elsewhere could provoke the type of antiwar violence prevalent during the Vietnam War. Finally, irrational acts by individuals who seek recognition, revenge and retaliation by hijacking airplanes, seizing hostages, assassinating government representatives, or bombing federal and state facilities must be anticipated.

REVIEW QUESTIONS

1. Why has indiscriminate terrorism been absent in the United States?
2. Identify the following Puerto Rican separatist groups:
   a. FALN
   b. MLN
   c. the Mac heteros
   d. FARP

3. Describe the terrorist attack on Muniz Air Base in Puerto Rico.

4. What is expressive symbolism?

5. Trace the historical antecedents of contemporary Armenian terrorism. Do you think Armenian terrorists are justified? Why or why not?

6. Who had the greatest influence on the growth of Armenian terrorism?

7. What are the three Armenian *r*'s?

8. What is the most significant difference between the ASALA and JCAG?

9. Why was the Ustasa Movement a failure? Describe the terror tactics of Ustasa.

10. Compare and contrast the political ideology of Croatian nationalists, Armenian extremists and Puerto Rican separatists.

11. Identify the following groups:
    a. Omega 7
    b. Alpha 66
    c. JDL
    d. Kach
    e. DGI

12. Recount the emergence of the WUO, BLA, RNA and May 19 CO.

13. Define the theory of internal colonialism. Do you think this theory is applicable to the United States? Why?

FIVE

INTERNATIONAL TERRORISM: THE MIDEAST AND WESTERN EUROPE

CHAPTER OBJECTIVES

The study of this chapter will enable you to:
■ Trace the historical antecedents of the Arab-Israeli conflict
■ Identify extremist groups affiliated with the PLO
■ Compare and contrast the Palestine question and the Irish troubles
■ Track the historical development of the Irish Republican Army (IRA)
■ Explore the escalation of terrorism in democracies
■ Review Euro-terrorism
■ Speculate as to the nature of terrorism in the 21st century

INTRODUCTION

In this chapter the focus is on international terrorism and the analysis of two case studies of terrorism: the Palestine question and the Northern Ireland troubles. In the first section, the organizational structure, motives, and methods of the Palestine Liberation Organization (PLO) will be explored. The second section will examine the activities of the Irish Republican Army (IRA). The evolutionary development of the IRA will be examined with emphasis on newly emerged splinter groups such as the Provos. The third section will present the activities of various terrorist groups active in other Western European countries. Some of the factors involved in the creation of the Basque separatist movement, the Red Brigades, the Red Army Faction, and Direct Action will be reviewed, partly to illustrate the diversity and motivations thought to contribute to the growth of terrorism and partly to acquaint students with the widespread nature of international terrorism. The suggestion has been made that the differences in motivation of international terrorist groups stem from the fact that terrorism is an ambiguous, emotionally laden term.

Palestine Resistance Movement

The most inventive, successful, and sometimes ruthless nonstate terrorists have been the various Palestinian extremist factions. The success of Palestinian terrorists has no doubt inspired other freedom fighters and rebels around the world. In fact, much of the increase in world terrorism can be directly traced to the success of the various Palestinian extremist groups.

For more than 20 years the world had ignored the fate of the displaced Palestinians. Then in 1968 the Palestinians carried their struggle from the borders of Israel to the rest of the world by capturing media attention for their cause. Spectacular hostage-taking episodes, outrageous bombings, and barbaric assassinations catapulted little-known, obscure, Palestinian extremist groups onto the world scene. Today the conflict between Israel and the Palestinians and the Arab world in general has become a central issue in international politics. At the forefront of this conflict is the Palestine Liberation Organization (PLO), which claims to represent the interests of all Palestinians.[1] The stated objective of the PLO is the "liberation of Palestine, the elimination of Israel as a political entity."[2] What follows is a brief history of the evolutionary development of the PLO and the Arab-Israeli conflict.

Historical Antecedents

Beginning in the late 19th century, two powerful political forces emerged in Palestine: political Zionism and Arab nationalism.[3] Political Zionism represented the yearning for Jewish political and religious self-determination in the

---

[1]Edward W. Said, *The Question of Palestine* (New York: Times Books, 1979), p. 25.

[2]John N. Moore, ed., *The Arab-Israeli Conflict, Volume III* (Princeton, N.J.: Princeton University Press, 1974), pp. 706–11.

[3]Fred J. Khouri, *The Arab Israeli Dilemma* (Syracuse, N.Y.: Syracuse University Press, 1985), pp. 1–3.

promised land. The ultimate objective of the Zionists was the creation of a Jewish state in Palestine. Arab nationalists, of course, had other ideas and as the Ottoman Empire began to disintegrate after World War I, both Zionist and Arab nationalists saw an opportunity to realize a passionate dream of self-determination in Palestine. However, as World War I ended, Palestine was placed under the administration of a British mandatory government that was officially committed to the creation of a Zionist/Jewish state in Palestine.[4]

British Foreign Secretary Lord Arthur Balfour stated in a written document that "Palestine shall be reconstituted as a national Home of the Jewish people."[5] This document was subsequently referred to as the Balfour Declaration. Although the Balfour Declaration was not a legally binding document, it did strengthen the cause of the world Zionist movement and stimulate Jewish immigration to the "Promised Land." The British also verbally promised to give the Arabs of Palestine the opportunity to once again become a nation in the world. For the next 30 years the British pursued an inconsistent policy in Palestine that permitted both the growth of a Zionist/Jewish economic and social infrastructure and the existence of a separate Arab national movement.

In short, the British mandate seriously underestimated both the rise of Arab nationalism and the determination of the Zionists to create a Jewish state in Palestine. It seems evident that Britain's conflicting promises and policies would ultimately lead to strife between Arabs and Jews and to endless problems for Britain in Palestine. Thus, the indecision of the British, the impatience of the Zionists, and the political immaturity of the Arabs helped to launch a chain of events that produced the "question of Palestine."

By 1947 the British mandate in Palestine found Arab and Jewish demands irreconcilable and turned the problem over to the newly formed United Nations. A UN Commission reviewed the question of Palestine and recommended partitioning the country. (See Figure 5-1). The United Nations was now committed in principle to a divided Palestine. The Partition Plan was eagerly accepted by the Zionists and unequivocally rejected by the Palestinian Arabs. The British mandate ended on May 14, 1948; the new Jewish state of Israel was proclaimed the following day. The Jewish assertion of statehood was immediately challenged by the invading armies of five surrounding Arab countries; but in this first of six major Arab-Israeli wars, Israel was able to consolidate its independence and extend its authority over all of Palestine except for the West Bank and Gaza. Palestine ceased to exist after the 1948 war, and more than 700,000 Palestinian Arabs fled or were forced out of their country or off their land by the new Israeli state.[6] The Palestinians were now stateless and rele-

[4]Mark A. Heller, *A Palestinian State: The Implications for Israel* (Cambridge: Harvard University Press, 1983), p. 1.

[5]Walter Laqueur, ed., *The Israeli-Arab Reader* (New York: Bantam, 1969), p. 18.

[6]Said, *The Question of Palestine,* p. 45.

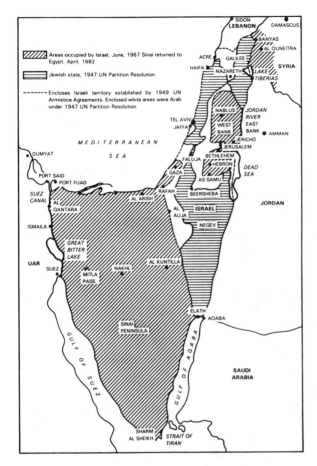

FIGURE 5-1   Israel's Changing Boundaries: 1948–1986

gated to refugee status. The diaspora, or dispersal, had passed from one people, the Jews, to another, the Palestinians.

Nevertheless, the end of the 1948 war did not bring peace; rather, it left a legacy of hate. The Arabs, defeated and humiliated, were determined to reverse the decision in future wars. Since the 1948 war, Israel has fought and won five major wars: 1956 Suez War; 1967 June War; 1968–70 War of Attrition; 1973 Yom Kippur War; 1982 PLO war and invasion of Lebanon.[7] According to Flapan, the Israelis believe that they have become a mini-super-power in the world and can continue indefinitely to rule over the Palestinians and to annex Palestinian land.[8] If this is so, then Israel ignores the historical

---

[7]For example, see, Howard M. Sachar, *Egypt and Israel* (New York: Richard Marek, 1982).

[8]S. Flapan, "Israelis and Palestinians: Can They Make Peace," *Journal of Palestine Studies* 15, no. 1 (Autumn 1985), p. 21.

context of the Jewish people, which contends that people suffering from dispersion, homelessness, and refugee conditions yearn for freedom and independence and that the oppression of another people can only lead to violence and terrorism.

Thus, Palestinian refugee camps administered by the United Nations have become breeding grounds for terrorism. The generation of Palestinians who were born and raised in the refugee camps has erupted on the world stage of international terrorism. Condemned to refugee status after the 1948 war, Palestinian social structure and political institutions were shattered and ceased to be a major factor in the Arab/Israeli conflict, at least until the formation of the Palestine Liberation Organization in 1964.

Palestine Liberation Organization (PLO)

In January 1964, the first Arab summit was held in Cairo, and steps were taken to create the Palestine Liberation Organization. The PLO was organized to provide greater unity to the fragmented Palestinian community and to adopt a new tougher strategy on the "liberation of Palestine." Ahmed Shuqairy, an articulate, resolute Palestinian diplomat, was assigned the task of developing the structure of the PLO. Wide disagreement about the formation, structure, and goals of the PLO made this a difficult task. Particularly vocal in its criticism of the planned organization of the PLO was a group of freedom fighters known as *Fatah,* led by Yasir Arafat. Nisan argues that Arafat and the leadership of Fatah wanted to begin an armed struggle with Israel in the form of guerrilla/terrorist attacks against "soft" Israel targets.[9] Fatah, which is an acronym formed by reversing the initial letters of Harakat Tahrir Filastin (the Palestine Liberation Movement), proclaimed through its official publication, *Filastinuna* (our Palestine), that the strategic use of terrorism should be to disrupt the Jewish state and that "Palestine is the only road to Arab unity."[10]

Even though Fatah would later develop a complex strategy of guerrilla warfare and suffer numerous internal conflicts, its political ideology was simple. The liberation of Palestine could only be accomplished by armed Palestinians, and the struggle with the Zionists could not be controlled by unstable Arab regimes. Fatah was greatly influenced by the success and simplistic terrorist strategy of the Algerian terrorist organization, the FLN. Miller writes that one of the reasons for the continued survival of Fatah has been the decision to avoid the "confusing ideological traps." that would be the downfall of other Palestinian resistance groups.[11]

[9]M. Nisan, "The PLO and the Palestinian Issue," *Middle East Review* 28, no. 2 (Winter 1985):55.

[10]James W. Amos, III, *Palestine Resistance: Organization of a Nationalist Movement* (New York: Pergamon Press, 1980), p. 56.

[11]Aaron D. Miller, *The PLO and the Politics of Survival* (New York: Praeger Pub., 1983), p. 19.

While Fatah emphasized the liberation of Palestine by Palestinians, the Arab Nationalist Movement (ANM) stressed that only through total Arab unity and power could Palestine be recovered from Israel. However, the ANM eventually split over a disagreement in ideology, and some members adopted a more radical position. For example, the two most ideological of the ANM resistance groups, the PFLP (Popular Front for the Liberation of Palestine), formed by Dr. George Habash, and the PDFLP (Popular Democratic Front for the Liberation of Palestine) adopted a Marxist political orientation. Both the PFLP and PDFLP were later to distinguish themselves by introducing the "new" terrorism onto the international scene. During the course of this bitter internecine warfare between the moderate leadership of the PLO, the ANM, and Fatah, Fatah began to escalate its guerrilla actions against Israel. By the end of 1965, Fatah had logged a total of 39 successful raids against "soft" Israeli targets.[12] Fatah had proved itself capable of sustaining a continued level of guerrilla/terrorist activity against Israel. While these guerrilla operations by Fatah did not destroy the Jewish state, they were a constant irritant and provided a source of pride for Fatah in the Palestinian "diaspora."

The guerrilla actions by Fatah eventually forced the Israelis to retaliate against Fatah bases in Syria, Egypt, and Jordan. These Israeli retaliation raids in turn prompted increased public clamor, particularly in Jordan, to finally destroy Israel. Thus, once again hostilities seemed imminent, and the outbreak of the third Arab-Israeli war seemed inevitable. When it came, the 1967 Arab/Israeli war was a devastating defeat of the armies of Syria, Egypt, and Jordan. The Arab defeat further aggravated the Palestinian people, forcing some 400,000 Palestinian Arabs to join the 700,000 refugees of 1948.[13] Israel now occupied the West Bank, Gaza, Golan Heights, and the Sinai Peninsula. (See Figure 5-1) But the humilitating Arab defeat catapulted Fatah and Arafat into the leadership of the PLO. The moderate leadership of the PLO was discredited after the 1967 war; and by July 1968, guerrilla groups took over the PLO and Arafat was elected chairman. The question of Palestine now exploded onto the international scene in a series of well-planned terrorist incidents designed to attract media attention for the Palestinian cause that continues to this day.

Palestinian Extremism and the 1973 War

In order to attract maximum world attention, the PLO-affiliated PFLP introduced the hijacking of aircraft. It was the first to do so. The PFLP planned and directed a series of "spectacular" air hijackings of international flights between July 1968, and September 1970. Fifty innocent people were killed and scores were injured. Despite the success of the well-staged hijack-

---

[12]Helen Cobban, *The Palestinian Liberation Organization: People, Power, and Politics* (Cambridge: Cambridge University Press, 1983), p. 33.

[13]Said, *The Question of Palestine,* p. 118.

ings, hijackers were apprehended and convicted in European countries; they were quickly released after other planes had been hijacked and hostages were exchanged for convicted hijackers.[14]

Again there was an escalation of Palestinian terrorism. Israeli retaliation and the continued Israeli occupation of Arab lands acquired during the 1967 war led to renewed military confrontation between Israel and its Arab neighbors. On October 6, 1973, Syria and Egypt invaded the "occupied terroritories of Palestine." Sachar considers the 1973 October War to be the most brutal of the six Arab-Israeli wars and the most traumatic experience for Israelis.[15]

For the first time the Arabs achieved significant military successes. Unlike the Israeli victories in 1948, 1956, and 1967, the 1973 war produced a credible military performance by the Arab forces and proved to the Arabs that the Israeli military machine was not invincible. The 1973 war restored Arab self-respect and produced a new pragmatism among Arab leaders based on the military superiority of Israel and the lack of unity in the Arab world. This new pragmatism also forced the PLO to review its strategy for the liberation of Palestine in order to meet the post-October war situation (1973).

Under the leadership of Yasir Arafat, the PLO National Council in 1974 agreed to pursue a diplomatic or political solution with Israel by opening up negotiations for a Palestinian homeland on the West Bank and Gaza. However, several members of Arafat's Fatah rejected any negotiations with Israel while the smaller, more extremist groups such as the Popular Front for the Liberation of Palestine, the Palestine Liberation Front (PLF), and the Arab Liberation Front withdrew from the PLO executive committee in protest. Arafat, in a desperate effort to prevent the disintegration of the PLO, reluctantly concluded that "half a loaf was better than none," while keeping alive the vision that someday Palestine would be returned to the Palestinians by peaceful means.

Even more important, by renouncing their more extreme terrorist tactics, the moderate PLO factions were able to win public support throughout the world since many countries were prepared to support a Palestinian national home. Thus, the PLO received recognition from more than 100 countries throughout the world, obtained overwhelming backing for favorable UN General Assembly resolutions, and also gained wide popular support, especially in the Third World. Then on November 17, 1974, Arafat addressed the U.N. General Assembly to a standing ovation, and the PLO obtained observer status at the U.N. The PLO now could attempt to influence and initiate U.N. resolutions on the "question of Palestine." A more favorable media image of the PLO began to appear. As a result, moderate Palestinian leaders encouraged their followers to pursue a path of diplomacy and negotiation in the hope

[14]Julian Becker, *The PLO: The Rise and Fall of the Palestine Liberation Organization* (New York: St. Martin's Press, 1984), p. 74.

[15]Sachar, *Egypt and Israel,* pp. 222–23.

that it would eventually pay off. Nonetheless, this path did not diminish Israel's opposition to the PLO and the creation of a Palestinian state, and did not win meaningful support from the U.S. for a Palestinian entity in Israel. Since the PLO's stated tactic of moderation has not yet resulted in any serious negotiations with Israel, increasing numbers of moderate Palestinians have joined the "rejectionists," leading to several splits in Fatah and the PLO.[16]

Rejectionist Front

Since 1974 the rejectionist PLO factions have been composed of two important factions. First, for ideological reasons, one faction has completely rejected the "half a loaf" idea, even if it were offered to them. Second, the other faction liked the "half a loaf" notion but was convinced that Israel would never voluntarily and peacefully surrender the "occupied" territories and that the United States would never pressure Israel into negotiations for a Palestinian state. Believing that no diplomatic solution was feasible for the recovery of Palestine, which nearly the entire world considered as legitimate, the rejectionists concluded that the only alternative open to them was armed struggle, i.e., terrorism. Thus, the rejectionists had nothing to lose by going for the "whole loaf." Arafat's position was widely criticized by extremist Palestinian elements, and he was accused of wasting precious time by pursuing the unattainable through peaceful diplomacy and negotiation.

Over the years, many of Arafat's most ardent followers have deserted him to pursue the escalation of violence and terrorism and no negotiations with Israel. For example, on December 27, 1985, Palestinian terrorists attacked the El Al ticket counter at the Rome and Vienna airports, randomly killing 17 innocent victims and seriously wounding 116 more. Responsibility for the unprovoked, indiscriminate shooting spree was claimed by the Abu Nidal faction, and the media quickly christened Abu Nidal the master terrorist of international terrorism.[17] Although little known in the West, Abu Nidal was well known within the PLO and by the Israeli Mossad. The Abu Nidal faction has claimed credit for hundreds of terrorist incidents and assassinations, including the attempted assassination of Arafat. Abu Nidal was eventually sentenced to death in absentia for his attempt to kill the PLO chairman, although other assassination attempts have been more successful.[18] An estimated 90 moderate PLO leaders and supporters have been murdered by the Abu Nidal faction. Equally ruthless have been random indiscriminate attacks against non-Palestinian targets. For example, the Abu Nidal faction killed several people in random grenade attacks on synagogues in Rome and Vienna in

---

[16]Alain Gresh, *The PLO: The Struggle Within: Towards an Independent Palestinian State* (London: Zed Bks, Ltd., 1985), pp. 146–49.

[17]T. L. Friedman, *New York Times,* January 1, 1986, sec. 1, p. 4.

[18]Yossi Melman, *The Master Terrorist: The True Story Behind Abu Nidal* (New York: Adams Bks., 1986), pp. 69–82.

1982.[19] But the most serious challenge to the existence of the PLO and the leadership of Arafat came with the Israeli invasion of Lebanon on June 6, 1982.

Invasion of Lebanon

The war in Lebanon, the sixth major Arab-Israeli war, was a large ground force operation launched by Israel into Lebanon to destroy the PLO and root out its infrastructure, which supported terrorist attacks on the settlements and civilian inhabitants of northern Israel. Israeli ground units struck with lightning speed and precision, destroying PLO training camps and capturing hundreds of international terrorists caught by the surprise Israeli blitzkreig. Eventually, after five days of fighting, the PLO was bottled up in West Beirut. The seige of Beirut lasted for several weeks and finally ended when U.N. negotiators planned the safe withdrawal of PLO fighters to several Arab host countries.[20]

The war in Lebanon became a turning point for both Israel and the PLO and generated an international crisis of unprecedented dimensions. Spontaneous protests erupted in Israel, Europe, and the United States in reaction to the blockade of Beirut and the savage massacre in the Sabra and Shatila Palestinian refugee camps. Approximately 1000 unarmed Palestinian refugees were killed by the Israeli-supported Lebanese right-wing Christian Phalangist militia. The Israel military was later charged with complicity in the atrocities at Sabra and Shatila, and Israeli citizens demanded a change in government.[21] But the Lebanon war dragged on for three years. All of the Israeli objectives of the war were shattered, including the destruction of the PLO, forcing Syria to evacuate its military from Lebanese soil, and a peace treaty with the Christian-dominated government in Lebanon. The initial promise by Israeli Prime Minister Begin of a two-day limited military action against PLO military bases resulted in Israel's longest war, with heavy Israeli, Palestinian, and Lebanese casualties. Finally, on June 7, 1985, the Israelis pulled most of their ground troops out of Lebanon, leaving reserve forces in southern Lebanon to prevent a return of the PLO. However, the distressing reality is that the destruction of PLO terrorist camps and the ejection of PLO fighters from Beirut have not diminished the PLO's leading role in the Palestinian struggle for independent nationhood.

In conclusion, six major Arab-Israeli wars have been fought, and on occasion the fighting threatens to erupt into a superpower confrontation between the United States and the Soviet Union. This superpower confrontation

[19]*Time* 127 (Jan. 13, 1986), pp. 31–32.

[20]Richard A. Gabriel, *Operation Peace for Gallilee: The Israeli-PLO War in Lebanon* (New York: Hill and Wang, 1985), pp. 53–57.

[21]Kahan Commission Report, *The Beirut Massacre* (Princeton, N.J.: Karz-Cohl, 1983), pp. 50–99.

remains an ominous undertone in any Arab-Israeli crisis, one of the few regional conflicts that could actually provoke a nuclear war. Despite the superpower rivalry and Arab intervention, the heart of the Israeli-Palestinian conflict is the dispute over what each considers its rightful homeland. Both sides, Palestinian and Israeli, are utterly convinced that the land is theirs. There is little agreement between Israelis and Palestinians, with no resolution in sight, but the alternative to peaceful negotiation is protracted regional wars and a continued escalation of international terrorism by desperate, revengeful Palestinians.

In sum, the PLO is an umbrella group consisting of eight major extremist groups and several minor factions. In addition, the PLO provides a general organizational framework for all Palestinian community life. The five major extremist groups are al Fatah, al Saiqa, PFLP, PDFLP, and the PFLP-GC. The PLO attempts to project a unified organization of Palestinian nationalists working for the liberation of Palestine and the destruction of Israel. Moreover, members of the PLO attempt to portray themselves as guerrilla fighters in the image of guerrilla movements in Latin America or Asia. However, this is not the case.

The PLO is splintered. In fact, the PLO does not appear to be unified on anything, including social outlook, economic interests, or relationship with Israel. Each group pursues its own self-interest; and group leaders view each other with deep suspicion, taking precautions against being assassinated by rival factions. Internal clashes by competing groups occur as frequently as clashes with Israelis. According to Gabriel, some PLO-affiliated groups often clash over the control of illegal drug traffic, prostitution, and smuggling, especially in Lebanon.[22] The Palestinian groups are also divided along ideological lines. They range from the nationalism of al Fatah to the Marxist PFLP, from the extremist terrorism of the PFLP-GC to the rejectionist front led by Abu Nidal. Table 5-1 outlines the extremist PLO-affiliated organizations.

The role of the PLO seems bound to change in reaction to the post-Beirut period. The reality of the situation is that both Israel and the Palestinians have a time bomb on their hands. Extremist elements on both fronts are becoming more vocal, and acts of terrorism are bound to increase within the "occupied territories" and on the international scene. On April 14, 1987, in an unprecedented meeting between Arafat and rival guerrilla groups, a bid was made to unite the once-powerful PLO. Rejectionist groups, such as the PFLP's George Habash, after four years of internal strife, have once again joined with Arafat in the armed struggle against Israel. Table 5-2 outlines the chronology of historical events in the continuing conflict between Israel, the Palestinians, and surrounding Arab nations.

This next section will examine the evolution of the Irish Republican Army (IRA).

---

[22]Gabriel, *Operation Peace for Gallilee,* p. 37.

TABLE 5-1   PLO-Affiliated Extremist/Terrorist Groups*

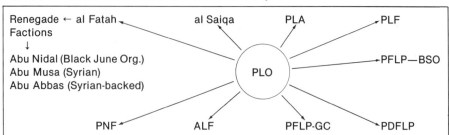

Renegade ← al Fatah · al Saiqa · PLA · PLF
Factions
↓
Abu Nidal (Black June Org.) · PFLP—BSO
Abu Musa (Syrian) · PLO
Abu Abbas (Syrian-backed)

PNF · ALF · PFLP-GC · PDFLP

1. al Fatah is the oldest and largest of the PLO organizations cofounded by Yasir Arafat. Fatah dominates the coalition of the PLO ever since Arafat has been the chairperson.

2. al Saiqa (Thunderbolt) is the second largest PLO-affiliated group formed after the 1967 June War. Although Saiqa is independent, most of its support comes from Syria. Saiqa has often been referred to as the terrorist arm of the Syrian Army.

3. The Popular Front for the Liberation of Palestine (PFLP), founded by George Habash, supports a Marxist ideology. The PFLP is highly ideological and radical; acts of spectacular terrorism are almost its exclusive activity.

4. The Popular Front of the Liberation of Palestine–General Command (PFLP-GC), led by Ahmed Jibril, has been responsible for numerous terrorist attacks against Israeli soft targets. PFLP-GC claims its major support comes from Libya.

5. The Popular Democratic Front for the Liberation of Palestine (PDFLP), formed by Nayef Hawatmeh, is a splinter group of the PFLP. The PDFLP is said to have close ties to the Soviet Union and Syria.

6. The Palestine Liberation Army (PLA) is a regular standing military force of some 15,000 Palestinians financed primarily by the PLO and Syria. The commander-in-chief of the PLA is Yasir Arafat.

7. The Arab Liberation Front (ALF), like Saiqa, is the terrorist strike force of the Iraqi military. The ALF conducts its operations almost exclusively against Israeli targets.

8. The Palestine National Front (PNF) is the newest PLO group formed after the 1973 October War. The PNF conducts its operations primarily in the "occupied territories," especially the West Bank.

9. The Palestine Liberation Front (PLF) is a splinter group of the PFLP-GC. The PLF sought to escape Syrian influence in favor of alliance with Iraq.

10. Renegade al Fatah factions consist of three primary groups: 1) Abu Nidal faction, 2) Abu Musa faction, and 3) Abu Mohammed Abbas faction. The Abu Abbas faction was responsible for the seajacking of the Achille Lauro in 1985.

11. The Black September Organization (BSO) was formed in 1970 after the Jordanian Army drove the PLO and affiliated groups out of Jordan. The BSO's most spectacular terrorist operation was the taking of Israeli athlete hostages at the Munich Olympic games in 1972.

*For a more comprehensive coverage of the geneology of the PLO, see J. W. Amos, III, *Palestine Resistance: Organization of a Nationalist Movement* (New York: Pergamon Press, 1980).

TABLE 5-2   Chronology of Significant Events

A.D. 70	Destruction of the 2nd Temple: Jewish Diaspora
6th Century	After death of Mohammed, Arabs conquer Palestine
1897	First Zionist Congress held in Switzerland
1917	Palestine becomes a British mandate: Balfour Declaration
1929	Jewish agency established: Haganah formed
1937	British Peel Commission proposes partition of Palestine
1947	UN recommends partition of Palestine
1948	State of Israel is created; first Palestine war
1950–55	Peace fails: border violence, blockade, boycott, and isolation of Israel
1956	Second Palestine War: Suez War
1957	Arafat forms al Fatah and the Palestine Liberation Movement
1964	PLO established
1967	Third Arab-Israeli war: June War; Israel expands territory; UN Security Council Resolution 242
1968–70	Escalation of terrorism by PFLP and Fatah; first terrorist skyjacking; Black September formed; War of Attrition, 4th Arab/Israeli conflict
1972	Munich Olympic massacre by Black September; Israeli retaliation
1973	Fifth Arab-Israeli war: Yom Kippur War
1974	Arafat addresses UN General Assembly and PLO given observer status at UN
1975	Civil war breaks out in Lebanon: Damour destroyed by Saiqa
1976	Entebbe hijacking/Israeli counterterrorist strike
1978	Bus incident: thirty killed by PDFLP; Israel retaliates and invades Lebanon
1980	Camp David peace talks; Israel and Egypt
1981	Annexation of Golan; Reagan Peace Plan; Fez Peace Plan
1982	Israeli occupation ends in Sinai; invasion of Lebanon and the dispersion of PLO; massacre at Sabra and Shatila
1983–84	Atrocities continue in Lebanon; PLO internal struggle; terror bombings of multinational force
1985	Terror attacks at Rome and Vienna Airports by Abu Nidal faction; seajacking of Achille Lauro by Abu Abbas faction; Israeli bombing of PLO headquarters in Tunisia
1986	U.S. bombing of PLO-supported terrorist training centers in Libya
1987	PLO reconciliation

The Irish Republican Army (IRA)

On March 1, 1985, IRA guerrillas launched several homemade mortar shells into a heavily fortified police barracks located in Newry, Northern Ireland.[23] Nine members of the Royal Ulster Constabulary were killed and 37 were seriously injured. A few hours later, a bomb exploded outside a Roman Catholic church in Newry, killing a British soldier and wounding two police officers on foot patrol. On May 22, 1986, three members of the British security forces were killed by a remote controlled bomb as they patrolled near the

[23]*San Francisco Chronicle,* March 2, 1985, sec. 1, p. 8.

Catholic community of Crossmaglen in south Armagh.[24] Aside from the killing of soldiers and policemen, IRA terrorists have also murdered judges, civil servants, prison officers, and Protestant paramilitaries. The terrorist strategy of the IRA is to provoke and force the British government to pull their security forces out of Northern Ireland. The methods, which the IRA has used in an attempt to demonstrate that the security in Northern Ireland is unsolvable as long as the British remain, include not only bombing of soldiers and police officers but (1) bombings designed to disrupt daily life and create a general feeling of insecurity, (2) demonstrations and communal/sectarian riots, (3) incitement of police officers and security forces to overreact, thus generating sympathy for the IRA and the Roman Catholic community, (4) attempts to get the Republic of Ireland involved in the crisis and set off a confrontation between the republic and Britain, (5) attempts to provoke Britain to enact emergency legislation that would alienate the Catholic community and stimulate widespread civil disorder, and (6) manipulation of the mass media to win support and sympathy for the Irish cause, especially in the United States.

Clearly, the IRA has succeeded in many of their tactical goals. By November 1985, the IRA terrorist offensive had inspired an Anglo-Irish summit between Britain and the Irish republic. The agreement would give the republic the right to eventually participate in the governance of Northern Ireland. This just may be the first step to allow British security forces to pull out of Northern Ireland. Even so, the IRA has not stopped the bombing and killing. For example, as church bells rang in the new year of 1986, the PIRA ambushed and killed three police officers in South Armagh. The IRA is the oldest active guerrilla/terrorist organization in the world today and has a long tradition of insurrection and civil war going back to the eighteenth century.

Historical Tradition of Insurrection

The present IRA can trace its roots to the Irish Republican Brotherhood (IRB), which arose in the 1860s from the American-financed Fenian Brotherhood.[25] By 1913, members of the IRB had joined forces with the Irish National Volunteers, which had been formed to combat the Protestant, extremist Ulster Volunteer Force. Both the IRB and the Irish Volunteers advocated the violent overthrow of British rule in Ireland and the importance of organizing to counteract the well-armed Protestant Ulster Volunteer Force (UVF). In 1914, then, Ireland appeared on the verge of civil war with Protestants in control of Ulster in the north, the IRB and the Irish Volunteers in control in the south of Ireland, and the British Parliament debating home rule for Ireland. However, the clouds of civil war vanished at the outbreak of World War I in 1914. Con-

---

[24]*Sacramento Bee,* May 23, 1986, sec. A, p. 7.

[25]Kevin Kelley, *The Longest War: Northern Ireland and the IRA* (Westport, Conn.: Lawrence Hill, 1982), pp. 18–19.

vinced that Britain and the Protestant UVF would be preoccupied in Europe during World War I, the IRB and Irish Volunteers, joined by the Irish Socialists, planned for the possibility of driving the British out of Ireland.

On April 24, 1916, the Easter Rising began after the rebels occupied the General Post Office in Dublin, and P. H. Pearse proclaimed the Irish Republic. Militarily, the Easter Rising was a failure; but it awakened the revolutionary spirit of the Irish people and provided a great stimulus to the independence movement. After 6 days of fighting, the rebellion was crushed by British armored military units. The leaders and seven signers of the proclamation were tried and executed by the British. However, the British spaced out the executions, allowing the media to dramatize the "martyrdoms" for Ireland. It was a significant turning point in the history of the creation of two separate entities in Ireland. Under pressure from the United States, the British stopped the executions and freed the remaining jailed rebels. The rebels gathered around the little-known and obscure, Irish nationalist political party, Sinn Fein (Ourselves Alone), founded in 1905 by A. Griffith.[26]

Sinn Fein won massive public support in the 1918 elections, but instead of taking their seats at Westminster, they convened a revolutionary parliament and proclaimed the Republic of Ireland. To the British, the whole enterprise seemed ludicrous; a declaration of independence by a nonexistent republic in the presence of overwhelming British political and military power! This was the time of the Empire and the British army was invincible. So the British began a massive roundup of Sinn Fein dissidents, who were arrested and jailed. Thus, the newly formed paramilitary wing of Sinn Fein, the Irish Republican Army (IRA), was called into action. The first task of the newly formed IRA was to neutralize the 9,000 armed Royal Irish Constabulary (RIC), the Irish police. Through a campaign of selective assassination, ambushes, coercion, intimidation, and terror, IRA gunmen effectively weakened the internal structure of the RIC. The British responded to the defeat of the Irish police by recruiting World War I veterans from the British army to counter the violence and terrorism of the IRA. In one sense, the first "counterterrorist" squad was organized to fight political violence. This counterterrorist squad eventually became known as the Black and Tans.

Between 1918 and 1921, the IRA waged the archetypical war of national liberation—the Tan War. Then in 1921, exhausted by the war and frustrated after centuries of Irish insurrections, the British sought a negotiated settlement. The IRA had in effect bombed the British to the bargaining table. What resulted was an Anglo-Irish treaty that divided the island into two distinct political entities. In the north, six counties from the nine in the province of Ulster remained within the United Kingdom. In the south, the Irish Free State emerged, controlling the remaining 26 counties. (See Figure 5-2.) However, the

[26]J. Bowyer Bell, *The Secret Army: The IRA 1916–1979* (Cambridge, Mass.: MIT Press, 1980), p. 8.

FIGURE 5-2   Ireland After Partition: December, 1921

acceptance of the partition plan ushered in a period of internecine Irish civil war between the pro-treaty and anti-treaty Irish forces.

The civil war between the pro-treaty wing of Sinn Fein, which formed the government of the Irish Free State, and the republican wing of Sinn Fein, supported by the IRA, ended in 1923 with the submission of the republicans. This brief and bloody Irish civil war fought between the IRA and the new Free State army was bloodier than the Tan War. The Free State army defeated the IRA on all fronts. However, the IRA did not disappear, but went underground and reorganized for another day. In order to counter the potential threat to the Free State from the IRA, legislation was passed that banned the IRA and permitted internment of known IRA members and sympathizers. Free State supporters, however, saw the partition of Ireland as only a temporary measure. Eventually the six northeastern countries would rejoin the Free State and Ireland once again would be united. But sectarian differences were stronger than national identity.

Northern Ireland After Partition

While the south of Ireland was fighting the Tans and then the civil war, the Unionist party in the six northeastern counties was working to consolidate its power. The Unionist party was an alliance of Protestants who supported union with Britain and resisted the demands of Irish nationalists. Although IRA activity was sporadic in Ulster during 1918–23, the area was the scene of numerous sectarian battles between Protestants and Catholics. Riots and sectarian shoot-outs were common during this turbulent period. Fearing the initial military successes of the IRA in the south, the Unionist Protestants introduced internment and banned membership in the IRA. The IRA was now outlawed in both the north and the Republic. But this did not prevent the Protestants in the north from further tightening the noose around the Catholic minority that continued to tighten until the growth of the civil rights movement in the mid-1960s.

For the IRA, however, the years leading up to the civil rights movement were marked by a steady decline in numbers and support. Internally, personal rivalries and ideological differences split the organization. During World War II some IRA leaders collaborated with Nazi Germany while the Marxist elements of the IRA remained stoic and impassive.[27] By 1950 the IRA was a fractionalized group of discontented ideologues, dominated by common criminals.

Then in 1956 the IRA reopened its campaign of violence in Northern Ireland. However, this new campaign, designed to harass the British security forces, was quickly repelled by the Royal Ulster Constabulary (RUC) and confined to a small section of the border. When the "Border War" ended in 1962, the IRA was discredited as a viable military force. The loss of military credibility prompted the Marxist element within the IRA to propose a diplomatic solution to the troubles. Hence, the IRA tacitly abandoned the use of violence in favor of negotiations with the Protestant majority of Northern Ireland and their British supporters. However, the Catholic civil rights movement was beginning to take shape in Northern Ireland; this movement would once again project the extremist element in the IRA onto the international scene.

The Northern Ireland Civil Rights Association (NICRA) was born out of frustration, anxiety, and hatred. The Roman Catholics of Northern Ireland compiled a long list of grievances against the oppressive rule of the Protestant majority. The Protestants of Northern Ireland enjoyed a monopoly of power since voting rights were based on property ownership, and electoral boundaries were deliberately gerrymandered to produce a Protestant electorate. Discrimination in jobs and housing was likewise flagrant. In addition, complaints of police brutality were widespread in Catholic ghettos of Belfast and Londonderry. The Northern Ireland government addressed the civil rights de-

---

[27]Carolle J. Carter, *The Shamrock and the Swastika* (Palo Alto, CA: Pacific Books, 1977), p. 27.

mands of the Catholics by establishing a reform program that removed the causes of the grievances. Discrimination in jobs and housing was made illegal, and an independent commission was established to investigate Catholic complaints of police brutality and electioneering. But these reforms did little to prevent the escalation of violence between Protestants and Catholics or the reemergence of the IRA.

IRA Gunman Take Over

Janke has outlined four stages in the escalation of contemporary political violence in Northern Ireland and the emergence of terrorism.[28] The first stage involved the eruption of spontaneous, communal disturbances, especially during civil rights marches; gangs of Protestant extremists would disrupt Catholic marchers. Protestants who felt threatened by growing Catholic agitation began to attack Catholic residential areas and even turned off the public utilities and water in Catholic communities. The Catholics responded by blowing up public utilities and destroying the water supply in Protestant communities. To protect key public installations against sabotage attacks by both Protestant extremists and retaliating Catholics, the British government agreed to send army units to Northern Ireland. The arriving British security forces were welcomed by both Protestants and Catholics. However, this pleasant reception for British army units was short-lived.

By 1969 the second stage of the violence escalated to planned sectarian attacks in Catholic residential and business areas by Protestant paramilitary groups. During one such sectarian battle in Belfast, the British army was summoned to separate the two factions—Protestants and Catholics. In the ensuing riot, British army units panicked and fired into a group of rioters. Eight unarmed Catholics were killed. The Catholic community demanded revenge, and the IRA was there in force.

In the third stage IRA gunmen were called into action and introduced snipers to pick off individual British soldiers. The security forces responded and by July 1970, gun battles were being fought throughout Northern Ireland. Then on Sunday, January 30, 1972, during a civil rights demonstration in Londonderry, British troops once again apparently panicked and fired into a crowd of dispersing Catholic demonstrators, killing 13 people and wounding 12 others.[29] In response to this Bloody Sunday, the IRA escalated its indiscriminate bombing campaign against British army units and their Protestant supporters.

This final stage was the introduction of the devastating car bomb, which caused a dramatic increase in property damage and doubled the number of

---

[28]Peter Janke, *Ulster: A Decade of Violence,* Conflict Studies 108 (London: Institute for the Study of Conflict, 1979), pp. 11–17.

[29]Alfred McClung Lee, *Terrorism in Northern Ireland* (New York: General Hall, Inc., 1984), pp. 179–80.

casualties. For example, during the communal and sectarian violence of 1969 and 1970, Northern Ireland recorded 25 deaths. In comparison, in 1972 after Bloody Sunday, 321 deaths were recorded.[30] The indiscriminate IRA bombing campaign continues to this day. However, this gradual escalation of political violence in Northern Ireland was largely due to an unprecedented split in the IRA.

The split occurred in 1969 when a group of fervent nationalists formed the nucleus of the Provisional IRA, dedicated to direct military action. The Provos, or PIRA, as they are called, initiated a terrorist campaign to "make Ulster ungovernable, to force the British to relinquish all responsibility, and to withdraw their armed forces."[31] The Provos are also strong critics of the Marxist ideology proclaimed by the Official IRA (OIRA). Additionally, while the OIRA does not avoid terrorism, it differs from the Provos in its use of terrorist methods on strictly tactical grounds. The Officials subscribe to the philosophy of Sun Zu, "kill one, frighten a thousand." Murder is, therefore, dignified as a political act, and premediated murder then becomes a killing with political implications. Crozier maintains that on the streets, the Officials and Provisionals have displayed deadly hostility towards each other.[32] If a United Ireland were possible in the foreseeable future, there would be no room for both factions. In 1973, the Officials declared a qualified ceasefire that has been generally observed to the present time.

Another split by a revolutionary branch of the Officials occurred in 1975 when the Irish National Liberation Army (INLA) emerged. The goals of INLA are quite candid. INLA expects to drive the British military from Northern Ireland through sustained military action and reunite the 32 counties of Ireland in a socialist state. Even though INLA remains dedicated to the principles of Marxism, it criticizes the pro-Soviet stance of the Official IRA. INLA has its organizational headquarters in Dublin, where recruits are selected from pockets of poverty in both the north and the republic. INLA's most startling act of terrorism occurred in March 1979, when the Conservative Party spokesperson in Northern Ireland was blown up in his car while parked in front of the British House of Commons. Throughout the 1980s INLA has continued to attack targets of opportunity, including Protestant paramilitaries.

Protestant Paramilitary Groups

Protestant paramilitary groups were formed largely to combat the terrorism of PIRA and INLA and to counteract the growing militancy in the Catholic community. The largest Protestant paramilitary group is an affiliation of

---

[30]The Royal Ulster Constabulary, *Chief Constable's Report: 1983* (Belfast, 1984), p. 11, table 6.

[31]Janke, *Ulster,* p. 8.

[32]Brian Crozier, *Ulster: Politics and Terrorism,* Conflict Studies #36 (London: Institute for the Study of Conflict, 1973), p. 14.

several Protestant defense associations formed in 1971 under the banner of the Ulster Defense Association (UDA). The UDA draws its major support from the Protestant working class in Belfast, where it began a random campaign of murder and no-warning bombs against Catholics in 1972.[33] The UDA also has attacked PIRA targets in the Republic, bombing known meeting places and assassinating known members of PIRA. The UDA also had within its ranks the equivalent of "Murder Incorporated." UDA murder squads attempted to kill as many Catholics as possible. Kelley writes that a kind of sectarian genocide existed in Northern Ireland in the early 1970s where often the only criteria for murder was whether or not the potential victim was Protestant or Catholic.[34] The UDA is the most active Protestant paramilitary group in Ulster, although other Protestant paramilitary groups, such as the Ulster Volunteer Force (UVF), the Ulster Freedom Fighters (UFF), and the Red Hand Commandos (RHC) are also active.

After being forced out of the UDA, John McKeague formed the clandestine paramilitary group, the Red Hand Commandos (RHC). The membership of the RHC consisted of the most extreme elements of the various Protestant paramilitaries. Their most vicious act of terrorism was the explosion of a car bomb during rush hour on a crowded Dublin street; 25 people were killed and 151 were injured.[35] In 1982, McKeague was finally arrested for his involvement in several sectarian murders; he was later acquitted by the court. Shortly after McTeague gained his freedom, he was reportedly assassinated by INLA. After his murder, acts of random terrorism by RHC began to decline, and several terrorists of the RHC were jailed by 1985. As a result, the terrorism attributed to the RHC has been greatly reduced, but other Protestant paramilitaries have picked up the slack.

The Ulster Freedom Fighters (UFF), founded in 1973, appears to be a splinter group of the UDA. Like the RHC, the UFF has been described as the "terrorist arm" of the UDA. Shortly after its formation, the UFF announced that it had compiled dossiers on known members of PIRA and would soon begin to kill them. Subsequently, seven Catholics were randomly killed; none had affiliation with the Republican movement. Sporadic terrorist activity by UFF continued through the early 1980s, rising briefly during the PIRA hunger strike of 1981 when four Catholics were randomly murdered. Lately, the terrorist acts of the UFF have also greatly declined; but their presence is a constant reminder of the terrorism that is possible if the British security forces completely withdraw from Ulster.[36]

---

[33]Kelley, *The Longest War,* p. 160.

[34]Ibid., p. 169.

[35]Richard Deutsch and Vivien McGowan, *Northern Ireland: 1968–73* (Belfast: Blackstaff Press, 1973–74), pp. 2, 59.

[36]Conflict Studies #135, *Northern Ireland: Problems and Perspectives* (London: Institute for the Study of Conflict, 1982), p. 27.

Another fringe, Protestant, paramilitary group is the Ulster Volunteer Force (UVF). The UVF can trace its origins back to the unionist resistance to home rule before World War I; the present UVF was established in 1966. On May 21, 1966, the UVF declared war on the IRA, claiming that known IRA members and collaborators "will be executed without hesitation." The victims of UVF assassination squads, whose only crime was that they were Catholic, became the latest casualties in this cycle of sectarian killing. In all, 19 Catholics were indiscriminately murdered. By 1979 British counterterrorist squads had penetrated the UVF, and 11 men, known to the media as "Shankill Butchers," were sentenced to life in prison.[37]

In summary, the Protestant paramilitaries are less well equipped than the nationalist PIRA and INLA. The Protestant paramilitaries, like British security forces, have had little success in destroying the Republican movement. Unlike the Republican groups, i.e., the PIRA and INLA, Protestant extremists seldom attack economic targets or members of the British security forces or the police. Figure 5-3 illustrates the relationship between Republicans, paramilitaries, security forces, and the police.

In conclusion, Northern Ireland has been torn apart fighting over religious differences for 300 years.[38] In the past 17 years, Northern Ireland has been the scene of an endless cycle of terrorism and counterterrorism. Certainly, sectarian differences play an important part in the troubles; but the Catholic community is also struggling for economic and social equality. Protestants outnumber Catholics two to one and in the past have used that majority to maintain political and economic dominance. For example, since Northern Ireland is part of Britain, it sends 17 representatives to the British

FIGURE 5-3 Conflict in Northern Ireland

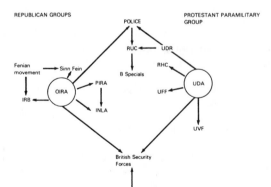

[37]Peter Janke, *Guerrilla and Terrorist Organizations: A World Directory and Bibliography* (New York: MacMillan, 1983), pp. 107–108.

[38]Richard Ned Lebow, "The Origins of Sectarian Assassination: The Case of Belfast," *Journal of International Affairs* 32 (1978), pp. 43–61.

Parliament; all but three are Protestants. On one hand, what the Protestants want is to be British; on the other, the Catholics want the British out of Northern Ireland and a reunification with the Republic. Table 5-3 presents a chronology of relevant historical events in Northern Ireland.

This next section briefly sketches the cycle of terrorism in western Europe.

Western Europe

Terrorism in western Europe appeared suddenly in the late 1960s in West Germany, France, Italy, and Spain. In Belgium, a new terrorist group announced its arrival in 1984 with a series of bombings. Scandinavia has escaped political violence and terrorism and so, to a large extent, have Switzerland and the Low Countries. The causes for this dramatic escalation of terrorism in Western Europe are varied and complex. Even though the causes in each country differ, unsuccessful attempts have been made to organize European terrorist groups into one coordinated unit. In some cases there are common factors that reach across borders, and certainly telecommunications and instantaneous

TABLE 5-3   Chronology of Significant Events in Northern Ireland

1690	Battle of Boyne
1916	Easter Rising
1921	Irish Free State established: Ireland is partitioned
1922	Civil War in Ireland: IRA goes underground
1939–45	IRA campaign against British military
1956–62	IRA border war with Ulster
1967	NICRA formed: Issues include
	*discrimination in jobs and housing
	*gerrymandering of voting district to exclude Catholics
	*voting which is based on property ownership
	*police brutality
1969	Split in IRA; Provisional Wing formed; British troops arrive in Ulster
1972	Bloody Sunday; U.K. begins direct rule of Ulster and establishes policy of internment
1974	INLA emerges advocating armed warfare with Britain
1975	Sectarian violence escalates with creation of Protestant Death Squads; IRA retaliates
1980	Assassination of Mountbatten and 18 British soldiers
1981	Hunger strike begins at Maze Prison; ten die
1982	Bombing campaign continues in United Kingdom: Crocus Street ambush
1983–84	Escape from Maze Prison; London bombings; attempt on British prime minister
1985	Bombing of Police Barracks; Anglo-Irish Treaty; Sinn Fein wins 11% Catholic vote in Ulster
1986	Protestant backlash to Anglo-Irish Treaty; United States ratifies new extradition treaty with United Kingdom
1987	Eight PIRA terrorists killed in shoot-out with British military in south Armagh

media coverage encourage international contacts between European terrorist groups. Yet the principal motivation of European terrorist groups remains characteristically individual.

European terrorism is motivated by two major themes: (1) the rise of nationalism, and (2) the influence of the political ideology of the extreme left. Neither theme has been successful in destroying "the system" or even in coexisting within established political frameworks. In other words, the themes of European terrorist groups are beyond the reach of compromise and negotiation; and an accommodation with these groups would upset the existing status quo. Therefore, a small number of fanatics are committed to violence and terrorism in order to forcefully impose their objectives upon resistant European governments.

Nationalism is the root cause for Basque terrorism in Spain and for the violent actions of Corsican and Briton separatists who feel ignored and threatened by France. On the other hand, the terrorism that motivates the Red Brigades of Italy, the Red Army Faction of West Germany, Direct Action of France, and the Communist Combatant Cells of Belgium is adherence to an intellectually weak revision of Marxist ideology.

By far the greatest threat to the stability of Europe has been the terrorism of the ideological left, or what is called Euroterrorism. Euroterrorism is a campaign of seemingly coordinated attacks against NATO and defense-related targets primarily in West Germany, France, and Belgium. According to the U.S. Department of State, there are disturbing indications that left-wing terrorists are perhaps beginning to cooperate and coordinate terrorist attacks against NATO facilities and related high-tech industries.[39] Table 5-4 is a compendium of the most active European terrorist groups.

In conclusion, the challenge in confronting terrorism in European democracies is likely to increase in the remaining years of this century. There appears to be a large cadre of extremists prepared to resort to the use of terrorism. There are numerous conflict issues, the availability of sophisticated weapons technologies, and the financial backing of state-sponsored terrorism. Such factors, together with the growing cooperation of international and transnational linkages, enhance the need to develop a strategy to prevent the escalation of terrorism in the 21st century.

CONCLUSIONS

For more than 20 years, the international community has been combating Palestinian terrorism; it is conceivable to assume that at least in the near future

---

[39]United States Department of State, *Patterns of Global Terrorism: 1984* (Washington, D.C.: Government Printing Office, 1985), p. 14.

TABLE 5-4   Most Active European Terrorist Groups

Spain

First of October Anti-Fascist Resistance Group (GRAPO). GRAPO is a Marxist-ideologically motivated terrorist group which derives its name from the killing of four police officers in Madrid on October 1, 1975. The assassinations were in retaliation for the execution of several GRAPO members by the Franco government.

Freedom for the Basque Homeland (ETA). The ETA is a Basque nationalist movement which seeks to create a separate Basque nation in the four Basque provinces of northwestern Spain. ETA's most outrageous terrorist act was the assassination of Spanish Prime Minister Admiral Carrero Blanco.[a]

France

Direct Action (DA). The DA is a collection of remnants of several French left-wing terrorist groups dedicated "to wreck society through direct action by destroying its institutions and the men who serve it." Since its founding in May of 1979, DA has taken credit for some 60 attacks.[b]

Breton Liberation Front (FLB). The FLB first appeared in 1966 seeking to create an autonomous Breton nation in northwestern France. Bombing was the primary activity of the FLB; however, by the 1980s, most members of the FLB were jailed and since then the separatist movement has been on the decline.[c]

Corsican Revolutionary Action (ARC). Like the FLB, the ARC is a separatist movement seeking to advance the cause of the Corsican people and freedom from French governmental influence.

Italy

Red Brigades (RB). The RB derives its name from the left-wing ideology it supports and the fact the RB is organized into individual brigades. The RB has been responsible for the deaths and injuries of thousands of victims since its appearance in late 1968.[d] Police have been able to penetrate the RB organization and some 500 have been imprisoned, but new recruits are always available to fill the void.

Belgium

The Communist Combatant Cells (CCC). The CCC first appeared in 1984. The group has a leftist orientation and closely resembles the Red Army Faction (RAF) of West Germany. The terrorist strategy of the CCC has been to attack NATO targets.[e]

West Germany

Red Army Faction (RAF). The RAF is an outgrowth of the Baader-Meinhoff Gang active between 1970 and 1973 in West Germany.[f] The RAF's principal target has been American military installations and private multinational corporations in West Germany who "support American imperialism."

[a]Peter Janke, *Spanish Separatism: ETA's Threat to Basque Democracy,* Conflict Studies 123 (London: Institute for the Study of Conflict, October, 1980), p. 2.
[b]Janke, 1983, p. 33.
[c]Vittorfranco S. Pisano, "France as an International Setting for Domestic and International Terrorism," *Clandestine Tactics and Technology* (Maryland: International Association of Chiefs of Police, 1985), pp. 3–6.
[d]Vittorfranco S. Pisano, *The Red Brigades: A Challenge to Italian Democracy,* Conflict Studies 120 (London: Institute for the Study of Conflict, July, 1980), p. 2.
[e]*San Francisco Chronicle,* March 2, 1985, Sec. 1, p. 8.
[f]Julian Becker, *Hitler's Children: The Story of the Baader-Meinhoff Terrorist Gang* (Philadelphia: Lippincott, 1977), p. 12.

Palestinian terrorism will continue. The tenacity of Palestinian terrorist activity has gained worldwide sympathy for the Palestinian cause and the PLO. More than 130 countries have officially recognized the PLO, which has a permanent representative at the United Nations. The PLO seeks to achieve its objectives through a strategy of "protracted struggle." This strategy is partly based on unprovoked attacks on civilian targets. There have been few attacks by Palestinian terrorist groups on military targets.

In implementing its strategy of protracted struggle, the PLO enjoys several important advantages that could continue indefinitely. First, the PLO has a large recruiting pool located in the many refugee camps throughout the Arab world and within the Palestinian diaspora. Second, the various Palestinian terrorist groups have been provided sanctuaries in several Arab countries, including Libya, Syria, Iraq, and Lebanon. Third, Palestinian terrorist groups enjoy financial, political, and military aid from the Arab world. The Soviet Union and Eastern Bloc countries also play an important part in the support and training of the PLO-affiliated terrorist groups.[40] Fourth, international terrorist groups, such as the Red Army Faction, United Red Army, and the IRA, have cooperated with Palestinian terrorist groups on a variety of random terrorist acts; one, for example, was the Lod massacre in 1974. This support can only strengthen and escalate worldwide incidents of Palestinian terrorism.

In the foreseeable future, all these advantages seem likely not to change. Although the Israeli military blitz of 1982 disrupted the PLO infrastructure, it is only a matter of time before the PLO is back to its pre-1982 stature. In general, Palestinian terrorist organizations are doing well and will continue to thrive.

Likewise, the protracted struggle of the Irish Republican movement has literally been centuries in the making and cannot easily be eliminated either through negotiation or by military force. The popularity of the Irish Republican Army has been strengthened by the uncompromising position of the British that has continued for at least two centuries. The IRA and Sinn Fein claim that the Republican revolutionary tradition has been responsible for the creation of the Republic of Ireland and that violence works. In other words, political agitation and civil disobedience have proved ineffective without the resort to physical violence, especially attacks against the military and police. Britain must solve the Irish troubles in such a manner that the IRA becomes irrelevant, and violence and terrorism are no longer seen as legitimate means of political expression in Northern Ireland. In Europe, the ideological left continues to attack U.S. military installations and NATO targets. No doubt this trend will continue well into the 1990s. In later chapters we will discuss some responses to PLO and IRA terrorism. The next chapter explores the dramatic increase in various types of hostage-taking events.

---

[40]Shlomi Elad and Ariel Merari, "The Soviet Bloc and World Terrorism," *Jaffee Center for Strategic Studies* (Tel Aviv: Tel Aviv University, 1984), pp. 12–19.

REVIEW QUESTIONS

1. Identify and define the following terms:
   a. Zionism
   b. Arab nationalism
   c. Diaspora
   d. Balfour Declaration
   e. British mandate colony
2. Describe the United Nations Partition Plan for Palestine in 1947.
3. Define the difference between a soft target and a hard target. Why do you think Palestinian terrorists concentrate on soft targets?
4. List Palestinian terrorist groups affiliated with the PLO.
5. Why was the war in Lebanon a failure for Israel?
6. Outline the elements of Fatah. What do you think of the future success of Fatah and the PLO?
7. Discuss the methods of terrorism used by the IRA.
8. Identify the following groups:
   a. IRB
   b. Sinn Fein
   c. Black and Tans
   d. RUC
   e. UVF
   f. UDA
   g. RHC
   h. UFF
9. Describe the civil rights grievances of Roman Catholics in Ulster.
10. Sketch the four stages of the escalation of political violence in Northern Ireland.
11. Explain the split between the OIRA, PIRA, and INLA.
12. Identify the country of origin for the following European terrorist groups:
    a. Red Army Faction
    b. Red Brigades
    c. Direct Action
    d. Communist Combatant Cells
    e. ETA (Basque Separatists)
    f. GRAPO

SIX

THE DYNAMICS OF HOSTAGE-TAKING AND NEGOTIATION

CHAPTER OBJECTIVES

The study of this chapter will enable you to:
- ■ Sketch the historical precedents of hostage-taking
- ■ Examine the Lindbergh Law
- ■ Describe at least three categories of hostage takers
- ■ Explain the Stockholm Syndrome
- ■ Recognize the need for hostage guidelines
- ■ Distinguish between hostage-taking and kidnapping
- ■ Review hostage survival strategies

INTRODUCTION

The last decade has witnessed a dramatic increase in hostage-taking as a preferred tactic of political terrorists. The theatrical nature surrounding terrorist hostage situations has also provided the stimulus for the expansion of criminal and psychotic hostage-taking episodes. The high visibility of instant media coverage of the hostage incident has also forced democratic governments and police administrators to develop extensive hostage anti-terrorist training programs. In this chapter, therefore, some of the basic factors related to government and police response to hostage-takings will be examined. Additionally, a typology of hostage-takers will be presented; furthermore, the psychological manifestations of the Stockholm Syndrome, identification with the aggressor, response of the hostage victim, and techniques for surviving a hostage-taking will be explored. The purpose here is to alert the reader to the complex problems associated with a variety of hostage-taking scenarios. But first, a brief historical review of hostage-taking is in order.

Early History of Hostage-Taking

Hostage-taking has a long relationship with rebellion and warfare. For example, the Roman Empire suppressed revolts in Italy, Spain, and Gaul by requiring the vanquished tribes to give hostages as a guarantee of their future good behavior.[1] Similar tactics were used in Ireland by the Earl of Tyrone during the sixteenth century and again during the French Revolution. More recently, during World War II, Nazi Germany would take hostages in retaliation for acts of sabotage and assassination. In one such incident, during the Nazi occupation of Czechoslovakia in 1942, 10,000 Czech hostages were taken by the Nazis and randomly executed in reprisal for the attempted assassination of Reinhard Heydrich.[2] Likewise, today nuclear strategy based on the alleged balance of power is as Schelling states, "simply a massive and modern version of an ancient institution: the exchange of hostages."[3]

However, a qualitative distinction in the selection of hostage victims appeared in the twelfth century. In Europe the hostage holding of a member of the nobility was considered to be effective, future bargaining tool. The best-known example was the abduction of Richard the Lionhearted by rival noblemen in Austria in 1193. In order to secure the release of Richard, a large ransom was paid to the Austrians. Similarly, Fredrich Barbarossa seized hundreds of noblemen and high-ranking military leaders in order to secure a favorable peace treaty with Milan in 1158. This pattern of holding powerful government officials as hostages has continued to the present, although today nonstate hostage-takers have become more widespread. The taking of hostages to achieve political objectives by nonstate hostage-takers has occurred with regularity in Northern Ireland, Spain, France, Italy, West Germany, and Central America.[4]

[1]Robert B. Asprey, *War in the Shadows: The Guerrilla in History* (London: MacDonald and Jane's, 1975), p. 20.

[2]J. Bowyer Bell, *Assassin: The Theory and Practice of Political Violence* (New York: St. Martin's Press, 1979), p. 102.

[3]Thomas C. Schelling, *The Strategy of Conflict* (London: Oxford University Press, 1973), p. 239.

[4]Clive C. Aston, "Political Hostage Taking in Western Europe: A Statistical Analysis," in *Perspectives on Terrorism*, eds. Lawrence Z. Freedman and Yonah Alexander (Wilmington, Delaware: Scholarly Resources, 1983), p. 100.

Meanwhile, in the United States, the incidences of hostage-taking or extortion-kidnapping began to escalate after World War I. Few kidnappings are recorded in the United States prior to World War I; but because of inadequate laws, lack of coordination among police jurisdictions, and increased mobility of kidnappers, the possibilities for the successful completion of kidnappings increased. For example, Gallagher presents data from 1931 which shows that 279 kidnappings had taken place with unreported cases estimated at three times that number. Thirteen victims were killed and only 69 offenders had been arrested and convicted.[5] In addition, ransom demands were often paid since families of victims preferred to pay rather than risk the life of a captive. By 1932, kidnapping had grown into a cottage industry in the United States. But one particular kidnapping case aroused the indignation of the American public, and steps were taken to strengthen kidnapping laws.

No other kidnapping in the United States quite compares with the taking of the Lindbergh baby on March 1, 1932. The Lindbergh case (1) dominated the news media for several months, (2) provoked the largest police search in American history, (3) established the Federal Bureau of Investigation (FBI) as a competent law enforcement agency, and (4) produced the Lindbergh Law. The popularly known Lindbergh Law provided for the death penalty in kidnapping cases if the victim was injured or still missing when sentence was passed on the perpetrator of the offense. Nevertheless, a large number of kidnappings for ransom took place in the United States between 1933 and 1935, and a number of the victims were killed after the payment of ransom to prevent the captive from testifying later as a witness.[6] The media referred to this epidemic of kidnappings in the United States as the "snatch racket." However, by the end of the 1930s, the incidents of kidnapping began to decline with improved investigative techniques by the FBI, cooperation between the FBI and local law enforcement agencies, and cooperation from the relatives of victims. The epidemic of kidnappings was over. But the cases that occurred in later years proved just as spectacular.

For example, on February 9, 1960, Adolph Coors was abducted and held for a $500,000 ransom demand. His body was later discovered by a hiker in Sedalia, Colorado. The suspect in the case was later apprehended by the FBI and tried in state court, where he received a mandatory life sentence. In another well-publicized case, Barbara Mackle, the daughter of a wealthy real estate broker, was abducted and entombed in a coffinlike box for 83 hours. She was released after a ransom demand of $500,000 was paid to the kidnappers. Her abductors were later apprehended and sentenced to life in prison by the Georgia State Court. In yet another sensational case, Samuel Bronfman,

[5]Richard J. Gallagher, "Kidnapping in the U.S. and the Development of the Federal Kidnapping Statute," in *Terrorism and Personal Protection,* ed. Brian M. Jenkins (Boston: Butterworth, 1985), p. 131.

[6]Richard Clutterbuck, *Kidnap and Ransom: The Response* (London: Faber & Faber, 1978), p. 20.

the son of the president of Seagrams, was kidnapped; a ransom demand of $2.3 million was paid for his release. The Bronfman kidnapper was later arrested and convicted of extortion and sentenced to state prison. In April 1968, the U.S. Supreme Court declared the capital punishment provision of the Lindbergh Law to be unconstitutional. Between 1930 and 1968, 22 convicted extortionist hostage-takers were executed for kidnapping. The FBI maintains that of the hundreds of kidnapping cases they have investigated, only two remain unsolved.[7] But federal and local law enforcement agencies in the United States, Europe, and Asia were ill prepared to cope with the variety of hostage-taking or kidnapping types that began to appear in the early 1970s.

Typologies of Hostage-Takers

There are a number of possible ways to categorize hostage-takers, each of which may be used for decision-making purposes, developing negotiating styles, or for academic analysis. Stratton has identified three broad categories and delineates them as follows: (1) the mentally ill hostage-taker, (2) the criminal hostage-taker, and (3) the social, political, religious, or ethnic crusader hostage-taker.[8] The mentally ill hostage-taker most often seeks recognition from the intense media exposure that follows the hostage episode. The mentally ill hostage taker also has the ability to exercise considerable power over the police. This is especially true in the barricade/hostage situation where the hostage-taker threatens suicide. This hostage-taking event can easily develop into a spectacle, emulating a Cecil B. deMille Hollywood production. For example, on April 3, 1986, a barricaded hostage-taker in a crowded South Chicago tenement killed two hostages and was holding one captive and threatening suicide.[9] The building was surrounded by 150 police officers. The hostage-taker demanded a pizza be delivered and vowed not to surrender until he had watched a movie on TV. The hostage-taker was permitted to watch his movie and eat his pizza uninterrupted by the police. In a related incident, a barricaded suspect holding two teenage hostages in a Newport, Kentucky, house held off police SWAT teams for over 30 hours, demanding heroin and $20,000 in ransom for the release of the hostages before being killed by a police sharpshooter.[10]

Virtually every police agency in the United States has its own version of the mentally disturbed hostage-taking scenario. The number of incidents is endless. Cooper suggests that the mentally disturbed hostage-taker is a person with limited individual power who feels persecuted by the world or a segment

---

[7]Caroline Moorehead, *Hostages to Fortune* (New York: Atheneum, 1980), p. 51.

[8]John G. Stratton, "The Terrorist Act of Hostage Taking: Considerations for Law Enforcement," *Journal of Police Science and Administration* 6 (1978), pp. 123–24.

[9]*Sacramento Bee*, April 4, 1986, sec. A, p. 10.

[10]*Sacramento Bee*, December 31, 1985, sec. A, p. 8.

of it and strikes back by attempting to physically control someone.[11] Mentally disturbed hostage-takers are the most difficult to negotiate with since their actions are irrational and unpredictable.

Criminal hostage-takers, on the other hand, are generally the most rational and predictable to negotiate with because they do not want to be arrested. Criminal hostage-takers account for approximately 60 percent of all hostage-taking incidents in the United States. Criminals who are fleeing the scene of a felony, such as an armed robbery, often take hostages as a last resort when faced with the unexpected arrival of the police. The fleeing felon can most likely be negotiated out of a potentially dangerous situation by delineating the seriousness of the crime of kidnapping or false imprisonment as well as the charge of armed robbery. However, some criminals may try to convince the police they are political terrorists rather than criminals, thus complicating the negotiating process. This was the case when a man claiming to be a Palestinian guerrilla burst into a French courtroom and attempted to free two of France's most notorious criminals.[12] The two French criminals who were on trial for a series of armed robberies were provided with guns, and 35 hostages were taken, including the judge and jury. During the course of the courtroom siege, hostages were released sporadically; after two days, French police negotiators were able to convince the hostage-takers that their escape was futile. The political cause proclaimed by the hostage-takers was obscure, and few people understood their political rhetoric. But what seemed to be yet another hostage tragedy ended with no injuries or deaths.

The social, political, religious, or ethnic crusader hostage-taker is most often a member of a group falling within our definition of terrorism. The terrorist hostage-taker generally has a strong commitment to a cause or a political ideology. Organizations that seek social change (for example, the Red Brigades in Italy), political change (the Sikhs in India and the Islamic Jihad of Lebanon), or independence for ethnic minorities (the ETA Basque separatist movement in Spain) are well known to the world because of their extranormal acts of terrorism and the publicity these acts generate through intense media involvement. Such groups are the most difficult to negotiate with because of their total commitment to a cause. The crusader terrorist is rational and often enters a hostage-taking situation with preconceived demands and identified limits as to how far the negotiator can be pushed in meeting the stated demands. Therefore, through extensive planning, individual determination, and the ability to manipulate the media, the negotiation process is quite complicated.

The three-way classification of hostage-takers has also been analyzed by other criminal justice writers. Middendorff has identified three types of hostage-takers: (1) politically motivated offenders, (2) those seeking to escape from

---

[11]H. H. A. Cooper, *The Hostage Takers* (Boulder: Paladin Press, 1981), pp. 53–61.
[12]*Time Magazine,* December 23, 1985, p. 35.

something to somewhere, and (3) those seeking personal gain. Middendorff argues that the classification of hostage-takers can only be based on motives.[13]

Like Middendorff and Stratton, the New York City hostage-negotiation training program identifies three categories of hostage-takers: (1) professional criminals, (2) psychotics, and (3) terrorists. Trainers from that program claim that each type of hostage-taker requires a different approach to handling the situation in the process of negotiation. In other words, different motives would require different response strategies by police negotiators. For example, a ransom demand can have quite a different meaning for the professional criminal and the terrorist. The professional criminal may use the ransom for personal gratification while the terrorist may use the ransom to purchase guns and explosives to further his terrorist activity.[14]

Richard Kobetz lists five types of hostage-taking situations: (1) prison takeovers and escape situations in which hostages are seized, (2) aircraft hijackings, (3) seizures of business executives, diplomats, athletes, and cultural personalities, (4) armed robberies in which innocent bystanders are seized to effect an escape, and (5) seizures of hostages by mentally disturbed individuals seeking personal recognition. Clearly, his typology involves a synthesis of hostage-taker, hostage, and motive. Each category has its own unique features that demand an individual response by police negotiators.[15]

Cooper maintains that hostages are seized by those who perceive the hostage-taking event as a way of setting up a bargaining position that cannot be achieved by other means. He argues for a typology of seven hostage-takers: (1) political extremists, (2) fleeing felons, (3) institutionalized persons, (4) estranged persons, (5) wronged persons, (6) religious fanatics, and (7) mentally disturbed persons. Cooper recognizes that his classification is subject to wide criticism since many categories may overlap. But from a police operational point of view, this classification can be used as a guide for action in organizing police/hostage training programs.[16]

Goldaber describes nine categories of hostage-takers: (1) suicidal personality, (2) vengeance seeker, (3) disturbed individual, (4) cornered perpetrator, (5) aggrieved inmate, (6) felonious extortionist, (7) social protestor, (8) ideological zealot, and (9) terrorist extremist. The value of Goldaber's typology is that it reveals the complexity of responsive action by the police. For example, negotiating with a suicidal bank robber as opposed to a nonsuicidal bank rob-

---

[13]Wolf Middendorff, *New Developments in the Taking of Hostages and Kidnapping: A Summary* (Washington, D.C.: National Criminal Justice Reference Service, 1975), pp. 1–9.

[14]Frank Bolz, Jr., "The Hostage Situation: Law Enforcement Options," in *Terrorism: Interdisciplinary Perspectives,* eds. Burr Eichelman, David A. Soskis, and William H. Reid (Washington, D. C.: American Psychiatric Association, 1983), pp. 99–116.

[15]Richard Kobetz, *Hostage Incidents: The New Police Priority* (Gaithersburg, MD: International Association of Chiefs of Police, undated mimeo.

[16]Cooper, *The Hostage Takers,* pp. 1–3.

ber, or a vengeance-seeking terrorist as opposed to a social protestor, requires an extraordinarily complex police response.[17]

The creation of a hostage typology is a useful first step in coordinating police responses. This is the case even though no natural categories of hostage-takers exist. The creation of any typology is bound to be arbitrary, reflecting the training and discipline of those who construct them. The most realistic arrangements are those that are able to reduce the subjectivity of the categories. Certainly, this is no easy task. Nonetheless, a typology clearly indicates that different responses (to different hostage types) require a wide variety of police strategies, negotiating skills, and tactical responses. Based on the previous review, we now seek to provide a reasonable typology of hostage-takers. The typology is based on the hostage-taker's motivation, with the creation of three broad categories and several subcategories. Conceivably, an individual hostage-taker could be a psychotic, criminally inclined, political terrorist. (See Table 6-1).

We will now review some of the general negotiating guidelines that apply most often to all hostage-taking situations.

Time, Trust, and The Stockholm Syndrome

The most important factor in any hostage negotiation situation is time. The first few minutes appear to be the most dangerous since the emotional level of both hostage-takers and hostages is extremely unpredictable. The confusion, fear, and anxiety at the initial stage of the hostage-taking event predominate and can produce injury and death. However, as time passes and the agitated emotions of the hostage-takers and the hostages subside, a period of calm begins. Generally, the longer the hostage-taking incident continues, the greater the probability the hostages will be released unharmed. This phenomenon can be explained in several ways. The passage of time allows the *Stock-*

TABLE 6-1 Typology of Hostage-Takers

CRIMINAL	POLITICAL TERRORIST	PSYCHOTIC
Fleeing felon	Seeking media recognition for a cause	Mentally deranged
Prison inmate riots	Social protestor	Suicidal
Extortionist kidnapper	Religious zealot	Angry
	Seeking vengeance	Seeking personal recognition
	Air hijacking	Estranged from family
	State as hostage-taker	

[17]Irving Goldaber, "A Typology of Hostage Takers," *Police Chief* June, 1979), pp. 21–22.

holm Syndrome an opportunity to manifest itself. The Stockholm Syndrome was first observed on August 23, 1973, when a single gunman intent on robbery entered a bank in Stockholm, Sweden. The robbery attempt was interrupted by the police, whereupon the gunman took four bank employees hostage and retreated into an 11-foot by 42-foot carpeted bank vault. The hostage-taking was to continue for 131 hours, affecting the lives of the hostages and giving rise to the psychological phenomenon eventually referred to as the Stockholm Syndrome.

The Stockholm Syndrome appears to be an unconscious emotional response to the traumatic experience of victimization. In the Stockholm bank robbery case, the armed bank robber was able to negotiate the release from prison of his former cellmate. This cellmate then joined the bank robber in the vault, thus further complicating negotiating procedures. Now there were four hostages and two hostage-takers. During the course of the negotiations it was discovered that the hostages feared the police more than they feared their captors. In a phone conversation with the prime minister of Sweden, one of the hostages expressed the feelings of the entire group when she stated, "The robbers are protecting us from the police." Eventually, after 131 hours, the bank siege ended; but for weeks after, the hostages complained to psychiatrists that they had chronic nightmares over the possibility that the hostage-takers might escape and abduct them again. Yet strangely enough, the hostages felt no hatred toward their abductors. In fact, they felt emotionally indebted to the hostage-takers for allowing them to remain alive and saving them from the police.

The Stockholm Syndrome has been observed around the world in a variety of hostage situations. Participants in the hostage drama are cast together in a life-threatening environment where each must adapt in order to stay alive. The positive bond that develops between hostages and hostage-takers serves to unite them against the outside influence of the police. Actually the Stockholm Syndrome has been known for quite some time to the psychiatric community, where it often is referred to as "identification with the aggressor." By any name, the syndrome works in favor of the police negotiator. The Stockholm Syndrome may manifest itself in three ways: (1) the positive feelings of the hostages toward the hostage-takers, (2) the reciprocal, positive feelings of the hostage-takers toward the hostages, and (3) the negative feelings of both the hostages and hostage-takers toward the police and the government.[18] Strentz defends the position that hostages regress to an earlier period of development when they are in a state of extreme dependence and fear.[19] This situation is not unlike a parent/child relationship in which the child is emotionally

---

[18]Murray S. Miron and Arnold P. Goldstein, *Hostage* (New York: Pergamon, 1979), p. 9.

[19]Thomas Strentz, "Law Enforcement Policy and Ego Defenses of the Hostage," *F.B.I. Law Enforcement Bulletin* (April, 1979), p. 4.

attached to its parents. The positive feelings act as a defense mechanism to ensure the survival of the hostage.

Despite the involuntary manifestation of the Stockholm Syndrome, it is not a magical relationship that affects *all* hostage-taking incidents. The positive contact between hostage-taker and hostages is largely determined by the absence of negative experiences during the hostage-taking incident. For example, if the hostages are beaten, raped, or physically abused, the Stockholm Syndrome is less likely to occur. In Iran, during the U.S. hostage crisis that lasted 444 days, few of the freed hostages had any favorable commentary about their captors. In order to prevent the positive feelings the hostage-takers might feel toward the hostages, Iranian hostage-takers would frequently change guards, and keep some hostages isolated and others blindfolded for long periods of time. In fact, one of the returning hostages stated that "students told him of being trained in the summer of 1979 at Palestine Liberation Organization camps on how to handle hostages."[20]

Aronson maintains that most people cannot harm another person unless the victim has been dehumanized.[21] When hostage-takers and hostages are isolated together in a building, airplane, or a bank vault, a process of humanization apparently occurs. A hostage can then build empathy with the hostage-taker while still maintaining his or her dignity and individuality, thus lessening the possibility of being physically abused or executed. The exception is the antisocial hostage-taker, demonstrated by four Iranians in December 1984.[22] The four seized a Kuwaiti airliner and took refuge in Tehran. Two American hostages were summarily executed and several other hostages reported being beaten, burned with cigarettes, and having their hair set on fire. Fortunately, this type of hostage incident is rare; and in most situations the Stockholm Syndrome will be present. As time passes and positive experiences begin to develop between hostage-takers and hostages, then the hostage's chance of survival becomes much greater.

Certainly the relevance of the Stockholm Syndrome to the police negotiation process is clear. The syndrome's presence may save the life of hostages as well as hostage-takers. Understanding the ultimate effects of the syndrome may also prevent the police from resorting too quickly to the use of deadly force. The experience of positive contact often prevents the hostage-taker from injuring a hostage he has come to know and in some cases to love. The police negotiator can foster the Stockholm Syndrome by: (1) asking to check on the health of a hostage, (2) discussing the family responsibilities of the hostage with the hostage-taker, and (3) requesting information on the treatment of the

---

[20]Robert D. McFadden, Joe B. Treaster and Maurice Carroll, *No Hiding Place* (New York: Times Books, 1981), p. 120.

[21]Elliot Aronson, *Social Animal* (San Francisco: W. H. Freeman, 1972), p. 168.

[22]*Sacramento Bee,* December 11, 1984, sec. A, p. 1.

hostage. The importance of the human qualities of the victim or hostage should not be understated by the police negotiator.

Time is also important because it allows a "friendly" relationship between the hostage-takers and the negotiator to develop. By stalling for time, the negotiator can use several strategies to build rapport and trust with the hostage-takers. The improvement of trust between hostage-takers and negotiator reduces the likelihood that victims or hostages will be harmed and increases the likelihood that the negotiator's suggestions will be seriously considered by the hostage-takers. Miron and Goldstein outline several techniques for developing trust and rapport between negotiator and hostage-takers, which include: (1) self-disclosure, (2) empathy, (3) being a good listener, (4) being understanding and showing personal interest in hostage-taker's problems, (5) reflecting on hostage-taker's feelings, and (6) not rejecting outright all demands.[23] The primary role of the negotiator is to establish a favorable and supportive climate with the hostage-takers. Even though time and trust are generally considered to be the most important factors in the hostage-taking episode, other "management" considerations are also very important.

Guidelines for Hostage Events

After the tragedy of the Munich Olympics in 1972, democratic nations recognized a need to deal with political hostage-taking incidents on more than an ad hoc basis. Eleven Israeli hostages, five Palestinian hostage-takers, and one police officer were killed when negotiations collapsed and Munich police attempted to rescue the hostages.[24] The Palestinian hostage-takers demanded the release of 200 "fedayeen" incarcerated in Israeli jails. The Israelis refused; but after a complicated negotiation process, the West Germans promised the Palestinian hostage-takers safe passage to Egypt with their hostages. When Israeli hostages and their Palestinian captors arrived at the Furstenfeldbruck airport, German police sharpshooters were waiting for them. In the ensuing gun battle, the terrorists threw hand grenades into the helicopters holding the Israeli hostages, killing all on board. Three terrorists were captured by police after the gun battle. The West German police were widely criticized for their use of deadly force. The massacre at Munich caused police administrators worldwide to review carefully and analyze police response to hostage-taking situations. Police and democratic governments suddenly became conscious of their lack of understanding of terrorist hostage-takers and the vulnerability of society's institutions. A series of well-trained, elite military units were organized (we will discuss the tactical response in a later chapter), and the improvement of hostage negotiation skills was undertaken in response to the newest form of criminality: hostage-taking.

---

[23]Miron and Goldstein, *Hostage,* pp. 101–102.

[24]Manfred Schreiber, *After Action Report of Terrorist Activities 20th Olympic Games Munich, West Germany* FRG, September 1972, p. 14.

The circumstances surrounding every hostage-taking situation are somewhat different; however, there are recommended guidelines appropriate for most hostage situations. The selection and training of negotiators is of crucial importance since they provide the link between police authorities and hostage-takers. Negotiators should be trained in hostage management strategy, terrorist ideologies, and the psychology of hostage-takers. In the case of the Munich Olympics no specifically trained negotiator was available. Several police and government officials representing West German, Israel, U.S. and Arab delegations attempted to negotiate the release of the Israeli hostages without success. One reason for this failure is that high-ranking officials acted as negotiators. Negotiators should be lower- or middle-ranking police officers who report to a decision-maker. This buys *time* since the negotiator must always consult with his or her superiors before a decision is made. Other advantages are that unfavorable decisions will be accepted as coming from "higher-ups" and not the negotiator and, therefore, will not influence the *trust* that has developed, it is hoped, between negotiator and hostage-taker. The negotiator can also direct his or her attention to the immediate task of building rapport with the hostage-takers and not be obstructed by management responsibilities.

Cooperation of the media is also essential not to reveal the tactical plans and resources of the police or military. In the Munich incident, no limit was placed on media reporting of West Germany's tactical response.

A chain of command must be established to ensure that communication among responding personnel is free of interference. Communications, firepower, assistance to negotiators, and related resources should be the responsibility of one ranking official.

All police and nonpolice personnel must be readily identifiable and distinguishable from hostages and hostage-takers. In the event of an unexpected firefight, police personnel obviously must not be mistaken for hostage-takers.

The exact number and identity of hostage-takers must be ascertained as quickly as possible. In the event of an assault, the police fire-team must be able to distinguish the difference between hostages and hostage-takers beyond mere clothing because hostage-takers can easily switch clothing or other similar items to confuse or test the trustworthiness of the police. For example, in Munich the police misjudged the number of Palestinian hostage-takers, assuming that there were only five holding the Israelis at the Olympic Village. Instead, there were eight. Five sharpshooters were stationed at strategic locations and instructed to "take out" the terrorists after they arrived at the airport with the hostages. Even under the best of conditions, it would have been difficult for the sharpshooters to kill all of the hostage-takers before they retaliated against the hostage Israeli athletes. The problem was compounded when one of the police sharpshooters prematurely opened fire. Three hostage-takers were disabled, but the others turned on the bound and helpless Israeli hostages with grenades, killing all. If possible, the negotiating team should make every effort actually to see all the hostages and hostage-takers.

The negotiator should avoid any shifts in location of hostages by the hostage-takers. Most likely this demand is for an airplane, bus, or car for the purpose of escape. Once the hostage-taking location is moved, the negotiator loses the control of the situation that might possibly have been established at the original location. The movement of hostages creates a setting of unpredictability and compounds the task of the negotiator. This loss of control by the negotiator may prompt the mistimed use of deadly force to rescue the hostages, since new resources and new people for the hostage-takers are now available. For example, as the hostages were being moved to the airport in Munich, the hostage-takers were joined by three companions, seemingly to help control the hostages.

If hostage-takers request others, such as relatives or friends, to be present at the scene, the negotiator should avoid this and stall the hostage-taker. Like shifts in location, the presence of hostage-takers' relatives or friends (religious or governmental) adds that element of unpredictability to the scenario. Friends or relatives may aid the hostage-taker, become hostages, or act as an audience for the hostage-taker who has suicidal tendencies. The way of handling such a request, rather than outright refusal, is to stall for time. However, there are exceptions, as with all guidelines. The Hanafi Muslim siege of Washington, D.C., in 1977, for example, was resolved only after three outside negotiators representing the Islamic faith were requested; they successfully negotiated the release of the hostages.[25]

Certain items are universally accepted as nonnegotiable. Obviously, you would not want to negotiate for new weapons, explosives, or more ammunition, which would increase the level of power or violence potential of the hostage-takers. Crelinsten and Szabo cite two additional nonnegotiable policies that are commonly adhered to by police negotiators throughout the world: (1) no exchange of hostages, and (2) no concessions without something in return.[26] Other nonnegotiable items are drugs, narcotics, and alcohol. A hostage situation becomes unpredictable and unduly dangerous when intoxicating substances are introduced. As with requests for others and shifts in location, the negotiator should stall for time.

The use of tricks and deceit by the negotiator during a hostage situation is yet another difficult management consideration. On the one hand, critics of the use of deception maintain that the negotiator must consider the long-term effects of dishonest negotiation because of widespread media reporting of the hostage incident. Then, hostage-takers involved in the next incident may not trust any negotiators, thereby reducing the probability of a peaceful resolution of the incident. On the other hand, tricks and deceit are viewed as viable strategies if they work and hostage lives are saved. Evidence indicates, however,

[25]Miron and Goldstein, *Hostage,* pp. 53–62.

[26]Ron A. Crelinsten and Denis Szabo, *Hostage Taking* (Massachusetts: Lexington Books, 1979), p. 53.

that tricks and deceit are likely to be more successful with psychotic and criminal hostage-takers than with fanatical and devoted political terrorists. The dilemma is a realistic one and ultimately the use of deception should be based on the circumstances of each individual hostage situation. Generally, the negotiator should avoid promising to meet demands he cannot deliver, especially if the hostage incident generates intense media coverage that is observed by future hostage-takers seeking to demonstrate the perfidy of a rival government or the treachery and brutality of the police.

Finally, a style of negotiation or overall hostage strategy based on mutual concession is recommended. After reviewing hundreds of hostage-taking incidents, three styles of negotiation have been observed: (1) win/lose, or agitation, (2) harmony, and (3) mutual concession. The agitation style forces the hostage-taker into a position where he has no other recourse but to harm the hostages. The negotiator who is more interested in harmony gives in easily, granting the demands of the hostage-taker. The preferred style is, of course, one based on compromise, problem solving, and mutual concession.

In sum, the few guidelines highlighted in this section point out the complexity of hostage negotiations. A hostage incident is more than a few "crazy people" seeking recognition. In effect, hostage incidents are contests of power between police and governments on the one hand and a variety of hostage-takers on the other hand, the latter representing criminals, political terrorists, and psychotics. The understanding of this power relationship should be an important element in formulating hostage-taking strategies by the police in order to cope with future hostage incidents.

Kidnapping and Terrorism

Moammar Gaddafi is not the only source of funding for international terrorist groups. The kidnapping of corporate executives has provided terrorist groups with a lucrative, low-risk source of revenues for the last 15 years. Wealthy businessmen have comprised 48 percent of all kidnap victims since 1970, and approximately $250 million in ransom has been paid by business firms to international terrorist groups.[27] Corporations almost always "buy back" their executives, no matter what the cost. For example, on December 6, 1973, Victor Samuelson, general manager of Exxon in Argentina, was kidnapped by the People's Revolutionary Army (ERP). The kidnapping was the beginning of five months of terror for Samuelson and Exxon. Exxon was told by ERP that if the ransom demands were not met, bombs would be placed at Exxon service stations throughout Argentina, other Exxon officials would be gunned down on the streets, and Samuelson would be killed. In the end, after the nightmarish negotiations for Samuelson's release, Exxon agreed to pay the

[27]Charles Russell, "Kidnapping as a Terrorist Tactic," in *Terrorism and Personal Protection,* ed. Brian M. Jenkins (Boston: Butterworth, 1985), p. 8.

ERP $14.2 million.[28] The ERP is an ultraleft terrorist organization formed in 1970.

By 1972 the ERP had developed into Latin America's most colorful and notorious terrorist organization. In February of 1971, the ERP successfully accomplished the largest bank robbery in the history of Argentina, obtaining $300,000. The ERP also created a "Robin Hood" image by seizing food trucks and clothing trailers and distributing the contents among the poor of Buenos Aires. An entire television station was overrun by ERP militants and the public was subjected to a 10-minute propaganda speech. The daring acts of terrorism of the ERP continue with the planned assassinations of Argentine military and political leaders. But the kidnapping of business executives netted the ERP funds far in excess of anything previously considered possible from bank robberies.[29]

Predictably, the notoriety and success of ERP bank robberies and kidnappings was a harbinger of things to come. Again, Argentina was the scene of another spectacular kidnapping that produced the largest recorded ransom payment in history. On September 16, 1974, two brothers, Juan and Jorge Born, heirs to the country's largest private industrial firm, were abducted by the Montoneros. The Montoneros used 19 terrorists to achieve the kidnapping on a busy Buenos Aires boulevard. The Born brothers were held for several months and released only after the completion of a very complicated process of negotiation. The ransom ultimately turned over to the Montoneros was a staggering $60 million.[30]

The Montoneros is the largest and most well known of all the Argentinian terrorist groups. The Montoneros first gained publicity by abducting and later killing the former president of Argentina, Pedro Aramburu, in May 1970. The political ideology supported by the Montoneros, like that of the ERP, is a mixture of socialist and Marxist ideas. In late 1976, the Montoneros announced the group would attempt to promote a popular war through the use of assassination, arson, sabotage, and kidnapping. To the developing countries and European socialists, the Montoneros presented themselves as the victims of military repression. In the hope of influencing western democracies, they even established aboveground offices in Rome and Paris with the money acquired from kidnapping victims.[31]

In fact, the terrorist kidnappings of wealthy corporate executives signal the beginning of terrorist insurgent movements. This has been the case in Central and Latin America. The tactics of kidnapping high-ranking corporate officials serve four important objectives for the newly emerging guerrilla organiza-

[28]*Wall Street Journal* (New York), December 2, 1983, p. 1.

[29]Peter Janke, *Guerrilla and Terrorist Organizations: A World Directory and Bibliography* (New York: Macmillan, 1983), pp. 428–30.

[30]Clutterbuck, *Kidnap and Ransom,* pp. 168–69.

[31]Janke, *Guerrilla and Terrorist Organizations,* pp. 424–26.

tion: (1) the acquisition of large sums of ransom money needed to finance the underground activities of the group, (2) the publicity generated by media exposure brings the group national and international recognition, (3) the ransom victim is often viewed as exploiting the Third World, thereby awakening the struggle between the "haves and have-nots," which translates into support for the terrorist group from the grass roots, and (4) the free enterprise economic system is weakened by intimidating foreign investors.

Although terrorist kidnapping was first introduced by Latin American insurgent groups, the tactic quickly spread to Western Europe and the Mideast. In Europe the Red Brigades, the ETA, and the Red Army Faction have repeatedly used kidnapping of nonbusiness targets to achieve a variety of political objectives. Rarely are nonbusiness targets kidnapped for a money ransom demand. Instead, the aim of the terrorist group is to force the state or a national government to: (1) release imprisoned terrorists, (2) publicize terrorist objectives, (3) humiliate the national government, and (4) change established social, political, or economic programs.

In order to accomplish these objectives, the selection of the hostage victim is of critical importance. The intended victim must be a well-known person of prestige, status, reputation, and a close political associate with the power elite. The abduction of Aldo Moro, a former Italian premier, or de Oriol y Urguijo, personal advisor to King Juan Carlos of Spain, represents the ideal type of hostage victim. In the absence of the ideal type, the abduction of a foreign diplomat can produce an equal amount of pressure on a national government. Therefore, it comes as no surprise to discover that nonbusiness kidnap targets are political leaders, foreign diplomats, ranking military or police officials, high-level government officials, and more recently, prominent academics and media personnel. Together, these target groups account for approximately 65 percent of all nonbusiness abductions since 1970. The remaining 35 percent include a wide variety of victims, including religious types, school administrators, personnel assigned to international organizations, students, sport celebrities, and "poor" people.[32]

At this point, to avoid confusion, let us consider the distinguishing differences between kidnapping and hostage-taking. In the world of terrorism and political violence, the distinction is often blurred. Nevertheless, we can identify some significant differences between the two concepts. The kidnapper most likely confines the victim in a secret location and makes some monetary ransom demands or the victim will be killed. Typically, the hostage-taker will openly confront military or police authorities. His or her location is known, and the ultimate objective is often maximum publicity for a political or religious cause. The hostage-takers' demands are designed to take full advantage of the media coverage of the hostage-taking incident. The hostage-taking

[32]Russell, "Kidnapping," p. 13.

drama is street theater. However, some incidents blend the elements of kidnapping and hostage taking.

The most notorious incident of this kind, which combined kidnapping with hostage seizure and hijacking, was the raid on the OPEC meeting in Vienna in December 1975, by an international band of terrorists led by Ilych Ramirez Sanchez, alias Carlos. Working with a joint team of terrorists composed of the Red Army Faction (RAF) and the Popular Front for the Liberation of Palestine (PFLP), Carlos held the oil ministers of all the mideastern oil-producing countries. The demands of the terrorists included several million dollars in ransom for the release of the oil ministers, a prepared propaganda message to be broadcast every 30 minutes denouncing the Zionist Israeli state and American imperialism and glorifying the Palestinian struggle, and a plan to transport hostages and hostage takers to a "friendly" mideast country. Eventually the terrorists were flown to Algeria with their hostages through a plan provided by the Austrian government. Once in Algeria, Carlos and his band collected the ransom money and the hostages were released. But, as Clutterbuck states, most certainly the objective sought by Carlos in the OPEC hostage incident was "exposure on world television."[33] Few other hostage-taking incidents have been so successful. The terrorists received the ransom demand, international recognition, and asylum in Algeria and later in Libya.

Russell argues that even though kidnappings have declined somewhat since 1979, they still remain an important terrorist tactic for obtaining operational funds.[34] Thus, corporate executives will continue to be the primary target of abduction, especially in Europe and Latin America. A single successful kidnapping operation can solve a terrorist group's financial problems for years to come. For example, in a series of kidnappings in El Salvador, a total of five executives with British, Japanese, Swedish, and Dutch firms were kidnapped for ransom between August 14 and December 8, 1978.[35] Known ransoms paid to the radical Marxist Armed Forces for National Resistance in El Salvador (FARN) for the release of the executives were $18 million. The ransom subsequently provided the expansion of the guerrilla efforts of FARN. Aside from the holding of corporate executives, other targets of opportunity have become more prevalent as corporations tighten their security measures. This being the case, what can the individual do to prepare for the sudden unpredictable captivity of the hostage-taking experience?

Surviving Hostage Situations

Past experience has shown that people who are prepared suffer the least physical abuse and emotional trauma when taken hostage. Even though every

---

[33]Clutterbuck, *Kidnap and Ransom,* p. 50.

[34]Russell, "Kidnapping," p. 20.

[35]Risks International, *Regional Risk Assessment: Latin America* (Alexandria, VA: Risks International, April 1979), p. 60.

hostage situation is somewhat different and every individual reacts differently, the following proposed guidelines may prove useful in surviving the growing threat of the sudden, unpredictable captivity of being held hostage. So, how does one prepare to be a hostage?

The most critical points of any type of hostage or kidnapping situation come at the moment of capture and release. The important thing is to remain calm and not to panic. During the capture phase of the incident, the hostage should avoid unnecessary or unexpected movements, crying out for help, or making loud noises. Obviously, the initial reactions of hostages are fear, disbelief, and shock. This fear must quickly be overcome so that the hostage can regain composure and recognize the reality of captivity. At the initial phase of captivity, should the hostage resist or surrender? Generally, this is a personal decision based on the circumstances and the amount of danger involved in trying to escape. Because of the uncertainty involved at the moment of capture, it is recommended that the hostage reassure the hostage-taker of his or her intention to cooperate. The potential hostage must also be psychologically prepared to cope with blindfolds, gags, being bound, and drugs. Blindfolds and hoods are used to disorient and confuse the hostage. Gags prevent talking or shouting out and being bound hand and foot prevents escape. Being blindfolded, gagged, and bound, the hostage then becomes a mere object, less than a human being, making it easier for the hostage taker to assault the hostage.

After the initial phase of captivity, the hostage must adjust to captivity. There are several recommendations: (1) exercise when possible and keep fit, (2) keep a sense of humor by remembering that others have survived similar or worse situations, (3) try to establish a routine; this gives the hostage the feeling of control over the environment, (4) try to keep a sense of time orientation by inwardly recording time, place, and routine of the hostage-takers, (5) if singled out, try to relate to the hostage-taker as a human being—for example, mention personal events, emphasizing children and family, (6) do not let hostage-takers dehumanize you, (7) when physically beaten, do not be a hero; show pain; if you have any medical problems, notify the hostage-takers immediately, (8) if interrogated by the hostage-takers, tell the truth; avoid embellishments that will cause damage later in the situation, and (9) do not try to escape unless the probability of success is high.

During the capture phase, the captors may also heighten fear by loading and unloading weapons in the presence of hostages, by staging mock executions, by dramatic displays of temper, by physical abuse, and by continually threatening to kill the hostages. But time is in the favor of the hostages. The longer the hostage situation continues, the greater the chance hostages will be released unharmed. Passage of time without rescue or release is quite depressing. To overcome this depression, the hostage can establish rapport with the hostage-taker but should not fake interest in support for the hostage-taker's cause. Terrorist hostage-takers will use that support for propaganda purposes.

The most dangerous phase of any hostage-taking situation is during a negotiated release or a tactical rescue attempt. Seventy-five percent of all casualties occur during release and rescue operations. If a negotiated release is agreed upon, hostage-takers may be nervous and fearful of a double cross—anxious to escape capture and punishment. Therefore, hostages must not act in any manner that would endanger their lives, such as an angry outburst toward the hostage-takers. In the case of a tactical rescue attempt, hostages must avoid panic and remain as calm as possible. The tactical rescue is based largely on surprise and shock. During the rescue phase, hostages and hostage-takers will experience momentary panic and fear. Confusion may also result from gunfire, explosions, and tactical team members shouting instructions to both hostages and hostage-takers. The hostage must avoid the impulse to flee during the rescue operation. Hostages can easily be mistaken for hostage-takers by rescue team members. The safest response for hostages is to immediately drop to the ground and lie as flat as possible. In later chapters we will discuss several hostage rescue attempts, some successful and others not so successful.

The experience of being a hostage does not end with the resolution of the situation either by negotiated release or tactical rescue. Generally, the victimization hostages live through can be either uncomplicated or pathological. Following the hostage crisis, many hostages develop a variety of psychological problems, including nightmares, phobias, depression, and startle reactions. For example, five years after the Iranian hostage episode, at least one-half of the American hostages reported still having nightmares about their captivity in Iran.[36] A hostage may not suffer depression until after the situation has ended. The intense media coverage of hostage incidents makes celebrities of some hostages. This certainly was the case during the 17-day captivity of TWA 847 in June 1985. However, as the celebrity status begins to recede, depression may occur. Ochberg identifies additional psychological manifestations of post-release hostages, including paranoid reactions, obsessions, idiosyncratic difficulties, and the Stockholm Syndrome.[37]

For some people (high-risk corporate executives, diplomats, and ranking military personnel) preparing for captivity is just as important as preparing tighter security measures to avoid being captured. Therefore, potential targets should realize what their own instinctive reactions will be during captivity, what hostage-takers or kidnappers might expect hostages to do, and what hostages can do to overcome the psychological and physical pressures of being held captive.

In sum, the psychological literature identifies five states of hostage reaction to captivity. The five states can be categorized into a normal response and

[36]*Sacramento Bee,* January 19, 1986, sec. A, p. 1.

[37]Frank Ochberg, "Hostage Victims," in *Terrorism: Interdisciplinary Perspectives,* eds. Burr Eichelman, David Soskis, and William Reid (Washington, D.C.: American Psychiatric Association, 1983), p. 86.

TABLE 6-2   Hostage Event

NORMAL RESPONSE	PATHOLOGICAL RESPONSE
Outcry Fear, sadness, anger, rage	**Overwhelmed** Emotional reaction of panic and fear
Denial "This cannot be happening to me"	**Extreme Avoidance** Using drugs and alcohol to avoid pain
Intrusion Voluntary thoughts of the event	**Flooded States** Disturbing nightmares and thoughts of the event
Working Through Facing reality of situation	**Psychosomatic Responses** Developing new ailments
Completion Going on with life	**Character Distortions** Long-term distortions of ability

a pathological response. The emotional impact of being held hostage has a devastating effect on some hostages—they never outlive the experience of having been held hostage. (See Table 6-2.)

CONCLUSIONS

Hostage-taking and kidnapping will continue to escalate because of the proven benefits of intense publicity and as a cost-effective method of extorting a ransom. Kidnapping and hostage-taking do work. It works for criminals except in those countries where the police are efficient and trusted by the populace. In recent years, for example, Italy has reported the kidnapping of 334 people by criminal gangs and ransoms of $185 million paid for the release of the victims.[38] It works for terrorists except where states are repressive. Hundreds of people have been kidnapped by terrorist groups and millions of dollars have been paid in ransom by businesses and private citizens. But above all, the taking of hostages brings terrorists, psychotics, and criminals publicity and recognition. For example, little was known of Palestinians, South Moluccans, or Croatians until their criminal acts of hostage-taking filled the media. One factor that could disrupt the trend of hostage-taking and extortionate kidnappings is to establish stringent security measures. More effective security measures should deter and reduce attacks on corporations, embassies, airlines, and individuals by raising the potential risks and the costs to hostage-takers in terms of death or imprisonment. Another factor that could impinge on the escalation of hostage-taking and kidnapping is the universal application of a

[38]Clutterbuck, *Kidnap and Ransom,* pp. 158–64.

no-ransom policy. If a policy of no ransom or no concessions were uniformly applied without major exceptions, then the probability of reducing hostage episodes might rise dramatically.

The possibility also exists that terrorists or psychotics could take mass hostages involving not just individual victims or corporations but the governments they represent. Nuclear threats by terrorists against major cities is not an unlikely scenario confined to paperback novels. Another reasonable conclusion is that as hostage-taking increases, governments will be forced to devote sizable resources and money to the protection of key communication networks, nuclear plants, and energy systems. Finally, the need to improve negotiation skills and tactical responses is imperative if we expect to effectively manage the hostage crisis. The next chapter will examine the most common act of terrorism in the world today—indiscriminate bombing.

REVIEW QUESTIONS

1. Why was the Munich Olympics a turning point in hostage negotiation strategies and tactical response?
2. Describe the Stockholm Syndrome.
3. How would you go about formulating a hostage-negotiating strategy?
4. How can you distinguish between hostage-negotiating strategies and policy guidelines?
5. Describe the hostage-negotiating style you would recommend in a political terrorist-hostage situation.
6. What distinguishes kidnapping and hostage-taking?
7. Identify the following:
   a. ERP
   b. Montoneros
   c. fedayeen
   d. OPEC
   e. Lindbergh Law
8. Develop your own typology of hostage-takers.
9. How should police administrators meet the challenge of increased incidents of hostage-taking and extortionate kidnapping?
10. List the objectives of hostage takers and kidnappers.
11. How would you prepare yourself to survive a hostage-taking incident?

SEVEN

CONTEMPORARY TERRORISM AND BOMBING

CHAPTER OBJECTIVES

The study of this chapter will enable you to:
- Identify the effects of an explosion
- Explore the historical antecedents of explosive materials
- Distinguish between low- and high-velocity explosives
- Describe the phases of blast/pressure
- Examine several vehicle bomb attack methods
- Outline a law enforcement strategy to cope with vehicle bombs
- Explore incidence of aircraft bombings
- Develop a security program to prevent injuries due to mail bombs

INTRODUCTION

In spite of the spectacular nature of hostage-taking incidents, nothing personifies contemporary terrorism more than indiscriminate bombing. Certainly everyone is familiar with the popular caricature of the nineteenth-century anarchist/terrorist, dressed in a long, black coat, broad-brimmed hat with eyes bulging, about to throw a round, black bomb with a fuse extending from the top into a crowd of unsuspecting victims. Unfortunately, the terrorist using the bomb is still the most important strategic attack method of modern terrorism. Slightly more than one-half of all recorded international terrorist incidents in 1984 were bombings.[1] Between 1977 and 1983, the U.S. State Department affirms that 63.5 percent of all recorded terrorist incidents were bombings.[2] According to Risks International, 10,107 terrorist bombings occurred worldwide between 1970 and 1984, recording 3,407 deaths, 15,111 injuries, and over $473 million in property damage.[3] Regardless of whose statistics we use, little doubt remains that bombing is the terrorist weapon of choice. Several factors have contributed to the escalation of bombing as a preferred tactic by today's terrorist groups.

First, bombings are the most effective method of launching a terrorist attack. Marighella writes, "Terrorism is accomplished by placing a bomb . . . so that its destructive power causes an irreparable loss of life to the *enemy* (my emphasis); committed with extreme cold-bloodedness, while acting with bold decisiveness."[4] Indeed, terrorist bombings are lethal, indiscriminate, and cold-blooded. Several examples illustrate the point. In September 1986, fourteen terrorist bombs indiscriminately exploded in French cities, killing 15; the U.S. embassies in Portugal, Peru, and Tokyo were bombed in March of 1986. In April 1986, a Berlin disco was bombed, killing two Americans; and a midair terrorist explosion aboard a TWA jetliner killed four Americans. In June 1986, Tamil terrorists in Sri Lanka randomly bombed trains, busses, and busy market plazas, killing more than 85 innocent victims. But the most devastating bombings over the last 4 years have occurred in Lebanon with the introduction of the deadly car bomb. Thousands of Lebanese civilians and militia have been killed by vehicle bombs. Nothing so symbolizes the Lebanese civil war as the ubiquitous car bomb.

Second, explosives and bomb technology are easily accessible to terrorist groups at a relatively low financial cost. In fact, several "mayhem" manuals are available, which graphically illustrate the simplicity of bomb-making.[5] Third, although the making of clandestine explosive devices requires some de-

---

[1] U.S. Department of State, *Patterns of Global Terrorism: 1984,* (Washington, D.C.: U.S. Government Printing Office, 1985), p. 8.

[2] U.S. Department of State, *Terrorist Bombings* (Washington, D.C.: U.S. Government Printing Office, 1983), p. 1.

[3] Risks International, *Terrorism 1970-1984* (Alexandria, VA: Risks International, Inc., unpublished report, 1985), p. 3.

[4] Carlos Marighella, *The Terrorist Classic: Manual of The Urban Guerrilla,* trans. Gene Hanrahan (Chapel Hill, N.C.: Documentary Pub., 1985), p. 84.

[5] William Powell, *Anarchist Cookbook* (New York: L. Stuart, 1971); Andrew MacDonald, *The Turner Diaries* (Arlington, VA: National Vanguard Books, 1985); Alberto Bayo, *150 Questions For A Guerrilla* (Colorado: Paladin Press, 1975); Joseph P. Stoffel, *Explosives and Homemade Bombs* (Springfield, Ill.: Charles C. Thomas, 1972).

gree of technical expertise, the entire process can easily be handled by one person. Fourth, bombings involve far less risk to the terrorist bomber since improved timing devices allow sufficient opportunity for the terrorist to escape detection or injury. Finally, the larger the terrorist explosion, the more vigorous the media coverage. Media interest is in "good" pictures. Indeed, bombings provide graphic scenes of mayhem, mutilation, and death.

The focus of this chapter is on types of explosives, effects of explosions, and terrorist attack methodologies. The purpose of the chapter is to provide criminal justice students with a general understanding of the nature of explosions and explosives. But first, a brief revew of the historical development of explosive devices is relevant.

Historical Perspective

The oldest known explosive and propellant is black powder. As with most discoveries that are centuries old, the name of the inventor and even the country of its origin remain in dispute. The principal claimants for the discovery of black powder are the Chinese, the Romans, the Hindus, the Greeks, the Arabs, the English, and the Germans. For example, the Chinese and the Romans of the fourth century were familiar with black powder pyrotechnic displays, while the ancient Greeks manufactured an incendiary composition, similar to that of black powder, referred to as "Greek Fire."

In England, Roger Bacon is generally credited with the invention of black powder in the thirteenth century. However, Bacon apparently was not aware of the projecting qualities of black powder although he was aware that black powder was unstable, made a thunderous noise when exploded, and terrified people. By the fourteenth century, Berthold Schwarz, a German friar, used black powder as a propelling agent; he is generally acknowledged as the inventor of firearms. Eventually, in Europe, black powder became known as Schwarzpulver. Until the seventeenth century, black powder was used as a propellant charge. Cannonballs, for example, were made of solid pieces of stone or iron. But the development of hollow cast iron balls introduced the use of black powder as an explosive filler, thus introducing crude bombs that could be thrown or used as mines. These bombs could easily be ignited by a time fuse.

Laqueur records several incidents where black powder bombs were used with great effect, especially in the terrorist Fenian bombing of Clerkenwell Prison in 1867 in which 12 persons were killed and 120 injured.[6] The unpredictable nature of black powder, however, made it extremely dangerous to handle, and many people blew themselves up while making bombs. Terrorist bombing was made much easier with the invention of nitroglycerine and dynamite.

Nitroglycerine, the basis of high explosives, was discovered in 1847 by

[6]Walter Laqueur, *Terrorism* (Boston: Little, Brown & Co., 1977), p. 92.

an Italian chemistry professor at the University of Turin.[7] But the discovery of nitroglycerine remained more or less a scientific curiosity until 1867, when the eminent scientist Alfred Nobel mixed nitroglycerine with an absorbent material, thus making it safer to handle. Nobel's epoch-making discovery of dynamite ushered in a new era of high explosives. Dynamite was widely believed to be the ultimate weapon, and anarchist/revolutionary groups of the period based their whole strategy on its use. However, terrorists, anarchists, and revolutionaries quickly discovered that they could not bomb their way into the hearts and minds of the people. The exaggerated hope of dynamite as the ultimate weapon was not fulfilled. Clearly, the dynamite bomb was not the all-destroying weapon of the future; but it had become a symbol of fear and intimidation. Dynamite continues to be one of the most popular high explosives used by modern terrorist groups.

With the introduction of military explosives shortly before the outbreak of World War I, the technological development of high explosives accelerated. Military explosives differ from commercial explosives such as black powder and dynamite in several respects. Military explosives: (1) have a much greater shattering effect, (2) have high rates of detonation, and (3) are relatively insensitive to impact, heat, shock, and friction. Military explosives also must be usable underwater and be of convenient size, shape and weight for combat use. The most widely used military explosive is TNT (trinitrotoluene). TNT is widely used as a main charge in aerial bombs, artillery shells, and mortar rounds. TNT cannot be detonated by heat, shock, or friction, as black powder or dynamite can.

Another popular military explosive, discovered during World War II and in wide use today, is the mysterious Composition 4 (C-4). C-4 is the notorious "plastic" explosive, a yellow, putty-like substance that closely resembles children's play dough. C-4 is easy and safe to handle and can be molded into a variety of shapes. It has no odor, has a greater shattering effect than TNT, and detonates at a much higher rate.[8] Yet another well-known military explosive is pentaerythritol-tetranitrate, commonly known as PETN.[9] PETN is a high explosive in linear form that has a variety of military as well as some commercial uses. PETN closely resembles ordinary clothesline and is also referred to as detacord, primex, or primacord. Like C-4, PETN is resistant to heat, shock, and friction.

The ample range of explosive materials now available to contemporary terrorist groups has produced a shock wave of worldwide bombings. The commercial explosives, black powder and dynamite, can be easily purchased or stolen from construction or mining sites while military explosives are provided

---

[7]Arthur P. Van Gelder and Hugo Schlatter, *History of the Explosives Industry in American* (New York: Arno Press, 1972), p. 315.

[8]Robert R. Lenz, *Explosives and Bomb Disposal Guide* (Springfield, Ill.: Charles C. Thomas, 1971), p. 56.

[9]H. J. Yallop, *Explosion Investigation* (Edinburgh, Scotland: Scottish Academic Press, 1980), p. 90.

to terrorist groups by "terrorist" nations such as Iran, Libya, or Syria.[10] New types of delayed fuses are also available to terrorist groups. These include electrically fired devices and bombs fired by pressure, by chemical methods, and by X-ray–sensitive fuses. Even the most powerful bombs can be easily concealed in letters, parcels, shopping bags, suitcases or vehicles. The technological advances in the manufacture of explosives has produced limitless opportunities for today's terrorist bombers. But the greatest threat of terrorist bombing comes from the very real possibility of nuclear terrorism. Jenkins warns the international community that nuclear blackmail by terrorists is the future threat to democratic nations.[11]

Several future nuclear terrorist scenarios have been identified. First, terrorists now have the technology to construct a fission-type nuclear device. Second, terrorists could contaminate a city with nuclear waste material by detonating a nuclear device in midair and allowing the wind to let the radiation drift over the target. Third, a terrorist group could seize a nuclear facility and cause a meltdown. Finally, a nuclear facility could be attacked by long-range missiles or mortars, causing widespread nuclear fallout. Theoretically possible, these nuclear scenarios pose a serious threat to the entire world.[12]

As the technology of bombing has become more complicated, terrorist groups have greatly increased their technical expertise and the competency required to handle sophisticated explosive material. When manufactured explosives are not available, the ingredients necessary to produce an improvised explosive device are easily obtained. The ingredients required to construct homemade bombs are virtually unlimited and can easily be obtained in hardware or drug stores without arousing much suspicion. Such seemingly innocuous items as starch, flour, sugar, and ammonia-nitrate fertilizers can be treated to become effective explosives. But still, the most widely used main charge explosive is black powder. The black powder pipe bomb is the most popular type of clandestine explosive device used in the United States. This next section will review the three primary effects of an explosion.

Effects of an Explosion

When an explosive is detonated, the black powder, stick of dynamite, block of TNT, or chunk of C-4 is instantaneously converted from a solid into a rapidly expanding mass of gases. The detonation will produce several secondary effects, but the greatest amount of damage is produced by three primary effects: fragmentation, blast pressure, and secondary fires, as illustrated in Figure 7-1.

[10]U.S. Department of State, *Terrorist Bombings,* p. 4.

[11]Brian Jenkins, "Terrorism and Nuclear Safeguards Issue," *Rand Paper Series P-5611* (Santa Monica: Rand Corp., 1984), p. 1.

[12]Neil C. Livingstone and Terrell E. Arnold, eds., *Fighting Back: Winning the War Against Terrorism* (Lexington, Mass.: D.C. Heath, 1986), pp. 32–33.

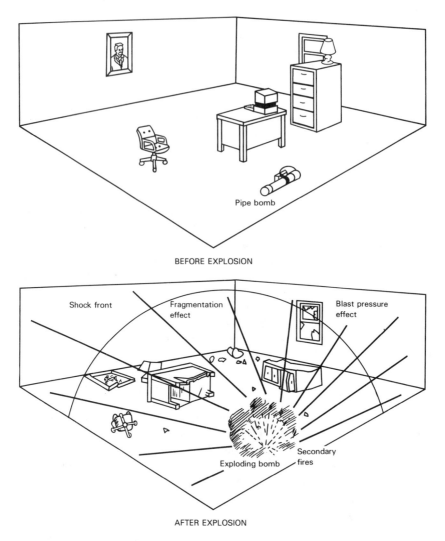

Pipe bomb

BEFORE EXPLOSION

Shock front   Fragmentation effect   Blast pressure effect

Secondary fires

Exploding bomb

AFTER EXPLOSION

FIGURE 7-1   Fragmentation, Blast Pressure, and Secondary Fires produced by an Explosion

Fragmentation.   A simple fragmentation bomb is a quantity of explosive filler placed inside a length of pipe capped at each end with a piece of time fuse used for detonation. Once detonated, the explosion will produce a number of shattered fragments of the pipe propelled outward from the point of detonation at extremely high velocity. These small, high-velocity fragments reach a speed of approximately 2700 feet per second.[13] The bomb fragments

[13]Yallop, *Explosion Investigation,* pp. 75–77.

travel in a straight line until they lose velocity and fall to the earth or become embedded in an object. In order to increase the number of small, high-velocity fragments flying through the air, the inside of the pipe is often filled with glass, nails, bullets, or staples, thereby increasing the number of people killed and injured. Another fiendish explosive device used by terrorist groups to increase the amount of fragmentation, or *shrapnel,* is one in which a couple of sticks of dynamite has a two-inch layer of nails or staples taped on the outside. This type of device is referred to as an IRA nail bomb. Figure 7-2 illustrates the typical pipe bomb and IRA nail bomb.

However, the most destructive fragmentation terrorist explosive device is the vehicle bomb. The configuration of a vehicle bomb is limited only by the imagination of the bomber. Whether a car, van, or truck is used, the consequences are overwhelming. Not only does the explosion create fragments from the vehicle, but in many cases the vehicle is loaded with bullets, scrap metal, or a large quantity of nails to increase the amount of fragmentation. Typically, vehicle bombs contain high explosives such as dynamite, TNT, or "plastic." For example, the FBI estimates that the truck driven into the Marine compound in Beirut in October 1983 contained approximately 12,000 pounds of TNT.[14] The explosion collapsed a four-story building, left a crater approximately 30 feet deep by 40 feet wide, and killed 241 Marines as they lay sleeping in their bunks. Despite injuries created by the fragmentation effect, the blast pressure effect can also contribute to increased casualties.

FIGURE 7-2   Black Powder Pipe Bomb and Dynamite Nail Bomb

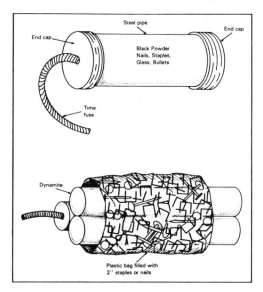

[14]*New York Times,* October 23, 1983, sec. 1, p. 1.

Blast pressure.   The detonation of an explosive charge produces very hot expanding gases. These gases exert pressures of approximately 700 tons per square inch and rush away from the point of detonation at velocities up to 7000 miles per hour. This mass of expanding gases travels outward in a concentric pattern from the point of origin of the explosion like an immense wave, destroying any object in its path. Similar to a giant ocean wave rushing to meet the beach, the further the pressure wave travels from the point of origin of the explosion, the less power it has until it disappears completely. This wave of pressure is called the blast pressure effect of an explosion. There are two distinct phases to the blast pressure effect: (1) positive pressure phase, and (2) negative pressure phase.[15]

The positive pressure wave is formed at the moment of detonation when the surrounding atmosphere is compressed into a rapidly expanding circle. The leading edge of the positive pressure wave is called the shock front. As the shock front begins to move outward from the point of detonation, closely followed by the positive pressure wave, it introduces a sudden, crushing one-two punch to any object in its path. Therefore, when the positive pressure wave struck, for example, the walls of the Marine compound, the shock front delivered a massive blow to the building followed instantly by the positive pressure phase. The shock front shattered the walls of the compound while the positive pressure waves violently pushed the walls outward in a radiating pattern away from the point of detonation. The entire process of shock front and positive pressure waves lasts only a fraction of a second. The positive pressure waves will continue to dissipate until all the wave's power is expended.

The negative pressure phase occurs as the outward compression of air by the positive pressure phase causes a partial vacuum at the point of detonation. The partial vacuum causes the displaced air to reverse its movement and rush inward to fill the void left by the positive pressure phase. The displaced air has mass and power as it returns toward the point of origin of the explosion. Even though the negative pressure phase is not as powerful as the positive pressure phase, it still has great velocity. In comparative terms, the positive pressure wave is comparable to a hurricane while the negative pressure phase can be compared to a high wind.

As the displaced air rushes toward the point of origin or detonation, it will strike and move objects in its path of destruction. For example, when negative pressure waves struck the already-damaged Marine compound, it caused additional portions of the battered building to topple. However, in the negative pressure phase, objects are pulled toward the center of detonation. The negative pressure phase lasts about three times longer than the positive pressure phase and is less powerful in its destruction.

---

[15]Charles L. Roblee and Allen McKechnie, *The Investigation of Fires* (Englewood Cliffs, N.J.: Prentice-Hall, 1981), p. 98.

Secondary fires.   The final effect produced by an explosion is the secondary fires, or thermal effect. The secondary fires created by the detonation of low- or high-velocity explosives vary greatly. At the instant of detonation, there is a bright flash, or fireball, that often causes a fire. Only when highly combustible materials are near the point of detonation will secondary fires erupt. For example, if a pipe bomb containing five pounds of black powder is detonated inside a building, the fires generally result from ruptured fuel lines or shorted electrical circuits. Generally, secondary fires cause the least amount of damage of the three primary detonation effects. The next section will clarify the distinction between low- and high-velocity explosives.

Velocity and Explosives

The most widely acclaimed system for the classification of explosives is according to the rate of velocity or detonation of explosion. Two major groups of explosives have been identified: (1) low-velocity explosives, and (2) high-velocity explosives.

Low-velocity explosives have rates of detonation below 3000 feet per second. For example, the most popular low-velocity explosive in use today is black powder, which has a velocity rating of approximately 1312 feet per second.[16] By comparison, straight dynamite, which is at the low end of high-velocity explosives, has a velocity rating of between 7000 and 18,000 feet per second. The primary use of low-velocity explosives is as a propellant. The expanding gases of a low-velocity explosive such as black powder has a pushing effect rather than the shattering effect of high-velocity explosives. Low-velocity explosives, i.e., black powder, gun powder, or smokeless powder, are used in a variety of legitimate ways such as the manufacture of fireworks, flares, sporting propellants, blasting and mining operations, and the construction of safety fuses.

Black powder is a mechanical mixture of three common ingredients: (1) potassium nitrate, or saltpeter, (2) charcoal or carbon, and (3) sulphur. The explosive characteristics of black powder occur only when the three ingredients are thoroughly mixed together. There are several recipes for the making of black powder. However, the most widely accepted formula is 75 percent saltpeter, 15 percent charcoal, and 10 percent sulfur. The composition of black powder has changed little since it was introduced in the thirteenth century in Europe. Black powder can also be found in a range of colors, from black to gray to brown. In addition, the form of black powder may differ: the grains range from very fine to very coarse. The size of the grains controls the burning speed of black powder; large grains burn more slowly than smaller grains, fine grains burn more rapidly and explode more quickly. Thus, the fine grain black powders are preferred by terrorists in making homemade pipe bombs.

[16]Van Gelden and Schlatter, *History of Explosives Industry,* p. 281.

Black powder is also one of the most hazardous low-velocity explosives. It is easily ignited and can explode, when not confined, for no apparent reason. It is susceptible to friction, heat, and static electricity. Black powder fires and explosions can easily be initiated by static electrical sparks. Therefore, police officers and other criminal justice personnel working with black powder should wear self-grounding shoes and static-free clothing and work with wooden tools. Additionally, unlike other explosives, black powder does not deteriorate with age.

As previously stated, the black powder pipe bomb is the most widely used clandestine explosive device in the United States, and a number of people have blown themselves up while attempting to make the device. For instance, in 1982, 35 percent of all recorded injuries in the United States due to bombings involved the persons who made the bombs.[17] Bombs show no allegiance to their makers. In sum, black powder is an extremely unpredictable low-velocity explosive that should be handled with extreme care.

The most widely used high-velocity explosive is dynamite, which is a combination of liquid nitroglycerine, oxidizers, and an absorbent material. Dynamite is relatively easy to obtain in the United States either by theft or through legal purchase. Consequently, it is preferred by terrorist and criminal bombers. Commercial dynamites differ widely in their strength and sensitivity. Straight dynamite, for example, is a mixture of liquid nitroglycerine, sodium nitrate, which supplies the oxygen for complete combustion, and wood pulp or ground meal to absorb the shock of the nitroglycerine. The strength of commercial straight dynamite is determined by the percentage of nitroglycerine by weight in the dynamite formula. For example, a 60-percent dynamite means the dynamite contains 60 percent nitroglycerine and is quite powerful. When detonated, dynamite gives off a gray-white smoke. Dynamite is usually found in stick form, wrapped in colored waxpaper, but is available in a variety of sizes, shapes, strengths, and packages. In addition to straight dynamites, ammonia dynamites, gelatin dynamites, and ammonia-gelatin dynamites are in wide use today in commercial operations.[18]

Other high-velocity explosives are manufactured for military use. These include TNT, C-4, and PETN. The TNT recovered by law enforcement personnel generally comes in the form of $\frac{1}{4}$-, $\frac{1}{2}$-, or 1-pound blocks. After TNT is exposed to sunlight, its light-yellow to light-brown color gradually turns to dark brown. TNT gives off a dirty gray smoke when detonated.

Composition 4 (C-4) is an improved version of Composition 3 (C-3). C-3 was developed for the Korean War but had a tendency to be brittle and break up. C-3 was difficult to handle in hot or cold environments. Subsequently, C-4 was developed for the Vietnam War. C-4 contains 90 percent of the explosive

---

[17]U.S. Bureau of Alcohol, Tobacco, and Firearms, *Explosives Incidents 1982* (Washington, D.C.: U.S. Government Printing Office, 1983), p. 6.

[18]Van Gelden and Schlatter, *History,* pp. 403–416.

TABLE 7-1 Types of Explosives

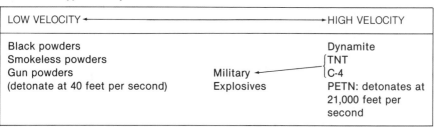

LOW VELOCITY ←		→ HIGH VELOCITY
Black powders Smokeless powders Gun powders (detonate at 40 feet per second)	Military ← Explosives	Dynamite [TNT [C-4 PETN: detonates at 21,000 feet per second

compound RDX, has no odor, and is white to light tan in color. Table 7-1 summarizes the types of explosives most commonly used by modern terrorist groups and criminal bombers.

Now that we have identified the effects of an explosion and the types of explosive materials, our attention turns to the diverse and innovative attack methodologies of modern terrorist groups and criminal bombers.

Vehicle Bombs

The use of a vehicle as a bomb delivery system is not new, but it has become the tactic most preferred by such terrorist groups as the IRA and various Mideast factions. Typically, the types of vehicles used to "deliver" explosive materials have been cars and vans. However, with the escalation of terrorism, explosive devices have also been planted on railway cars, busses, and airplanes to create increased casualties and to attract greater media attention.

The attack methodologies used to date by terrorists and criminal bombers include the following: (1) placing explosive materials on or in a car to kill the occupants, (2) the use of a vehicle as a launching system for rocket-propelled munitions, (3) the use of a vehicle as a booby trap or antipersonnel device to ambush law enforcement personnel, members of the military, or bomb disposal experts, (4) the use of a hostage for the transportation and delivery of explosives, (5) the use of a vehicle as a fragmentation device when a large amount of explosives is used, (6) the use of multiple vehicle bombs in a coordinated terrorist strike, and (7) the use of a vehicle in a suicide, or "kamikaze," attack. All these methods are used by terrorist groups today, but the trend seems to be toward the indiscriminate car bomb, loaded with explosives, parked on a busy commercial street with the purpose of killing a large number of innocent bystanders. A review of car-bomb attack methods follows.

Historically, car bombs have been used for the purpose of killing the occupants. The car served merely as another location for the act of murder. The motives for such killings were no different than other types of murders that were committed with guns, knives, or poisons. These motives included retaliation, revenge, anger, suicide, financial gain, or hate-love triangles. The procedure for many of these car bombings was to place 2 to 5 pounds of dynamite under the hood on the left side of the engine, under the front seat, on the gas tank, under the dashboards, or any place on the car that would have the greatest killing effect on the intended target.[19]

Organized crime figures of the 1920s, 1930s and even the 1980s are notorious for using car bombs to intimidate rival gangs and to eliminate competition. The practice is still used today. In one incident in 1985, a car bomb was used to murder a government witness who agreed to testify against organized crime figures in a Chicago gambling case.

Likewise, hundreds of accounts exist in which car bombs were used in domestic arguments. In one case, known as the "baby food bombing," the bomber placed two explosive devices contained in baby food jars under the front seat of his spouse's car. The jars were wired to the car's ignition system. Brodie maintains that the most effective place to hide a bomb is under the driver's seat, which is also the most common area for bombs to be placed in domestic quarrels.[20]

Car bombs have also been used in the selective assassination of political figures throughout the world. For example, Orlando Letelier, the former Chilean ambassador to the United States, was killed by a remote-controlled bomb as he drove through a quiet residential street in Washington, D.C. The bomb, a 1.5-pound mixture of TNT and plastic explosive, was fastened to the undercarriage of Letelier's car. The explosion killed Letelier and two passengers as they unsuspectingly drove to work.[21]

Another fairly common terrorist bomb attack method is to place an explosive charge inside a vehicle and park the vehicle along the route of the intended victim. Using a remote control switch, the terrorist bomber needs only await the arrival of the intended victim. When the victim is within range, a signal is transmitted to the explosive charge, causing detonation. The remote-controlled car bomb is a popular Provisional IRA tactic.

On August 27, 1979, 18 British paratroopers were killed by a cleverly planned double car bombing on the border between Northern Ireland and the Republic of Ireland. A vehicle containing 1100 pounds of explosives was parked inconspicuously on a country road. As a British troop convoy passed the vehicle, the PIRA bombers detonated the bomb by remote control. Ten British soldiers were killed, and the force of the blast hurled their vehicle 50 feet into the air. British reinforcements quickly arrived at the scene, and a second 800-pound bomb was detonated remotely, killing another eight British paratroopers. The use of two explosive devices in conjunction is a frequently

---

[19]Thomas G. Brodie, *Bombs and Bombings* (Springfield, Ill: Charles C. Thomas, 1972), p. 92.

[20]Ibid., p. 98.

[21]John Dinges and Saul Landau, *Assassination on Embassy Row* (New York: Pantheon, 1980), pp. 2–15.

used PIRA tactic. This PIRA attack inflicted the heaviest loss of life on British soliders since 1921, when 35 British troopers were killed in an ambush by Irish Republican rebels.[22]

A second variation of the vehicle bomb attack method is to use the vehicle as a munition launching system. This terrorist strategy is used to fire rockets and mortars at the intended target; again, a favorite strategy of the Provos.

A stolen flatbed truck that concealed a makeshift mortar-launching system welded to the truck's frame was used by the PIRA to attack a heavily fortified police barracks in Newry, Northern Ireland.[23] Nine shells were launched from a distance of 250 yards away, scoring a direct hit on the Royal Ulster Constabulary police barracks, killing 9 police officers and seriously wounding 37 others. Police in Northern Ireland suspected the mortars were fired by remote control. The stolen flatbed truck had been parked on a hill overlooking the rear entrance of the police barracks, making an easy target for the PIRA bombers. Mortar attacks by the PIRA are quite frequent in Northern Ireland but in the past have been notoriously inaccurate. For example, the PIRA fired 18 mortar rounds from a flatbed truck at a police station and training center in Belfast.[24] The mortar rounds fell harmlessly and no one was seriously injured. Such attacks, whether successful or not, receive significant media attention, again publicizing the cause of the Republican movement and the "courageousness" of the Irish Republican Army.

The third variation of the vehicle bomb attack method involves the use of the bomb-ladened vehicle to ambush law enforcement and military personnel. The ambush attack method usually involves a stolen car or rental vehicle expertly wired with a remote-control firing device. The vehicle bomb is then parked near a police station house or along routes frequented by police or military personnel. As security vehicles approach, the vehicle bomb is detonated without warning, usually killing the unsuspecting security officers.

In July of 1986 the PIRA detonated a booby-trapped truck in Belfast, Northern Ireland, while four British security officers were inspecting it, killing two and seriously wounding the others. Hundreds of British soldiers and police officers of the Royal Ulster Constabulary have been killed by such devices. The tactic has also been used recently in Spain, Greece, Australia, and the United States. For example, on July 27, 1986, Basque separatists or terrorists in Spain killed two police officers with a remote-control vehicle bomb as they were about to investigate a complaint of a suspicious vehicle.[25] In Athens, Greece, a car bomb was detonated by remote control as a police bus was passing, killing 2 and wounding 14. In Melbourne, Australia, two rental cars packed with explosives were parked at the front entrance to police headquar-

[22]*The London Times,* August 28, 1979, p. 1.

[23]*San Francisco Chronicle,* March 2, 1985, sec. A, p. 8.

[24]*Sacramento Bee,* September 5, 1985, sec. A, p. 12.

[25]*New York Times,* July 27, 1986, sec. 1, p. 2.

ters. The first car bomb was detonated, causing little damage and few injuries; however, the second car bomb was detonated 15 minutes later after a large crowd had gathered at the scene of the first bomb. This second car bomb, or double bomb, caused many casualties, including the serious wounding of 15 police officers. In the United States the booby-trapped car bomb has also been used by the FALN. In one such incident a number of police officers and fire-fighters were injured by an exploding van while responding to a fire alarm. Eyewitness accounts indicate that the van was parked and then set on fire. As firefighters attempted to put out the flames, the van was detonated by a remote-control firing device. The FALN later claimed credit for the blast in a tele-phone call to the *New York Times.*

The fourth type of vehicle attack bomb uses the vehicle to deliver or gain access to the intended target. The PIRA was the first terrorist group to popularize this method, which uses the following strategy. In order to pene-trate security checkpoints and gain a closer position to the intended target, the PIRA would kidnap a close family member of a legitimate employee (such as a government employee or prison guard) of the bombing target. The legitimate employee would then be instructed to deliver the bomb vehicle to his place of employment. If the employee refused, then the family member being held hos-tage would be threatened with injury or death. With few choices, the employee would deliver the explosive device using his legitimate identification to pene-trate security checkpoints. The tactic has also been used repeatedly in the Mid-dle East with a slight difference.

In the October 1983 bombing of the French embassy in Beirut, explosives were surreptitiously planted in the vehicle of an embassy employee. Unaware that the vehicle contained a large quantity of explosives, the unsuspecting em-ployee was allowed to pass a security checkpoint and park the vehicle on the embassy grounds where sometime later the explosives were detonated.

In the fifth variation of the vehicle terrorist attack method, large quan-tities of explosives are used; and glass, bullets, or small pieces of metal are contained inside the bomb vehicle. Bomb vehicles containing explosive sub-stances in excess of 100 to 500 pounds and randomly parked in a heavily resi-dential area to maximize the killing of innocent civilians are not unusual.

The tragic civil war in Lebanon has witnessed hundreds of such bomb attacks. During one 17-day period in July and August 1986, various Lebanese militias detonated 9 vehicle bombs, killing 103 people and injuring 596. These vehicle bombs were parked on busy commercial and residential streets, thereby increasing the number of civilian casualties.

The sixth vehicle attack method uses multiple bombs hidden on vehicles of public transportation. This terrorist attack method involves placing explo-sive devices, timed to explode during rush hours, on busses or trains, thereby creating mass casualties of innocent civilian bystanders. The method has been used by various Palestinian factions, the PIRA, and more recently by Tamal separatists in Sri Lanka and Sikhs in India. The intent of such indiscriminate bombings is to gain media attention and create intense fear in the general community. There is no doubt that the selective terrorist bombing of public transportation will continue to escalate. The establishment of effective security controls for all public transportation is difficult to institute.

The seventh bomb attack method involves vehicle bombs containing large quantities of explosives driven by suicide bombers. The most sensational suicide bombings have occurred in the Middle East and have been directed against U.S. targets. On October 23, 1983, a truck loaded with the equivalent of 12,000 pounds of TNT was driven into the Marine compound in Beirut.[26] According to the FBI, this vehicle bomb created the largest conventional blast ever seen by explosive experts. In a simultaneous attack on the French multinational peacekeeping force, a suicide truck bomber killed 58 French paratroopers. Then, on November 5, 1983, a suicide truck bomber penetrated the Israeli military compound in Tyre, Lebanon, killing 60 people.[27] In less than two weeks, suicide truck bombers had killed 359 members of the military forces of the United States, France, and Israel.

The suicide bomb attack method has fully emerged as a strategic weapon that enables nations with inferior military forces to gain a degree of strategic equality with more powerful military forces. Defenses against the suicide car or truck bomb are difficult to maintain. They consist of physical barriers, vehicle mazes, use of increased buffer distances, and well-armed security guards instructed to fire on suspicious vehicles. The fear of the vehicle bomb exists not only in the Middle East. Washington, D.C., has been given the look of a government under siege with dump trucks filled with dirt, highway barriers, and armed security guards protecting entrances to the White House, U.S. Capitol, and other important government structures. The psychological impact of the suicide bomber has created a situation of overwhelming fear in the United States as well as the Middle East. One must remember that the focus and direction of terrorism is to create fear. Certainly the suicide vehicle bomb accomplishes this major objective of terrorist violence.

In sum, the evolution of the vehicle bomb attack method has produced some definitive trends. The bigger the explosion the greater the casualties, and the more intense the media coverage the greater the publicity for the terrorist group. Since we concluded in earlier chapters that terrorist groups are imitative rather then innovative, they have certainly monitored the successes of vehicle bomb tactics. Most likely we can anticipate the increased use of vehicle bombs by terrorist groups around the world.

As the use of vehicle bombs escalates, law enforcement personnel must devise alternative tactics to identify practical ways to stop the bombing—obviously an extremely difficult responsibility. In some cases, such as with the

[26]Report of the DOD Commission on Beirut International Airport Terrorist Act, October 23, 1983 (Washington, D.C.: U.S. Government Printing Office, 1983), pp. 84–86.

[27]New York Times, November 5, 1983, sec. 1, p. 14.

suicide bomber, it becomes a formidable task to prevent or deter infiltration into an area without seriously disrupting daily routines. However, security forces (law enforcement, military, or sentries) must be on the alert and have sufficient training to handle the vehicle bomb on an individual basis. From the terrorist perspective, the true genius of the vehicle attack method is that the objective and the means of attack are often beyond the imagination of those responsible for providing security and establishing bomb-training curriculums. Security personnel must understand that the vehicle bomb is a fully established mode of indiscriminate political violence. But the use of deadly parcel bombs is probably the most heinous bomb attack method.

Letter Bombs

According to Laqueur, the terrorist tactic of preparing letter bombs was first introduced by Russian terrorists of the 1880s. Russian terrorists made plans to conceal small quantities of explosives in little parcels, then mail the parcels to the tzar and other government officials. However, because of the insurmountable technical difficulties in handling explosives, this plan apparently was not carried out. Additionally, anarchist writers of the 1880s, such as Most, Bakunin, and Nechaev, recommended sending letters and small parcels containing incendiary explosives as a tactic to spread fear among government leaders and bureaucrats. Nonetheless, the first recorded use of a letter bomb or parcel bomb occurred in 1895 when a young German anarchist sent a 25-pound black powder bomb to a Berlin police officer. The bomb was intercepted at the Berlin post office and rendered harmless. By the beginning of the World War I some of the technical difficulties of making letter bombs were overcome, and several prominent European political leaders were killed or seriously injured by exploding parcels. Through the years various terrorist groups, including the Irgun, the Palestine resistance groups, and the IRA, have used letter bombs to spread fear and to introduce ''new'' terror tactics since the police and potential targets were alert to most of the old terror bomb attack methods.[28]

Through trial and error the technological problems associated with the construction of letter bombs have been greatly reduced. Explosive devices now can easily be concealed within letters and small packages. The letter bomb creates a far greater security risk than the car bomb or planted bomb. Letter bombs are antipersonnel devices and serve two offensive terrorist functions. First, they may be designed to kill or maim a specific target. Since letter bombs contain only a small amount of explosive material, their intended effect is to injure and maim. Injury from an exploding letter bomb is caused by the explosive shock and the blast pressure, not from fragmentation. Second, letter bombs may be used to harass and intimidate the general public.

[28]Laqueur, *Terrorism,* pp. 94–95.

Even though the use of letter bombs is an ideal terrorist attack method, they are used infrequently compared to other bomb attack methods, such as the vehicle bomb. Letter bombs tend to be the preferred terrorist tactic during periods of a brief, intensive terrorist bombing campaign directed against specific targets. Such a terrorist letter bomb campaign was waged by Palestinian terrorists against Israeli and American targets in 1972. As with other bomb attack methods, the high-risk targets of letter bombs are embassies, corporations, defense-related industries, police, and government offices.

Between 1977 and 1983, for example, 84 recorded letter bomb incidents occurred in 23 different countries. The United States was the favorite target, with 19 incidents reported, while 47 letter bombs were mailed to Western European targets. By far the favored addresses for letter bombs have been diplomats, to whom 40 of the 84 letter bombs were sent. Seven people were killed and 51 others injured in the 84 reported letter bomb attacks. Terrorist groups representing 18 different ethnic identities claimed credit for 43 (51.1 percent) of the 84 letter bombs, with the senders of the remaining 41 undetermined. Various Irish extremist groups and individuals sent 11 of the deadly letter bombs to British targets, accounting for the largest number of letter bombs sent among known ethnic terrorists.[29]

Letter bombs or parcel bombs may be constructed to fit within almost any familiar container. This list includes all types of mail deliveries. Mail bombs are designed to detonate as the letter or package is opened. The explosive charge is activated by the release of a spring-loaded striker system or an electrical circuit. The most common type of mail devices encountered by postal security officers have been sent in large envelopes or small packages. The typical terrorist letter bomb weighs between two and three ounces and fits neatly into an envelope approximately 5 3/4 inches by 4 inches by 1/4 inches.[30]

In order to function, letter bombs must contain an explosive charge, a detonator, and a fuse to set off the detonator. The type of explosive preferred by letter bombers is C-4, but if C-4 is unavailable, other fast-burning explosives, including various black powder mixtures, can also be used. The most common type of fuse used in letter bomb construction is the percussion fuse. The percussion fuse operates on the same principle as a firing pin in a gun. The spring is released carrying a striker that impacts upon the detonator, igniting the explosive charge. The detonator most commonly discovered in letter bombs is the type used in commercial mining operations. This type of detonator is cylindrical in shape, has a very thin copper casing, and is about 3/16 inch (5 millimeters) in diameter. It is hoped that the identification and understanding of these principles of letter bomb construction will help security and police officers to detect and recognize suspected mail explosive devices.

Some specific things to look for in a suspected letter bomb are the fol-

---

[29]U.S. Department of State, *Terrorist Bombings,* pp. 4–6.

[30]Graham Knowles, *Bomb Security Guide* (Los Angeles: Security World, 1976), p. 93.

lowing: (1) letters bombs cannot be constructed of extremely small size or placed in very thin, ordinary envelopes, (2) letter bombs are generally unbalanced, and are heavier on one side or the other, (3) an explosive mail device may have wires or spring holes in its outer wrapping, (4) certain categories of explosives may leave a greasy film on the envelope or paper wrapping, which may indicate also that the explosive is extremely unstable, (5) an unusual odor such as an almond smell may be present, (6) if the envelope is taped down on all sides, it may contain a spring-loaded booby trap, and (7) inspection of the stiffness of the contents of the envelope may reveal the presence of folded paper, cardboard, or an explosive device. The key indicator that an explosive device may be present in an envelope is *feel*. If the suspected letter bomb does not bend or flex and has a feeling of springiness at the top, bottom, or sides of the envelope, this is a clear sign that an explosive device is present.

As in other bomb attack methods, the target of the bombers should not assume that only one explosive device exists. Letter bombers have been known to send several explosive devices to the same address. Therefore, all mail deliveries for several weeks should be carefully examined. There are several excellent books, monographs, and pamphlets that outline the correct procedure for handling suspected letter bombs and parcel bombs.[31]

Letter bombs are a continued hazard to the high-risk population of diplomats, corporate executives, government officials, and police officers. Therefore, the risks of receiving letter bombs must be continually reevaluated and updated. Criminal justice management and rank-and-file employees alike must be trained in letter bomb recognition and the proper emergency procedures for handling explosive mail devices.

Bombings Aboard Aircraft

The bombing of inflight aircraft is yet another extranormal terrorist attack method. Modern high-performance civil aircraft are extremely vulnerable to inflight bombing attacks. There are numerous ways of planting bombs on aircraft, even with the heightening of security measures. The motivations behind such terrorist attacks are many; but regardless of the motive, it is apparent that bombers of aircraft hope to destroy all tangible evidence by creating midair explosions. The design of the explosive device and methods of concealment are limited only by the ingenuity of the bomber. Therefore, security arrangements and technical methods of detecting hidden explosive devices on board aircraft must be superior to that of the skillful bomber. If, however, bombers of aircraft are able to penetrate security measures and the aircraft is destroyed, then every effort must be made to quickly recover victims and debris from the explosion. At times the problems of recovery may seem insur-

---

[31]For example, see Knowles, *Bomb Security Guide,* pp. 96–102; Frank Moyer, *Police Guide to Bomb Search Techniques* (Boulder: Paladin Press, 1981), pp. 137–46; Richard Clutterbuck, *Living with Terrorism* (London: Faber & Faber, 1976), pp. 83–91.

mountable, especially if the explosion occurred over deep ocean waters or the aircraft is widely scattered over desert or jungle landscapes. Such was the case after a midair bomb explosion occurred off the coast of Ireland on September 21, 1985.

An Air India Boeing 747 en route to London disintegrated in midair about 110 miles off southwestern Ireland, killing all 329 people on board.[32] The midair explosion occurred less than an hour after another explosive device detonated at the Air India baggage check station in Tokyo, seriously wounding several workers. Both bombings were claimed by Sikh extremists seeking political autonomy from India. After a lengthy investigation, Air India officials concluded that a plastic explosive device that escaped metal detectors was the cause of the midair explosion. Indian forensic scientists reconstructed the debris and examined the remains of victims recovered at the scene of the explosion and further determined that two bombs were used by the Sikh terrorists.

In yet another recent midair explosion, this one inside a TWA jetliner bound for Athens, four people were hurled to their deaths.[33] The explosion blew a 9- by 3-foot hole in the side of the aircraft; the four innocent victims were sucked out of the hole at approximately 15,000 feet and fell to their deaths. Palestinians claimed credit for the TWA bombing, saying it was in retaliation for a U.S.-military strike against Libya. Fortunately, this type of terrorist bombing attack is rare compared to car bombs and letter bombs.

Statistics on explosions aboard aircraft between 1949 and 1984 indicate that 80 aircraft were damaged or destroyed by the detonation of an explosive device while in flight. Of the 80 aircraft damaged or destroyed, 17 aircraft were totally destroyed. In all, 1,148 passengers and crew lost their lives. The bombings occurred in various parts of the world covering 38 countries and affecting 43 airlines. During that same period, the United States recorded the damage or destruction of 15 aircraft with a total loss of 126 lives.[34]

Details of these statistics are portrayed in Table 7-2, while illustrates the annual incidence of explosions aboard civil aircraft and the number of fatalities. To some extent the increase in fatalities can be attributed to the larger size of aircraft used by civil air carriers rather than the increased effectiveness of terrorist bombers. An analysis of the statistics also reveals that the three most popular areas to secrete explosive devices aboard aircraft are cargo-baggage holds, the passenger cabin, and the lavatory.

In view of the little information available to students of criminal justice, a brief review of several inflight aircraft bomb attacks is presented.[35] A total of 754 people lost their lives.

[32]*New York Times,* September 21, 1985, sec. 1, p. 1.

[33]*New York Times,* June 24, 1985, sec. 1, p. 1.

[34]U.S. Department of Transportation, Federal Aviation Administration, Office of Civil Aviation Security, *Explosions Aboard Aircraft* (Washington, D.C.: U.S. Government Printing Office, 1985), pp. 1–13.

[35]Ibid.

TABLE 7-2 Explosions Aboard Civil Aircraft
Number of Incidents and Persons Killed by Year*

YEAR	NUMBER OF INCIDENTS	NUMBER KILLED	YEAR	NUMBER OF INCIDENTS	NUMBER KILLED	YEAR	NUMBER OF INCIDENTS	NUMBER KILLED
1949	2	36	1965	1	52	1975	4	1
1950	1	0	1966	1	28	1976	5	168
1952	1	0	1967	4	66	1977	1	0
1955	2	60	1968	1	0	1978	3	5
1956	1	0	1969	4	33	1979	2	0
1957	2	1	1970	9	84	1980	1	0
1959	1	1	1971	3	25	1981	3	2
1960	2	47	1972	7	114	1982	2	1
1962	1	45	1973	5	92	1983	2	112
1964	1	15	1974	5	161	1984	3	0
						Total	80	1,149

*Source: U.S. Department of Transportation, Federal Aviation Administration, Office of Civil Aviation Security, *Explosions Aboard Aircraft* (Washington, D.C.: U.S. Government Printing Office, 1985), pp. 1–13.

1. United Airlines DC-68 (November 1, 1955)
   This aircraft was on a scheduled flight to Portland, Oregon. Approximately 11 minutes after takeoff from San Francisco an explosion disintegrated the aircraft. A dynamite bomb located in the number 4 *baggage compartment* detonated, killing 39 passengers and 5 crew.

2. Canadian Pacific Airlines DC-68 (July 8, 1965)
   An explosive device planted in the *passenger cabin* area detonated, separating the tail section from the aircraft. All 52 aboard were killed. The explosion occurred over British Columbia.

3. British Airways Comet 48 (October 12, 1967)
   On a scheduled flight to Nicosia, Cyprus, at about 28,000 feet an explosion ripped through the tourist passenger cabin. All 66 aboard were killed. The recovery of victims and debris revealed evidence of an explosion.

4. Cathway Pacific Airways CV 880 (June 15, 1972)
   En route from Thailand to Hong Kong a bomb in a suitcase under the *passenger seat* exploded killing 81 passengers and crew.

5. Air Vietnam B-727 (September 15, 1974)
   A skyjacker boarded the aircraft in Saigon and ordered the flight to go to Hanoi. The pilot convinced the skyjacker that the plane was low on fuel and therefore a forced landing was necessary. While in the landing pattern the skyjacker for some reason detonated two hand grenades in the *cockpit*. The pilot lost control of the aircraft and 70 passengers and crew were killed.

6. Gulf Air Bahrain B-737 (September 23, 1983)
   About 30 miles from the airport in Kuwait, a bomb exploded in the *baggage compartment*. While attempting a forced landing in the desert, the aircraft crashed, killing 112 people.

7. Air India B-747 (June 21, 1985)
   Approaching the coast of Ireland at approximately 30,000 feet, the aircraft disintegrated, killing 329 people. Subsequent investigation revealed plastic explosives had been planted in the *baggage compartment* and the *lavatory*.

In sum, the effectiveness of civil-aviation security measures will continue to test the determination of terrorist bombers. Acts of aircraft bombings and attempted bombings are on the increase. This increase in the number of explosions and the number of explosive devices detected by airport security indicates that perhaps aircraft bombings may become the primary threat to civil air carriers as opposed to hijackings. Despite the preventive measures taken of strengthening security systems, it is believed that civil aviation will remain a tempting and vulnerable target to the mentally disturbed, criminal, and terrorist bomber.

CONCLUSIONS

We have reviewed the effects of explosions, types of explosive devices, and bomb attack methodologies, including the use of car bombs, letter bombs, and the bombing of aircraft. This review suggests that terrorist bombers have demonstrated clearly and convincingly that they are willing to escalate the threshold of violence beyond what was previously believed attainable because of stricter police and military security measures. However, stricter security measures have not prevented terrorist bombers from turning Paris into a city of fear. During the month of September in 1986, Lebanese terrorists, in an attempt to coerce the French government to release a jailed comrade, detonated six bombs in Paris in one ten-day period. Fifteen people were killed and scores were injured. Although the Paris bombings were serious, they were not catastrophic; and the French government did not capitulate. Nevertheless, the terrorist bombings in Paris may be a harbinger of a more lethal future for democratic countries. Intensive terrorist bombing campaigns could easily be mounted by dedicated terrorist groups.

Therefore, police officers and government security personnel need technical training in bomb recognition, indentification of explosive materials, and bomb contruction. Too often law enforcement agencies wait until a tragedy occurs before a decision is made to take precautionary measures for the future. There is no substitute for the well-informed and well-trained police officer.

The next chapter will explore a special kind of murder—terrorist assassination.

REVIEW QUESTIONS

1. List at least five factors that have contributed to the escalation of terrorist bombing.
2. Describe the difference between commercial and military explosives.
3. Explain the effects of an explosion.
4. Distinguish between the positive and negative pressure phase of an explosion.
5. Discuss the difference between low- and high-velocity explosives.
6. Identify and explain at least five terrorist vehicle bomb attack methods. What strategies would you suggest to prevent the recurring problem of vehicle bombs?
7. Compare and contrast the car bomb and letter bomb methodologies.
8. Describe several techniques for identifying suspected letter bombs.
9. Why are aircraft so vulnerable to terrorist attack?
10. Outline a bomb training program for police and security personnel.

EIGHT

ASSASSINATION AND POLITICAL MURDER

CHAPTER OBJECTIVES

The study of this chapter will enable you to:
- Explore several definitions of assassination
- Develop a typology of assassins
- Distinguish between assassination in the Middle East and the United States
- Describe the motivation of U.S. assassins
- Cite the assassinations of American political figures
- Compare and contrast conspiracy theory and the lone assassin

INTRODUCTION

On February 28, 1986, Olaf Palme, the prime minister of Sweden, was assassinated by a lone gunman after he left a movie theater in midtown Stockholm. The assassination of Palme shattered two centuries of peaceful politics in Sweden. No head of state in Sweden had been slain since King Gustaf III in 1792.[1] Even in recently terrorist-plagued Europe, Sweden has largely escaped terrorist attacks. Several groups took credit for the assassination of Palme, including the Red Army Faction and the Croatian organization Ustasa. Both groups threatened Palme in the past; however, police investigators have little evidence to link the RAF or Ustasa to the murder. Other Swedish police investigators have concluded that Palme was slain by a psychopathic killer seeking revenge. Nonetheless, the assassination of Palme remains a baffling mystery.

In Bonn, Germany, on October 12, 1986, the West German foreign minister was slain after he emerged from a taxi outside his residence. The Red Army Faction took credit for the assassination, claiming the foreign minister played a key role in Western Europe's "imperialist war strategy."[2] The assassination of Palme and the West German foreign minister are but the latest in the growing number of terrorist attacks on world political leaders.

The past 60 years have witnessed a quantitative increase in assassination so great that it poses a global problem. Murder has plagued people since biblical times and murder for political reasons nearly as long. The list of slain political leaders is endless. For example, the last several years has witnessed the assassination of Indira Gandhi, Anwar Sadat, and Benigno Aquino and the attempted murder of Margaret Thatcher, Pope John Paul, and Ronald Reagan. Murder related to political motivations includes everything from the random killings of government officials to the well-planned murder of powerful political elites. Yet the act of murder that ties the brutal killing of Anwar Sadat and the carefully planned assassination of Olaf Palme, or the murder by Protestant death squads and the random killing of top-ranking government officials in the United States is little understood. Even so, the academic analysis of assassination and the psychological evaluation of the mind of the assassin has long intrigued scholars.

Despite the dramatic escalation of assassination in recent years and a concurrent scholarly interest, there is little agreement on a general definition of assassination. In fact, the terms assassination, terrorism, and political murder are frequently used interchangeably with considerable overlap in meaning.[3] Beyond the fact that assassination is a specific category of murder, there seems to be little consensus as to what constitutes an assassination.

The purpose of this chapter is to explore several definitions of assassination, review assassinations and attempted assassinations in the modern world, particularly those occurring after 1960, and to analyze the assassination of prominent American political figures.

[1]Franklin L. Ford, *Political Murder: From Tyrannicide to Terrorism* (Cambridge: Harvard University Press, 1985), pp. 205–206.

[2]*Sacramento Bee,* October 12, 1986, sec. A, p. 4.

[3]David C. Rapoport, *Assassination and Terrorism* (Toronto: Canadian Broadcasting Corporation, 1976), p. 1–8.

What is Assassination?

The word assassination first appeared in western Europe at the time of the first Crusades. The Crusaders established contact with a ubiquitous Shi'ite Ismaili sect called the hashish eaters.[4] The hashish eaters (identified in Chapter 2) were a radical religious sect who slew "enemies of the faith" while they were reportedly under the influence of hashish. The hashish eaters strongly believed they were perfectly justified in slaying the infidels who challenged their religious dogmas. The first reference to the word in a western language appeared in Dante's *Inferno* with the phrase "lo perfido assassin," which translated means "one who kills others for money."[5] Thus, Dante is the first westerner to introduce the concept of the professional hit man. Lerner's definition of assassination is "the killing of a person in private life from a political motive and without legal process."[6] Still others have defined assassination simply as "the trucidation of a political figure without due process of law."[7] Jaszi and Lewis are somewhat more articulate and define assassination as the "premediated killing of an individual . . . in order to get, maintain, or extend the power of the state in the interest of an individual or a group. When the killing is directed to well-defined individuals, it would be a political assassination."[8] Bell concludes that "assassination is simply a violent crime with political implications."[9]

Obviously assassination is not an easy term to define precisely. Most definitions of assassination treat it as a unique category of the crime of murder, generally committed against individuals of prominent political standing. The murder or assassination of political leaders has for many years been known as tyrannicide. However, in the vast literature on tyrannicide, there are writers who claim that the tyrant, by his oppression or by his corruption, violated the laws of God so that killing him was no murder but a just punishment for treason against God.[10] In fact, ancient Greek and Roman scholars regarded tyrannicide with general approval. Seneca, the great Roman philosopher, was credited with introducing the formula that no sacrifice was more pleasing to God than the death of a tyrant. However, Ford reminds us that even though ancient scholars supported the right of resistance to tyranny by assassination, they also believed that assassination was bad politics and could lead to a recur-

---

[4]Ford, *Political Murder*, p. 1.

[5]Bernard Lewis, *The Assassins: A Radical Sect in Islam* (New York: Basic Books, 1968), p. 2.

[6]*Encyclopedia of the Social Sciences* (New York: Macmillan, 1937), 1, 271.

[7]Saul K. Padover, "Patterns of Assassination in Occupied Territory," *Public Opinion Quarterly*, 7 (1943), p. 680.

[8]Oscar Jaszi and John D. Lewis, *Against the Tyrant: The Tradition and Theory of Tyrannicide* (Glencoe, Ill: Free Press, 1957), pp. 150–51.

[9]J. Bowyer Bell, *Assassin! The Theory and Practice of Political Violence* (New York: St. Martin's Press, 1979), p. 24.

[10]Walter Laqueur, *The Terrorism Reader* (New York: New American Library, 1978), p. 21.

ring cycle of violence and counterviolence.[11] Through the centuries those of the church and philosophers alike, rather than attempting to follow the legal process for removing the tyrant, have justified the death of the tyrant. Admittedly, when the legal process is controlled by the tyrant, political assassination may be the only alternative to free the oppressed.

Clearly there is only limited consensus as to what constitutes an assassination. Scholarly writing is no doubt shaped by individual perceptions of assassinations as they apply to a set of political events. For example, depending on which set of victims the scholar is analyzing, the semantics of assassination will be quite different. One investigator may view tyrannicide as justifiable homicide while another may see all political homicide as premeditated murder. However, at least seven separate elements appear to be correlated with the concept of assassination that identifies it as a special category of murder:

1. The target is a prominent public figure of political importance.
2. The motive for the killing is political in nature.
3. The killing occurs outside the context of war, revolution, insurrection, or coup d'état.
4. The legal procedures for establishing guilt of the tyrant are nonexistent or controlled by the potential victim.
5. The target of the assassination is carefully selected.
6. The act of murder is committed in a public place; thus, the assassin takes a much greater risk.
7. The potential political impact of the assassination, for example, the killing of a head of state, is great.

Unmistakably, many different types of assassination exist. In order to develop a clearer understanding of political murder, terrorism, and assassination, several scholarly typologies will be examined.

Types of Assassinations

The National Commission on the Causes and Prevention of Violence identifies five types of assassination.[12] The major thrust of the commission's report was to examine the experience of the United States with assassination in reference to the five types.

The first type of assassination is by one political elite to replace another without a concomitant change in either political structure or political ideology. The object of the assassination is to change the ruling power and the identity of the person at the top. This type of assassination is most common in the

---

[11]Ford, *Political Murder,* p. 46.

[12]James F. Kirkham and others, *Assassination and Political Violence: A Report to the National Commission on the Causes and Prevention of Violence* (New York: Bantam Books, 1970), pp. 3–7.

Middle East and in Latin America. The success of this type of assassination depends on how much support the government has in the grass roots community. Assassination of this type has not appeared in the United States.

The second type of assassination, designed to create intense fear and demoralize the legitimacy of the ruling power in order to effect systematic governmental change, has been quite successful in several countries. Most notably, the British presence in Aden, Cyprus, and Palestine in the 1940s produced a wave of terrorist assassination attacks against individual British soldiers and minor government officials. In spite of all the counterstrategies to eradicate the terrorist attacks, the British eventually abdicated and removed their troops. Terrorist assassination appears to be most effective in countries where the government is viewed as a colonial power or otherwise illegitimate by a substantial portion of the population. In the United States this type of assassination was prevalent throughout the South after the Civil War. The assassination of Northern officeholders and the emergence of the KKK eventually forced the "foreigners" from the South.

The third type of assassination is carried out by government agents in order to suppress political challenges from rival political groups or individuals. In many respects this type of assassination is reserved for Nazi Germany and Soviet Russia. Under Stalin the Russian secret police carried out thousands of executions for crimes against the state. The most celebrated was the assassination of Leon Trotsky at his home outside Mexico City in 1940. Trotsky's son was also murdered by Russian assassins in Paris. Not to be outdone, once Hitler was in power, he silenced dissent within his own party ranks by mass executions. In one murderous assault, known as the "Night of the Long Knives," Hitler killed more than 200 "close allies" he considered to be potential political enemies.[13] Nazi and Soviet internal terror was designed not only to intimidate their own ranks but also to create fear in the larger society. The National Commission maintains that this type of assassination has not occurred in the United States.

The fourth type of assassination is propaganda by deed. The purpose is to dramatize and publicize a perceived injustice. This terrorist strategy was popular with turn-of-the-century anarchist movements. Laqueur writes that it is doubtful whether "selective assassinations" or propaganda by deed had any lasting political effect on government stability or change.[14] The attempted assassination of some U.S. Presidents may fall within this category. Assassination of U.S. political figures will be reviewed in later sections of this chapter.

Finally, the type of assassination unrelated to "rational" political objectives deserves a special place in U.S. history. This is the typically mentally deranged assassin of U.S. Presidents. Bell euphemistically refers to this type

---

[13]Bell, *Assassin!,* p. 132.
[14]Laqueur, *Terrorism,* pp. 49–53.

of assassination as "murder as a form of personal therapy."[15] The assassin, while under the grip of a strange obsession, can only be free of the obsession by resorting to violence. Therefore, the motive for the assassination is neither pleasure, profit, passion, pain, or revenge, but rather a form of possession by evil demons, spirits, or instructions from God. The well-publicized case of the attempted assassination of Sir Robert Peel, the founder of modern police agencies in 1843, by Daniel MacNaughton, is such an example. MacNaughton claimed he was being pursued by "a parcel of devils" who instructed him to kill Peel. Eventually, the trial produced the famous legal precedent known as the MacNaughton Rules. MacNaughton was found not guilty by reason of insanity.

The verdict is still being discussed by legal scholars today. Other scholars have also attempted to categorize types of assassinations. Gross distinguishes three types of assassination.[16] Gross is concerned primarily with the murder of leading political personalities. He identifies the isolation act of political assassination frequently accomplished by the mentally disturbed person as his first type of assassination.

The second type is defined as a sultanism, the assassination of a king or sovereign from an Islamic state. This category of assassinations is related to the acquisition of power by murdering political elites and securing political power through the use of threats, coercion, and intimidation.

The third type of assassination discussed by Gross is the selective and tactical assassination directed against the officials of the ruling party of government. The objective of such an assassination tactic is to weaken the governmental structure by individual acts of terrorism. As individual government agents are murdered, other governmental agents will then become intimidated, which in turn cripples the ability of the government to react in a crisis situation. That is the strategy. As mentioned previously, such a strategy was successful in Aden, Cyprus, and Palestine as frustrated British troops withdrew.

Gross maintains the importance of ideological and ethnic/national tensions as the basis for campaigns of indiscriminate terrorism rather than deteriorating economic and social conditions.[17] Gross's observations and typology are accurate, even though the focus of his research is on nineteenth-century eastern European and Mid-East assassinations. It appears to apply to other areas of the world where widespread terrorism is prevalent, particularly Northern Ireland.

Crotty divided assassinations into five distinct types.[18] Crotty's typology

---

[15]Bell, *Assassin!* pp. 63–66.

[16]Feliks Gross, "Political Assassination" in *International Terrorism in the Contemporary World,* ed. M. H. Livingston (Westport, Conn.: Greenwood Press, 1978), pp. 312–16.

[17]Feliks Gross, *Violence in Politics: Terror and Political Assassination in Eastern Europe and Russia* (The Hague: Monton, 1972), p. 94.

[18]William J. Crotty, ed., *Assassinations and Their Interpretation Within the American Context* (New York: Harper & Row, 1971), pp. 10–13.

closely resembles the National Commission report and the types of assassinations explored by Gross.

Crotty's first classification, which involves the murder of a political leader for essentially private motives, is anomic. The murder appears to be irrational and the link between assassin and victim is locked in the fantasies of the killer.

Elite substitution, the second category, is the murder of a politically powerful leader in order to replace that leader with the leader of an opposing political faction.

The third classification is tyrannicide, which occurs when a despot is murdered and replaced with a leader who exhibits more compassion for the people of the country. The purpose of this type of murder is to destabilize, weaken, and eventually incapacitate the state. This, in turn, leads to the fourth type of assassination.

The fourth category is terroristic. The focus of terroristic assassination of government officials is to demonstrate the government's inability to control the "insurgents" and to neutralize the allegiance of the general population to the government. For example, the Vietcong reportedly killed approximately 10,000 village elders during the late 1950s, thus preparing the way for a takeover from within. Again, in the words of Sun Zu, "kill one, frighten a thousand."

Propaganda by deed is Crotty's fifth classification. The purpose of this type of assassination is to direct attention to a broader national or political problem, for instance, the oppression of a specific ethnic group. The assassination of Senator Robert Kennedy by Sirhan Sirhan fits well into this type. Sirhan killed Senator Kennedy because he blamed the U.S. government for neglecting the Palestinian issue.

Similar to Gross, Crotty uses the murder of Russian tsars as examples of his five types of assassination. Furthermore, Gross and Crotty view the planned murder of Russian political leaders as more than an isolated act of political assassination. The assassination of members of the Russian autocracy provides the basis for the development of a theory of political struggle based on political assassinations. In essense, terrorism is directed at a corrupt system, which the assassin attacks a corrupt person. Other scholars also share this interpretation of political events during the time of the tsars and the strategy of planned terroristic assassinations.

Rapoport maintains that the objectives of terrorism can only be achieved by continued assassinations over long periods of time, since fear (the purpose of terrorism) dissipates when assassinations occur irregularly.[19] Therefore, terroristic assassination is directed toward the system, and any representative of that system is a potential target. In this way the IRA directs a campaign of assassination against British security forces and police officers in Northern

---

[19]Rapoport, *Assassination and Terrorism,* p. 38.

Ireland. Moreover, according to Crenshaw, the victims of terroristic assassination represent certain categories of people; thus attacks on one member of the group are a threat to all other members of the same group.[20] Thus, terroristic assassination generates fear among the victim's reference group. Terroristic assassinations, then, are designed to create the question, "Will I be next?"

In sum, from a review of the typologies suggested by the National Commission report, Gross, and Crotty, we may safely conclude that the interaction between victim and assassin is quite different for terroristic assassination and other types of political murder. The assassin is motivated by a desire to eliminate the direct influence of the victim on the political scene or obsessed with fantasies of immediate recognition. The terrorist is motivated by the demonstrative effect and the impact that the assassination of the victim will have. In view of the several types of assassination, let us now turn our attention to two areas of the world, the Mideast and the United States, in order to explore specific examples of assassination and where they fit in the typologies discussed. Mideast assassinations that occurred between 1951 and 1980 will be reviewed.

The cradle of assassination and political murder appears to be in the predominantly Islamic Middle East. The Middle East, with its seemingly endless political violence, has the distinction of surpassing all other areas of the world in the recorded number of assassinations. Africa and Asia have been preoccupied with factional disputes for control over newly independent states, and European countries have suffered through sporadic episodes of anarchism and social revolutionary violence. But the Middle East has been a kaleidoscope of power conflicts, religious hatred, ethnic dislocation, disagreements over foreign policy, and economic deprivation. According to Franklin Ford, 24 percent of all recorded assassination attempts between 1951 and 1980 occurred in the Middle East.

Assassination in the Middle East

From the assassination of King Abdullah of Jordan on July 20, 1951, by a dispossessed Palestinian refugee who accused the king of secret negotiations with the Israelis, to the sensational murder of Anwar Sadat, the Mideast has witnessed countless political assassinations inspired by a variety of motives. (See Table 8-1.) Numerous palace revolutions and assassinations have occurred both within and between nations in the Middle East since 1951. On July 9, 1958, King Faisal II of Iraq was killed during a coup d'état and General Karim Kassem took control.[21] Kassem was killed in another coup on February 9, 1963, when a group of army generals revolted and Abdul Arif became Presi-

---

[20]Martha Crenshaw, *Revolutionary Terrorism: The FLN in Algeria, 1954-1962* (Stanford: Hoover Institute, 1978), pp. 19-20.

[21]Willard A. Heaps, *Assassination: A Special Kind of Murder* (New York: Meredith Press, 1969), pp. 100-102.

TABLE 8-1 Assassination Attempts: 1951–1980

DECADE	EUROPE	MIDEAST	AFRICA	ASIA	LATIN AMERICA	UNITED STATES	TOTAL
1951–60	26 (18)	30 (21)	4 (0)	24 (8)	26 (13)	8 (4)	118 (64)
1961–70	10 (7)	25 (19)	18 (16)	24 (17)	30 (22)	16 (15)	123 (96)
1971–80	34 (30)	36 (27)	15 (12)	20 (14)	30 (24)	3 (1)	138 (108)
Total	70 (55)	91 (67)	37 (18)	68 (39)	86 (59)	27 (20)	379 (258)
% Fatal	78.6	73.6	48.7	57.3	68.6	74.0	

Source: Ford, *Political Murder*, p. 300.

dent. Arif subsequently was deposed by General Hassan al Bakr, who became president and prime minister. Bakr crushed a coup attempt in 1973 and executed 36 coup leaders. Eventually, Iraq's vice president emerged as the new force in Iraqi politics. Saddam Hussein remains today one of the dominate figures of Mideast politics. This now familiar pattern of palace revolutions and political assassination is well-established in several Middle Eastern countries. Political life in the Middle East is haunted by the reality of assassination, terrorism, and political murder.

Such assassination attempts on other Muslim monarchs were to be frequently repeated, often successfully. King Faisal of Saudi Arabia was slain by his nephew, who proclaimed that Faisal was getting too powerful. Several assassination attempts were made on King Farouk of Egypt. In July of 1952, Farouk was forced into exile and Lt. Col. Gamal Nasser eventually became premier.[22] At least two reported attempts were made on Nasser's life. King Hassan II of Morocco survived an attack in 1971 when three escorting jet fighters tried unsuccessfully to shoot down the royal Moroccan aircraft as it approached Hassan's capital, Rabat.

In the bitterly divided Yeman Arab Republic and Southern Yemen, numerous personal assaults are tied to disagreements over foreign policy. In June of 1978 President Ahmed Hussein al-Ghashni of Yemen Arab Republic was murdered while receiving the credentials of the ambassador of Soviet-influenced Southern Yemen. As the new ambassador opened his briefcase, a bomb exploded, killing the ambassador and the president of Yemen Arab Republic. Two days later the president of Southern Yemen, Salem Robaya Ali, was deposed and executed by a rival faction within his own political party. Both assassinations were blamed on pro-Soviet factions in Southern Yemen seeking to unite the Yemen Arab Republic and Southern Yemen. Closely related to the Yemeni crisis is the upheaval in Soviet-dominated Afghanistan. In December 1979, Premier Hafizullah Amin, a pro-Soviet dictator, was executed for crimes against the state and replaced by another pro-Soviet leader who sanctioned the invasion of Afghanistan by the Red Army to bring Afghans under closer Soviet domination.[23]

Meanwhile in Lebanon, Muslims and Christians have been locked in a religious civil war since 1975, and the Israelis have waged a continuing struggle with the forces of the PLO. Both the Christians and Muslims are vehemently divided into smaller religious sects. For example, the Muslims are divided into Shi'ite, Sunni, Druse, and numerous smaller groupings. Sectarian hatred in Lebanon is widespread and incessant. Long before an assassin's bomb killed Bashir Gemayel, the president-elect of Lebanon, and 26 members of his Christian right-wing party, the Phalangists, on September 14, 1982, several notable

[22]Donald Neff, *Warriors at Suez* (New York: Simon and Schuster, 1981), pp. 68–70.
[23]Ford, *Political Murder*, p. 330.

Lebanese political figures had been assassinated.[24] Lebanon's first casualty was Premier Riad Sohl, who attempted to bring Muslims and Christians together by proclaiming the brotherhood of all Lebanese no matter what sect they supported. Next, President Camille Chamoun was slain by members of a left-wing, rival Christian sect who claimed he was planning to bring neutral Lebanon into the Western sphere of influence. Then in August 1977, Kamal Jumblat, a prominent Druse leader, was shot to death in Beirut. The assassination of Jumblat touched off several days of vengeance rioting, in which numerous Christians reportedly lost their lives. A recent victim was Sunni Moslem Prime Minister Karami, killed by a bomb hidden in his helicopter in June 1987. The number of victims of the Lebanese civil war has been estimated at close to 100,000 killed. In Lebanon, the wave of sectarian political murders continues unabated and may be expected to escalate in the future.

But the most sensational Middle East assassination occurred on October 6, 1981, when Anwar Sadat, the president of Egypt, was slaughtered by gunfire and shrapnel as he sat in a VIP stand reviewing a military parade. Four assassins dressed in army uniforms suddenly leaped from a passing military vehicle and assaulted the reviewing stand with automatic weapons and grenades. The assassins belonged to a fundamentalist Muslim sect that announced that Allah had instructed them to kill Sadat. Sadat had been labeled as a heretic and a traitor to Islam for his belief in détente with Israel and the adoption of Western ways that were contrary to Islamic beliefs.[25]

Amid this atmosphere of religious bloodletting and power conflicts, several wars of national liberation have escalated Middle Eastern political violence. Most notably, the successful terrorist campaign of assassination by Zionist gangs in Palestine offers the best instructive model for other liberation movements of the Middle East. The Irgun and Stern Gang carried out numerous raids on British garrisons and tactical assassinations of individual British soldiers. They also attempted to assassinate the British high commissioner of Palestine, Sir Harold MacMichael, who was shot from ambush. MacMichael represented a symbolic target of the British treachery which closed the gates of Palestine, condemning thousands of Jews to Hitler's death camps. Others were not so lucky. Lord Moyne, Winston Churchill's chief administrator outside London and one of the wealthiest men in Great Britain, was murdered in Cairo by the Stern Gang for refusing to admit Jewish refugees into Palestine. Count Folke Bernadotte, UN mediator for Palestine, also fell under the guns of Stern Gang assassins. The Stern Gang was infuriated with Bernadotte's peace plan for Palestine because it appeared to favor the Arabs. The Zionist gangs of Palestine argued that they did not murder political figures unless

[24]Kahan Commission Report, *The Beirut Massacre* (Princeton, N.J.: Karz-Cohl, 1983), p. 13.

[25]*Newsweek,* October 19, 1981, pp. 26–31.

history could be changed, but they did murder as revolutionaries and terrorists. The British were driven out of Palestine, but an accommodation with the Arabs has not been reached. Now there is a new diaspora and a new Palestinian dream. Israel has been the principal enemy of Arab states since the moment it attained sovereignty.[26]

As for the Palestinians and the activities of the PLO, including Fatah, Black September, PFLP, and the rejectionist front, their deeds have already been discussed in Chapter 5. It remains only to recall that some of the leading players in the drama for control of the PLO between Arafat and his challengers have themselves been victims of internecine warfare and assassination plots. Rejectionist Palestinans led by the Abu Nidal faction have claimed responsibility for hundreds of murders and attempted assassinations. Among the victims of rejectionist assassination schemes have been moderate PLO representatives, ambassadors and foreign service officers from Jordan, Saudi Arabia, Syria, Iraq, Kuwait, Egypt, and Israel. On October 17, 1974, there was an abortive attempt to assassinate the chairman of the PLO, Yasir Arafat. The enemies of the rejectionists have been anyone—Middle Eastern or western, Arab or Jew—who advocates a conciliatory policy or accommodation with the "Zionist entity" of Israel. Undoubtedly, this conflict between moderation and extremism in the Palestinian movement will continue and just may create a new generation of Palestinian Abu Nidal-type assassins.[27]

Political murder and assassination in Iran illustrate a case study in which a combination of factors appears to be interacting. In no other region of the world can we observe the interaction of deadly power politics, religious fanaticism, ethnic hostility, minority grievances, and terrorist acts carried out across national borders. Long before the shah fled and the Ayatollah Khomeini came to power, Iran had witnessed numerous assassinations and terrorist plots. In 1951 Prime Minister Ali Rasmara was slain by an assassin while attending services at a mosque. Rasmara's assassin belonged to a group favoring the nationalization of Iran's oil industry. In 1965 Premier Hassan Ali Mansour was shot to death by a disgruntled Muslim fundamentalist student who viewed the regime of the shah as evil and undemocratic. Iran played host to many violent incidents including the reign of terror by the ruthless Iranian political police, Savak, who tortured and killed hundreds of political dissidents. But the flight of the Shah dramatically escalated the level of assassination, terrorism, and political murder.

Once the theocracy of ayatollahs came to power, under the leadership of Khomeini, terrorism and assassination were elevated to new heights. By mid-1981, under the combined influence of total war with Iraq, the activities of

---

[26]For example, see J. Bowyer Bell, *Terror Out of Zion: The Shock Troops of Israeli Independence* (New York: St. Martin's Press, 1978).

[27]Yossi Melman, *The Master Terrorist: The True Story Behind Abu Nidal* (New York: Adama Books, 1986), pp. 201–207.

political exiles, continuous Kurdish uprisings, Baluch, Arab and Turkish resistance, countless assassinations of agents of the Khomeini regime, increasing economic chaos, and widespread terrorism, the Khomeini government announced the start of an "inquisition" to purge the revolution of suspected traitors. Hundreds of people were executed in a reign of terror that lasted approximately four years. The Forghan Fighters, a group of fanatical Kurdish fundamentalists, assassinated several members of the Khomeini clergy on the grounds that the clergy interfered with man's individual relationship with God.[28] The Forghan Fighters were eventually crushed and a reported 500 Kurds were shot by firing squads. Although the Kurds remain rebellious, the greatest threat to the Khomeini regime came from a group of ethnic Iranians called the People's Mujahideen.

The Mujahideen fought openly with the Khomeini Revolutionary Guards on the streets of Tehran and other cities of Iran. The Mujahideen assassinated several key figures in the Khomeini government.[29] Khomeini retaliated, destroying the infrastructure of the Mujahideen and forcing its leaders to flee the country. Even though Khomeini has now consolidated his power base in Iran, he appears no closer to solving the problem of total obedience to Allah. Khomeini rode to power preaching death for all enemies of Allah and Islam. This has led to the accusation by the United States that Iran now sponsors, assists, and actively engages in terrorist assassination attacks against the "infidels."

According to the CIA, Iranian assassins have killed more people than any other group. Further, Iranian assassination teams operate out of Iranian embassies, and the Khomeini government provides the direct financial and military support to several terrorist groups. Terrorist groups such as Islamic Jihad, Islamic Amal, Hesbollah, or Party of God, and Al Dawa conduct acts of terrorism and assassination as a strategy to accomplish the objectives of the Khomeini government. Livingstone argues that Iran is the principal sponsor of terrorism and murder throughout the world in its effort "to internationalize the Iranian revolution."[30]

Certainly, we can anticipate a continuation of assassinations throughout the Middle East. The instability of Mideast politics makes a fertile ground for assassination and terrorism. With the exception of democratic Israel, all other governments of Mideast nations are either monarchies, military dictatorships, or controlled by religious fundamentalists. The *Report to the National Commission on the Causes and Prevention of Violence* lists three preconditions for assassination when there is oppressive or authoritarian rule: (1) the establish-

[28]Peter Janke, *Guerrilla and Terrorist Organizations: A World Directory and Bibliography* (New York: Macmillan, 1983), p. 229.

[29]Ford, *Political Murder*, p. 335.

[30]Neil C. Livingstone and Terrell E. Arnold, "The Rise of State Sponsored Terrorism," in *Fighting Back: Winning the War Against Terrorism*, eds. Neil C. Livingstone and Terrell E. Arnold (Lexington, Mass.: D. C. Heath, 1986), pp. 15–18.

ment of a political party with an ideology based on direct action; (2) existence or perception of oppression, and (3) people willing to resort to violence in order to overthrow oppressive rules.[31] All three conditions exist in the Middle East and the roll of assassination victims will continue to grow. The region is in a spasmodic period of sorting out its political and ideological future.

Assassination in the United States

As you may recall from Chapter 2, the history of the United States contains many examples of civil disobedience and urban rioting. The nation was conceived by colonial rebellion and united together by the Civil War. Throughout the colonial period of approximately 150 years, many violent demonstrations were recorded, but no member of the British crown was ever assassinated. After the creation of the United States, violent outbreaks continued; but still, political murder by surprise or stealth, i.e., assassination, was conspicuously absent. Then, on January 30, 1835, a would-be king attempted to assassinate President Andrew Jackson. Between 1835 and 1986, sixteen assassination attempts have been directed against nationally prominent political figures in the United States. In a sense, the assassination of political figures in a nation where the transfer of power is achieved in an orderly fashion seems paradoxical. Nonetheless, since 1835 and the attempt on President Jackson, assassinations represent a recurring phenomenon in American politics. (See Table 8-2.) Unlike assassinations which occur regularly in the Middle East and other parts of the world to secure political power, U.S. assassinations are overwhelmingly connected with the irrational or pathological needs of mentally disturbed assailants.

After attending a funeral for a deceased congressman, President Jackson was returning to his office through the Capitol rotunda when he was approached by Richard Lawrence. Lawrence drew a single-shot pistol and fired at the president from approximately 8 feet; the pistol misfired. Lawrence then attempted to fire a second single-shot pistol that also misfired. Fortunately for Jackson, both weapons misfired because the powder and ball ammunition had apparently fallen out of the pockets of the would-be assassin. Lawrence, who had been born in England, had hallucinations and the obsessive belief that he was King Richard III and as such had a valid claim against the U.S. government. Today Lawrence would be classified a paranoid schizophrenic. His family history also revealed several cases of severe mental illness. In the end Lawrence was committed to a mental facility, where he died in 1861. The United States was about to enter a terrible struggle that threatened to permanently divide the country. The Civil War and its aftermath produced several assassinations and attempted assassinations. Most notable, of course, was the assassination of the sixteenth president of the United States.

---

[31]Kirkham, *Assassination and Political Violence*, p. 7.

TABLE 8-2 American Assassins: Summary

YEAR	VICTIM	ASSASSIN	MOTIVE	WEAPON	DISPOSITION
1835	Jackson	Lawrence	Wanted to be King	Two single-shot pistols	Mental facility
1865	Lincoln	Booth	Agent of God	.44 derringer	Suicide
1881	Garfield	Guiteau	Agent of God	.44-cal. revolver	Hanged
1901	McKinley	Czolgosz	Anarchist/ Agent of God	Handgun	Electrocuted
1912	T. Roosevelt	Schrank	3rd Term President	.38-cal. revolver	Mental facility
1933	F. D. Roosevelt	Zangara	Anarchist	.38-cal. revolver	Electrocuted
1935	Long	Weiss	Personal	.32-cal. pistol	Killed by body guards at scene
1950	Truman	Collazo/ Torresole	Puerto Rican nationalism	Handguns	Killed at scene Sentenced to life
1963	J. F. Kennedy	Oswald	Personal	Rifle shots	Killed while in jail by gun shot
1968	King	Ray	Racism	Rifle shot	Sentenced to life
1968	R. F. Kennedy	Sirhan	Palestinian cause	.22-cal. revolver	Sentenced to life
1972	Wallace	Bremer	Personal recognition	.38-cal. revolver	63 years in prison
1974	Nixon	Byck	Personal recognition	Kamikaze style attack	Suicide
1975	Ford	Fromme	Agent of God	.45-cal. automatic	Sentenced to life
1975	Ford	Moore	Personal	.38-cal. revolver	Sentenced to life
1981	Reagan	Hinckley	Personal recognition	Pistol	Mental facility

On April 14, 1865, John Wilkes Booth entered the unguarded presidential box at the Ford Theater and shot President Lincoln in the head with a single-shot derringer. Booth then leaped onto the stage, amid startled performers, shouting "sic semper tyrannis." Breaking his leg in the leap, Booth, now disabled, hobbled off the stage. The selection of a public theater for the assassination was a well-planned, calculated decision by Booth. As a well-known actor, he had the freedom to enter and leave the theater without arousing the suspicion of security guards. Therefore, he had access to climb the stairs and enter the president's box. Booth's leap to the stage was not so much for notoriety as escape—it was the most direct route from the theater. To leave the scene of the murder by any other route meant certain capture.[32]

The assassination of President Lincoln was part of a larger conspiracy that involved the planned murder of William Seward, the secretary of state; Vice President Andrew Johnson, and General Ulysses S. Grant, commander in chief of the Union army. Booth and his conspirators hoped to eliminate in one coordinated strike the political and military leadership of the federal government. The conspirators were successful in wounding Seward but missed Johnson and Grant. Thus, only President Lincoln died.

The conspirators were quickly captured, convicted, and executed. Booth escaped into the Maryland swamps and after 12 days was cornered by Union soldiers who surrounded a barn in which he had taken refuge. Booth refused to surrender and the barn was set ablaze. His body was later discovered with a gunshot wound behind his right ear. Apparently he died by his own hand, although a Union soldier claimes to have shot Booth when he attempted to flee the burning barn.

Booth's diaries and letters revealed that he seriously believed he had acted as an agent of God. Few Southerners loved the Confederacy and hated Abraham Lincoln more than John Wilkes Booth. Booth's hatred for the sixteenth president was both personal and political. He felt that Lincoln was unqualified by birth to be president, and he held Lincoln responsible for the bloodiest war in the brief history of the United States. In the end Booth maintained that Lincoln was a tyrant; Booth desired to proclaim himself king of the "new" United States. The cost of the Lincoln assassination to the now reunited nation was an epidemic of political murders. According to the violence commission's report, in the decade preceding the assassination of President Lincoln, 32 high-ranking political officials were attacked in the United States, and 23 of them died of their wounds.[33] But the murder of the country's chief executive did not remain an isolated American trauma.

On July 2, 1881, less than four months after his inauguration, President James A. Garfield was fatally shot by Charles Julius Guiteau, a self-styled

---

[32]James W. Clarke, *American Assassins: The Darker Side of Politics* (Princeton, N. J.: Princeton University Press, 1982), p. 35.

[33]Kirkham, *Assassination and Political Violence,* pp. 13–59.

"lawyer, theologian, and politician." President Garfield had arrived at the District of Columbia railroad station to take a train to Massachusetts to attend his 25th college class reunion. As the president walked through the station waiting room, Guiteau, waiting in ambush, shot him twice in the back with a .44 British revolver. The assassin was quickly overpowered and taken into custody. The president died from his wounds 80 days after the attack.

Guiteau had planned the murder of President Garfield for several months, believing that "if the President was out of the way everything would go better." Guiteau's life was a series of failures, which he largely blamed on the president. His marriage had failed, and he had incurred numerous debts, dropped out of college, written political speeches for leading politicians that were never used, could not maintain a steady job, and briefly supported a religious utopian community that sought his resignation after a confrontation with group elders. Like Richard Lawrence, Guiteau had delusions of grandeur, having decided that an ambassadorship to Paris or Vienna was proper reward for his contributions to the Republican presidential campaign. In his deranged state, he believed the president owed him a debt of gratitude. Receiving no such ambassadorship, he blamed Garfield, thus setting the stage for the eventual assassination. At his trial, which was the first in the United States to involve the question of insanity, Guiteau had a public forum that provided much evidence of his demented condition. He claimed that he had been chosen by supreme powers to kill the president and thus save the nation. God had instructed him to become a presidential assassin. The question of Guiteau's sanity was never resolved, and he received the death sentence and was hanged. Psychologists argue that Guiteau suffered from a psychological aberration called "magnicide," the desire to kill a person of social prominence.[34]

The next victim to be felled by an assassin's bullet was President William McKinley. On September 6, 1901, as McKinley was greeting a group of constituents at the Pan American Exposition in Buffalo, New York, he was approached by Leon Czolgosz, who shot and fatally wounded him. Czolgosz concealed his weapon under a handkerchief and, while shaking hands with the president, fired two shots at very close range, striking McKinley in the chest and the abdomen. The president succumbed 8 days later. Czolgosz was apprehended at the scene, tried, convicted of first-degree murder, and executed 44 days later. He freely admitted his guilt without remorse, offering no defense after his initial plea; and he refused to cooperate with his court-appointed attorneys. Shortly before being electrocuted, he told several witnesses he "killed the President because he was the enemy of the good people—the good working people."

At the time many believed Czolgosz was an anarchist who was pro-

---

[34]Charles E. Rosenberg, *The Trial of the Assassin Guiteau* (Chicago: University of Chicago Press, 1968), pp. 23–46.

foundly influenced by the writings and speeches of Emma Goldman.[35] As a result, Czolgosz was suspected as being part of an anarchist conspiracy, although one was never uncovered. During the trial, Czolgosz was examined by five psychiatrists, and all concluded that they could find no indication of insanity. However, later independent psychological evaluations of his life history concluded that he was confused, remote, and moody, which eventually led to a nervous breakdown and long periods of depression, which produced his unstable mental condition.[36] On the other hand, Clarke argues that the insanity label is not supported by empirical evidence, and Czolgosz was more a product of the times than a demented psychotic killer.[37] Sane or insane, Leon Czolgosz was not the last paranoid assassin to attack a prominent American political figure.

On the evening of October 14, 1912, while attending a political rally in Milwaukee, former President and Bull Moose Party candidate Theodore Roosevelt was shot in the chest by a German immigrant, John Schrank. After exiting his hotel, Roosevelt was greeted by a large crowd of supporters. As he climbed into an open car for the short trip to his political headquarters, a shot was fired from the crowd. The bullet struck Roosevelt in the chest, but the impact of the projectile was absorbed by a spectacle case, his heavy woolen jacket, and a folded 50-page speech he carried in his left breast pocket. These items saved the former president's life. The assassin fired one round from a .38 Colt at a distance of approximately 6 feet from the intended target. He was set upon by the crowd before he could fire a second shot.

John Shrank later confessed that he had been visited by the ghost of William McKinley, who proclaimed that Roosevelt had killed him and further that it was vital that there never be a third-term President. Shrank's interpretation of the vision surely meant that he was intended to be an agent of God. He began to follow Roosevelt's campaign tour as it crisscrossed eight states, the last stop in Milwaukee. After the arrest, Shrank was examined by a team of psychiatrists who declared him insane. He was subsequently confined to a mental facility until his death 30 years later.

The next attempted assassination occurred 21 years later in Miami. On February 15, 1933, an Italian immigrant named Guiseppe Zangara suddenly leaped up onto an empty chair so he could position himself to get a good shot at President-elect Franklin D. Roosevelt. The incapacitated Roosevelt was attending a political rally in Miami, and as he drove up in an open touring car to greet supporters, Zangara fired five wild shots. Miraculously, Roosevelt escaped injury, but Anton Cermak, the mayor of Chicago, was fatally

[35]Ford, *Political Murder,* pp. 360–61.

[36]Walter Channing, "The Mental State of Czolgosz, the Assassin of President McKinley," *American Journal of Insanity* 58 (October 1902), p. 274.

[37]Clarke, *American Assassins,* p. 61.

wounded. Four other bystanders were also wounded. Zangara was set upon by the crowd and later hauled off to jail.

Zangara was eventually sentenced to die in the electric chair. His only regret was that he had missed killing Roosevelt. Zangara was described by the media as a dedicated anarchist. However, Clarke reasons that Zangara's motives were more an expression of personal outrage against a society he despised.[38] Zangara hated the capitalist system. He especially hated American society, which he blamed for all his personal and medical problems. He expressed that outrage by attempting to assassinate the symbolic leader of capitalism, Franklin D. Roosevelt. Zangara, unaided, walked to the electric chair; his final words were "Go ahead, push the button."[39]

Unlike previous assassinations and attempts on American political figures by mentally unstable and deranged persons, the primary motive for the attack on President Truman was Puerto Rican nationalism. On November 1, 1950, Oscar Collazo and Griseilio Torresola attacked the Blair House, intending to kill Truman. In the ensuing shootout, 27 shots were fired. In the first volley of shots, a White House police officer and Torresola were killed. Two other security guards and Collazo were wounded. The president, asleep in an upstairs bedroom overlooking the front portico of the Blair House, was awakened and witnessed the brief exchange of gun fire.

The would-be assassins, Collazo and Torresola, were fervent Puerto Rican nationalists. The purpose of the attack was to draw media attention to the cause of Puerto Rican self-determination. The nationalists believed that only through some tremendous act of political violence would the U.S. government and people realize that Puerto Ricans were willing to die to secure Puerto Rican self-determination. The surviving assassin, Collazo, was convicted of first-degree murder and sentenced to die. However, his sentence was commuted by Truman, without explanation, to life imprisonment. Then on September 10, 1979, President Carter, for an unexplained reason, commuted the sentence of the now 64-year-old Collazo. An estimated crowd of 5000 supporters greeted Collazo when he returned to San Juan, Puerto Rico, on September 12, 1979.[40] Collazo refused to denounce the use of violence and terrorism and vowed the nationalist movement would continue its struggle until Puerto Rico gains independence. The movement continues to this day. The violence commission's report concluded that a political conspiracy, "although a singularly inept one," did exist.[41]

The next presidential assassination was that òf President John F. Kennedy on November 22, 1963, in Dallas, Texas, by Lee Harvey Oswald.

[38]Ibid., p. 174.

[39]Kirkham, *Assassination and Political Violence,* p. 73.

[40]*New York Times,* September 13, 1979, sec. B, p. 23.

[41]Kirkham, *Assassination and Political Violence,* p. 75.

Oswald fired three rifle shots from a 6.5 Mannlicher rifle that he had purchased by mail order. President Kennedy was struck by two of the shots. Unlike other presidential assassins, Oswald used a rifle instead of a handgun, and he steadfastly denied any involvement in the murders of John Kennedy or Officer J. D. Tippit. However, before Oswald could describe his true motives for killing Kennedy, he was shot to death by Jack Ruby in the Dallas County jail. More is known about the John F. Kennedy assassination and the assassin than about any other political assassination in the history of the United States. The details are presented in the now well-reviewed *Warren Commission Report,* which concluded that Lee Harvey Oswald acted alone. The Warren Commission is considered the final authority on the John F. Kennedy assassination, but the commission's findings have not gone unchallenged.

Critics have accused the Warren Commission of dismissing too quickly the possibility of several scenarios that definitely pointed to a conspiracy.[42] After much heated debate, another government commission, the Select Committee on Assassinations of the U.S. House of Representatives, presented a summary of its conclusions which stated that Kennedy's murder was the work of a major conspiracy. The committee was, however, unable to identify the extent of the conspiracy although they did rule out several popular conspiracy theories, including the involvement of the Soviet government, the Cuban government, anti-Castro groups, the national syndicate of organized crime, and even the FBI and CIA.[43] Were others involved in the assassination of John F. Kennedy?

Clarke agrees with the Warren Commission and thinks it unlikely that Oswald was part of a foreign or domestic conspiracy. Like other U.S. assassins, Oswald's life was a series of failures and followed a well-established pattern of behavior. His childhood was filled with unhappiness, and school officials saw Lee as an "emotionally disturbed youngster." He attempted suicide after the Soviet Union rejected his services as a spy and after unsuccessful attempts to join the Cuban revolution. His wife, a Soviet citizen, was indifferent and refused to live with him. He had a short and uneventful tour in the Marine Corps, spending four weeks in the brig and later securing an early discharge. As yet, no convincing supportive evidence has surfaced to support the conspiracy theory.[44]

The murder of Dr. Martin Luther King on April 4, 1968, by James Earl

---

[42]For example, see Thomas Buchanan, *Who Killed Kennedy?* (New York: Putnam, 1964); Mark Lane, *Rush to Judgment* (New York: Holt, Rinehart & Winston, 1966); Richard Popkin, *The Second Oswald* (New York: Avon, 1966); Edward J. Epstein, *The Secret World of Lee Harvey Oswald* (New York: McGraw-Hill, 1978). Henry Hurt, *Reasonable Doubt: An Investigation into the Assassination of John F. Kennedy* (New York: Holt, Rinehart, and Winston, 1986).

[43]*Report of the Select Committee on Assassinations, U.S. House of Representatives, Ninety-fifth Congress, Second Session: Findings and Recommendations* (Washington, D.C.: U.S. Government Printing Office, 1979), Vols 1–26.

[44]Clarke, *American Assassins,* pp. 126–28.

Ray also suggested through a considerable amount of circumstantial evidence that a conspiracy existed. The famous nonviolent, black civil rights leader was fatally shot by one rifle bullet while standing on the balcony outside his motel room in Memphis, Tennessee. Except for John Wilkes Booth, Ray is the only other assassin who planned an elaborate escape. Ray was apprehended 65 days later by British police at London's Heathrow Airport. Returned to the United States, Ray pleaded guilty, but 2 days later, under advice from his attorney, the well-known Percy Foreman, changed his plea to not guilty. Nonetheless, Ray was convicted and sentenced to 99 years in prison.

Ray's biographers conclude that he acted alone and was not part of some grand conspiracy, but they disagree as to Ray's motive for the murder. On the one hand, Huie maintains that Ray killed King in order to achieve instant fame and recognition.[45] On the other hand, McMillan argues that Ray was an obsessive racist who despised the black civil rights leader for *his* fame and recognition.[46] Despite the conclusions of Ray's biographers, the Select Committee on Assassinations believes that Ray assassinated King as a result of a planned conspiracy.[47] Like the John F. Kennedy assassination, no conclusive evidence has surfaced to lend credibility to the conspiracy theory.

However, the murder of King did touch off a black rampage that subjected the United States to the most widespread spasm of violence, rioting, and disorder in its history. Large-scale riots occurred in every major American city, causing millions of dollars in property damage and hundreds of deaths. Some communities still have not recovered from the aftermath of King's assassination.

On the same day that James Earl Ray was captured, June 5, 1968, Senator Robert F. Kennedy, a candidate for the presidential nomination of the Democratic party, was murdered by a Palestinian refugee, Sirhan Bisbara Sirhan. Shortly after midnight, the jubilant but fatigued Robert Kennedy addressed his supporters in the Ambassador Hotel in Los Angeles. He had just won the California presidential primary election. Moments later, to avoid a large crowd of supporters, Robert Kennedy made his way through a food service corridor to exit the hotel. Anticipating Kennedy's departure, Sirhan concealed himself behind a food-tray rack in the food service area. As Kennedy moved slowly through the food service corridor greeting food service workers, Sirhan leaped from his hiding place shouting, "Kennedy, you son of a bitch." Sirhan then raised a .22-caliber Iver Johnson revolver within an inch of the victim's head and fired. The first round entered Kennedy's head. As the senator began to fall to the floor, two more rounds entered his right armpit. With the senator mortally wounded, Sirhan fired five additional shots that wounded

---

[45] William B. Huie, *He Slew the Dreamer* (New York: Delacorte, 1970), p. 173.
[46] George McMillan, *The Making of an Assassin* (Boston: Little, Brown, 1976), p. 70.
[47] *Select Committee,* 1979, p. 3.

five bystanders. Sirhan was wrestled to the floor and held securely until the arrival of the police. These scenes were witnessed on national television.

Sirhan was motivated by an abiding and deep hatred of the Zionists. The 24-year-old assassin, born and raised on the West Bank, was an ardent Palestinian nationalist who saw Robert Kennedy as an assiduous collaborator with Israel. Sirhan kept a detailed notebook in which he recorded his feelings. In one such notation, he became enraged when Kennedy proposed the sale of high-performance jet fighters to Israel. His rage intensified after the humiliating Arab defeat in the 1967 Six Day War between Israel and the Arabs. Sirhan held Kennedy responsible for that defeat and planned his murder to coincide with the anniversary of the June 5, 1967, Israeli invasion of the Sinai. Senator Kennedy was killed one year later to commemorate the Arab defeat. No evidence of a conspiracy was found. Sirhan only wanted to make his mark on history and "do something" for the Palestinian cause. He is now serving a life sentence at Soledad State Prison.[48]

Arthur Bremer also wanted personal recognition, and on the humid afternoon of May 15, 1972, he attempted to assassinate George Wallace, governor of Alabama and presidential candidate. Wallace was in Laurel, Maryland, attending an open-air rally. Following his address to a large crowd of supporters, the governor moved from the safety of his bulletproof podium to shake hands with admirers. The heat had been so oppressive on the fateful day that Wallace had decided not to wear his bulletproof vest, a precaution regularly followed by the governor. As he walked toward the loudly cheering crowd, Bremer shouted, "Over here, over here." Wallace extended his hand in the direction of Bremer, and Bremer responded by firing a .38 caliber bullet into his midsection. Bremer continued to fire four more rounds, hitting Wallace in the right arm, shoulder, and chest. Two security guards and a bystander were also wounded before Bremer was disarmed and taken into custody.[49]

Bremer kept a diary that revealed a firsthand look at the perversity, frustration, and anxiety that motivated him. The diaries also contained passages of how he stalked President Nixon and Democratic presidential hopeful Hubert Humphrey. Governor Wallace was apparently a target of opportunity. In an effort to convince the jury that Bremer surely was insane, his attorney recited the entire diary in court. The jury, however, believed that Bremer's diary disclosed a violent, antisocial personality, not the psychotic, insane killer portrayed by his defense. Certainly, Bremer anticipated the publicity that his act of murder would generate. But Clarke insists that Bremer's primary motive was to outrage society and to show his utter contempt for a political and social

---

[48]For a detailed account of the Robert F. Kennedy murder, see Robert B. Kaiser, *RFK Must Die! A History of the Robert Kennedy Assassination and its Aftermath* (New York: Dutton, 1970).

[49]Gore Vidal, "Now for the Shooting of George Wallace," *New York Review of Books,* 20 (December 13, 1973), pp. 17–19.

system that he hated.[50] Despite the contemptuous nature of Bremer's personality and his fascination with the simulated violence of his favorite movie, *A Clockwork Orange,* Bremer also read about the lives of Booth, Sirhan, and Oswald.[51] Not surprisingly, he selected a prominent and controversial political personality to kill. Based largely on the information contained in his diaries, Bremer was found guilty and sentenced to 63 years in Maryland State Prison.

Probably the most bizarre assassination attempt occurred February 22, 1974, when Samuel Byck planned to hijack a jumbo jet and crash the aircraft Kamikaze-style into the White House, killing President Nixon. As Byck was in line waiting to board a Delta flight to Atlanta from the Baltimore-Washington International Airport, he suddenly produced a .22-caliber pistol, shooting a security guard twice in the back. With other security guards in pursuit, he ran down the boarding ramp and entered the plane. Confronting the crew, Byck ordered the pilot to take off. When the pilot hesitated, the now enraged Byck shot the copilot twice, killing him. Suddenly a shot was fired through the cabin window of the plane, causing Byck to panic and shoot the pilot. A second and third shot were fired through the broken cabin window, striking Byck in the chest and stomach. Byck, mortally wounded, fell to the floor. He then reached for his own pistol, rested the barrel against his right temple, and pulled the trigger. Security guards later discovered an improvised gasoline bomb under his body.[52]

In one of his many tape recordings, Byck outlined his security project of assassination, entitled "Operation Pandora's Box." Byck planned to force the crew to fly toward the executive mansion, shoot the pilot, seize control of the plane, and crash-dive into the White House, killing Nixon and everyone on the aircraft. Byck was distressed by what he perceived as unfair treatment by the Nixon administration. Byck had a strong compulsion for personal recognition and to be heard on political issues such as the oil crisis, Watergate affair, and the Israeli occupation of the Sinai. Although this double murder and suicide startled security personnel, it is the least talked about attempted political assassination in U.S. history.[53]

The instances of attempted murder by Lynette "Squeaky" Fromme and Sara Jane Moore are more well known. Fromme and Moore, the first American women convicted of attempted assassination, were involved in separate instances within a $2\frac{1}{2}$-week period in September 1975. On September 5, 1975, as President Gerald Ford was walking from his hotel to address the California State Legislature in the Capitol building in Sacramento, Squeaky Fromme suddenly appeared, pointing a .45-caliber automatic at the chief executive. A Se-

[50]Clarke, *American Assassins,* p. 187.

[51]Arthur H. Bremer, *An Assasin's Diary* (New York: Harpers Magazine Press, 1972).

[52]Clarke, *American Assassins,* pp. 128–42.

[53]Ibid.

cret Service agent leaped in front of the president and grabbed the weapon, wrestling the would-be assassin to the ground.

There is some speculation about whether Fromme intended to kill the president. But there is no doubt she was motivated by her devotion to Charles Manson.[54] She directed all her efforts toward gaining a new trial for Manson. Frustrated in her attempts to attract the media for Manson, Fromme assaulted President Ford in order to focus the attention of the nation on her forthcoming trial. She incorrectly assumed that Manson would be called as a witness by her defense counsel. This court appearance by Manson would eventually provide him with a forum to explain his vision of world order. Fromme summed up her feelings in the following statements: "Until our Christ (Manson) is taken off the cross," the world would continue on a self-destruct course, and "Charlie could do a lot for the world if given the chance."[55] Lynette Fromme was moved by a missionary zeal to spread the gospel according to Charles Manson, even if it included the attempted murder of President Ford.

On September 22, 1975, President Ford was once again the target of an attempted assassination. As the president exited the St. Francis Hotel in San Francisco amid heavy security, Sara Jane Moore fired a single shot from a .38-caliber revolver, narrowly missing him.[56] Police quickly subdued Moore, disarming her before another shot could be fired. Unlike Fromme, Moore was motivated by a desire to show "friends" on the far left that she was a fervent supporter of radical politics. Moore had previously acted as an informer for the FBI. After being dropped from their list, she confessed to the Bay-area radical community that she had informed for the FBI. Fearing retaliation for having failed her friends, Moore needed to demonstrate her loyalty to the radical left and to seek forgiveness for acting as an FBI informant. To that extent, only through personal sacrifice could she convey her sincerity and support of radical Bay-area politics. What better way than to attempt the murder of the symbol of a hated political system. Moore, now a certified revolutionary, is doing her penance—life in prison.

Finally, on March 30, 1981, John W. Hinckley shot President Reagan in the chest. The president left a Washington hotel and was about to enter his waiting limousine when several shots rang out. Besides the president, his chief press aide was shot in the head and two security guards were wounded. The would-be assassin, Hinckley, was apparently motivated by his infatuation with his favorite movie actress, Jodie Foster. Hinckley spent much of his spare time writing love letters to Foster, which she ignored. Feeling rejected by her, Hinckley wanted to do something outrageous so that Foster would recognize the depth of his passion for her. Inspired by the film *Taxi Driver,* Hinckley

---

[54]For example, see Vincent Bugliosi and Curt Gentry, *Helter Skelter: The True Story of the Manson Murders* (New York: W.W. Norton, 1974).

[55]*Sacramento Bee,* September 7, 1975, sec. A, p. 3.

[56]*Newsweek,* October 6, 1975, p. 24.

decided to assassinate President Reagan, thus ensuring the applause of Jodie Foster. Hinckley was eventually found not guilty by reason of insanity and ordered to undergo treatment in a mental hospital. He has been confined indefinitely to St. Elizabeth's Hospital in Washington, D.C.

In conclusion, with the exception of the attempted assassination of President Truman, assassins of U.S. political figures have acted alone and not as part of a political conspiracy. In brief, U.S. assassins came from disorganized and broken families, where they were often brutalized. Their life was a series of failures in which they exhibited little talent. They were marginal people who did not adjust easily to societal change. Most were short and slightly built. Their sexual lives were unfulfilled; all were lonely and had difficulty maintaining normal interpersonal relations with family and peers. They all believed that God was responsible for their actions. In sum, most U.S. assassins decided it was better to be wanted for murder than not wanted at all.[57]

CONCLUSION

Similar to terrorism, assassination is a difficult concept to define. No universally accepted definition of assassination can be found. In fact, considerable overlapping in meanings exists. Additionally, social scientists have also been concerned with the construction of a consistent typology of assassinations, and several ingenious classifications have emerged. Of particular interest for us is the fact that in almost all the proposed typologies, American assassins surface as a unique category of political murderers. Overwhelmingly, American assassins acted alone, as distinct from extended conspiracies. Conspiracy is not the common motivation for the murder of U.S. political figures despite the eagerness of many observers to find elaborate deception even in cases where little evidence for it exists. The preponderance of single assassins over theories of conspiracy has been most pronounced in instances of successful political assassination in the United States. Of all the proposed conspiracies (Lincoln, JFK, RFK, or King), only one *group* actually carried out a well-planned, although inept, assassination of an American political figure. Puerto Rican extremists attempted to assassinate President Truman.

Political assassination is undeniably dramatic. Predicting the next event is impossible. The ranks of the emotionally disturbed have been joined by the growing numbers of well-organized terrorist groups. We can only wait for the next casualty.

[57]Clarke, *American Assassins,* pp. 258–70.

REVIEW QUESTIONS

1. Distinguish between assassination and murder.
2. Define assassination.
3. Describe the typology of assassination outlined by the *National Advisory Commission on the Causes and Prevention of Violence.*
4. How are the typologies of Gross and Crotty different or similar?
5. Why is the Middle East a fertile arena for political assassination?
6. Identify the following and define:
   a. MacNaughton Rule   d. Tyrannicide
   b. Irgun/Stern Gang   e. Conspiracy theory
   c. Ustasa   f. Sultanism
7. Compare and contrast assassination in the Middle East and the United States.
8. Match U.S. assassination victims with offenders.
9. Do you think that handgun control would reduce the instance of assassination and murder in the United States? Explain.
10. Discuss similarities and differences between the Abraham Lincoln, John F. Kennedy, and Martin Luther King assassinations.
11. Describe the attempted assassination of President Truman. How does the Truman attempt differ from other U.S. political assassinations?
12. What security measures would you prescribe to reduce or eliminate attacks on U.S. political elites?

NINE

COUNTERTERRORIST MEASURES: THE RESPONSE

CHAPTER OBJECTIVES

The study of this chapter will enable you to:
- ■ Understand the major trends in counterterrorist tactics that may have an impact on future policy decisions
- ■ Differentiate between reactive and proactive counterterrorist strategies
- ■ Identify steps in the intelligence-gathering process
- ■ Describe the difficulties in the application of covert hostage rescue attempts
- ■ Explain the need for a legal framework that increases the opportunity of prosecution of terrorists
- ■ Discuss the various strategies for defeating the spread of terrorism

INTRODUCTION

In the preceding chapters it was stated that contemporary terrorism produces a credible threat to the security and stability of democratic nations. The social impact of an indiscriminate terrorist campaign of bombing or assassination cannot be overstated. Democratic governments must respond to the nature of the potential threat of terrorism. However, since contemporary terrorism first erupted onto the world stage in the late 1960s, that response has been less than adequate. In 1970 the U.S. State Department recorded 302 terrorist incidents around the world.[1] Democratic governments reacted in near panic since they had neither a common response nor the resources or equipment to counter terrorism. This lack of a coordinated response became particularly evident during the Munich Olympic hostage-taking incident. The result has been a critical examination of counterterrorism strategies and governmental policy decisions regarding a viable response to the growing threat of terrorism.

In attempting to provide that response, police and government officials may take positive action at three different stages of possible involvement in combating terrorism. The first stage is to deter acts of terrorism before they occur. Several options can be identified: (1) tighten security measures at airports, nuclear plants, or any critical industry, (2) design a general public awareness program to reduce sympathy for the terrorist cause, (3) develop effective intelligence gathering that leads to the apprehension of terrorists, and (4) find the causes of increased terrorist activity, particularly terrorist acts directed at democratic nations. If these steps fail, then police and government officials must "manage" the terrorist incident or respond with the maximum use of force.

The second stage involves such strategies as improving hostage negotiation skills and the use of various elite military units, either working within existing armed forces or as an auxiliary to counterterrorist police squads. The responsibility of these specialized military units is to provide a quick reaction force to respond to skyjackings, kidnappings, bombings, and assassinations. By the late 1970s no self-respecting democratic nation or police agency was without its own highly trained, elite, counterterrorist SWAT team. By 1984 the use of a military counterterrorist strike force was expanded to include preemptive or retaliatory measures to prevent terrorist attacks or to punish terrorist organizations.

Finally, if the act of terrorism is successfully completed and the terrorist escapes from the scene, then law enforcement authorities must locate, apprehend, prosecute, and convict the terrorist. Therefore, the third stage involves the enactment of domestic antiterrorist legislation and the acknowledgement of international treaties. In sum, the focus of this chapter is to examine several policy options open to police and government officials in their efforts to combat terrorism. The intent is not to analyze specific policies in depth but rather to explore several possible considerations for controlling, combating, and reducing terrorist acts.

---

[1]Secretary of Defense, *Annual Report to Congress*, Fiscal Year 1986, February 4, 1985, p. 23.

Security Measures

Typically, security measures include intrusion detection systems, barriers, panic alarms, uniformed guards, and a highly visible patrol force. The concept of deterring acts of terrorism is based on the old police formula for preventing crime, i.e., *desire plus opportunity = crime*. The police have little effect on controlling the desire to commit crime, but the opportunity to carry out a criminal event can be greatly reduced by a highly visible patrol force. Likewise, the opportunity to execute a terrorist act can be significantly reduced by tightening the security around potential targets. For example, once security measures were adopted seriously by commercial air carriers and airports, skyjackings were reduced by 65 percent.[2] In 1973 the introduction of metal detectors and uniformed security guards reduced the number of skyjackings of domestic and international flights. Approximately 30 skyjackings a year have been recorded worldwide since 1973.[3] Undoubtedly the number of skyjackings can be reduced further or perhaps completely eliminated if airport security management would consider adopting additional options.

Several policy options for enhancing air travel security are available. First, security managers may consider the use of more efficient explosive-detection devices. The technology is now available to identify particles from specific explosive substances that provide information about the kind of explosive, who made it, when it was manufactured, and who sold it. The process is called *microtagging*.[4] In this process, tiny chips of microtaggants are blended into the explosive substance and color coded to identify the manufacturer and the batch of explosives. These microtaggants are also magnetic and fluorescent to aid in discovery and bomb-scene reconstruction. Another innovative technological discovery, even more impressive than microtagging, is dielectric analysis. According to Gregory, all material has dielectric properties that can be easily identified.[5] Under careful laboratory conditions Gregory maintains the dielectric properties of explosive materials are as distinctive as individual fingerprints.[6] The proposal is that dielectric detectors may be installed at airports, providing immediate identification of explosive substances hidden in carry-on luggage. Yet another bomb detector claims to detect the chemical signature of virtually every known explosive substance.

Second, the inspection of not only passenger luggage but also mail, catering supplies, airport vehicles, and all cargo is advocated. Third, in the near

[2]Federal Aviation Administration, *Semiannual Report to Congress on the Effectiveness of the Civil Aviation Security Program* (Washington, D.C.: Federal Aviation Administration, April, 1985), p. 8.

[3]Ibid.

[4]A. Atley Peterson, "A Report on the Detection and Identification of Explosives by Tagging," *Journal of Forensic Sciences* 26 (April 1981), pp. 313–18.

[5]Quoted by Stephen Kindel, "Catching Terrorists," *Science Digest* 94 (September 1986), p. 78.

[6]Ibid, pp. 77–79.

future there certainly will be a need to develop detection devices for high-density plastics. The appearance of the now notorious Glock-17 plastic pistol developed by Gaston Glock presents new problems for security-conscious airports.[7] Although an assembled Glock-17 can be detected by conventional security measures since it contains approximately a pound of metal, the weapon can easily evade detection when broken down into smaller parts. The Glock-17 may be only the beginning of plastic guns. A more advanced design made of high-strength plastics is certain to be marketed soon.

Fourth, the stationing of sky marshals on flights along with the installation of high-tech devices designed to incapacitate skyjackers is yet another option. Fifth, the use of closed-circuit TV monitors on board high-risk overseas flights and imposing security clearance checks on all airport personnel may also reduce skyjackings. Sixth, a closer scrutiny of passports with a pre-flight check of all suspicious passengers; and for better identification the inclusion of fingerprints on passports may assist security in reducing the instance of skyjacking.

In the long term, the establishment of such security options would restrict the easy access to aircraft and airports by determined skyjackers. Unquestionably, the proposed options would increase the risk for skyjackers and decrease the possibility of carrying out a successful skyjacking. Certainly passenger morale and sense of security would improve with the presence of sky marshals, television monitors, and "disabling" devices. The proposed security options can help solve the problem of skyjacking, but it is not without some drawbacks. Airport security managers must also consider possible disadvantages that on the surface may not be as readily apparent.

The proposed security options are expensive, inconvenient to passengers, time-consuming to implement, and may infringe upon individual rights in a free and open society. The development of sophisticated detectors requires high-cost research. The presence of sky marshals may endanger the lives of passengers since an armed confrontation with skyjackers is more likely. For example, most airports would probably resist any increased security measures because passengers dislike being searched or having their behavior monitored by television cameras. Increased security measures also result in displacement so that terrorists shift from high-security targets to less likely ones. The clandestine nature of terrorist groups poses difficult problems for security personnel. In order to deal successfully with the potential threat of terrorism, security authorities need information. The planning of preventive security measures requires solid information-gathering techniques.

Relevant information must also be provided to the general public. It is a well-documented psychological observation that individuals who are threatened react more confidently to the threat if their awareness is heightened

[7]Nora Underwood, "Fear of Plastic Pistols," *MacLeans* 99 (March 10, 1986), p. 61; "Packing Plastic Pistols," *Science Digest* 94 (June 1986), p. 15.

by practical information. The type of information that could be most useful in desensitizing the general public about terrorism falls into three broad categories. First, the historical background of specific terrorist organizations can reduce the mystery of clandestine operations and political objectives of a campaign of terrorism. However, the dissemination of such information may provide terrorist groups with much-needed publicity. The information highlighted must, then, emphasize the indiscriminate nature of the extranormal violence of the terrorist act and not the propaganda designed to generate sympathy for freedom fighters.

Second, information about counterterrorist strategies can reassure the general public that active steps are being taken to reduce the threat of future terrorist actions. Third, forecasts about the capacity, frequency, and intensity of future terrorist operations may reduce the individual fear and general feelings of dread in democratic countries under siege by terrorism. Without such information, the public may envision an escalation of terrorism more threatening than what has actually occurred. In sum, the mass media must provide reliable, factual, and accurate information about terrorism and the political objectives of terrorist groups. Factual information is also required in the gathering of accurate intelligence data on the nature of terrorist groups and potential terrorist targets.

Intelligence Function

The need for adequate intelligence is of vital importance. Intelligence information is the first line of defense against political terrorism. The organizational structures, methods of operation, and political objectives of terrorist groups must be fully understood by police and government authorities. This is a difficult undertaking since terrorist groups strive for secrecy in order to ensure the advantage of the element of surprise. Terrorist tactics depend on the use of surprise to achieve tactical objectives. Wardlaw suggests that by utilizing surprise terrorists achieve the following goals:

1. Force police and military personnel into unplanned actions;
2. create violent situations that police and security planners are unprepared to deal with;
3. capitalize on the use of unexpected tactics;
4. disperse security personnel by diversionary tactics; and
5. create the illusion of the relative strength of the terrorist group.[8]

Obviously the element of surprise puts police and security forces at a great disadvantage; thus the need for pertinent intelligence information. But surprise is not the only disadvantage.

[8]Grant Wardlaw, *Political Terrorism: Theory, Tactics, and Countermeasures* (Cambridge: Cambridge University Press, 1982), pp. 131–34.

Terrorist groups are typically small and their clandestine operations are organized in such a manner as to limit the flow of information even within the terrorist organization itself. Contemporary terrorist groups prefer the cellular model of organization with three to ten members in each cell. The cellular organization places its greatest emphasis on the secrecy and security of group communication. Therefore, before any counterterrorist measure can be undertaken, overt or covert, police and government planners must have in their possession solid documentation of terrorist objectives. So when U.S. State Department officials, for example, argue about a military strike against terrorist training camps, how do they locate these terrorists?

Historically, a covert operator, whether a government agent or an informant, has proven to be the most valuable in obtaining intelligence information on terrorist groups. However, the use of undercover operatives is extremely dangerous. The fanaticism and intensity of terrorist groups today make covert penetration of terrorist groups especially difficult. Most terrorist groups to some extent have international ties and therefore are suspicious of new group members. An alternative to the undercover operative is the cultivation of an informant who is an active member of the terrorist group. Several democratic countries, including the United Kingdom, have used this strategy successfully.

In the early 1980s police in Northern Ireland broke through the organizational structure of the Provisional IRA. Under intense questioning and the promise of immunity from prosecution, several Provisional IRA men agreed to inform. Acting on information supplied by informers, the RUC have been able to make a number of arrests and uncover several weapons caches.[9] The use of informants continues to be an important tactic in attempts by British intelligence, the British army, and the RUC to curtail the terrorist campaign of various IRA-affiliated terrorist groups. Wilson reminds us that having productive informants is essential and indispensable in virtually all criminal terrorist cases.[10] If, however, the use of undercover agents or the development of informants proves to be too dangerous and difficult, other sources of intelligence-gathering may be pursued.

A variety of intelligence information useful to police and government officials can be found in an analysis of the political, military, economic, and scientific and technical operations of proclaimed terrorist groups.

Political intelligence includes intelligence about the terrorist group's support for a specific political ideology or philosophy. A variety of issues might be relevant: the group's relations with the Soviet Union, Iran, Syria, Libya,

---

[9]"Provos Versus the Crown: A Review of Contemporary Terrorist and Antiterrorist Operations in Northern Ireland," *Clandestine Tactics and Technology,* Update Report 8, No. 7 (1983), p. 2.

[10]James Q. Wilson, *The Investigators: Managing F.B.I. and Narcotics Agents* (New York: Basic Books, 1978), p. 61.

or Cuba; policies and attitudes relating to the Israeli-Arab conflict; support for other terrorist or revolutionary groups; and the perception of the United States, particularly related to the presence of military bases on foreign soil.

Military intelligence is required for several situations. For example, what type of weapons are preferred by terrorist groups and who supplies those weapons? In addition, the size and capability of terrorist forces as well as the location of training bases and readiness to carry out acts of violence must be continually monitored. William Casey stated that the free world is engaged in a new form of low-intensity warfare carried out by highly trained and dedicated terrorists under the military control of various nations that sponsor surrogate warfare.[11] This low-intensity conflict is directed by an enemy that is difficult to locate and even more difficult to defend against; thus there is a need for relevant military intelligence information.

Economic intelligence involves the evaluation of evidence concerning financial resources. How do terrorists get their money and how do they spend it? Adams insists that no serious study on how terrorists obtain funding existed until he published *The Financing of Terror*.[12] In this excellent volume, Adams describes several strategies terrorists use to fatten their war chests. These strategies include the sale of illegal narcotics, armed robbery, kidnapping for ransom, control of illegal activities, donations from individual contributors, lotteries and raffles, and gifts from states that sponsor terrorism.

Scientific and technical intelligence includes monitoring the development and availability of new technologies to terrorist groups. The capability of acquiring nuclear weapons should receive intelligence priority. The unknown factor revolves around the question: What are the possibilities that a terrorist group can somehow obtain a nuclear weapon? According to the U. S. Office of Nuclear Material Safety and Safeguards, hundreds of pounds of weapons-grade uranium and plutonium have disappeared and are unaccounted for.[13] It is not unreasonable to assume that some of the missing weapons-grade material has fallen into the hands of political terrorists or states that sponsor terrorism. The collection of terrorist intelligence information is costly, and a plethora of intelligence organizations disseminate intelligence information to various police and military authorities.

In the United States, intelligence information is collected via aircraft, ships, reconnaissance satellites, radar, clandestine operations, and covert intelligence stations. In general terms, the cost of collecting *all* kinds of intelligence information exceeds $10 billion per year in the United States. Surprisingly,

---

[11]William Casey, "The International Linkages—What Do We Know," in *Hydra of Carnage: International Linkages of Terrorism*, eds. Uri Ra'anan and others (Lexington, Mass.: Lexington Books, 1986), pp. 5–15.

[12]James Adams, *The Financing of Terror: Behind the PLO, IRA, Red Brigades, and M19 Stand the Paymasters* (New York: Simon and Schuster, 1986).

[13]Ovid Demaris, *Brothers in Blood: The International Terrorist Newtork* (New York: Charles Scribner's Sons, 1977), p. 392.

the number of intelligence agencies involved in the collection of information concerning terrorist activities is unknown. Some intelligence organizations are well known, such as the Central Intelligence Agency (CIA), the National Security Agency (NSA), the State Department Bureau of Intelligence and Research (INR), the National Reconnaissance Office (NRO), and the Defense Intelligence Agency (DIA). However, other intelligence agencies, services, and offices exist that only marginally collect and disseminate intelligence on terrorism. For example, the U.S. Air Force publishes *Current News: Summaries of Terrorist Incidents,* and the International Association of Chiefs of Police provides update reports on terrorism in *Clandestine Tactics and Technology.*[14]

Regardless of the source of data used, the process includes the collection, collation, analysis, and dissemination of data gathered on terrorism incidents and terrorist organizations. Figure 9-1 describes the intelligence information cycle. The first step in the process is to collect information, data, and intelligence. The next step is the analysis of the information. Some information may be difficult to analyze since terrorist groups often conceal their true objectives by engaging in media campaigns of disinformation. The analyst must decide the validity and reliability of each piece of information. Then that information must be compared with existing information to determine new trends and to specifically identify individuals and terrorist or criminal organizations. The final step is to disseminate relevant information to police and military personnel in the most expedient and secure means available. Only by carefully analyzing terrorist information can command authorities conduct a relevant threat analysis.

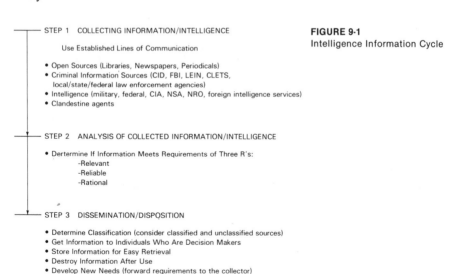

STEP 1   COLLECTING INFORMATION/INTELLIGENCE

    Use Established Lines of Communication

- Open Sources (Libraries, Newspapers, Periodicals)
- Criminal Information Sources (CID, FBI, LEIN, CLETS, local/state/federal law enforcement agencies)
- Intelligence (military, federal, CIA, NSA, NRO, foreign intelligence services)
- Clandestine agents

STEP 2   ANALYSIS OF COLLECTED INFORMATION/INTELLIGENCE

- Dertermine If Information Meets Requirements of Three R's:
  -Relevant
  -Reliable
  -Rational

STEP 3   DISSEMINATION/DISPOSITION

- Determine Classification (consider classified and unclassified sources)
- Get Information to Individuals Who Are Decision Makers
- Store Information for Easy Retrieval
- Destroy Information After Use
- Develop New Needs (forward requirements to the collector)
- Forecast Trends and Developments
- Evaluate Problems
- Conduct Threat Analysis

FIGURE 9-1
Intelligence Information Cycle

[14]Jeffrey T. Richelson, *The U.S. Intelligence Community* (Cambridge, Mass.: Ballinger, 1985), p. 11.

A threat analysis is a comprehensive review of all available intelligence information in order to evaluate security measures in terms of potential terrorist targets and vulnerabilities. The elements of a complete threat analysis are included in the following proposition:

$$\text{Threat analysis} = \text{terrorist information/intelligence} + \text{threat} + \text{vulnerabilities}$$

The failure to review continuously the organization's overall threat assessment could seriously restrict police and military antiterrorism measures and the ability to mount counterterrorist operations. If security measures prove inadequate and potential targets easy for terrorist groups to penetrate, and if intelligence indicates a dangerous threat to the safety and security of the state, then police and security managers must consider the use of elite military or police forces.

Counterterrorist Operations: Retaliation and Preemption

Despite improved physical security around potential terrorist targets, a public somewhat better informed about terrorism, and the collection of relevant intelligence information, acts of political terrorism continue to escalate in both numbers and ferocity. Terrorist groups now appear to be more inclined to conduct large-scale, indiscriminate attacks against completely innocent victims. The trend in the 1980s is to attack public places such as airport terminals, trains, department stores and public gatherings. Such attacks are calculated to kill as many innocent people as possible. This lethality of terrorist assaults has led democratic nations to consider the use of retaliation and preemptive military strikes against terrorist bases, training facilities, and countries that sponsor terrorism.

Since 1981 U.S. government officials have declared that the United States would employ force to preempt or retaliate for terrorist attacks. The purpose of such retaliation is to punish terrorists or criminals who have committed terrorist assaults and retreated to the safety of bases beyond the reach of conventional police or military forces. The guiding example of this type of retaliation is the Israeli commando raids on suspected Palestinian Liberation strongholds.

Israel was the first nation to articulate a deliberate and official policy of retaliation against terrorism. However, there certainly is a great deal of moral ambiguity about preemptive strikes. Many innocent bystanders have become victims of Israeli preemption. At times retaliatory strikes seem as terroristic as random car bombings. Since 1951 the Israeli Defense Forces have conducted large reprisal raids and preemptive strikes against Palestinian guerrilla bases and hostile Arab countries. In practice, Israel frequently goes beyond the principle of "an eye for an eye," seeking to inflict maximum casualties on the Palestinians. Such was the case in October, 1953, at the Arab village of Qibya, where Israeli forces killed 42 men, women, and children in retaliation for the terrorist murder of an Israeli woman and two children.[15] In June, 1981, the Israelis destroyed an Iraqi nuclear facility in a preemptive bombing raid. Israel claimed Iraq was close to attaining a nuclear military option that they would unleash against the state of Israel. Israel has conducted hundreds of retaliatory raids and preemptive strikes against "hostile" Arab targets. The practice was sanctioned by the Israeli people and was especially popular among the nationalistic elements of the population. This has not been the case in the United States.

Although public support in the United States for retaliatory strikes against terrorist groups and sponsoring nations is strong in the wake of a major terrorist episode, that support quickly vanishes once the terrorist incident ends. Many government officials and citizens of the United States are uncertain about the use of military force to cope with terrorism. There is no doubt that the democratic principles embraced by the United States create ambiguities about the moral aspects of using military force, particularly bombing raids. One school of thought argues that retaliation only invites terrorists to escalate their strategy of indiscriminate violence. Another school of thought believes that retaliation is necessary to demonstrate American resolve not to be passive victims of indiscriminate acts of terrorist violence. During the course of intense debate and heated rhetoric on this issue, President Reagan signed, on April 3, 1984, the National Security Decision Directive 138, which permits the United States to use retaliatory military force legally against terrorists who attack U.S. citizens, interests, or allies.[16] United States targets of retaliation have been identified as individual terrorists, terrorist training camps, or any country that sponsors, aids, or abets terrorist organizations.

Even though the United States is now committed to a policy of retaliation, the concept has been vigorously resisted by White House staff members, especially Vice President Bush and Secretary of Defense Caspar Weinberger. Motley summarizes the opinion of many observers who feel that because of a lack of information it is doubtful that the United States will ever carry out a successful retaliatory military strike against terrorist bases.[17] The lack of detailed intelligence information prevents the use of retaliatory or preemptive military actions against terrorists by U.S. forces. President Reagan acknowledged this fact, stating that the lack of precise information regarding terrorists keeps the United States from retaliating against known terrorist strongholds.[18]

[15]Fred J. Khouri, *The Arab-Israeli Dilemma* (Syracuse, N.Y.: Syracuse University Press, 1985), pp. 187–88.

[16]*Public Report of the Vice President's Task Force on Combating Terrorism* (Washington, D.C.: U.S. Government Printing Office, February, 1986), p. 15.

[17]James B. Motley, "Target America: The Undeclared War," in *Fighting Back: Winning the War Against Terrorism,* eds. Neil C. Livingstone and Terrell E. Arnold (Lexington, Mass.: Lexington Books, 1986), p. 73.

[18]*New York Times,* January 27, 1985, p. 12.

But on April 4, 1986, U.S. intelligence services allegedly intercepted several messages between Gaddafi of Libya and his agents in West Berlin.[19] According to the U.S. State Department, the intercepted messages provided the first clear and detailed evidence of Libyan participation in a terrorist attack. Libyan terrorists had bombed a Berlin nightclub frequented by U.S. servicemen. One U.S. soldier was killed and several were seriously injured. The evidence of Libyan complicity in terrorist attacks directed against U.S. citizens was viewed as irrefutable by the Reagan administration. Amid controversy and internal dissension, President Reagan made plans for a retaliatory air strike against suspected Libyan terrorist training bases.

The planned "surgical" air strike, code-named "Operation El Dorado Canyon," began on Monday, April 14, 1986. Twenty-four F-111s from the 48th Tactical Fighter Wing along with various support aircraft left southern England and headed towards the Mediterranean and Libya. Five hours later, after a 2,800-mile flight, the aircraft, now reduced to thirteen fighters, began their attack on Tripoli, Libya. The targets consisted of two military airfields, a military barracks, a training center for elite naval personnel, and Gaddafi's headquarters. While all the targets were hit, several non-targets came under attack as well. The fears expressed by critics of the retaliatory strike were all too accurate. The primary fear concerned the impossibility of reliably distinguishing between military targets and civilian areas. Several civilian houses were hit as well as the French and Swiss embassies, a community park and a children's playground. Six men, three women, and two children were killed, including Gaddafi's 15-month-old adopted daughter. Sixty civilians were injured, including two of Gaddafi's other children. Later it was reported that 40 people were killed. The Libyans were to use the casualties to great political advantage. The world's press focused on the injuries to the innocent victims, visiting hospitals and photographing dead children. These pictures were spread throughout the world, depicting the United States as a military superpower that badly overreacted.[20]

All aircraft, except one F-111 that had been hit by antiaircraft fire and crashed, returned safely to their bases.[21] The mission, viewed in strictly military terms, was deemed a success. But the political fallout that resulted from the raid was far greater than the military success. The raid was condemned by the United States NATO allies in Europe. Politicians and citizens in Britain, France, Spain, and Italy overwhelmingly opposed the raid. In contrast, the raid was hailed by Americans, and support for President Reagan's tough, new stand against terrorism was high.

More practically, the immediate aftermath of the raid seemed to confirm

[19]*Sacramento Bee,* April 15, 1986, sec. A, p. 8.

[20]*New York Times,* April 15, 1986, p. 1; *Time,* April 21, 1986, pp. 17–29; *Newsweek,* April 21, 1986, pp. 21–26.

[21]*Sacramento Bee,* April 16, 1986, p. 1.

earlier observations that retaliation equals greater retaliation and escalation. Two British and one American hostage being held for several months in Lebanon were executed. The British ambassador's residence in Beirut was attacked; also in Beirut a British journalist was hanged and another was taken hostage. A U.S. employee was shot in Khartoum, and an attempt to bomb London's Heathrow Airport was uncovered by security police. Attacks were made on U.S. embassies in Mexico, Indonesia, and Tokyo, and U.S. military bases in West Germany, Spain, and Japan. Certainly this violence was in reprisal for the U.S. raid on Libya. A well-planned terrorist assault takes months to set in motion, so the response to the U.S. raid could manifest itself at some time in the future. Undoubtedly the U.S. attack on Libya will act as a future rallying cry for international terrorist groups, and terrorism against American targets will escalate. Given the high cost of the U.S. air raid on Libya, did the benefits make it worthwhile?

On the one hand, Adams concludes that the United States made a serious political, military, and moral mistake by bombing Libya.[22] He concludes that the result of the bombing raid will result in new complications within the NATO alliance and an escalation of terrorism against NATO targets; the distinction between state-sponsored terrorism and reprisals by democratic nations will become difficult to evaluate. On the other hand, secretary of state Schultz argues that terrorists are murderers and lawbreakers, and the United States should take forceful action against them.[23] Schultz claims there is no moral question. The United States merely responds to acts of indiscriminate murder by considering both the use and effectiveness of military force as a weapon against future attacks. The argument maintains that failure to strike back forcefully encourages more attacks against Americans. A policy of retaliation would make it clear to international terrorist groups that Americans traveling abroad are not soft targets and that the United States has an obligation to its citizens to punish murderers beyond the reach of the U.S. legal system.

There is little doubt that Libya was an easy target. Repeating such attacks to counter an expected rise in anti-American terrorism in the future would be extremely difficult. The United States is not Israel. The Israelis are determined to destroy the PLO and refuse to yield to hostage-takers, skyjackers, or bombers. But Israel is engaged in an undeclared war with the PLO and various Arab nations, and as such has no moral ambiguity over the use of retaliation or preemptive air strikes. Like Israel, Livingstone and Arnold believe that the United States and other western democracies are involved in a state of war with nations that sponsor international terrorism.[24] Only by

[22]Adams, *The Financing of Terror,* pp. 31–32.

[23]George P. Schultz, "The U.S. Must Retaliate Against Terrorist States," in *Terrorism: Opposing Viewpoints*, eds. David L. Bender and Bruno Leone (St. Paul, Minn.: Greenhaven Press, 1986), pp. 197–203.

[24]Neil C. Livingstone and Terrell E. Arnold, "The Rise of State-Sponsored Terrorism," *Fighting Back: Winning the War Against Terrorism,* eds. Neil C. Livingstone and Terrell E. Arnold (Lexington, Mass.: Lexington Books, 1986), pp. 11–23.

acknowledging the magnitude of the terrorist problem can the United States take active steps to combat it. The United States and its NATO allies are only now beginning to realize that a state of low-intensity warfare exists with nations that support terrorist activities. Israeli ambassador to the United Nations Netanyahu unequivocally states that the United States and other western democracies are clearly justified in waging defensive as well as offensive war against nations such as Libya, Syria, and Iran, which sponsor international terrorism.[25] The current rhetoric proposed by the U.S. State Department, no doubt influenced by Israel, supports not only retaliatory air raids but also the organization of a covert counterterrorist squad that would infiltrate and make preemptive military strikes against terrorist training facilities.

Covert Military Operations: Proactive Measures

The objectives of commando-type assaults would be to inflict casualties on terrorists and destroy their base of operation. The plan would use a clandestine military force to track down and penetrate terrorist groups in an effort to defeat the terrorist threat. This clandestine, or Special Operations Force (SOF), is not new to U.S. military adherents of guerrilla-style warfare. However, military traditionalists who prefer to plan for an all-out, conventional-style war oppose the formation and use of small guerrilla-type commando forces. High-ranking military-staff planners opposed to special operations are concerned that an emphasis on clandestine tactics will reproduce Central Intelligence Agency (CIA) involvement in minimilitary projects. Military planners fear that the misuse of such Special Operations Forces by the CIA will create long-term problems for the United States by contributing to the escalation of terrorism and low-intensity warfare.

CIA covert actions have been directed at all major areas of conflict in the world—Africa, the Middle East, Eastern Europe and the Soviet Union, Asia, and Latin America. Covert actions by the CIA include a wide range of activities: (1) political advice, (2) subsidies to individuals, (3) financial support to political "democratic" groups, (4) disinformation and propaganda campaigns, (5) private training of insurgent forces, (6) paramilitary operations designed to overthrow a government, and (7) assassinations.[26] Probably the best-known of the CIA covert actions are the ones directed at Cuba. Not only did the CIA attempt to assassinate Castro several times but it also planned the Bay of Pigs invasion, trained guerrilla forces in the swamps of Florida for that invasion, conducted sabotage and economic warfare, and was involved in a

---

[25] Benjamin Netanyahu, *Terrorism: How the West Can Win* (New York: Farrar, Straus & Giroux, 1986), pp. 204–208.

[26] Victor Marchetti and John Marks, *The CIA and the Cult of Intelligence* (New York: Knopf, 1983), p. 334.

variety of propaganda and disinformation activities.[27] But the covert action that has generated the greatest publicity has been the one directed at the Sandinista government in Nicaragua. The Nicaraguan-CIA paramilitary operation clearly highlights the issues involved in covert activities.

The issues of adopting a policy of covert operations in the United States are both ethical and practical. Under what conditions are covert actions morally justified? Does the history of U.S. covert operations suggest that such actions have a long-term benefit for U.S. national interersts in the complicated world of foreign policy in efforts to defeat international terrorism?

Several U.S. presidents have sanctioned military covert operations. President Kennedy authorized a program of sabotage against Cuba. President Ford argued that covert military operations were acceptable international strategies. President Reagan stated that "every country" has the right to use covert actions when it believes its national interests are threatened.[28]

The implication of such presidential remarks is the acceptability of covert military operations when there is a direct, immediate threat to the national security of democratic nations. There is no doubt that the U.S. government feels physically threatened by a variety of international terrorist groups and the countries that support them. The benefits of adopting covert military operations as a planned governmental policy are several:

1. The directness of the military assault would cause the terrorists to lose face and prestige;
2. covert operations would be less objectionable than air strikes and would likely lessen world criticism;
3. more precise assaults would reduce the damage to civilian property and eliminate unnecessary civilian casualties;
4. actions could be accomplished with military forces already trained and in position to act;
5. military objectives would be selective and attacks on specific terrorist targets would lessen operations casualties;
6. the costs would be much lower than air strikes; and
7. democracies are not morally, ethically, or legally bound to deal in a civilized fashion with those who seek to destroy the democratic way of life.

On the other side of the issue, it is difficult to justify a policy of covert military operations to attack terrorists or their sponsors. Such a policy has several pitfalls:

1. The operations unit would be in danger of capture;
2. a failed mission would be embarrasing to the United States and discredit a policy of planned retaliation;

[27]Warren Hinckle and William Turner, *The Fish is Red: The Story of the Secret War Against Castro* (New York: Harper and Row, 1981), p. 106; John Ranelagh, *The Agency: The Rise and Decline of the CIA* (New York: Simon and Schuster, 1986), pp. 349–82.

[28]*New York Times,* October 21, 1983, sec. A, p. 35.

3. if the commando unit is withdrawn before completion of the mission, policy-makers run the risk of escalation of the problem;
4. intelligence information in covert operations often is inadequate and inaccurate;
5. the cooperation of friendly forces and nations is essential for success; however, most nations would not support such covert U.S. actions for fear of retaliation by terrorists or their sponsors;
6. small wars have a tendency to escalate into larger wars; and
7. the history of U.S. covert operations does not support the view that such operations serve the long-term interests of the United States.

For example, the Green Berets were often misused, many becoming on-loan members of the CIA's secret army in Vietnam and Laos, a situation encouraging the rejection of future Special Operations Forces in the Pentagon.

The issue of covert military operations has been debated for decades. But until the policymakers face up to the realities of terrorism and low-intensity conflict, the United States will remain a highly visible and too often helpless target. Traditionally, the role of the military in counterterrorist operations has been one of "reaction" rather than "proaction."

Counterterrorist Operations: Reactive Measures

In the recent past, the deployment of military forces for internal security duties in democratic nations has produced much controversy. The increase of random political terrorism has caused the governments of Britain, Canada, West Germany, Australia, France, and Italy to call out the troops to provide internal protection and to assist the police in searching for terrorist hideouts. In 1970 the Canadian government invoked the War Measures Act, enabling government troops to conduct a search of residential areas of Montreal in an attempt to apprehend terrorist hostage-takers of the Front Liberation du Quebec (FLQ), who had abducted James Cross, the British Trade Commissioner. The War Measures Act gave Canadian government forces broad legal powers of detention for questioning and abrogated individual rights related to search and seizure. The act remained in force for approximately 6 months. Since 1969 British Security Forces have seen duty in Northern Ireland attempting to defeat the terrorist activities of the Provisional IRA and various reactionary, Protestant paramilitary groups. In West Germany and Italy government troops have been called into action to provide security for airports, to guard transport routes, to protect government officials, and to search the countryside for terrorist bases and safe houses. In May 1980, elite British troops of the Special Air Service (SAS) regiment were used to rescue hostages being held by terrorists in the Iranian Embassy in London. All of these incidents have caused heated arguments about the role of governmental armed forces in support of civil authorities responding to terrorist attacks. In sum, what are the specific roles of the armed forces and the police in internal security problems in a democracy?

Nearly all writers on terrorism are concerned with the need to maintain a balance between security measures used to protect against terrorism and individual rights of liberty and freedom. Wardlaw argues that as far as possible the local police should provide for the internal security of citizens, and that the distinctive roles of police and military security forces need to be clearly defined.[29] Heavily armed detachments of military troops responding to control local internal matters, whether terrorism or public order, only serve to incite the citizenry against the government. The military is incapable, by their mission, philosophy, and training, to adequately respond to an internal security matter involving a terrorist attack. In assessing the capabilities of the United States, the federal government is guided by the Constitution. The protection of life and property and the maintenance of public order are the responsibilities of state and local government police forces. The federal government can assume police responsibilities only in certain limited circumstances.

Acts defined as terrorism are crimes already proscribed by state and local statutes. Certain terrorist acts also violate federal criminal statutes. These include hijacking, kidnapping, hostage-holding, bombing, and assassination. The lead agency for the management of terrorist incidents is the FBI. The initial tactical response and the resolution of incidents defined as terrorism are also the responsibility of the FBI. However, in the event that a prolonged terrorist attack erupts and exceeds the capacity of local civil police agencies or the FBI to control and resolve the incident, then the president has the option to use specially trained and equipped military forces to restore order and preserve life. This presidential option was used during the urban riots of the 1960s when President Johnson stationed federal troops throughout the United States. The use of military forces is necessary only in extreme circumstances. In such extreme cases, the United States does have a counterterrorist military unit ready to respond anywhere in the world to protect U.S. interests and to attempt the rescue of U.S. citizens being held hostage outside the United States. This military unit is called the Delta Force.

As you recall, military actions may serve to deter future terrorist acts and could also encourage other nations to adopt a no-concessions policy. Successful employment, however, depends to a large extent on timely and refined intelligence and prompt positioning of forces. Counterterrorism missions are high risk–high gain operations that can have a severe negative impact on U.S. prestige if they fail. An example was the abortive rescue mission in Iran.

After 5 months of stalled negotiations to free the American hostages in Iran in 1980, President Carter severed diplomatic relations and gave the go-ahead for an attempted military rescue. The rescue mission was to be carried out by the newly formed U.S. counterterrorist team—Delta Force. On April 25, 1980, eight helicopters were to rendezvous with six C-130 tactical air transports about 200 miles southeast of Tehran. In brief, the plan was to refuel the

---

[29]Wardlaw, *Political Terrorism*, p. 89.

aircraft, then under the cover of darkness fly to the outskirts of Tehran, rest until the following evening, and then in buses and cars provided by CIA-supported agents, drive to the U.S. Embassy and rescue the American hostages. However, from the start, several unfortunate circumstances prevented the successful completion of the rescue mission.[30]

Two of the helicopters experienced engine trouble and were forced to land in the Iranian desert where they were abandoned by the crew. The remaining six helicopters flew directly into a fierce, unpredicted sandstorm. The helicopters had to fly at a lower altitude through the sandstorm in order to avoid Iranian radar detection. The helicopter crews momentarily lost their direction and failed to arrive at the rendezvous at the appointed time. The six C-130s encountered no difficulties en route. But sometime after the C-130s were in position, an Iranian bus, fuel truck, and pickup truck came down a nearby road. The vehicles refused to stop. Warning shots were fired by the rescue team and eventually the passengers on the bus were held hostage, the fuel truck exploded into flames, and the pickup escaped.[31]

In the meantime, a third helicopter broke down and was judged unsafe. This left five remaining helicopters, one below the minimum outlined by operational planners. Not wanting to attempt the rescue with less than the minimum number of aircraft, President Carter gave the order to cancel the mission. As one of the helicopters moved into position for refueling, it collided with a C-130. Both aircraft burst into flames, and exploding shell casings and burning ammunition endangered the other aircraft.

Eight members of the team died in the crash and their remains were left behind. The decision to leave the bodies of rescue team members behind was based on both the urgent need to leave the area before Iranian military spotted the flames and the fact that it would have taken too much time to wait until the aircraft cooled sufficiently to recover the bodies. Almost 4 hours after the first contingent arrived at the rendezvous location, the remaining 200-member military task force left the Iranian desert. In their haste to make a quick getaway, the rescue team left behind on the abandoned helicopters numerous classified materials, including alternative escape routes, personnel lists, planning documents, and lists of undercover agents operating inside Iran.[32]

There is little doubt that the Iranian hostage rescue mission was an utter failure. In fact, many high-ranking military officials decided early in the planning stages that the mission would fail.[33] American hostages scattered through-

[30]Charles A. Beckwith and Donald Knox, *Delta Force* (New York: Dell, 1983), pp. 233–36.

[31]Hamilton Jordan, *Crisis: The Last Years of the Carter Presidency* (New York: Putnam, 1982), pp. 254–63.

[32]Gary Sick, *All Fall Down: America's Tragic Encounter with Iran* (New York: Random House, 1984), pp. 84–96.

[33]Paul Ryan, *The Iranian Rescue Mission: Why It Failed* (Annapolis, Md: Naval Institute, 1985), pp. 17–45.

out Tehran also believed the rescue team had little chance of success.[34] The Iranian military recovered the eight bodies of the rescue team and put them on display for the entire world to see. The failed rescue mission was a great propaganda victory for Iran. However, the United States is not the only nation that has experienced humiliation and defeat attempting to rescue hostages with reactive counterterrorist military forces.

In February, 1978, Egyptian commandos attempted to rescue hostages in Cyprus; the result was an equally spectacular failure. Palestinian hostage takers skyjacked a Cyprus Airways jetliner and forced it to land at Larnaca Airport, Cyprus. An Egyptian hostage who was a close friend of President Sadat was slain by the hijackers. An Egyptian military counterterrorist team landed at Larnaca and attempted to storm onto the aircraft and rescue the hostages. However, the Egyptian commando team did not receive or arrange the proper clearance with Cypriot authorities. Upon seeing Egyptian forces and apparently not having any knowledge of the rescue mission, the Cypriot National Guard attacked the commandos. The Egyptians lost 15 men in the brief but deadly firefight and failed to gain entrance into the aircraft. The Palestinian skyjackers eventually surrendered to Cypriot police. The Larnaca and Tehran rescue attempts illustrate the difficulties involved in planning a long-range military intervention in a terrorist hostage situation.[35]

Short-range rescue attempts have also presented problems for Egypt. In a more recent Egyptian commando-style raid to rescue hostages on board an Egyptian jetliner, 60 hostages were killed. On November 23, 1985, three Palestinians of the Abu Nidal faction diverted an Egyptian aircraft to the island of Malta. Unlike the Cyprus fiasco, the Maltese government had permitted the Egyptian commandos to undertake a rescue of the hostages. In the confusion, as the commandos stormed the aircraft, the hostages got caught in a crossfire between the rescue squad and the hostage-takers. Thirty-eight hostages survived. The three hostage-takers were slain. The Egyptians, with the backing of the United States, proclaimed that the rescue mission was a success.[36]

Despite the failures, there have been some counterterrorist, military rescue missions that have been described by the media as successful. However, upon closer review, the reader can only conclude that successful rescue missions have also been failures. The most well known is the Israeli commando-style raid on Entebbe Airport in Uganda. On June 27, 1976, terrorist skyjackers, under the sponsorship of the PFLP, hijacked an Air France jet from Athens and diverted it to Entebbe. Fearing that Israeli and Jewish hostages

---

[34]Robert D. McFadden and others, *No Hiding Place: Inside Report on the Hostage Crisis* (New York: Times Books, 1981), pp. 87–100. See also accounts by former hostages Kathryn Koob, *Guest of the Revolution* (New York: Thomas Nelson, 1982); Barry Rosen, Barbara Rosen, and George Feifer, *The Destined Hour: The Hostage Crisis and One Family's Ordeal* (New York: Doubleday, 1982).

[35]*Newsweek,* March 6, 1978, pp. 33–34; *Time,* March 6, 1978, pp. 40–45.

[36]*New York Times,* November 26, 1985, p. 1.

would be killed, the Israelis mounted a bold and successful rescue mission. Under the cover of darkness and catching the hostage-takers completely by surprise, the Israelis assaulted the hostage location. After a brief but furious gun battle, 7 hostage-takers, 20 Ugandan soldiers, and 3 Israeli hostages were killed. The remaining hostages were freed and returned to Israel.[37]

On October 18, 1977, a similar rescue was accomplished by members of the West German counterterrorist squad, GSG-9 (Grenzschutzgruppen). Four skyjackers forced a Lufthansa jet to land at Mogadishu Airport in Somalia. The West German commando group stormed the aircraft and, in a firefight that lasted approximately 9 minutes, killed three of the hostage-takers, seriously wounded another, and rescued the terrified hostages.[38]

More recently, military counterterrorist groups have been used to effect the rescue of hostages in domestic hostage-taking incidents. The results have been far from successful. On November 6, 1985, leftist terrorists of the Colombian M-19 movement shot their way into the Palace of Justice in Bogota and held over 100 hostages. Colombian counterinsurgency military units stormed the palace, and in the ensuing gun battle a staggering 93 people were massacred, including 12 Supreme Court judges, 23 hostage-takers, and 58 completely innocent hostages. More than 3000 counterterrorist soldiers backed by tanks, artillery, and heavy machine guns took part in the assault.[39]

Pakistan was confronted with a similar hostage situation on September 6, 1986. The hijackers were four Abu Nidal Palestinians who boarded and seized the plane in Karachi. After several hours of unproductive negotiations, Pakistani counterterrorist commandos were called into action. As the commandos prepared to assault the aircraft, a generator on board the plane failed, plunging the cabin into darkness. The hostage-takers, sensing a commando-style attack to free the hostages, turned their weapons on the passengers. The hostage-takers began to fire indiscriminately into the helpless hostages who had been collected in the center of the cabin. In the end the arrival of the commando force further jeopardized the lives of the hostages, for now they became caught in a crossfire. Eighteen hostages were killed, approximately 325 were wounded, and the 4 Palestinian hijackers were apprehended.[40]

The use of the military in a counterterrorist role has thus far proven unsatisfactory, particularly the use of heavily armed troops to rescue hostages. Military forces are not trained to handle domestic police problems. Schoch writes that "counterterrorism is basically a police function at which regular

---

[37]For example, see William Stevenson, *Ninety Minutes at Entebbe* (New York: Bantam, 1977); Ze'ev Scheff, *Entebbe Rescue* (New York: Dell, 1977).

[38]Peter Koch and Kai Hermann, *Assault at Mogadishu* (London: Corgi Books, 1977); *Time*, October 31, 1977, pp. 42–45.

[39]*New York Times*, November 7, 1985, p. 1; *San Francisco Examiner*, November 10, 1985, sec. A, p. 18.

[40]*San Francisco Examiner*, September 7, 1986, p. 1; *Time*, September 15, 1986, pp. 30–35.

military units have generally shown themselves to be inept."[41] Several problems can be identified. First, the deployment of large numbers of uniformed troops implies a serious terrorist threat exists that could be used to the propaganda advantage of terrorist groups. Second, the presence of military troops may incite violence rather than prevent it. Third, the commitment of troops indicates that less violent methods, such as negotiation, have failed and terrorism cannot be controlled no matter how much force the government has at its disposal. Fourth, armed troops are more likely to be used for political reasons unacceptable in a democratcy, where the roles of police and military are significantly different. Finally, counterterrorist operations should be limited to specific strike actions where there is no other option, and not expanded to include order maintenance or security responsibilities. In the case of skyjackings, every effort should be made to peacefully negotiate the release of hostages.

The containment of terrorism, as far as police are concerned, should be a police function handled by police agencies. Each police agency should have a specialized unit prepared to deal with explosives, hostage negotiations, and firearms. Only in extreme situations that the police are unable to handle should armed military troops be called out. In the absence of widespread social unrest, there is no justification for the use of large numbers of military troops or specialized counterterrorist units to respond to terrorism incidents. The military should be assigned as a counterterrorist reaction force and again only in the most extreme circumstances. Presently in the United States and other democratic nations with the exception of Israel perhaps, no situations exist that the police cannot cope with, although admittedly that could change. In the event that it does change and acts of terrorism present widespread threats to social order, then the use of elite military counterterrorist units may be needed. As long as democratic nations can avoid the use of military forces, they should do so. Terrorism is a law enforcement problem, and the use of military forces, whether proactive or reactive, is unwarranted in the present circumstances. Attempts to control terrorism will always focus on the police response and the legal and treaty obligations rather than action-oriented military responses.

Legal Framework: Apprehension, Prosecution, and Punishment

The international community has considered several treaties or conventions specifically to fight the growing threat of terrorism. The central problem confronting the international community is agreeing on a common definition of terrorism. Since most treaties or conventions are formalized legal proceedings, all participants must accept a common definition of terms. The issue of what constitutes an act of terrorism is the most perplexing, unresolved prob-

[41]Bruce P. Schoch, "Four Rules for a Successful Rescue," *Army* 16 (February 1981), pp. 22–26.

lem in arguments about terrorism. Undoubtedly, the dissent and confusion surrounding an agreement on terrorism for the purpose of international conventions has contributed to the escalation of terrorism.

The precedent for establishing antiterrorist cooperation is the 1937 Convention for the Prevention and Punishment of Terrorism.[42] This Convention was initiated after the assassination of King Alexander I of Yugoslavia and French Foreign Minister Louis Barthou in Marseilles in 1934. The assassins represented an obscure group of Croatian freedom fighters, or terrorists, depending upon how terrorism is defined. The 1937 convention defined it as "criminal acts directed against a state and intended or calculated to create a state of terror in the minds of particular persons, or a group of persons, or the general public."[43] The 1937 convention considered two provisions relating to terrorism: (1) that attacks on heads of state or internationally protected persons are a criminal act regardless of motivation; (2) that the destruction of public property or the willful endangering of citizens of one country by another be proscribed under international law.[44] The most controversial issue of the convention was the extradition of offenders. Most countries refused to extradite offenders for political crimes. Because of these problems—lack of a precise definition, how to handle the extradition of offenders, and the impending signs of world war—the 1937 convention was never ratified, thus making it impotent and unenforceable.

Since 1937 and the escalation of international terrorism, the United Nations has adopted six antiterrorist treaties or conventions. These include three conventions ratified under the direction of the International Civil Aviation Organization and three adopted by the United Nations.[45] They are:

1. The Convention of Offenses and Certains Acts Committed on Board Aircraft, Tokyo Convention, September 14, 1963.

2. The Convention for the Suppression of Unlawful Seizure of Aircraft, The Hague Convention, December 16, 1970.

3. The Convention for the Suppression of Unlawful Acts Against the Safety of Civilian Aircraft, Montreal Convention, September 23, 1971.

4. The Convention on the Prevention and Punishment of Crimes Against Internationally Protected Persons, including Diplomatic Agents, New York Convention, December 14, 1973.

5. The International Convention Against the Taking of Hostages, West Germany Convention, 1979.

6. The Convention on the Physical Protection of Nuclear Material, International Atomic Energy Commission, March 3, 1980.

---

[42]Yonah Alexander, Marjorie Ann Brown, and Allen S. Nanes, eds., *Control of Terrorism: International Documents* (New York: Crane, Russak, 1979), pp. 19–31.

[43]Ibid., p. 21.

[44]Ibid., pp. 21–24.

[45]Ibid., pp. 45–113.

The focus of these conventions is to establish a formalized structure for international cooperation among nations to prevent and suppress international terrorism. The New York convention, for example, requires the cooperation by all signatories to prevent attacks on diplomats, to coordinate administrative measures against such assaults, and to exchange information on terrorist groups and individual offenders. In the event that a diplomat is attacked and the offender flees the country where the attack occurred, the signatories are obliged to make every effort to identify the offender and assist in determining his whereabouts. Additionally, if the offender successfully flees the country where the attack occurred and takes refuge in another country and is apprehended, then the offender must either be extradited or prosecuted for his crime.[46]

The most controversial issue of these conventions is the extradition of offenders. Strictly speaking, the extradition of offenders is not required in them. Rather they contain language that strongly induces nations to extradite the accused offender; and if extradition fails, the accused must be prosecuted in the country where apprehension took place. In a more practical sense, the conventions also obligate the signatories to apprehend and detain the suspect. However, there is no general agreement that absolutely obliges the requested country to return the accused to the requesting country to stand trial for the crimes. Usually countries will have agreed upon extradition treaties for the return of fleeing felons.

These treaties can often prove hypercritical, embarrassing, and contradictory. For example, at about the same time the United States was demanding the extradition of two Iranian hijackers who murdered two American civilians, a U.S. federal judge invoked the "political exception" rule and refused to return to the United Kingdom a Provisional IRA member who escaped while on trial for murdering a British soldier. The British requested that the PIRA revolutionary be extradited to serve his prison sentence for the murder. The PIRA escapee who had taken refuge in the United States resisted extradition on the grounds that his crimes were political, citing a treaty between the United States and Britain that forbids extradition for crimes of a "political character." The political exception rule has been used by several IRA guerrillas, allowing the United States to become a haven for Irish political terrorists. However, by July 17, 1986, the United States and the United Kingdom ratified a new treaty that would prohibit criminals, particularly IRA revolutionaries, from taking refuge in either country. On October 21, 1986, the United States finally extradited a PIRA assassin to the United Kingdom to stand trial for the murder of a London police officer.[47]

In this way western democracies retain their discretion to grant political

---

[46]Ibid., pp. 77–85.

[47]*Sacramento Bee,* July 18, 1986, sec. A, p.1; *Sacramento Bee,* October 21, 1981, sec. A, p. 8.

asylum to offenders when they consider the offense to be of a political nature. According to framers of the conventions, the entire extradition process is ambiguous, time-consuming, and cumbersome.[48]

To overcome some of the problems of international conventions, three conventions with a regional scope have attempted to fight the spread of international terrorism. These include:[49]

1. The Convention to Prevent and Punish Acts of Terrorism Taking the Form of Crimes Against Persons and Related Extortion That Are of International Significance, OAS Convention, Washington, D.C., February 2, 1971.
2. The European Convention on the Suppression of Terrorism, European Convention, United Kingdom, October 25, 1978.
3. The Agreement on the Application of the European Convention for the Suppression of Terrorism, Dublin Agreement, 1980.

The basic focus of these three conventions is somewhat different in their approach to combat the threat of terrorism.

The OAS convention, for example, in spite of its lengthy title, is limited to the protection of diplomatic personnel. The convention is also ambiguous with reference to establishing workable extradition treaties. In fact, a country is not obligated to extradite the alleged offender; and it may also refuse to prosecute the alleged offender without violating the provisions of the Convention.

The European convention deals directly with the most frustrating international problem in combating terrorism—the "political offense exception" rule. Extradition treaties commonly provide an exception for political offenses. Unfortunately, the convention fails to define what constitutes a political offense. The approach of the convention is to list a series of crimes that are to be excluded from the political offense exception rule. The convention failed to agree on the distinction between political crime and common crime. Equally, the convention failed to provide a definition of terrorism acceptable to all participants.

The Dublin accords attempted to strengthen the provisions of extradition outlined by the European convention. First, the conditions of extradition would apply to all signatories without reservations, even if one state has enacted a political offense exception. Second, any dissent made to the European convention would not apply in extradition proceedings. Nine European nations participated in the Dublin accords and have yet to ratify the proceedings. Again, a disagreement over the definition of terrorism and political crime has prevented the extradition of terrorists.

Both international and regional conventions have taken only a limited

---

[48]John F. Murphy, *Punishing International Terrorists: The Legal Framework for Policy Initiatives* (New Jersey: Rowman and Allanheld, 1985), pp. 9–11.

[49]Ibid., pp. 11–16.

approach toward reducing the incidence of political terrorism, and cover only specific manifestations of international terrorism. Accordingly, when a terrorist commits an act of terrorism in one country and flees to another, he or she can be prosecuted only if the country where he or she is apprehended agrees to return him or her to the country where the offense was committed. In today's world, return is highly unlikely, since terrorism to some is heroism to others. In the absence of strong international provisions against terrorism, some democratic countries have enacted tough antiterrorist legislation and invoked emergency powers.

Unfortunately, the emergency powers that democracies must enact to defeat terrorism are the same powers that totalitarian states use to subjugate entire populations. In West Germany, terrorist groups have forced the federal government to enact antiterrorist emergency legislation that is the most repressive in a liberal democracy.[50] Even the names given to these emergency powers connote a need for extreme action to cope with outbreaks of terrorism. In Spain a "State of Exception" exists; in Northern Ireland, "Special Powers" have been enacted; in India certain areas are declared "Terrorist Affected"; and in Uruguay, "Prompt Security Measures" resulted in the defeat of the Tupamaros and also the end of constitutional democracy for 12 years. Typically, in an emergency situation democratic governments will enact the following broad categories of draconian legislation to defeat terrorist threats to internal security:

1. All citizens are required to carry identity cards that include a photograph, fingerprints, and signature. Identity cards, for example, were required in Italy and Spain during the most recent outbreaks of terrorism. In West Germany police can establish roadblocks to make identity checks.

2. Firearms, ammunition, and explosives are controlled. The tactic is to make the legal acquisition of weapons as difficult as possible.

3. Special courts are established to try suspected terrorists for heinous political crimes. In India special courts try offenses that impinge on the security and territorial integrity of the country. India also imposed the death penalty for terrorist acts. France has abolished jury trials involving charges of terrorism. Northern Ireland has abolished jury trials also in terrorist cases.

4. Other harsh penalties were enacted in hopes of deterring future acts of terrorism. Italy now imposes a mandatory life sentence for the killing of a police officer. In Northern Ireland suspects can be interned indefinitely for possession of firearms or explosives. In West Germany anyone who disseminates "terrorist" literature can be imprisoned for three years.

---

[50]For example, see M. Radvanyi, *Antiterrorist Legislation in the Federal Republic of Germany* (Washington, D.C.: Law Library, Library of Congress, 1979); Herman Blei, "Terrorism, Domestic, and International: The West German Experience," *Report of the Task Force on Disorders and Terrorism* (Washington, D.C.: U.S. Government Printing Office, 1976), pp. 497–506; Karlheinz Gemmer, "Problems, Means, and Methods of Police Action in the Federal Republic of Germany," In *Hostage Taking,* eds., Ronald D. Crelinsten and Denis Szabo (Lexington, Mass.: D.C. Heath, 1979), pp. 119–26.

5. Security forces are now permitted in several countries to arrest and question people without charge, to search houses and vehicles without warrants, to intern suspects, and to impose curfews. The situation in Northern Ireland is an example of this type of infringement of rights.

6. Substantive rights such as free speech and the right of assembly are curtailed; censorship and the banning of organizations are frequently imposed. In Northern Ireland the assembly of three or more people is a violation of Special Powers.

The obvious question concerns the effectiveness of emergency legislation. Does the enactment of emergency provisions to fight terrorism have a greater impact than international or regional treaties? Hewitt states that the results are mixed but most often emergency legislation has no discernible impact on terrorism.[51] Wardlaw argues that democracies should not arbitrarily disregard all emergency legislation as ineffective.[52] Extreme circumstances may exist in which security forces need extensive powers to stop, search, question, or detain people suspected of terrorist involvement. The proper evaluation of terrorist legislation, emergency powers, and international treaties is an important consideration for U.S. lawmakers. The U.S. Congress only recently began to vigorously pass legislation to improve the apprehension, prosecution, and punishment of terrorists and the control of terrorism.

In 1984 the U.S. Congress passed several antiterrorist bills. This legislation made it a federal offense to commit an act of violence against any passenger on board civilian or government aircraft. Hijackers can now be prosecuted for the destruction of foreign aircraft outside the United States if they take refuge in the United States. Crimes against high-ranking federal government officials can now be prosecuted under special legislation. The new "Murder for Hire" legislation makes it possible to prosecute persons who travel interstate or use foreign transportation for the purpose of murder or assassination. Congress has posted reward money under the direction of the FBI for information leading to the arrest and conviction of international terrorists. Laws concerning traffic in arms have been expanded to make it illegal to train any foreign national in the use of firearms, munitions, and explosives. The death penalty has been approved in hostage-taking situations where hostages are deliberately murdered. Anyone who kills, assaults, or kidnaps a U.S. citizen outside the United States can be prosecuted if returned to the United States. The most difficult legislation has involved the debate over extradition proceedings. The United States currently is negotiating with several countries to revise the extradition process and the political offense exception rule.[53]

The continental United States has not been exposed to the widespread random terrorism that many other liberal democracies have had to cope with.

---

[51]Christopher Hewitt, *The Effectiveness of Anti-Terrorist Policies* (New York: University Press of America, 1984), pp. 61–67.

[52]Wardlaw, *Political Terrorism*, 1982, p. 130.

[53]*Vice President's Task Force*, 1985, pp. 15–16.

Despite 1985 being considered the worst year yet for recorded acts of international terrorism, the FBI reported only seven terrorist incidents in the United States. Therefore, in the United States the rule of constitutional law still prevails. There has been no need for emergency powers or the diluting of individual and civil rights. However, this situation could change in the near future.

CONCLUSION

So what do we have to do to fight and defeat the spread of terrorism? The first line of defense against terrorism is to tighten security measures. The protection of people and places is quickly evolving from the total reliance on poorly trained, undereducated, and underpaid security guards to the development of high-technology intrusion systems. The media's concentration on terrorism has provided the general population with current information on terrorism, even though media coverage of terrorist incidents sensationalizes the violence. The effective management of the many diverse components and assets of the intelligence community is crucial in order to acquire the most pertinent, relevant information on terroristic activities.

The second line of defense in response to widespread terrorism is the use of elite military forces for retaliation, preemption, or prevention. The willingness to use the armed forces in such actions as air strikes or covert operations is indispensable to defeat terrorism. Otherwise, the deterrent capability of liberal democracies would be nonexistent. Commando-style raids against known terrorist installations are considered by the United States and other democracies to be a credible alternative in the fight against terrorism. However, it must be remembered that military force should be used only as a last resort.

Nations typically respond to terrorism by strengthening existing laws and enacting emergency legislation. Often this emergency legislation deprives the population of various individual and civil liberties. Detention without trial, warrantless searches and seizures, establishment of special courts, and other extreme legal measures should be used with great caution. However, emergency powers may be justified to illustrate the government's determination to defeat terrorism; and the enactment of such legislation provides a proscribed legal framework for security forces, police or military, to respond to the potential threat of terrorism. Finally, the improvement of extradition treaties would enhance the prospects of bringing international terrorists to justice. The U.S. Congress needs to reform the extradition laws of the United States to make them more effective to combat the spread of international terrorism.

As of this writing, there certainly appears to be a great deal of confusion and hypocrisy on the appropriate U.S. response to terrorism. The foreign policy crisis over the U.S. sale of arms to Iran raises some confounding questions. The response to terrorism must be unambiguous and most of all consistent if the United States and its allies hope to defeat terrorism in the 1990s.

REVIEW QUESTIONS

1. Describe the intelligence information function.
2. Do you believe the United States should pursue a policy of retaliation or preemption? Why or why not?
3. What major measures can the international community take to prevent terrorism?
4. Define the following terms:
   a. Extradition
   b. Covert operations
   c. Dielectric analysis
   d. Microtagging
   e. Civil liberties
5. Do you think the United States should follow Israel's example in fighting terrorism? Explain fully.
6. What is the most insidious consequence of responding to the potential spread of terrorism? Discuss your response.
7. Respond to the following statements:
   a. Most politically motivated murders of U.S. citizens in recent years have come as a result of international terrorism.
   b. Violent actions conducted by surrogates are preferable to direct U.S. attacks on terrorists.
   c. Terrorism is low-intensity warfare in which innocent civilians are targets.
8. Identify and explain at least three international conventions organized to suppress terrorism.
9. Describe the various intelligence-gathering methods.
10. Discuss the impact of emergency powers on defeating terrorism.

TEN

FUTURE OF TERRORISM

CHAPTER OBJECTIVES

The study of this chapter will enable you to:
- Reexamine the Palestine question
- Explore the growth of Islamic fundamentalism
- Discuss the theory of state-sponsored terrorism
- Describe low-intensity warfare
- Discuss the future prospect of "super terrorism"
- Evaluate the influence of terrorism on the quality of life in the United States
- Estimate the future of terrorism and political violence

INTRODUCTION

After nearly 20 years of political and criminal terrorism, there can be few who have not been exposed to the atrocities and fanaticism waged by commandos, freedom fighters and guerrillas throughout the world. The ritualized massacre of hundreds of innocent civilians is all too well known. Terrorist shooting sprees in Rome, Vienna, and Lod, bombings so numerous that today several are recorded each day, and the monthly hostage-taking incidents have brought the drama of terrorism into sharp media focus. The media has made certain that millions are now familiar with the dreams of Palestinians and obscure Islamic religious fundamentalists, with the fantasies of the Red Army Faction and the Red Brigades, and with the alphabet of murder—PFLP, PIRA, FALN, and ASALA. Lebanon, Syria, and Iran are now found in daily media headlines of terrorism instead of travel brochures depicting the exotic Middle East. Terrorist attacks are planned for the prime-time viewer, and after each attack there is a plea for vengeance or at least for instituting tighter security measures. The repetition of terrorist attacks has become so ritualized that now each terrorist drama is a rerun. The script seems never to change. The deaths of innocent victims of terrorism are brought to us close up and made very personal by the media.

Capturing the attention of an audience may be easy, but terrorist groups need to heighten the drama in order to sustain that interest. This requires changing demands, locations, performers, and types of terrorist incidents. The most ingeniously contrived terrorist action can, if repeated too often, cause the intended audience to become bored and disinterested in the grievances of the terrorist group. To be effective, then, terrorists cannot attack the same target or continually use the same strategy.

Both sides, government and terrorists, like to be able to predict within reason the outcome of a terrorist incident. A government's interest in predictability is to reduce the element of surprise that gives terrorists a great advantage, but terrorists are equally interested in predictability. Terrorists want to attract media attention and create interest in their cause without damaging their image as freedom fighters or inviting massive government retaliation such as the Israeli retaliation against the PLO. The inevitable outcome of a terrorist incident in no way detracts from government involvement; if anything, predicting the outcome of a terrorist incident heightens anticipation and involvement for both terrorists, government, and police officials.

The prediction of future directions in terrorism and the threat that acts of indiscriminate violence will pose for democratic societies is an obvious consideration for government planners. The attempt to forecast future terrorist actions is an exercise ladened with danger and uncertainty, for the ability to accurately predict future events may be a form of crystal-ball gazing that produces an unrealistic picture of increased terrorism.[1] There is little agreement among scholars whether terrorism will continue to escalate or decline. Jenkins predicts that by the end of the century a new generation of terrorists will have taken the field, compelled to escalate their terrorism so as to maintain public

[1]David Carlton, "The Future of Political Substate Violence," in *Terrorism: Theory and Practice,* eds. Yonah Alexander, David Carlton, and Paul Wilkinson (Boulder, Colo.: Westview Press, 1979), pp. 201–4.

attention or to react to restrictive governmental power.[2] Apter argues that terrorism will gradually decline as terrorist groups recognize the futility of indiscriminate campaigns of violence that only serve to alienate the general society.[3] Still others conclude that the prospect of nuclear terrorism poses the greatest threat to the stability of the world.[4] Bearing in mind these conflicting observations, can we accurately predict the future directions of terrorism?

In this chapter we focus on the factors presented in earlier chapters that are currently thought to contribute to the escalation of world terrorism. In the first section, the continuation of the Palestinian problem is explored. The second section contains a review of Islamic fundamentalist terrorism in the context of the Iranian revolution. The third section will attempt to evaluate the concept of terrorism as a form of low-intensity warfare and the role of state-sponsored terrorism. The prospect of super terrorism is detailed in the fourth section. How accurate are earlier warnings that terrorists will inevitably go nuclear? Finally, the influence that terrorism has on the quality of life in a democracy is examined.

Israel versus Palestinian Resistance Movement

The Palestinian Resistance Movement is no closer today in recovering Palestine than it was in 1948 when Israel first proclaimed its statehood. Unmistakably, the Palestinians and the Israelis are implacable enemies, and they will remain so for considerable time to come. Netanyahu maintains that the spark of contemporary terrorism was ignited by Palestinian attacks against soft Israeli targets.[5] Eventually, Palestinian terrorism directed against Israeli targets expanded to include attacks against moderate Arab nations, moderate Palestinians, and the United States. Israel and the Palestinians have been engaged in an undeclared "underground" war since the mid-1960s. In June, 1982, that war was broadened when Israeli Defense Forces launched a blitzkrieg-style assault across the Lebanese border to finally destroy the infrastructure of Palestinian unity—the PLO. In the process the Israelis captured several documents that revealed the central role played by the PLO in contributing to the escalation of worldwide terrorism. The PLO had apparently created a miniterrorist state in Lebanon, where training centers and launching areas of international terrorism had been established.[6] However, the Israeli raid developed

[2]Brian Jenkins, "The Future Course of International Terrorism," *TVI Report* 6 (Fall 1985), S3–7.

[3]David E. Apter, "Notes on the Underground: Left Violence and the National State," *Daedalus* 108 (Fall, 1979), pp. 155–72.

[4]See, for example, Richard Barnet, "Nuclear Terrorism: Can It Be Stopped," *Current* 211, (March/April 1979); 30–40: David M. Krieger, "What Happens If . . . ? Terrorists, Revolutionaries, and Nuclear Weapons," *The Annals* 430 (March, 1977), pp. 44–57.

[5]Benjamin Netanyahu, ed., *Terrorism: How the West Can Win* (New York: Farrar, Straus & Giroux, 1986), p. 11.

[6]Ibid., pp. 11–13.

into a full-scale war lasting for 3 years. The major objective of the Lebanon war—the destruction of the PLO—was never accomplished. In fact, it is doubtful whether the Israeli blitzkrieg strategy had any effect at all on the PLO. Adams reports that the assets of the PLO exceed an impressive $6 billion.[7] With that kind of money, it will not take the PLO long to rebuild. Thus, the armed struggle to liberate the "occupied territories" and all Palestine will undoubtedly continue. However, the PLO has accomplished little by terrorism or violence. The Palestinians have not regained one acre of the land lost in the Palestinian diaspora of 1948, or the devastating defeat in 1967. Even so, the Palestinians have informed the world through incredible acts of violence that a great injustice has been done to the Palestinian people. Can Israel and the PLO, "the sole legitimate representatives of the Palestinian people," end the bloodshed and terrorism as so many statesmen and writers believe and urge?

Several peace plans for a reduction of hostilities between the PLO and Israel have been proposed—the Reagan Plan, the Soviet Plan, the Fez Plan, and the Saudi Plan. The best-known variant of all plans advocating the territorial compromise is the so-called Allon Plan.[8] All plans support the concept of "territory for peace." The major conclusion of the plans is that the creation on the West Bank and Gaza of an independent Palestinian state that meets certain minimal requirements would do much to bring peace not only to Israel but to the entire Middle East. However, almost all Israelis regard the creation of a Palestinian state as an immediate threat to their security and a long-term threat to the existence of the state of Israel.

Critics of territory for peace believe that the PLO would use the territory as a base for the destabilization of both Israel and Jordan.[9] They point to the PLO's constitution, which is clearly incompatible with the existence of the Israeli state. Still others write that Israeli fears are unwarranted and that a Palestinian state could peacefully and easily coexist if the Israelis would withdraw to their pre-June 1967 borders.[10] Even if the Israelis and the PLO were able to come to terms over the West Bank and Gaza, extremists within the PLO would certainly attack the Palestinian "traitors." Long before the Palestinian state could attack or destabilize Israel, it would likely destabilize itself through continuing internecine warfare. Chances are that a Palestinian state would likely collapse before it could launch successful attacks against Israel.

Attractive as the territory for peace sounds, it does not appear to be a feasible option for the West Bank, Gaza, or other occupied territories. Israel will remain in control of the West Bank and Gaza for a long time to come. As Conor Cruise O'Brien writes, "The idea of Israel withdrawing to its pre-

[7]James Adams, *The Financing of Terror* (New York: Simon & Schuster, 1986), pp. 83–131.

[8]Mark A. Heller, *A Palestinian State: The Implications for Israel* (Cambridge, Mass.: Harvard University Press, 1983), p. 35.

[9]Ibid., pp. 55–104.

[10]For example see, Noam Chomsky, *The Fateful Triangle: The United States, Israel and the Palestinians* (Boston: South End Press, 1983).

June 1967 territory and living there behind secure and recognized frontiers, in peace with all its neighbors, is an agreeable international pipedream. The reality is that Israel will stay in the West Bank where its presence will continue to be challenged from within and without."[11] The presence of Israel on the West Bank is likely to be continuously challenged by the PLO. In December, 1986, for example, there were several days of uncontrolled rioting on the West Bank after Israeli occupation troops killed a Palestinian student. Several Palestinians were subsequently killed as the rioting escalated throughout the West Bank and Gaza. The West Bank could become another Northern Ireland and Jerusalem another Belfast.

Additionally, as the years of Israeli occupation of the West Bank continue, the controversy over the establishment of Jewish settlements will also continue. The Palestinian Arabs, of course, strongly oppose any Jewish settlements in the "occupied territories." The Palestinians are supported by the international community, where it is widely believed that Jewish settlements on the West Bank are illegal and violate international law and the Geneva Convention. Israeli opinion supports the position that the West Bank is part of the sovereign state of Israel; and further, if Jews want to settle on the West Bank, they have the legal right to do so. There is fairly widespread agreement within Israel on the intrinsic right of Jews to settle in "Judea and Samaria," the land of the ancient Hebrews. Some of the settlements are little more than paramilitary outposts, while others are substantial agricultural or residential ventures, often with mystical Jewish historical connotations. A Palestinian state would surely prevent further Jewish settlement and might possibly mean the relocation of those Jewish settlements already established on the West Bank.

However, several Jewish religious fundamentalist groups vowed never again to be driven out of "Judea and Samaria." For example, the issues of religion and land are inseparable to the Gush Emunim (Block of the Faithful). Members of the Gush Emunim strongly believe that both the Jewish nation and the Jewish land are sacred, since they were both chosen by God. The Gush maintain they are fulfilling a religious prophecy and reviving the Jewish spirit of pioneers by settling on the West Bank, that is, Judea and Samaria. The ultimate objective of the Gush is to drive all Arabs out of the West Bank and reestablish a secular Jewish nation.[12]

The combination of religious fervor and the question of Israeli security make the establishment of a Palestinian state in the West Bank and Gaza a highly unlikely proposition at this time. Furthermore, Heller observes that the

---

[11]Conor Cruise O'Brien, *The Siege: The Saga of Israel and Zionism* (New York: Simon & Schuster, 1986), p. 650.

[12]David Newman, *Jewish Settlement in the West Bank: The Role of Gush Emunim* (Durham, N.C.: University of Durham Centre for Middle Eastern and Islamic Studies, 1982), pp. 27–30.

physical characteristics of the West Bank complicate the task of defending Israel's vital core area in which over 60 percent of its population and 80 percent of its industry are concentrated.[13] The geographic features of the West Bank, then, make it a formidable defensive asset for Israel and a definite threat if occupied by hostile Palestinian forces.

In sum, after nearly 2000 years, the Jews had finally regained Jerusalem, Judea, and Samaria; and to expect the Jews to hand over Jerusalem (the ancient city of David), the home of the ancient Hebrews, is to ask the impossible. Realistically, the Israelis will continue to dominate the West Bank and Gaza; and the 1.3 million Palestinians living under Israeli occupation will undoubtedly continue to resist. Most Palestinians living on the West Bank and Gaza are loyal to the PLO. One can only conclude that this loyalty will continue, and terrorism and resistance supported by various PLO-affiliated groups will continue to escalate. The debate over the illusory and highly publicized pursuit of territory for peace is likely to continue. The critical question of how to make the sharing of territory less dangerous and less uncomfortable for Israelis and Palestinians will continue to dominate international politics. Most likely, the Israelis will not yield and the Palestinians will continue their struggle to recover Palestine. Terrorism can, then, be expected to escalate as desperate Palestinian extremist groups fight for self-determination. In spite of the Palestinian-Israeli conflict and widespread acknowledgement of the justification of Palestinian political violence, a new strain of terrorism has spread throughout the Middle East. The results have been more deadly than any trend in international terrorism since the Palestinian-Arab-Israeli conflict began in 1948.

Islamic Extremism

After the 1979 Iranian revolution, the Middle East erupted into a spasm of political violence and terrorism that continues to this day. The early targets were not U.S. citizens or Europeans but Middle Easterners. The terrorist incidents were dramatic attention-getting events designed to provide maximum publicity to yet unknown Islamic religious fundamentalist groups. The assassination of Egyptian President Anwar Sadat, the attempted assassination of the president of Iraq, the 1981 plot to overthrow the government of Bahrain and install an Islamic republic, the plot to overthrow the Kuwaiti government in 1982, the 1987 seizure of the Grand Mosque in Mecca, and the Islamic uprisings in Saudi Arabia, Lebanon, Egypt, and Syria have all generated extensive news coverage. But other less publicized terrorist incidents have passed and been forgotten. Skyjackings of Arab jetliners, kidnappings of Arab government officials, assassinations of Arab civilians, and attacks on Arab businesses and cultural centers have become commonplace in the Middle East.

Amorphous groups with exotic-sounding names such as Islamic Amal,

---

[13]Heller, *A Palestinian State,* pp. 12–14.

Islamic Jihad and Hizballah began to attract media attention in the early 1980s. Little is known about the groups responsible for this new surge in Mideast terrorism except that they are thought to be Shi'ite Muslims. Islamic Amal of Lebanon, for example, attracted worldwide attention after involvement in several well-staged skyjackings. One Amal skyjacker has become a legend in the Shia community of the Middle East for successfully hijacking an astonishing six aircraft. The largest Shia movement in Lebanon is Amal. Amal is the Arabic word for "hope" as well as an acronym for the "Lebanese Resistance Battalions." Nabih Berri took over the leadership of Amal after the disappearance of Imam Sadr, the founder of Amal. Wright reports that by 1982 Amal split into two factions, and a more extremist faction called Hizballah, or "Party of God," emerged.[14]

Hizballah derives its name from a verse in the Koran which promises eternal life for those who join the Party of God and spread the message of Islam. With the support of Iran, Hizballah has grown among the disaffected Shi'ite minority, especially in Lebanon. Proclaiming world Islamic revolution and martyrdom, Hizballah followers represent a variety of Muslim fundamentalist beliefs. Attempts to understand the religious crusade of both Amal and Hizballah led to predictions that a revengeful Islamic world is preparing for a *jihad,* or holy war, against Christianity, Judaism, capitalism, and godless communism. The extremist Islamic world allegedly mobilized for such a jihad against the Israel presence in Lebanon in the early 1980s. Eventually Israel withdrew most of its military forces from Lebanon. Jihad, or holy war, promotes the concept of conscious martyrdom or purification through death, which is apparently the core belief of the radical Shi'ite sects of Amal, Hizballah, and Islamic Jihad.[15]

Only when the United States and other Westerners came under attack was the concept of jihad taken more seriously. Suicide car bombers attacked the U.S. Embassy, the U.S. Marine Command Center, and the French, British, and Italian multinational peacekeeping force in Lebanon. The French and U.S. embassies in Kuwait were also blown up by suicide car bombers and several theatrical skyjackings were staged between 1983 and 1986. At one point, Iranian officials were quoted as saying that 1000 suicide bombers were prepared to strike targets in the United States. By the end of 1983, the Reagan administration labeled the attacks on western targets as "state-sponsored terrorism." The United States charged that Iran was providing the financial and technical support for terrorist acts directed against the United States. Eventually, the Shi'ite Islamic sect became synonymous with the term *terrorism* in the United States. In some respects the Shi'ites had replaced extremist Palestinian groups as the most determined of international terrorist groups. The growth

---

[14]Robin Wright, *Sacred Rage: The Wrath of Militant Islam* (New York: Simon & Schuster, 1986), p. 82.

[15]Ibid., pp. 104–6, 236–38.

of Shi'ite extremism is complex, but undoubtedly the Lebanese civil war has contributed to the escalation of Shi'ite terrorism.

As the cycle of international terrorism shifts from one group to another, terrorist attacks usually become more devastating. Iran, under the Ayatollah Khomeini, has emerged as the leading patron of international terrorism; his support for terrorism is potentially more damaging than anything experienced by the PLO or PIRA. Unlike most terrorist organizations which have definite objectives—the recovery of Palestine or a united Ireland, the Iranian-sponsored extremist groups divide the entire world into two distinct categories: enemies of Iran and enemies of Islam. However, the two categories are not mutually exclusive. Since the U.S. Embassy was overrun in Tehran in 1979, U.S. citizens have become a prime target of Iranian-sponsored terrorists. Several Americans have been kidnapped in Lebanon by Iranian-sponsored terrorist groups such as Islamic Jihad and Amal. Iranian surrogates have also attacked U.S. interests in Europe and North Africa.[16]

The Shi'ites of Iran are convinced that they have been unfairly treated by the Arab countries of the Middle East and manipulated by the West. Khomeini has apparently taken Shi'ite discontent and molded it into a combination of religious fervor and national pride. Khomeini apparently views his destiny as one of destroying the heretics of Islam and diminishing the seductive influence of the "Great Satan," the United States. Since November 1981, Shi'ite Iranian-sponsored terrorists have carried out 32 terrorist attacks. Six attacks involved the newest terrorist strategy—suicide vehicle bombers. The majority of these attacks were directed against American targets in the Middle East.[17]

The growth of Iranian extremism is particularly alarming to western nations because Shi'ite fanatics are willing to sacrifice their lives for religious beliefs. Previously, all terrorists had carried out their terrorist attacks with well-devised plans of escape. Such logical planning does not apply to most Shi'ite terrorism. In many cases, in fact, the opposite seems true. Some Shi'ite martyrs choose death and gladly welcome the opportunity to enter paradise in exchange for the killing of western unbelievers and the eradication of Islamic heretics.

There seems to be little disagreement that Iran has planned for some time to export its revolution to other parts of the Islamic world, especially Middle Eastern countries. Casey noted that leaders of Shi'ite extremist movements recently met in Tehran to discuss the role of the Iranian government in spreading the true word of Islam throughout the world and the allocation of money to establish terrorist training camps and fund specific acts of terrorism.[18] The

---

[16]Neil C. Livingstone and Terrell E. Arnold, "The Rise of State-Sponsored Terrorism," *Fighting Back: Winning the War Against Terrorism* (Lexington, Mass.: Lexington Books, 1986), pp. 15–22.

[17]Wright, *Sacred Rage,* pp. 15–45.

[18]William J. Casey, "The International Linkages—What Do We Know," in *Hydra of Carnage: International Linkages of Terrorism,* eds. Uri Ra'anan, et al (Lexington, Mass.: Lexington Books, 1986), pp. 5–15.

cash allocation apparently contributed to the formation of Amal, Hizballah, and Islamic Jihad in Lebanon, and a series of suicide vehicle bomb attacks in Lebanon and Kuwait. Moreover, Ra'anan presents two credible documents, one containing the top secret minutes of a meeting of Iranian government leaders held on May 26, 1984, in which they outline the creation of a brigade-sized terrorist unit to destabilize and attack targets throughout the Middle East.[19] The second document, which Ra'anan and his colleagues at the Fletcher School of Law and Diplomacy present, claims to contain the manifesto of Hizballah, which emphatically states that it is directly linked to and receives support from Khomeini's Iran.[20] The Hizballah document openly proclaims responsibility for the suicide bombing of the Marine command center and the U.S. Embassy in Lebanon in 1983.

Western society, particularly the United States, is ill-prepared to combat the twentieth-century strategy of Iranian-sponsored terrorism, which draws heavily on its eleventh-century religious philosophy. Religious zealotry and suicidal fanaticism are virtually unknown to the United States. The Shi'ites, under the guidance of Iran, may now have a chance to influence the Islamic world by their dedication to fanatical religious principles. Iranian-sponsored terrorism will undoubtedly continue for some years to come. The state sponsor plays an important role in the formation of international terrorist groups. Nonetheless, if Iran is considered by the U.S. Department of State, the CIA, and President Reagan to be the principal sponsor of terrorism directed against the United States, then the United States has made a terrible blunder in its stated foreign policy and antiterrorism and counterterrorism strategy.

As of this writing, several high-ranking U.S. government officials have approved the sale of weapons and spare parts to Iran. The alleged sale of the weapons is in direct violation of an arms embargo that the United States placed on Iran in 1982. The sale to Iran also contradicts the antiterrorist policy of the United States which has attempted to isolate Iran from the rest of the world, claiming Iran sponsored international terrorism. The evidence linking Iranian-sponsored terrorism to attacks on U.S. targets in the Mideast and Europe is irrefutable. Further, the U.S. arms deal demonstrated the hypocrisy of the U.S. antiterrorism policy when President Reagan proposed that it would be unlawful for an American citizen to provide maintenance (mechanical or other services) to specified terrorist groups.[21] Certainly providing weapons to the enemy is in violation of that proposal. In fact, Casey stated that "more blood has been shed by Iranian-sponsored terrorism during the last few years than by all other terrorists combined."[22]

[19]Ibid., pp. 480–87.

[20]Ibid., pp. 488–92.

[21]*Public Report of the Vice President's Task Force on Combating Terrorism* (Washington, D.C.: U.S. Government Printing Office, 1986), pp. 7–17.

[22]Casey, *Hydra of Carnage*, p. 6.

What has come to be called Iranscam is just beginning to unfold. The Iran Contra hearings have exposed an administration engaged in the consistent withholding of information and repeated attempt at misleading Congress and the American people. Trails have led to a dozen countries, expanding the cast of characters, preoccupying Congress, and damaging U.S. antiterrorism and foreign policy. There are still far more questions than answers, and it may take several years to piece together this complex puzzle. But one thing is certain, the credibility of the U.S. antiterrorism policy has been badly damaged. President Reagan has repeatedly castigated France, Italy, Spain, and other NATO allies for making secret deals with Iran and Libya, when in fact Reagan himself signed an arms for hostages agreement. This ambivalence of U.S. antiterrorism policy could lead to an increase of terrorism against U.S. targets, both civilian and military.

Besides Iran, the U.S. government has also identified Syria and Libya as state sponsors of international terrorism. The theory of state-sponsored terrorism suggests that the bombings, kidnappings, and assassinations are directed by a single source attempting to destabilize western democratic nations. This conspiracy theory is supported by the U.S. Department of State, which proclaims, "The Soviet Union and its allies (Libya and Syria) have provided training, arms, and other direct and indirect support to a variety of national insurgent and separatist groups. Many of these groups commit international terrorist attacks as part of their program of revolutionary violence."[23] The Reagan administration is convinced that the mastermind of world terrorism is the Soviet Union and furthermore, that countries like Iran, Syria, Libya, and the PLO are the surrogates of an overall Soviet strategy to escalate low-intensity conflicts throughout the world by sponsoring terrorist organizations.

Low-Intensity Warfare

Several commentators maintain that the Soviet Union positively supports a variety of terrorist groups, particularly in Europe where the focus of terrorist attacks is directed toward destabilizing NATO countries.[24] Conventional warfare has become extremely dangerous for both superpowers, and an apparent nuclear power balance prevails between the United States and the Soviet

---

[23]U.S. Department of State, *Patterns of International Terrorism: 1982* (Washington, D.C.: U.S. Government Printing Office, 1983), Doc. #5, p. 18.

[24]For example, see Netanyahu, *Terrorism: How the West Can Win,* pp. 104–6; Ra'anan, et al, *Hydra of Carnage: International Linkages of Terrorism* (Lexington, Mass.: Lexington Books, 1986); Livingstone and Terrell, *Fighting Back: Winning the War Against Terrorism,* pp. 63–76; Claire Sterling, *The Terror Network: The Secret War of International Terrorism* (New York: Holt, Rinehart and Winston, 1980); Galia Golan, *The Soviet Union and the Palestine Liberation Organization* (New York: Praeger, 1980); Ray S. Cline and Yonah Alexander, *Terrorism: The Soviet Connection* (New York: Crane, Russak, 1984); Roberta Goren, *The Soviet Union and Terrorism* (London: Allen & Unwin, 1984); John Barron, *KGB Today: The Hidden Hand* (New York: Berkley Books, 1985).

Union. This nuclear standoff has led the Soviet Union to support international terrorism, insurgency, guerrilla wars, and wars of national liberation as a substitute for traditional warfare that could quickly escalate into nuclear war. Goren adds that the Soviet role in state-sponsored international terrorism should not be misunderstood since Soviet support of terrorist groups, whether extreme right or extreme left, is essentially to attain its political and military objectives.[25] Those objectives are to destabilize the free world, spread Soviet influence throughout the world, and assist pro-Soviet "liberation" movements to gain power. More pragmatic objectives involve the use of terrorism to eliminate anticommunist forces in various countries, to provoke western democracies to overreact, and to disrupt the military establishment and the criminal justice system. A variety of unconventional conflicts and episodes of indiscriminate terrorism are currently a permanent feature of the international community. Whether the Soviet Union is directly responsible for *all* of these conflicts is still debatable. Herman argues that it is absurd to place the blame for the increase of worldwide, unconventional conflicts on the Soviet Union.[26] There is, however, considerable disagreement regarding the definition and nature of unconventional conflicts and Soviet support for such conflicts.

The term *low-intensity conflict* is widely used to describe various forms of unconventional wars. The U.S. Army defines low-intensity conflicts as "conflicts ranging from terrorism, revolution, counterrevolution to limited small war operations conducted by a political group to achieve a major political goal that can include the overthrow of the existing system and replacing it with a new leadership and political-social order."[27] Other writers give little credence to the notion of unconventional conflicts and divide all violent political conflicts, including international terrorism, into low-intensity and high-intensity areas.[28] In the end, unconventional conflicts include a broad range of extranormal types of political violence. The most common and damaging to the survival of democracies is terrorism/counterterrorism and revolution/counterrevolution. Terrorism is a strategic and tactical concept fundamental to the success of a well-planned guerrilla war, insurgency or revolution. Marighella reminds us that "terrorism is an arm the revolutionary can never relinquish."[29]

Sarkesian presents a unique model for categorizing unconventional conflicts. He argues that to respond effectively to acts of political violence, a more comprehensive understanding of unconventional conflicts is necessary. He

[25]Goren, *The Soviet Union and Terrorism,* pp. 196–98.

[26]Edward S. Herman, *The Real Terror Network: Terrorism in Fact and Propaganda (Boston: South End Press, 1983), pp. 54–63.*

[27]*Low Intensity Conflict,* Army FM 100–30 (Washington, D.C.: Department of the Army, 1981), p. 24.

[28]*Executive Risk Assessment* (Alexandria, Va.: Risks International, 1986).

[29]Carlos Marighella, *The Terrorist Classic: Manual of the Urban Guerrilla* (Chapel Hill, N.C.: Documentary, 1985), p. 84.

identifies five types of world conflict. At one end of his conflict spectrum are conflicts unlikely to escalate into total warfare, that is, terrorism; and at the other end is the ultimate conflict—nuclear holocaust.[30] (See Table 10-1.)

In sum, as yet the concept of low-intensity conflict and Soviet involvement is ill defined. However, even as the Soviet Union officially denounces the use of terrorism as a tactic of state policy and proclaims noninvolvement in unconventional world conflicts, it still proclaims military support for Libya, Syria, and the PLO. Currently, 46 countries[31] are engaged in some type of unconventional warfare, ranging from the indiscriminate terrorism of Peru's Communist-inspired Sendero Luminoso (Shining Path) to the several guerrilla wars being waged in Africa to the conventional land wars inspired by territorial conquest, such as the Iran-Iraq war, or the Soviet Union–Afghan rebel war. Both conventional wars (Iran-Iraq and Soviets-Afghans) are now in their seventh year with little possibility of resolving the conflicts in the near future. Moreover, Janke identifies 568 terrorist guerrilla organizations that have been active throughout the world since the end of World War II and have posed a dangerous threat to the overthrow of established governments.[32] The motivation of terrorist guerrilla activity is indeed complex, covering such concepts as colonialism, ethnic separation, religious fundamentalism, and ideological convictions. To say that the Soviet Union has organized and planned the operations of the many world conflicts and financially and ideologically supported terrorist guerrilla groups that exist in the world seems somewhat farfetched. However, documentary evidence is available that indicates that once unconventional conflicts begin or terrorist groups emerge, the Soviet Union surely will attempt to exploit the situation.[33]

The Soviet Union does, indeed, have a terrorist strike force of approximately 30,000 men and women controlled by GRU, Soviet military intelligence known as SPETNAZ. During wartime SPETNAZ units would operate behind enemy lines conducting terrorism, assassinations, reconnaissance and direct action in support of frontal military attacks. In peacetime SPETNAZ units have been known to support various terrorist groups, national liberation movements, and revolutionaries. This support generally involves training, technical assistance, and at times direct participation. SPETNAZ forces, for example, have participated in terrorist attacks on U.S. military bases in Europe in support of communist-led terrorist groups in West Germany, Italy, France, and Belgium. According to Dziak, the Soviet Union has organized SPETNAZ into a highly specialized and trained force capable of conducting

---

[30]Sam C. Sarkesian, *America's Forgotten Wars: The Counterrevolutionary Past and Lessons For the Future* (Westport, Conn.: Greenwood Press, 1984), pp. 229–48.

[31]*Sacramento Bee,* January 20, 1985, Forum, p. 1.

[32]Peter Janke, *Guerrilla and Terrorist Organizations: A World Directory and Bibliography* (New York: Macmillan, 1983).

[33]Ra'anan, et al, *Hydra of Carnage,* pp. 301–621.

TABLE 10-1 The Conflict Spectrum*

TERRORISM	COUNTER TERRORISM	LOW-INTENSITY CONFLICT	CONVENTIONAL WARFARE	NUCLEAR WARFARE
Indiscriminate acts of political violence Attacks on "soft" targets (civilian or military) (PFLP, IRA, ETA RAF, criminal acts)	Special tactics (Delta Force SAS, GSG-9 Private militias Vigilante groups)	Revolution/ Counterrevolution (Nicaragua Wars of national liberation, civil war, ethnic and religious turmoil)	Major land wars (Iran/Iraq Soviets in Afghanistan)	First strike options? (Total destruction)

*Sam C. Sarkesian, *America's Forgotten Wars: The Counterrevolutionary Past and Lessons for the Future* (Westport, Conn.: Greenwood Press, 1984), pp. 229–48.

low-intensity warfare in peacetime and as a major disruptive force during the course of conventional wars.[34]

Jenkins insists that the future course of unconventional conflicts will involve an escalation in international terrorism, guerrilla war, and limited conventional war.[35] In some respects, the future course of low-intensity conflicts is reflected in the Lebanese civil war. Political violence in Lebanon encompasses four levels of Sarkesian's conflict spectrum. It involves indiscriminate terrorist bombings, private militias, regular military forces, guerrillas, revolutionaries and counterinsurgency forces, some of which are assisted by foreign states, by other terrorist groups, or political religious fanatics. But the most dangerous future escalation of international terrorism is the growing fear that terrorists, guerrillas, revolutionaries or insurgents will use nuclear weapons.

Super Terrorism

Among all forms of terrorist activity, there is little doubt that terrorist acquisition of weapons of mass destruction is the most threatening to the security of the world, specifically nuclear, biological, or chemical weapons. Symbolic terrorist attacks such as hostage-taking, bombing, murder and assassination, carried out for a variety of political motivations, have killed thousands of innocent people. However, no mass casualties have as yet resulted from a single terrorist attack using weapons of mass destruction. Terrorist groups prefer automatic weapons and bombs and seldom use more sophisticated weapons, although Palestinian terrorists have attacked Israeli El-al jetliners with RPG-7 (Rocket-propelled Grenades) rockets and SA-7 (Surface-to-Air) missiles. Livingstone reports that today it is not uncommon to find rocket-propelled grenade antitank missile launchers or Soviet-built SA-7 antiaircraft guided missiles in the arsenals of at least a dozen international terrorist groups.[36] But according to Dobson and Payne, high-tech weapons are least preferred by terrorist groups since tactical success has been achieved by using more conventional weapons.[36a] Nonetheless, the vulnerabilities of a high-tech attack are so obvious and so threatening that real security measures are needed even if the threat remains theoretical. The greatest threat comes from the possibility of some type of nuclear terrorism.

In the years since India's single nuclear test in 1974, the spread of nuclear weapons has slowly gone underground. The declared nuclear weapon states of the United States, Soviet Union, United Kingdom, France, and China an-

---

[34]John J. Dziak, "Military Doctrine and Structure," in *Hydra of Carnage,* eds. Uri Ra'anan et al, pp. 84–86.

[35]Jenkins, *TVI Report,* p. S10.

[36]Neil C. Livingstone, "The Impact of Technological Innovation," in *Hydra of Carnage,* eds. Uri Ra'anan et al, p. 139.

[37]Christopher Dobson and Ronald Payne, *The Never Ending War: Terrorism in the 80's* (New York, Facts on File, 1987), pp. ix-xx.

nounced their membership in the nuclear club by openly testing nuclear weapons. Thereafter, they publicly acknowledged the progress of nuclear weapons research as it advanced to hydrogen bombs, neutron bombs, strategic defense initiative (SDI), long-range missiles, and other high-tech weapons systems.

In contrast, the emerging nuclear weapon states of India, Israel, Iraq, South Africa, Pakistan, Argentina, Taiwan, and Brazil have concealed their programs of nuclear weapons testing; none acknowledges testing nuclear weapons with the objective of creating a nuclear military option in the event of war with hostile nations. In fact, emerging nuclear states deny any interest in the development of nuclear weapons. Fortunately, not all emerging nuclear states have the capacity to test or construct nuclear weapons. Nevertheless, the testing of nuclear weapons can be achieved through computer simulations, and reliable nuclear weapons can be developed without a test explosion. Clearly, a few nuclear weapons could have a devastating impact on regional global conflicts, which could escalate the risk of superpower involvement. Moreover, the clandestine development of nuclear weapons technology heightens the underground proliferation of unrestricted nuclear weapons programs. This global trend toward the secret development of nuclear weapons is a matter of grave concern for the planet.

Israel, for example, is believed to have acquired nuclear weapons in the late 1960s. However, in the absence of a known test, the certainty of Israeli possession of nuclear weapons is unknown. In addition, Israel has never proclaimed publicly that it now has a nuclear military option. Today, the possible size of the Israeli nuclear military arsenal and the capacity of delivering nuclear warheads to a projected target are a mystery although evidence suggests both are growing.[37] The Israeli government has maintained a well-planned, ambiguous position about its ownership of nuclear weapons, neither confirming nor denying their existence.[38] There is no doubt Israel has used this ambiguity as a veiled threat against hostile Arab nations. Of all parts of the globe where nuclear proliferation could occur, none is more volatile than the Middle East. Israeli nuclear development has provided a justification for several Middle Eastern nations to seek nuclear weapons. The race is on. The list of nations includes the key opponents of Israel: Iraq, Syria, Libya, Egypt, and Iran. As long as the status and self-determination of the Palestinians and Arab hostility toward Israel exist, there may be little that can be done to stop the escalation of nuclear proliferation in the Middle East.

The increase in the number of nations experimenting with nuclear

[38]Thomas C. Schelling, "Who Will Have the Bomb?" in *Studies in Nuclear Terrorism,* eds. Augustus R. Norton and Martin H. Greenberg (Boston, Mass.: G. K. Hill, 1979), pp. 42–43.

[39]Leonard S. Spector, *The Nuclear Nations* (New York: Vintage Books, 1985), pp. 129–149.

weapons also increases the number of nations in the world handling weapons-grade, enriched uranium and plutonium. Emerging nuclear powers may also have fewer security measures to protect such weapons-grade fuel. Obviously, if such weapons-grade material were obtained by a fanatical terrorist group, it could pose a significant threat to the entire world.

The spread of nuclear weapons to terrorist groups requires that terrorists possess at least two essential elements. First, the knowledge of how to construct a nuclear weapon is an obvious requirement. However, this is no longer a serious obstacle. Mullen points out that unclassified material is readily available to provide enough technical information for terrorists to manufacture a crude nuclear device that has a known probability of detonation.[39] Furthermore, states that sponsor terrorism have access to trained physicists who can probably figure out how to build a workable nuclear weapon. The technology could then be shared with terrorist groups. Logic suggests that sooner or later terrorist bombs will be nuclear.

Second, sufficient quantities of weapons-grade material are necessary to manufacture a nuclear weapon. Experts are in general agreement that terrorists would require not only design information but fissionable material, high explosives, a high-tech laboratory, extremely tight security, years of dedicated effort, advanced education in physics, and millions of dollars.[40] With this in mind, the possibility of terrorists building a workable, fissionable nuclear device seems remote. Nevertheless, Willrich and Taylor argue that the acquisition of nuclear material and the construction of a nuclear device are not beyond the capacities of most terrorist groups.[41] Willrich and Taylor estimate, for example, that nuclear terrorists would require no more than 4 kilograms of plutonium or 11 kilograms of highly enriched uranium to construct a crude fission bomb that upon detonation would produce an explosion equal to 100 tons of TNT or any high explosive and would be small enough to transport in a compact automobile.[42]

Awareness of the danger of terrorists acquiring a nuclear weapon has been growing for some time. Warnings in the United States and abroad have continually been issued that thefts from nuclear plants could provide the fissionable material to construct a terrorist nuclear device. In an effort to reduce the availability of weapons-grade materials, the United States and the Soviet Union have cooperated more than on any other issue during the postwar pe-

[40]Robert K. Mullen, "Mass Destruction and Terrorism," *Studies in Nuclear Terrorism,* eds. Norton and Greenberg, p. 247.

[41]For example, see Neil C. Livingstone and Joseph D. Douglass, Jr., *CBW: The Poor Man's Atomic Bomb* (Cambridge, Mass.: Institute for Foreign Policy Analysis, Inc., 1984); Stanley P. Berard, "Nuclear Terrorism: More Myth Than Reality," *Air University Review* 36 (July-August 1985), pp. 30–36.

[42]Mason Willrich and Theodore B. Taylor, "Nuclear Theft: Risks and Safeguards," *Studies in Nuclear Terrorism,* eds. Norton and Greenberg, pp. 59–84.

[43]Ibid.

riod. The two nuclear superpowers have a clear interest in keeping the nuclear weapons club as small as possible, both for security reasons and political power. Nuclear proliferation not only implies that terrorists could easily penetrate lax security systems, but it also entails a geometrical increase in the number of pairs of nations that could engage in a nuclear confrontation. To date, there have been no known attempts of terrorist groups to either steal fissionable materials or to construct a nuclear device.

By contrast, a real threat exists that terrorists might capture an intact nuclear weapon. The possession of such a nuclear weapon could undoubtedly create an international crisis, even if the terrorists could not overcome the technical security systems required to fire or launch the weapon. The United States now has commando teams equipped with "backpack nuclear weapons" designed to be planted in Warsaw Pact nations in the event of war with the Soviet Union.[43] If such small, easily concealable nuclear weapons were to fall into the hands of terrorists, they could be used to hold the United States hostage for a considerable time.

Numerous scenarios of nuclear terrorism have been proposed by scholars as well as authors of popular literature.[44] Some obvious possibilities that appear technically possible and politically convincing include a group of religious fanatics with suicidal tendencies who adhere to a belief that preaches heavenly rewards; antinuclear activists attacking nuclear facilities as an act of symbolic violence; organized criminal gangs attempting to extort large sums of money from affluent nations; emerging Third World nations seeking to influence international policy; revolutionaries, insurgents, or terrorists engaged in a low-intensity conflict with a strategic desire to escalate that conflict; or a band of highly trained terrorists who could take over a nuclear facility near a major city and destroy it, resulting in the deaths of millions of people.[45]

The scenarios should be taken seriously. Norton and Greenberg have identified 194 threats of violence against licensed nuclear facilities in the United States between 1969 and 1977, although few threats originated from organized terrorist groups. The overwhelming majority have been bomb threats; however, pipe bombs were discovered at four nuclear facilities, and

---

[44]*Time,* June 3, 1985, p. 52.

[45]Some examples of scholarly scenarios: Louis Rene Beres, "Terrorism and the Nuclear Threat in the Middle East," *Current History,* 70 (January, 1976), 27–29; Augustus R. Norton, *Understanding the Nuclear Terrorism Threat* (Gaithersburg, Md.:IACP, 1979); Robert H. Kupperman, "Fighting Terrorism: A National Security View," *Georgetown Center for Strategic International Studies,* Public Broadcasting Stations, September 17, 1986. The popular literature has produced hundreds of nuclear scenarios: Larry Collins and Dominque La Pierre, *The Fifth Horseman* (New York: Simon & Schuster, 1981); Karl Lorimar, *Special Bulletin* (movie) (Irvine, Ca: Lorimar Home Video, 1986); Christopher Matthews, *The Butcher* (New York: Stein and Day, 1986); *Final Option* (movie) (MGM/UA, 1984); Alistair MacLean, *Goodbye California* (New York: Doubleday, 1978).

[46]*Los Angeles Times,* October 16, 1974, p. 6.

automated intrusion security systems were penetrated at 15 others by unauthorized personnel.[46]

The seizure or theft of nuclear weapons in the United States and from NATO military installations has also been the object of many scenarios. One scenario explores the takeover of a Minuteman missile site by a dedicated team of terrorists, thus providing the terrorists with the means to launch a nuclear strike.[47] Jenkins hypothesizes that a dedicated team of three to five terrorists armed with automatic weapons and explosives could easily mount a surprise attack on a nuclear power plant or a nuclear military facility.[48] Recognition of these highly probable scenarios has led to the development of increased security measures at U.S. nuclear plants and military installations that have available strategic nuclear weapons systems. The increasing size, complexity, and sophistication of nuclear arsenals potentially increases the risk of nuclear terrorism.

Countering any future nuclear terrorist threat requires teamwork by federal, state, and local law enforcement agencies. The FBI maintains federal jurisdictional responsibility for the investigation of nuclear extortion threats or any incident involving radioactive materials or the attempted construction of nuclear explosives. The Department of Energy is also responsible for the security and management of nuclear materials. Search personnel with high-tech detection equipment, known as the Nuclear Emergency Search Team (NEST), are trained to respond when nuclear incidents include improvised nuclear weapons, lost or stolen radioactive material, or improvised radiation devices.[49] NEST can be mobilized and transported to a nuclear crisis scene anywhere in the United States in two hours. The role of NEST is to assist the FBI and local law enforcement in a search for suspected nuclear explosives material. Because of the dangerousness of the nuclear terrorist threat, criminal justice students and law enforcement personnel should be familiar with at least a few of the technical terms associated with nuclear weapons technology. The following terms are described:[50]

Enriched uranium—uranium that contains a U-235 concentration, which is the only naturally occurring fissile isotope.

Plutonium-239—a fissile isotope created by the use of U-238. Excellent material for construction of nuclear weapons that are manmade and radioactive.

[47]Augustus R. Norton and Martin H. Greenberg, eds., *Studies in Nuclear Terrorism* (Boston, Mass.: G. K. Hill, 1979), pp. 429-37.

[48]Bruce G. Blair and Gary D. Brewer, "The Terrorist Threat to World Nuclear Programs," *Journal of Conflict Resolution* 21 (September 1977), pp. 386-89.

[49]Brian Jenkins, *Terrorism and the Nuclear Safeguards Issue* (Santa Monica, Ca: Rand Corporation, March, 1976), pp. 2-7.

[50]William R. Farrell, "Organized to Fight Terrorism," in *Fighting Back: Winning the War Against Terrorism,* eds. Livingstone and Arnold, p. 52.

[51]Norton and Greenberg, *Studies in Nuclear Terrorism,* pp. 443-46.

Special Nuclear Material (SNM)—fissionable material in the form of uranium enriched isotopes consisting of Uranium–233 and Uranium–235 or Plutonium–239.

Radioactive Dispersal Device—any nuclear device containing radioactive material designed to spread contamination.

Weapons-Grade Plutonium—plutonium that contains approximately 7 percent of Plutonium–240 used in the design of nuclear weapons.

According to Butler, spokesman for the U.S. Energy Department, the United States now has two nuclear facilities to manufacture enriched uranium for eventual use in U.S. nuclear strategic weapons.[51] As production and supply centers increase, serious security and control problems also increase the possibility of the theft of weapons-grade material. For the first time in the evaluation of nuclear weapons technology, any nation with an advanced industrial base, a corps of nuclear scientists and technicians, and a modern military establishment familiar with weapons-delivery systems can build a formidable nuclear strike force. This obviously creates additional opportunities for terrorists to "go nuclear." Cranston points out, however, the real threat to the security of the world lies not with the acquisition of nuclear weapons by some fanatical terrorist group, but by the formation of a nuclear terrorist state such as Iran.[52]

Nevertheless, nuclear weapons represent only one dimension of the threat of so-called super terrorism. Other weapons of mass destruction include the introduction of biological and chemical agents into the target population by terrorist groups. Livingstone estimates that over 50 chemical or biological incidents involving terrorist groups have been recorded by the United States in recent years.[53] The use of chemical or biological weapons, like nuclear weapons, can produce several million casualties in a single episode, causing widespread public fear and disruption of normal governmental operations. Unlike nuclear weapons, no insurmountable technological problems exist. Chemical and biological agents are easy to obtain, the methods of delivery are manageable, and they can be dispersed over a wide area. Thus, the resort to chemical or biological weapons can be accomplished with the minimum of risk by terrorists.

Several chemical terrorist incidents have been recorded. For example, in 1975 West German police received several threats from the Red Army Faction that mustard gas stolen from the military would be used against the German people unless all "political prisoners" were released and granted amnesty.[54] In another incident Mideast terrorists mailed a Jewish target a parcel bomb that

[52]*San Francisco Chronicle,* December 21, 1986, p. AA4.

[53]Alan Cranston, "The Nuclear Terrorist State," *Terrorism: How The West Can Win,* ed., Netanyahu, pp. 177–81.

[54]Neil C. Livingstone, "The Impact of Technological Innovation," *Hydra of Carnage,* pp. 142–44.

[55]*Washington Post,* May 13, 1975, p. 22.

was designed to detonate a vial of nerve gas when the parcel was opened.[55] More recently, European police discovered a clandestine laboratory in Paris producing *clostridium botulinum,* which secretes botulinal toxin (BTX), considered to be the most lethal toxin known.[56] Hersh maintains that BTX is so lethal that it would require only 8 ounces dispersed by vapor or aerosol to kill every living creature on earth.[57]

There exist a substantial number of highly toxic chemical agents available to terrorists or criminals. The use of such toxic chemicals is widely discussed in the available literature. Books, monographs, and professional papers are easily obtainable at most university libraries. The information needed to synthesize toxic chemical agents from raw materials is, therefore, available, and the determined terrorist, in the privacy of his own kitchen, could easily brew up a chemical weapon capable of killing thousands of people. Four methods of dissemination of chemical weapons appear possible: (1) contamination of beverages and food products, (2) spreading lethal vapor concentrations in an enclosed location, (3) dispersal of aerosols in an enclosed location, and (4) widespread dispersal of vapors or aerosols in open locations.[58]

Mengel asserts that even though the threat of chemical or nuclear terrorism can be devastating, the greatest casualty-producing potential appears to be the threat of biological agents available to terrorists. The most lethal of these biological agents are anthrax and cryptococcosis. Terrorists could easily disperse anthrax by a truck-mounted spray. Once the anthrax was inhaled, it would take about 2 minutes for infection to set in. Not all victims would die, but sufficient casualties would produce chaos and confusion. In a more confined space, such as domed athletic stadiums, lethal doses of anthrax could be spread by aerosols. Mengel further estimates that in a domed stadium one fluid ounce of anthrax would infect 70,000 people in less than one hour.[59]

Although the threat of super terrorism covers a broad spectrum of probable events and the nuclear and chemical weapons club continues to grow, how realistic is the threat? Mengel argues that the probability of terrorist groups successfully combining the proper skills, material resources, and motivations necessary to carry out an act of super terrorism is extremely low.[60] Nonetheless, it must be recognized that in the event of a successful act of super terrorism, the results could be catastrophic, causing death, injury, and destruction beyond the magnitude of any past terrorist attack. The concept of super terrorism represents an unknown but realistic future terrorist threat that merits

[56]Ibid.

[57]Livingstone, *Hydra of Carnage,* pp. 142–43.

[58]Seymour N. Hersh, *Chemical and Biological Warfare* (Garden City, N.Y.: Doubleday, 1969), p. 83.

[59]R. W. Mengel, "Terrorism and New Technologies of Destruction: An Overview of the Potential Risk," *Studies in Nuclear Terrorism,* eds. Norton and Greenberg, pp. 195.

[60]Ibid., p. 196.

[61]Ibid., pp. 244–45.

the attention of law enforcement officials at all levels of government. Regardless of the type of terrorism, whether conventional or super, the results could be devastating to the future of democracy in the United States. What influence would a sustained terrorist climate have on the quality of life in the United States?

Influence of Terrorism on Democracy

The use of indiscriminate and random acts of terrorism has the potential to influence future U.S. society in the following ways. First, tighter security measures will continue to predominate strategies to defeat terrorism. The sight of dump trucks filled with sand stationed outside the White House reflects the heightened concern about terrorism in the United States that has also contributed to the growth of the domestic security industry. Government and private corporations now spend approximately $21 billion yearly to strengthen security systems against possible terrorist assaults.[61] The U.S. State Department currently spends 15 percent of its budget on security, and George Shultz recently asked Congress for an additional $4.4 billion over the next five years to strengthen embassy security.[62] Surveillance security systems, their maintenance, and the specialized personnel required to operate them are all very expensive. Additionally, kidnap and ransom insurance has become a growth industry in several European countries and the United States.[63] Private corporations are now taking out insurance policies to help cover possible ransom payments for high-risk employees. In sum, the increased security costs for both government and private corporations would be reflected in higher taxes and higher costs for consumer items. Most experts believe this trend will continue well into the 1990s.[64] The escalation of the potential threat of terrorism has created a new industry that could involve a combination of security systems that dramatically increases consumer prices.

Second, a prolonged campaign of terrorism in the United States would undoubtedly result in changes in the legal system. Legal concepts of habeas corpus, intent, individual rights, and precedent reflect the character of the legal system in the United States. Given a terrorist campaign of indiscriminate bombing and assassination, would the U.S. legal system strictly adhere to the principles of constitutional law and the protection of individual rights? Thus far, there has been no need to invoke emergency powers in the United States to defeat a campaign of random terrorism. However, there have been a number of incidents in the United States where normal legal procedures were suspended to prevent widespread disorder.

[62]Brian Jenkins, ed., *Terrorism and Personal Protection* (Boston: Butterworth, 1985), pp. xxi–xxii.

[63]*Sacramento Bee,* February 9, 1986, p. 1.

[64]*San Francisco Chronicle,* June 29, 1986, This World section, p. 15.

[65]Jenkins, *TVI Report,* p. S3.

For example, in May 1971 in Washington, D.C., the police reacted in an unusual way to quell a massive anti-Vietnam War demonstration. Fearing uncontrollable rioting, the police began arresting anyone they found in the streets. The dragnet sweeps resulted in 13,400 arrests in a 4-day period—a record that still stands.[65] Few arrestees were ever charged with any crime; in fact, most were peacefully demonstrating and a good number were totally uninvolved. But order was preserved, violence was kept to a minimum, and the chief of police was congratulated for taking such decisive action. Two years later a federal judge declared the arrests unconstitutional and awarded monetary damages to those individuals who were illegally arrested.[66] This example could well prove to be a model for future responses to random terrorism in the United States. Unquestionably, a campaign of prolonged terrorism in the United States would result in the federal government assuming direct police powers; and the temporary suspension of civil liberties would be deemed necessary to maintain order and locate offenders.

Third, a campaign of terrorism certainly can affect the general mental health of a community living in a terrorist "war zone." General feelings of dread and fear result from prolonged exposure to bombings, arson, assassination, and hostage-taking. Fanon observed that continued exposure to acts of extranormal violence creates mental disorders that he referred to as "reactionary psychoses."[67] Inner feelings of fear take on an apocalyptic sense in which eventually everyone will be consumed by the "fires" of violence and terrorism. The effect on children is especially acute. Children exhibit a noise phobia so intense that an unexpected sound often triggers a panic reaction, and their often chronic, sadistic behavior can manifest itself in the torture of small animals or other children.[68] In the terrorist war zones of Beirut, Belfast, Israel (West Bank and Gaza), Cambodia, or Central America, children often display nervous depression, motor instability, chronic apathy, and loss of appetite.[69] The symptoms are not unlike those associated with battered children.

The effect of a terrorist campaign on U.S. citizens could be even more profound. It is well documented that Americans already suffer from a wide variety of mental illnesses, including severe forms of neurosis and paranoid schizophrenia. The impact of an indiscriminate terrorist campaign could conceivably be more devastating on the mental health of Americans than, say, citizens of Belfast or Beirut, where intercommunal violence has become almost a way of life and part of traditional culture. Just how Americans would re-

[65]*Newsweek*, May 17, 1971, p. 250.

[67]*Time*, April 30, 1973, p. 66.

[68]Frantz Fanon, *The Wretched of the Earth* (New York: Grove Press, 1968), p. 251.

[69]*San Francisco Chronicle,* November 11, 1984, This World section, pp. 7–8.

[70]For example, see Johnathan Kozol, *Children of the Revolution: A Yankee Teacher in Cuban Schools* (New York: Delacorte, 1978); Howard Tolley, *Children and War: Political Socialization to International Conflict* (New York: Teachers College Press, 1973); Roger Rosenblatt, *Children of War* (Garden City, New York: Anchor/Doubleday, 1983).

spond to indiscriminate terrorist attacks is difficult to evaluate. But one thing seems certain. General feelings of fear, hopelessness, and dread would surely intensify.

Fourth, the growth of paramilitary groups to counter the actions of an indiscriminate terrorist campaign would intensify the violence. In the United States there are several well-known "paramilitary" organizations that could be quickly mobilized into reactionary vigilantes. These include right-wing groups such as the American Nazi party, the KKK, the Order, the CSA, the Jewish Defense League, and/or left-wing groups such as the United Freedom Fighters or the Black Liberation Army. In addition, there are armed groups that support no political ideology but have a penchant for terror and violence. A variety of prison gangs, like the Aryan Brotherhood, Mexican Mafia, and Black Guerrilla Family, or a host of juvenile gangs and motorcycle clubs, which are made up of elements of criminal society looking for opportunities to exploit, could easily be mobilized into vigilantes.

An indiscriminate terrorist campaign could mobilize groups like these and possibly produce anarchic situations of the kind that exist in Lebanon. For example, as terrorism escalates, a "warlord" mentality could emerge where communities and urban neighborhoods would "contract" paramilitary groups, for example, juvenile gangs, to protect lives and property. In its final stages, such as in Beirut, foreign intervention would be required to restore some semblance of order, although social deterioration such as this in the United States does seem somewhat remote.

Finally, demographic changes would occur as potential victims of terroristic violence flee areas where random terrorism is prevalent. As people flee, real estate values decline along with the tax base of the community. Eventually, businesses and industry will move to safer locations since increased terrorism prohibits people from daily shopping or attending their jobs. The result is chronic, high unemployment and economic chaos. Conditions like these exist in several parts of the world, most notably in Northern Ireland and Lebanon, where political terrorism has strangleholds on communities. There is no reason to believe that a terrorist climate in the United States could not produce similar conditions.

In brief, the future influence of terrorism on the quality of life in the United States could have the most profound effects in the following areas: (1) increased security costs, (2) changes in the legal system reflecting a loss of civil liberties, (3) increased mental health problems associated with the fear of terrorism, (4) growth of paramilitary groups that would heighten the level of violence, and (5) demographic changes reflected in patterns of settlement and commerce.[70]

[71]H. C. Greisman, "Terrorism and the Closure of Society: A Social Impact Projection," *Technological Forecasting and Social Change* 14 (1979), pp. 135-46.

CONCLUSIONS

If the future appears dismal, what measures are likely to be the most appropriate to defeat terrorism? The liberal view is that objective causes of terrorism should be overcome. Therefore, the focus could be on the establishment of a Palestinian homeland or the settlement of the justified claims of a variety of ethnic, religious, and racial issues. For example, Catholics in Northern Ireland, Shi'ite Muslims in Lebanon, and blacks in South Africa all strongly believe that they have been unjustly treated by the established governmental system. Obviously, justice for all people should be pursued with vigor if terrorism is to be defeated. However, the reality is that the concept of justice for all will probably never be achieved and certainly not quickly enough to raise the hope of "disadvantaged" groups.

The most difficult problem in attacking terrorism is still agreeing on a definition of terrorism. The Reagan administration has yet to define terrorism, scholars have yet to define terrorism, and the mass media, which exploits terroristic violence, has yet to adequately define terrorism. For example, non-aligned nations representing 70 countries recently condemned the repeated U.S. aggressions and provocations against Libya, Iran, and Syria as acts of state-sponsored terrorism. Arnold states that there is no universally accepted definition of terrorism.[71] This lack of a precise definition makes it virtually impossible for established governments to pursue policies that will remove many of the conditions or grievances, real or imagined, that motivate terrorists.

The future of international terrorism is bound to escalate as forms of low-intensity conflict increase. Terrorism, as a strategy of low-intensity warfare, is a serious threat to open democratic societies, and one that will be exacerbated in the future. Failure to respond firmly to the threat would be to give up a way of life based on individual and civil liberties. Democracy must not overestimate the threat nor overreact, but keep the violence associated with terrorism in perspective. In the end, acts of terrorism, i.e., bombing, assassination or murder, hostage-taking, and other criminal acts, are law enforcement problems. Therefore, the law enforcement community and more specifically the criminal justice system must be prepared to defeat the newest form of criminal behavior—terrorism. It is hoped that the considerations outlined in this text will contribute toward an understanding of the causes of terrorism, strategies of terrorism, and responses to terrorism.

[72]Quoted in Christopher Hitchens, "Wanton Acts of Usage: Terrorism, a Cliché in Search of a Meaning," *Harpers* (September 1986), p. 66.

REVIEW QUESTIONS

1. Describe the concept of "territory for peace." How would you solve the Israeli-Palestinian problem?
2. Who are the Gush Emunim? Why are Judea and Samaria so important to Jewish fundamentalists?
3. Identify the following Islamic groups:
   a. Amal
   b. Hizballah
   c. Islamic Jihad
4. What is state-sponsored terrorism? Does the Soviet Union use "surrogates" to foment international terrorism? Be specific.
5. Discuss Sarkesian's conflict spectrum.
6. What should the United States do to counter Soviet support for world terrorism? Does the United States support terrorism as many nations claim?
7. What is the likelihood that terrorists will go nuclear? Be specific.
8. Define the following terms:
   a. Fission
   b. Enriched uranium
   c. Plutonium–239
   d. Anthrax
   e. NEST
   f. Radioactive
   g. Clostridium botulinum
   h. Cryptococcosis
9. What changes would most likely occur in the United States if a sustained campaign of terrorism were initiated?
10. What can the law enforcement community do to meet the future threat of terrorism in the United States?
11. Describe briefly the Iranscam incident. Do you think the United States is hypocritical in its policy to defeat international terrorism?
12. Finally, define terrorism.

BIBLIOGRAPHY

■

ADAMS, JAMES, *The Financing of Terror: Behind the PLO, IRA, Red Brigades, and M19 Stand the Paymasters*. New York: Simon & Schuster, 1986.

ALEXANDER, YONAH, MARJORIE ANN BROWN, and ALLEN S. NANES, eds., *Control of Terrorism: International Documents*. New York: Crane, Russak, 1979.

AMOS, JAMES W., III, *Palestine Resistance: Organization of a Nationalist Movement*. New York: Pergamon Press, 1980.

ANDERSON, ROBERT W., *Party Politics in Puerto Rico*. Stanford: Stanford University Press, 1965.

"Anti-Soviet Zionist Terrorism in the U.S." *Current Digest of the Soviet Press,* 23 (1971), pp. 6–8.

APTER, DAVID E., "Notes on the Underground: Left Violence and the National State," *Daedalus,* 108 (Fall, 1979), 155–72.

"Armenian Allegations and Some Facts," *ATA-USA: Bulletin of the Assembly of American Turkish Associations,* Washington, D.C., April, 1980, p. 4.

ARONSON, ELLIOT, *Social Animal*. San Francisco: W. H. Freeman, 1972.

ASPREY, ROBERT B., *War in the Shadows: The Guerrilla in History*. London: MacDonald and Jane's, 1975.

ASTON, CLIVE C., "Political Hostage Taking in Western Europe: A Statistical Analysis," in *Perspectives on Terrorism,* eds. Lawrence Z. Freedman and Yonah Alexander. Wilmington, Delaware: Scholarly Resources, 1983.

ATTHOWE, PATRICIA, "Terrorism: The FALN's Undeclared War," *Defense and Foreign Affairs Digest,* 1978, p. 48.

AUDONIAN, ARAM, ed., *The Memoirs of Naim Bey: Turkish Official Documents Relating to the Deportation and Massacres of Armenians*. Pennsylvania: American Historical Review Association, 1964.

AVERY, JAMES, *The Sky Pirates*. London: Ian Allan, 1973.

BARNET, RICHARD, "Nuclear Terrorism: Can It Be Stopped," *Current* 211 (March/April 1979): 30–40.

BARRON, JOHN, *KGB Today: The Hidden Hand*. New York: Berkley Books, 1985.

BAYO, ALBERTO, *150 Questions For a Guerrilla*. Colorado: Paladin Press, 1975.

BECKER, JULIAN, *Hitler's Children: The Story of the Baader-Meinhoff Terrorist Gang*. Philadelphia: Lippincott, 1977.

———, *The PLO: The Rise and Fall of the Palestine Liberation Organization*. New York: St. Martin's Press, 1984.

BECKWITH, CHARLES A., and DONALD KNOX, *Delta Force*. New York: Dell, 1983.

Beer, W. R., *The Unexpected Rebellion*. New York: New York University, 1980.

BEGIN, MENACHEM, *The Revolt: Story of the Irgun* (rev. ed.). New York: Nash, 1977.

BELL, J. BOWYER, *Assassin: The Theory and Practice of Political Violence*. New York: St. Martin's, 1979.

———, *A Time of Terror: How Democratic Societies Respond to Revolutionary Violence*. New York: Basic, 1978.

———, *IPI Report* 25 (June, 1976), 4.

———, *Terror Out of Zion: The Shock Troops of Israeli Independence*. New York: St. Martin's Press, 1978.

———, *The Secret Army: The IRA 1916–1979*. Cambridge, Mass.: MIT Press, 1980.

———, *Transnational Terror*. Washington, D.C.: American Enterprise Institute, 1975.

BERARD, STANLEY P., "Nuclear Terrorism: More Myth Than Reality," *Air University Review*, 36 (July-August, 1985), 30–36.

BERES, LOUIS RENE, "Terrorism and the Nuclear Threat in the Middle East," *Current History*, 70 (January, 1976), 27–29.

BLAIR, BRUCE G., and GARY D. BREWER, "The Terrorist Threat to World Nuclear Programs," *Journal of Conflict Resolution*, 21 (September, 1977), 386–89.

BLEI, HERMAN, "Terrorism, Domestic, and International: The West German Experience," *Report of the Task Force on Disorders and Terrorism*. Washington, D.C.: U.S. Government Printing Office, 1976.

BOLZ, FRANK, Jr., "The Hostage Situation: Law Enforcement Options," in *Terrorism: Interdisciplinary Perspectives*, eds. Burr Eichelman, David A. Soskis, and William H. Reid. Washington, D.C.: American Psychiatric Association, 1983.

BOWDEN, TOM, *The Breakdown of Public Security*. Beverly Hills: Sage, 1977.

BRANDON, SAMUEL G., *Jesus and The Zealots: A Study of the Political Factor in Primitive Christianity*. New York: Scribner, 1967.

BREMER, ARTHUR H., *An Assassin's Diary*. New York: Harpers Magazine Press, 1972.

BRODIE, THOMAS G., *Bombs and Bombings*. Springfield, Ill.: Charles C. Thomas, 1972.

BRODY, DAVID, *Steelworkers In America*. Cambridge: Harvard University Press, 1960.

BROHLE, DAVID, *The Molly Maguires*. London: Oxford University, 1964.

BROOKS, JOHN G. *American Syndicalism: The IWW*. New York, Macmillan, 1913.

BROWN, DEE, *Bury My Heart at Wounded Knee: An Indian History of the American West*. New York: Bantam, 1972.

BROWN, WALLACE, *Victorious in Defeat The American Loyalists in Exile*. New York, Facts on File, 1984.

BRUSE, GEORGE, *The Stranglers: The Cult of Thuggee and Its Overthrow in British India*. New York: Harcourt, Brace and World, 1969.

BUCHANAN, THOMAS, *Who Killed Kennedy?* New York: Putnam, 1964.

BUGLIOSI, VINCENT, and CURT GENTRY, *Helter Skelter: The True Story of the Manson Murders*. New York: W. W. Norton, 1974.

BURGOYNE, ARTHUR G., *The Homestead Strike of 1892*. Pittsburgh: University of Pittsburgh, 1979.

California Peace Officers Association, *Law Enforcement Media Relations: Model Policy Manual*. Sacramento: California Peace Officers Association, 1983.

CARLTON, DAVID, "The Future of Political Substate Violence," in *Terrorism: Theory and Practice*, eds. Yonah Alexander, David Carlton, and Paul Wilkinson. Boulder, Colo.: Westview Press, 1979.

CARTER, CAROLLE J., *The Shamrock and the Swastika*. Palo Alto, Calif.: Pacific Books, 1977.

CASEY, WILLIAM, "The International Linkages—What Do We Know," in *Hydra of Carnage: International Linkages of Terrorism*, eds. Uri Ra'anan and others. Lexington, Mass.: Lexington Books, 1986.

CASTELLUCCI, JOHN, *The Big Dance: The Untold Story of Kathy Boudin and the Terrorist Family that Committed the Brink's Robbery Murders*. New York: Dodd, Mead, 1986.

Central Intelligence Agency, *International and Transnational Terrorism: Diagnosis and Prognosis*. Washington, D.C.: U.S. Government Printing Office, 1976.

CHALMERS, DAVID M., *Hooded Americanism: The First Century of the Ku Klux Klan 1865-1965*. Garden City, N.Y.: Doubleday, 1965.

———, *Hooded Americanism: The History of the Ku Klux Klan*. New York: Franklin Watts, 1981.

CHANNING, WALTER, "The Mental State of Czolgosz, the Assassin of President McKinley," *American Journal of Insanity* 58 (October 1902):274.

CHESNEAUX, JEAN, ed., *Popular Movements and Secret Societies in China, 1840-1950*. Stanford: Stanford University Press, 1972.

CHOMSKY, NOAM, *The Fateful Triangle: The United States, Israel and the Palestinians*. Boston: South End Press, 1983.

CLARKE, JAMES W., *American Assassins: The Darker Side of Politics*. Princeton, N. J.: Princeton University Press, 1982.

CLINE, RAY S., and YONAH ALEXANDER, *Terrorism: The Soviet Connection*. New York: Crane, Russak, 1984.

CLISSOLD, STEPHEN, *Croat Separatism: Nationalism, Dissidence, and Terrorism*. London: Institute for the Study of Conflict, 1979.

CLUTTERBUCK, RICHARD, *Kidnap and Ransom: The Response*. London: Faber & Faber, 1978.

———, *Living with Terrorism*. London: Faber & Faber, 1976.

COBBAN, HELEN, *The Palestinian Liberation Organization: People, Power, and Politics*. Cambridge: Cambridge University Press, 1983.

COLLINS, LARRY, and DOMINQUE LA PIERRE, *The Fifth Horseman*. New York: Simon & Schuster, 1981.

Conflict Studies #135, *Northern Ireland: Problems and Perspectives*. London: Institute for the Study of Conflict, 1982.

COOPER, H. H. A., *The Hostage Takers*. Boulder: Paladin Press, 1981.

CORSUN, ANDREW, "Armenian Terrorism: A Profile," *U. S. Department of State Bulletin*, August, 1982, pp. 31-35.

COXE, JOHN E., "The New Orleans Mafia Incident," *La. Hist. Q.* 20 (1937), 1067.

CRANSTON, ALAN, "The Nuclear Terrorist State," *Terrorism: How the West Can Win*, ed., Benjamin Netanyahu. New York: Farrar, Straus & Giroux, 1986.

CRELINSTEIN, RONALD D., and DENIS SZABO, *Hostage Taking*. Lexington, Massachusetts: Lexington Books, 1979.

CRENSHAW, MARTHA, "The Causes of Terrorism," *Comparative Politics*, 13 (1981), 374, 396.

———, *Revolutionary Terrorism: The FLN in Algeria, 1954-1962*. Stanford: Hoover Institute, 1978.

CROTTY, WILLIAM J., ed., *Assassinations and Their Interpretation Within the American Context*. New York: Harper & Row, 1971.

CROZIER, BRIAN, *Ulster: Politics and Terrorism*. Conflict Studies #36. London: Institute for the Study of Conflict, 1973.

DANIELS, STUART, "The Weathermen," *Government and Opposition*, 9 (1974) pp. 430-59.

D'ARCY, WILLIAM, *The Fenian Movement in the U.S.: 1858-1886*. Washington: Catholic University Press, 1947.

DAWSON, HENRY B., *The Sons of Liberty in New York*. New York: Arno, 1969.

DEBRAY, REGIS, *Revolution In the Revolution: Armed Struggle and Political Struggle in Latin America*. New York: Grove, 1967.

DEMARIS, OVID, *Brothers in Blood: The International Terrorist Network*. New York: Charles Scribner's Sons, 1977.

DEUTSCH, RICHARD, and VIVIEN MCGOWAN, *Northern Ireland: 1968-73*. Belfast: Blackstaff Press, 1973-74.

DICKSON, GRIERSON, *Murder by Numbers*. London: Robert Hall, 1958.

DINGES, JOHN, and SAUL LANDAU, *Assassination on Embassy Row*. New York: Pantheon, 1980.

DOBSON, CHRISTOPHER and RONALD PAYNE, *The Carlos Complex: A Pattern of Violence*. London: Hodder and Stroughton, 1977.

DOBSON, CHRISTOPHER and RONALD PAYNE, *The Never Ending War: Terrorism in the 80's*. New York: Facts on File, 1987.

DUGARD, JOHN, "International Terrorism and the Just War," *Stanford Journal of International Studies* 12 (1977):21.

DZIAK, JOHN J., "Military Doctrine and Structure," in *Hydra of Carnage: International Linkages of Terrorism,* eds. Uri Ra'anan et al. Lexington, Mass.: Lexington Books, 1986.

EBENSTEIN, WILLIAM, *Today's isms: Communism, Fascism, Capitalism, Socialism.* Englewood Cliffs, N.J.: Prentice-Hall, 1985.

ELAD, SHLOMI, and ARIEL MERARI, "The Soviet Bloc and World Terrorism," *Jaffee Center for Strategic Studies.* Tel Aviv: Tel Aviv University, 1984.

Encyclopedia of the Social Sciences. New York: Macmillan, 1937.

EPSTEIN, EDWARD J., *The Secret World of Lee Harvey Oswald.* New York: McGraw-Hill, 1978.

ETHEREDGE, LLOYD S., *Can Governments Learn: American Foreign Policy and Central American Revolutions.* New York: Pergamon Press, 1985.

Executive Risk Assessment. Alexandria, Va.: Risks International, Inc., 1986.

FANON, FRANTZ, *The Wretched of the Earth.* New York: Grove Press, 1968.

FARRELL, WILLIAM R., "Organized to Fight Terrorism," in *Fighting Back: Winning the War Against Terrorism,* eds. Neil C. Livingstone and Terrell E. Arnold. Lexington, Mass.: Lexington Books, 1986.

Federal Aviation Administration, *Semi-annual Report to Congress on the Effectiveness of the Civil Aviation Security Program.* Washington, D.C.: Federal Aviation Administration, April, 1985.

FENYVESI, CHARLES, *The Media and Terrorism.* Chicago: Field Enterprises, 1977.

Final Option (movie). MGM/UA, 1984.

FIORILLO, E., "Terrorism in Italy: Analysis of a Problem," *Terrorism* 2 (1979): 261-70.

FLAPAN, S., "Israelis and Palestinians: Can They Make Peace," *Journal of Palestine Studies* 15, no. 1 (Autumn 1985):21.

FOGELSON, EDWARD, *Big City Police.* Cambridge: Harvard, 1978.

FONER, PHILIP S., ed., *Black Panthers Speak.* Philadelphia: J. B. Lippincott, 1970.

FORD, FRANKLIN L., *Political Murder: From Tyrannicide to Terrorism.* Cambridge: Harvard University Press, 1985.

FRANKFORT, ELLEN, *Kathy Boudin and The Dance of Death.* New York: Stein and Day, 1983.

FRANZIUS, ENNO, *History of the Order of Assassins.* New York: Funk and Wagnalls, 1969.

FRIEDLANDER, ROBERT A., *Terrorism and The Law: What Price Safety?* Gaithersburg, Md.: IACP, 1981.

——, "Iran: The Hostage Seizure, the Media and International Law," in *Terrorism, the Media and Law Enforcement,* ed. A H. Miller. Washington, D.C.: Government Printing Office, 1983.

FRIEDMAN, T. L., *New York Times,* January 1, 1986, sec. 1, p. 4.

GABRIEL, RICHARD A., *Operation Peace for Gallilee: The Israeli-PLO War in Lebanon.* New York: Hill and Wang, 1985.

GALLAGHER, RICHARD J., "Kidnapping in the U. S. and the Development of the Federal Kidnapping Statute," in *Terrorism and Personal Protection,* ed. Brian M. Jenkins. Boston: Butterworth, 1985.

GEMMER, KARLHEINZ, "Problems, Means, and Methods of Police Action in the Federal Republic of Germany," in *Hostage Taking,* eds., Ronald D. Crelinsten and Denis Szabo. Lexington, Mass.: D. C. Heath, 1979.

GERSTEIN, ROBERT S., "Do Terrorists Have Rights," in *The Morality of Terrorism: Religious and Secular Justifications,* eds. David C. Rapoport and Yonah Alexander. New York: Pergamon Press, 1983.

GOLAN, GALIA, *The Soviet Union and the Palestine Liberation Organization.* New York: Praeger, 1980.

GOLDABER, IRVING, "A Typology of Hostage Takers," *Police Chief* (June 1979): 21-22.

GOREN, ROBERTA, *The Soviet Union and Terrorism.* London: George Allen and Unwin, 1984.

Great Britain Parliamentary Papers, *The Treatment of Armenians in the Ottoman Empire, 1915-16.* London: Cavston, 1916, No. 31.

GREGOR, A. JAMES, *The Ideology of Fascism: The Rationale of Totalitarianism.* New York: Free Press, 1969.

——, "Fascism's Philosophy of Violence and the Concept of Terror," in *The Morality of Terrorism: Religious and Secular Justifications,* eds. David C. Rapoport and Yonah Alexander. New York: Pergamon Press, 1983.

GREISMAN, H. C., "Terrorism and the Closure of Society: A Social Impact Projection," *Technological Forecasting and Social Change* 14 (1979): 135–46.

GRESH, ALAIN, *The PLO: The Struggle Within: Towards an Independent Palestinian State.* London: Zed Books, Ltd., 1985.

GRISWOLD, WESLEY S., *The Night the Revolution Began: The Boston Tea Party.* Brattleboro, Vermont: S. Greene, 1972.

GROSS, FELIKS, "Political Assassination" in *International Terrorism in the Contemporary World,* ed. M. H. Livingston. Westport, Conn.: Greenwood Press, 1978.

——, *Violence in Politics: Terror and Political Assassination in Eastern Europe and Russia.* The Hague: Monton, 1972.

GUEVARA, ERNESTO (Che), *Episodes of the Revolutionary War.* New York: International, 1968.

GUNTER, MICHAEL M., "The Armenian Terrorist Campaign Against Turkey," *Orbis* 27 (1983): 447–77.

HACKER, FREDERICK J., *Crusaders, Criminals, Crazies: Terror and Terrorism in Our Time.* New York: Bantam, 1978.

HARDMAN, J. B. S., "Terrorism," *Encyclopedia of the Social Sciences,* eds. E. R. A. Seligman and A. Johnson. New York: Macmillan, 1934, 14, 575–76.

HEAPS, WILLARD A., *Assassination: A Special Kind of Murder.* New York: Meredith Press, 1969.

HEATH, G. LOUIS, ed., *Off the Pigs!: The History and Literature of the Black Panther Party.* New Jersey: Scarecrow Press, 1973.

——, *Students For a Democratic Society.* New Jersey: Scarecrow Press, 1976.

——, *Vandals in the Bomb Factory: The History and Literature of the Students for a Democratic Society.* New Jersey: Scarecrow Press, 1976.

HELLER, MARK A., *A Palestinian State: The Implications for Israel.* Cambridge, Mass.: Harvard University Press, 1983.

HERMAN, EDWARD S., *The Real Terror Network: Terrorism in Fact and Propaganda.* Boston: South End, 1983.

HERSH, SEYMOUR N., *Chemical and Biological Warfare.* Garden City, N.Y.: Doubleday, 1969.

HEWITT, CHRISTOPHER, *The Effectiveness of Anti-Terrorist Policies.* New York: University Press of America, 1984.

HINCKLE, WARREN, and WILLIAM TURNER, *The Fish is Red: The Story of the Secret War Against Castro.* New York: Harper & Row, 1981.

HITCHENS, CHRISTOPHER, *"Wanton Acts of Usage: Terrorism, A Cliché in Search of a Meaning,"* Harper's (September 1986):66.

HODGSON, M.G.S., *The Order of Assassins.* The Hague: Morton, 1955.

HOLLAND, CAROLINE, "The Black, the Red and the Orange: System Terrorism Versus Regime Terror," unpublished manuscript, 1982.

HOWE, DANIEL W., *The Political Culture of American Whigs.* Chicago: University of Chicago, 1979.

HUBBARD, DAVID, *The Skyjacker: His Flights of Fancy.* New York: Macmillan, 1973.

HUIE, WILLIAM B., *He Slew the Dreamer.* New York: Delacorte, 1970.

HUNT , HENRY, *Reasonable Doubt: An Investigation into the Assassination of John F. Kennedy.* New York: Holt, Rinehart Winston, 1986.

INGRAHAM, BARTON L., *Political Crime in Europe.* Berkeley: University of California Press, 1979.

IVIANSKY, ZE'EV, "Individual Terror: Concept and Typology," *Journal of Contemporary History* 12 (1977): 43, 50.

——, "The Moral Issue: Some Aspects of Individual Terror," in *The Morality of Terrorism: Religious and Secular Justifications,* eds. David C. Rapoport and Yonah Alexander. New York: Pergamon Press, 1983.

JACKSON, BRIAN, *The Black Flag: A Look Back at the Strange Case of Nicola Sacco and Bartolomeo Vanzetti.* Boston: Routledge & Kegan Paul, 1981.

JACOBS, HAROLD, ed., *Weathermen.* Berkeley: Ramparts, 1970.

JAEGER, GERTRUDE, and PHILLIP SELZNICK, "A Normative Theory of Culture," *American Sociological Review* 29 (1964):653–69.

JANKE, PETER, *Guerrilla and Terrorist Organizations: A World Directory and Bibliography.* New York: Macmillan, 1983.

——, *Spanish Separatism: ETA's Threat to Basque Democracy,* Conflict Studies 123. London: Institute for the Study of Conflict, 1979.

——, *Ulster: A Decade of Violence,* Conflict Studies 108. London: Institute for the Study of Conflict, 1979.

JASZI, OSCAR, and JOHN D. LEWIS, *Against the Tyrant: The Tradition and Theory of Tyrannicide.* Glencoe, Ill.: Free Press, 1957.

JENKINS, BRIAN, *International Terrorism: A New Mode of Conflict.* Los Angeles: Crescent, 1975.

——, "Terrorism and Nuclear Safeguards Issue," *Rand Paper Series P-5611.* Santa Monica, Calif.: Rand Corporation, 1984.

——, ed., *Terrorism and Personal Protection.* Boston: Butterworth, 1985.

——, *Terrorism and the Nuclear Safeguards Issue.* Santa Monica, Calif.: Rand Corporation, March, 1976.

——, "The Future Course of International Terrorism," *TVI Report* 6 (Fall 1985): S3-7.

JENNINGS, PETER, *Hostage: An Endless Terror.* ABC Documentary Film, 1978.

JOLL, JAMES, "Anarchism: A Living Tradition," In *Anarchism Today,* eds. David E. Apter and James Joll. New York: Anchor, 1972.

——, *The Anarchists.* Cambridge: Harvard University Press, 1980.

JORDAN, HAMILTON, *Crisis: The Last Years of the Carter Presidency.* New York: Putnam, 1982.

JORDAN, WINTHROP D., *White over Black: American Attitudes Toward the Negro.* Chapel Hill: University of North Carolina Press, 1968.

Kahan Commission Report, *The Beirut Massacre.* Princeton, N.J.: Karz-Cohl, 1983.

KAISER, ROBERT B., *RFK Must Die! A History of the Robert Kennedy Assassination and its Aftermath.* New York: Dutton, 1970.

KELLEY, KEVIN, *The Longest War: Northern Ireland and the IRA.* Westport, Conn.: Lawrence Hill, 1982.

KERNER, OTTO, *Report of the National Advisory Commission on Civil Disorders.* New York: Bantam Books, 1968.

KHOURI, FRED J., *The Arab Israeli Dilemma.* Syracuse, N.Y.: Syracuse University Press, 1985.

KINDEL, STEPHEN, "Catching Terrorists," *Science Digest* 94 (September 1986): 78.

KINROSS, LORD J. P., *The Ottoman Centuries: The Rise and Fall of the Turkish Empire.* New York: Morrow, 1977.

KIRKHAM, JAMES F., and others, *Assassination and Political Violence: A Report to the National Commission on the Causes and Prevention of Violence.* New York: Bantam Books, 1970.

KNOWLES, GRAHAM, *Bomb Security Guide.* Los Angeles: Security World Publishing Company, 1976.

KOBETZ, RICHARD, *Hostage Incidents: The New Police Priority.* Gaithersburg, Md.: International Association of Chiefs of Police, undated mimeo.

KOCH, PETER, and KAI HERMANN, *Assault at Mogadishu.* London: Corgi Books, 1977.

KOHL, JAMES, and JOHN LITT, eds., *Urban Guerrilla Warfare in Latin America.* Cambridge: MIT Press, 1974.

KOOB, KATHRYN, *Guest of the Revolution.* New York: Thomas Nelson, 1982.

KOZOL, JONATHAN, *Children of the Revolution: A Yankee Teacher in Cuban Schools.* New York: Delacorte, 1978.

KRIEGER, DAVID M., "What Happens If? Terrorists, Revolutionaries, and Nuclear Weapons," *The Annals of the American Academy of Political and Social Sciences* 430 (March 1977): 44-57.

KUPER, LEO, *Genocide.* New Haven, Conn.: Yale University Press, 1981.

KUPPERMAN, ROBERT H., "Fighting Terrorism: A National Security View," *Georgetown Center for Strategic International Studies,* Public Broadcasting Stations, September 17, 1986.

LANE, MARK, *Rush to Judgment.* New York: Holt, Rinehard & Winston, 1966.

LANGER, WILLIAM, *The Diplomacy of Imperialism: 1890-1902.* Boston: Knopf, 1951.

LAQUEUR, WALTER, "The Futility of Terrorism," *Harper's,* (March, 1976) 104.

——, *Terrorism.* Boston: Little, Brown, 1977.

——, ed., *The Israeli-Arab Reader.* New York: Bantam Books, 1969.

——, *The Age of Terrorism.* Boston: Little Brown, 1987.

——, *The Terrorism Reader.* New York: New American Library, 1978.

LEBOW, RICHARD NED, "The Origins of Sectarian Assassination: The Case of Belfast," *Journal of International Affairs* 32 (1978): 43-61.

LENZ, ROBERT R., *Explosives and Bomb Disposal Guide.* Springfield, Ill.: Charles C. Thomas, 1971.

LEWIS, BERNARD, *The Assassins: A Radical Sect in Islam.* New York: Basic Books, 1968.

LIVINGSTONE, NEIL C., and JOSEPH D. DOUGLASS, Jr., *CBW: The Poor Man's Atomic Bomb.* Cambridge, Mass.: Institute for Foreign Policy Analysis, Inc., 1984.

——, and Terrell E. Arnold, eds., *Fighting Back: Winning the War Against Terrorism.* Lexington, Mass.: D.C. Heath, 1986.

——, and Terrell E. Arnold, "The Rise of State-Sponsored Terrorism," eds., Neil C. Livingstone and Terrell E. Arnold, *Fighting Back: Winning the War Against Terrorism.* Lexington, Mass.: Lexington Books, 1986.

——, "The Impact of Technological Innovation," in *Hydra of Carnage: International Linkages of Terrorism,* eds. Uri Ra'anan et al, Lexington, Mass.: Lexington Books, 1986.

LODGE, JAMES, ed., *Terrorism a Challenge to the State.* Oxford: Martin Robertson, 1981.

LORIMAR, KARL, *Special Bulletin* (movie). Irvine, CA: Lorimar Home Video, 1986.

Los Angeles Times, October 16, 1974, p. 6.

Low Intensity Conflict, Army FM 100–30. Washington, D.C.: Department of the Army, 1981.

MACDONALD, ANDREW, *The Turner Diaries.* Arlington, Va.: National Vanguard Books, 1985.

MACLEAN, ALISTAIR, *Goodbye California.* New York: Doubleday, 1978.

MARCHETTI, VICTOR, and JOHN MARKS, *The CIA and the Cult of Intelligence.* New York: Knopf, 1983.

MARIGHELLA, CARLOS, *The Terrorist Classic: Manual of the Urban Guerrilla,* trans. Gene Hanrahan. Chapel Hill, N.C.: Documentary Publishing, 1985.

——, "The Mini-Manual of Urban Guerrilla Warfare," in *Urban Guerrilla Warfare,* ed. Robert Moss. London: Institute for Strategic Studies, 1971.

MATTHEWS, CHRISTOPHER, *The Butcher.* New York: Stein and Day, 1986.

MAY, W. F., "Terrorism as Strategy and Ecstasy," *Social Research,* 41 (1974), 277.

MCADAMS, C. MICHAEL, *White Paper on Dr. Andrija Artukovic.* California: Croatian Information Series, 4 (July, 1975), 4–11.

MCCLUNG, ALFRED L., *Terrorism in Northern Ireland.* New York: General Hall, 1983.

MCFADDEN, ROBERT D., JOE B. TREASTER, and MAURICE CARROLL, *No Hiding Place.* New York: Times Books, 1981.

MCLELLAN, VIN, and PAUL AVERY, *The Voices of Guns.* New York: Putnam, 1977.

MCMILLAN, GEORGE, *The Making of an Assassin.* Boston: Little, Brown, 1976.

"Meir Kahane: A Candid Conversation with the Military Leader of the Jewish Defense League," *Playboy,* (October 1972):69.

MELMAN, YOSSI, *The Master Terrorist: The True Story Behind Abu Nidal.* New York: Adama Books, 1986.

MENGEL, R. W., "Terrorism and New Technologies of Destruction: An Overview of the Potential Risk," *Studies in Nuclear Terrorism,* eds. Augustus R. Norton and Martin H. Greenberg. Boston, Mass.: G. K. Hill, 1979.

MERARI, ARIAL, "Classification of Terrorist Groups," *Terrorism,* 1 (1978), 331.

MIDDENDORFF, WOLF, *New Developments in the Taking of Hostages and Kidnapping: A Summary.* Washington, D.C.: National Criminal Justice Reference Service, 1975.

MILLER, AARON D., *The PLO and the Politics of Survival.* New York: Praeger, 1983.

MILLER, DAVID, *Anarchism.* London: J. M. Dent and Sons, 1984.

MIRON, MURRAY S., and ARNOLD P. GOLDSTEIN, *Hostage.* New York: Pergamon Press, 1979.

MONACO, JAMES, *Celebrity: The Media as Image Maker.* New York: Delta, 1978.

MOODIE, MICHAEL, "The Patriot Game: The Politics of Violence in Northern Ireland," In *International Terrorism in the Contemporary World,* ed. Marius H. Livingston. Connecticut: Greenwood, 1978.

MOORE, Jr., BARRINGTON, *Terror and Progress—U.S.S.R.* New York: Harper, 1954.

MOORE, JOHN N., ed., *The Arab-Israeli Conflict, Volume III.* Princeton, N.J.: Princeton University Press, 1974.

MOOREHEAD, CAROLINE, *Hostages to Fortune.* New York: Atheneum, 1980.

MORGENTHAU, HENRY, *Ambassador Morgenthau's Story.* New York: Doubleday, 1918.

MOSSE, WILLIAM E., *Alesander II and the Modernization of Russia.* New York: Macmillan, 1958.

MOTLEY, JAMES B., "Target America: The Undeclared War," in *Fighting Back: Winning the War Against Terrorism,* eds. Neil C. Livingstone and Terrell E. Arnold. Lexington, Mass.: Lexington Books, 1986.

MOYER, FRANK, *Police Guide to Bomb Search Techniques.* Boulder: Paladin Press, 1981.

MUHAMMED, ASKIA, *The Nation* 224 (June 1977): 721.

MULLEN, ROBERT K., "Mass Destruction and Terrorism," *Studies in Nuclear Terrorism,* eds. Augustus R. Norton and Martin H. Greenberg. Boston, Mass.: G. K. Hill, 1979.

MURPHY, JOHN F., *Punishing International Terrorists: The Legal Framework for Policy Initiatives.* New Jersey: Rowman and Allanheld, 1985.

National Advisory Committee on Criminal Justice Standards and Goals, Law Enforcement Assistance Agency, *Disorders and Terrorism.* Washington, D.C.: U. S. Government Printing Office, 1976.

National Commission on Causes and Prevention of Violence, *Assassination and Political Violence.* Washington, D.C.: U. S. Government Printing Office, 1968.

NEALE, WILLIAM D., "Terror: Oldest Weapon in the Arsenal," *Army,* August, 1973, pp. 10–17.

NECHAEV, SERGEI, "Catechism of the Revolutionist," in *Daughter of a Revolutionist,* ed. M. Confino. London: Alcove, 1982.

NEFF, DONALD, *Warriors at Suez.* New York: Simon & Schuster, 1981.

NELDHARDT, WILFRIED, *Fenianism in North America.* University Park: Pennsylvania State University, 1975.

NETANYAHU, BENJAMIN, *Terrorism: How the West Can Win.* New York: Farrar, Straus & Giroux, 1986.

NEWMAN, DAVID, *Jewish Settlement in the West Bank: The Role of Gush Emunim.* Durham, N.C.: University of Durham Centre for Middle Eastern and Islamic Studies, 1982.

Newsweek, May 17, 1971, p. 250.

——, October 6, 1975, p. 24.

——, March 6, 1978, pp. 33–34.

——, May 22, 1978, p. 35.

——, October 19, 1981, pp. 26–31.

——, April 21, 1986, pp. 21–26.

New York Times, March 1, 1971, p. 2.

——, October 27, 1974, pp. 1, 64.

——, January 25, 1975, pp. 1, 10.

——, September 12, 1976, p. 3.

——, September 13, 1979, sec. B, p. 23.

——, December 4, 1979, pp. 1, A10.

——, March 3, 1980, p. 2.

——, March 16, 1980, pp. 1, 45.

——, April 5, 1980, pp. 1, 7.

——, January 13, 1981, pp. 1, A12.

——, October 20, 1981.

——, March 1, 1982, pp. 1, D11.

——, January 1, 1983, pp. 1, 23.

——, October 21, 1983, sec. A, p. 35.

——, October 23, 1983, sec. 1, p. 1.

——, November 5, 1983, sec. 1, p. 14.

——, February 19, 1984.

——, September 23, 1984, p. 2.

——, October 10, 1984.

——, January 27, 1985, p. 12.

——, June 24, 1985, sec. 1, p. 1.

——, September 21, 1985, sec. 1, p. 1.

——, November 7, 1985, p. 1.

——, November 26, 1985, p. 1.

——, April 15, 1986, p. 1.

——, July 27, 1986, sec. 1, p. 2.

NISAN, M., "The PLO and the Palestinian Issue," *Middle East Review,* 28, 2 (Winter, 1985), 55.

NORTON, AUGUSTUS R., and MARTIN H. GREENBERG, eds., *Studies in Nuclear Terrorism.* Boston, Mass.: G. K. Hill, 1979.

——, *Understanding the Nuclear Terrorism Threat.* Gaithersburg, Md.: IACP, 1979.

O'BRIEN, CONOR CRUISE, *The Siege: The Saga of Israel and Zionism.* New York: Simon & Schuster, 1986.

OCHBERG, FRANK, "Hostage Victims," in *Terrorism: Interdisciplinary Perspectives,* eds. Burr

Eichelman, David Soskis, and William Reid. Washington, D.C.: American Psychiatric Association, 1983.

O'FARRELL, PATRICK, *Ireland's English Question.* New York: Schocken, 1972.

PADOVER, SAUL K., "Patterns of Assassination in Occupied Territory," *Public Opinion Quarterly* 7 (1943):680.

PAPANIKOLAS, ZEESE, *Buried Unsung: Louis Tikas and the Ludlow Massacre. Salt Lake City, University of Utah Press, 1982.*

PAUST, JORDAN J., "International Law and Control of the Media: Terror, Repression and the Alternatives," *Ind. Law Journal* 53 (1978):644–45.

PAYNE, ROBERT, *The Life and Death of Lenin.* New York: Simon & Schuster, 1964.

PETER, LAURENCE J., *Peters' Quotations.* New York: Morrow, 1977.

PETERSON, A. ATLEY, "A Report on the Detection and Identification of Explosives by Tagging," *Journal of Forensic Sciences* 26 (April 1981):313–18.

PISANO, VITTORFRANCO, "France as an International Setting for Domestic and International Terrorism," *Clandestine Tactics and Technology,* (1985), pp. 3–6.

———, *The Red Brigades: A Challenge to Italian Democracy.* London: Institute for the Study of Conflict, July, 1980.

PHILLIPS, DAVID, *Skyjack.* London: Hairap, 1973.

PINKOWSKI, EDWARD, *The Latimer Massacre.* Philadelphia: Sunshine, 1950.

PONTECORRO, GILLO, *Battle of Algiers,* film written by Franco Solivar. New York: Scribner, 1973.

POPKIN, RICHARD, *The Second Oswald.* New York: Avon, 1966.

Powell, William, *Anarchist Cookbook.* New York: L. Stuart, 1971.

"Provos Versus the Crown: A Review of Contemporary Terrorist and Antiterrorist Operations in Northern Ireland," *Clandestine Tactics and Technology,* Update Report, 8, no. 7 (1983): 2.

Public Report of the Vice President's Task Force on Combating Terrorism. Washington, D.C.: U.S. Government Printing Office, February, 1986.

RA'ANAN, URI, et al, eds., *Hydra of Carnage: International Linkages of Terrorism.* Lexington, Mass.: Lexington Books, 1986.

RADVANYI, M., *Antiterrorist Legislation in the Federal Republic of Germany.* Washington, D.C.: Law Library, Library of Congress, 1979.

RANDEL, WILLIAM P., *The Ku Klux Klan: A Century of Infamy.* Philadelphia: Chilton, 1965.

RANELAGH, JOHN, *The Agency: The Rise and Decline of the CIA.* New York: Simon & Schuster, 1986.

RAPOPORT, DAVID C., *Assassination and Terrorism.* Toronto: CBC, 1976.

———, "The Politics of Atrocity," in *Terrorism: Interdisciplinary Perspectives,* eds. Yonah Alexander and S. M. Finger. New York: John Jay, 1977.

———, and Yonah Alexander, eds., *The Morality of Terrorism: Religious and Secular Justifications.* New York: Pergamon Press, 1983.

———, and Yonah Alexander, eds., "Document on Terror," in *The Morality of Terrorism: Religious and Secular Justifications.* New York: Pergamon Press, 1983.

———, "Terror and the Messiah: An Ancient Experience and Some Modern Parallels," in *The Morality of Terrorism: Religious and Secular Justifications,* eds. David C. Rapoport and Yonah Alexander. New York: Pergamon Press, 1983.

Report of the DOD Commission on Beirut International Airport Terrorist Act, October 23, 1983. Washington, D.C.: U.S. Government Printing Office, 1983.

Report of the Select Committee on Assassinations, U.S. House of Representatives, Ninety-Fifth Congress, Second Session: Findings and Recommendations. Washington, D.C.: U. S. Government Printing Office, 1979, Vols 1–26.

RICHELSON, JEFFREY T., *The U.S. Intelligence Community.* Cambridge, Mass.: Ballinger, 1985.

RIDENOUR, ROBERT, "Where Are the Terrorists and What Do They Want," *Skeptic* 11 (1976): 18–23.

Risks International, *Regional Risk Assessment: Latin America.* Alexandria, Va: Risks International, April 1979.

———, *Terrorism 1970–1984.* Alexandria, Va: Risks International, unpublished report, 1985.

ROBLEE, CHARLES L., and ALLEN MCKECHNIE, *The Investigation of Fires.* Englewood Cliffs, N.J.: Prentice-Hall, 1981.

ROSEN, BARRY, BARBARA ROSEN, and GEORGE FEIFER, *The Destined Hour: The Hostage Crisis and One Family's Ordeal.* New York: Doubleday, 1982.

ROSENBERG, CHARLES E., *The Trial of the Assassin Guiteau.* Chicago: University of Chicago Press, 1968.

ROSENBLATT, ROGER, *Children of War.* Garden City, New York: Anchor/Doubleday, 1983.

RUSSELL, BERTRAND, *Roads to Freedom: Socialism, Anarchism, and Syndicalism.* London: Allen & Unwin, 1919.

RUSSELL, CHARLES, "Kidnapping as a Terrorist Tactic," in *Terrorism and Personal Protection,* ed. Brian M. Jenkins. Boston: Butterworth, 1985.

RYAN, PAUL, *The Iranian Rescue Mission: Why It Failed.* Annapolis Md.: Naval Institute, 1985.

SACHAR, HOWARD M., *Egypt and Israel.* New York: Richard Marek, 1982.

Sacramento Bee, September 7, 1975, sec. A, p. 3.

——, October 21, 1981, sec. A, p. 8.

——, December 11, 1984, sec. A, p. 1.

——, January 20, 1985, Forum p. 1.

——, September 5, 1985, sec. A, p. 12.

——, December 31, 1985, sec. A, p. 8.

——, January 19, 1986, sec. A, p. 1.

——, February 9, 1986, p. 1.

——, April 4, 1986, sec. A, p. 10.

——, April 15, 1986, sec. A, p. 8.

——, April 16, 1986. p. 1.

——, May 23, 1986, sec. A, p. 7.

——, July 18, 1986, sec. A, p. 1.

——, October 12, 1986, sec. A, p. 4.

SAID, EDWARD W., *The Question of Palestine.* New York: Times Books, 1979.

SALE, KIRKPATRICK, *S.D.S.* New York: Random House, 1973.

SALTMAN, RICHARD B., *The Social and Political Thought of Michael Bakunin.* Westport, Conn.: Greenwood, 1983.

SANDMAN, PETER M., and others, *Media.* Englewood Cliffs: Prentice-Hall, 1976.

San Francisco Chronicle, November 11, 1984, This World section, pp. 7-8.

——, "War Crimes Extradition Hearing Begins," February 28, 1985, p. 7.

——, March 2, 1985, sec. A, p. 8.

——, June 29, 1986, This World section, p. 15.

——, December 21, 1986, p. AA4.

San Francisco Examiner, November 10, 1985, sec. A, p. 18.

——, September 7, 1986, p. 1.

SARKESIAN, SAM C., *America's Forgotten Wars: The Counterrevolutionary Past and Lessons For the Future.* Westport, Conn.: Greenwood Press, 1984.

SCHAFER, STEPHEN, *The Political Criminal.* New York: Free Press, 1974.

SCHAPP, WILLIAM, "New Spate of Terrorism: Key Leaders Unleashed," *Covert Action Information Bulletin* (December, 1980):7-9.

SCHEFF, ZE'EV, *Entebbe Rescue.* New York: Dell, 1977.

SCHELLING, THOMAS C., "Who Will Have the Bomb?" in *Studies In Nuclear Terrorism,* eds. Augustus R. Norton and Martin H. Greenberg. Boston, Mass.: G. K. Hill, 1979.

——, *The Strategy of Conflict.* London: Oxford University Press, 1973.

SCHMID, ALEX P., *Political Terrorism.* New Brunswick: Transaction, 1983.

——, and JANNY DE GRAAF, *Violence as Communication: Insurgent Terrorism and the Western News Media.* Beverly Hills: Sage, 1982.

SCHOCH, BRUCE P., "Four Rules for a Successful Rescue," *Army* 16 (February 1981): 22-26.

SCHREIBER, JAN, *The Ultimate Weapon: Terrorists and World Order.* New York: Morrow, 1978.

SCHREIBER, MANFRED, *After Action Report of Terrorist Activities 20th Olympic Games Munich, West Germany* FRG, September, 1972, p. 14.

Secretary of Defense, *Annual Report to Congress,* Fiscal Year 1986, February 4, 1985, p. 23.

SETH, RONALD, *The Russian Terrorists: The Story of Narodniki.* London: Barrie and Rockliff, 1967.

"Setting the Record Straight on Armenian Propaganda Against Turkey" *ATA-USA: Bulletin of the Assembly of American Turkish Associations,* Washington, D.C., Fall, 1982.

SHULTZ, GEORGE P., "The U.S. Must Retaliate Against Terrorist States," in *Terrorism: Opposing Viewpoints,* eds. David L. Bender and Bruno Leone. St. Paul Minn.: Greenhaven Press, 1986.

SHULTZ, RICHARD, "Conceptualizing Political Terrorism: A Typology," *Journal of International Affairs,* 32 (1978), 7.

SICK, GARY, *All Fall Down: America's Tragic Encounter with Iran.* New York: Random House, 1984.

SILBERMAN, CHARLES E., *Criminal Violence Criminal Justice.* New York: Random House, 1978.

SMALLWOOD, E. M., *The Jews Under Roman Rule.* Leiden, Netherlands: Brill, 1976.

SMITH, DESMOND, *The Nation,* March 30, 1974, pp. 392–94.

SMITH, ROBERT W., *The Coeur d'Alene Mining War of 1882: A Case Study of an Industrial Dispute.* Corvallis: Oregon State College, 1961.

SOBEL, LESTER A., ed., *Political Terrorism.* New York: Facts on File, 1975.

SPECTOR, LEONARD S., *The New Nuclear Nations.* New York: Vintage Books, 1985.

STEIN, DAVID L., *Living the Revolution: Yippies in Chicago.* Indianapolis: Bobbs-Merrill, 1969.

STEPNIAK, T., *Underground Russia: Revolutionary Profiles and Sketches from Life.* New York: Scribner, 1892.

STERLING, CLAIRE, *The Terror Network: The Secret War of International Terrorism.* New York: Holt, Rinehart & Winston, 1980.

STERN, JEFF, "An Army in Exile," *New Yorker,* September 10, 1979, pp. 42–6.

STEVENSON, WILLIAM, *Ninety Minutes at Entebbe.* New York: Bantam, 1977.

STOFFEL, JOSEPH P., *Explosives and Homemade Bombs.* Springfield, Ill.: Charles C. Thomas, 1972.

STRATTON, JOHN G., "The Terrorist Act of Hostage Taking: Considerations for Law Enforcement," *Journal of Police Science and Administration,* 6, (1978), 123–34.

STRENTZ, THOMAS, "Law Enforcement Policy and Ego Defenses of the Hostage," *F.B.I. Law Enforcement Bulletin* (April 1979): p. 4.

STYRON, WILLIAM, *The Confessions of Nat Turner.* New York: Random House, 1967.

TAFT, PHILIP, *History of Labor in the U.S.* New York: Macmillan, 1935.

"Terror," *Webster's Ninth New Collegiate Dictionary.* Springfield, Mass.: Merriam and Webster, 1983.

The London Times, August 28, 1979, p. 1.

The National News Council, "Paper on Terrorism." In *Terrorism, The Media and Law Enforcement,* ed. A.H. Miller. Washington, D.C.: Government Printing Office, 1983.

The Royal Ulster Constabulary, *Chief Constable's Report: 1983,* (Belfast, 1984), p. 11, table 6.

The Split of the Weather Underground Organization. Seattle, Wash.: John Brown Book Club, 1977.

THOMPSON, JERRY, *My Life in the Klan.* New York: Putnam, 1982.

THORNTON, THOMAS P., "Terror as a Weapon of Political Agitation," in *Internal War,* ed. H. Eckstein. New York: Free Press, 1964.

Time, April 30, 1973, p. 66.

———, March 28, 1977, p. 13.

———, October 31, 1977, pp. 42–45.

———, March 6, 1978, pp. 40–45.

———, August 13, 1984, p. 26.

———, October 22, 1984, p. 50.

———, June 3, 1985, p. 52.

———, December 23, 1985, p. 35.

———, January 13, 1986, pp. 31–32.

———, April 21, 1986, pp. 17–29.

———, September 15, 1986, pp. 30–35.

To Die For Ireland. ABC Documentary Film, 1980.

TOLLEY, HOWARD, *Children and War: Political Socialization to International Conflict.* New York: Teachers College Press, 1973.

TRICK, MARCIA M., "Chronology of Incidents of Terroristic Quasi-Terroristic and Political Violence in the u.s.: january 1965 to march 1976," in *Disorders and Terrorism.* Washington, D.C.: U. S. Government Printing Office, 1977.

TUGWELL, MAURICE A. J., "Guilt Transfer," in *The Morality of Terrorism: Religious and Secular Justifications,* eds. David C. Rapoport and Yonah Alexander. New York: Pergamon Press, 1983.

TURK, AUSTIN T., *Political Criminality.* Beverly Hills: Sage, 1982.

UNDERWOOD, NORA, "Fear of Plastic Pistols," *MacLeans* 99 (March 10, 1986): 61.

———, "Packing Plastic Pistols," *Science Digest* 94 (June 1986): 15.

United States Air Force Special Operations School, Hurlburt Field, Florida, July 1985.

United States Bureau of Alcohol, Tobacco, and Firearms, *Explosives Incidents 1982.* Washington, D.C.: U.S. Government Printing Office, 1983.

United States Congress, House, Committee on Internal Security, *Terrorism,* Hearing, 93rd Congress, 2nd Session. Washington, D. C.: Government Printing Office, 1974.

United States Congress, Senate, Committee on the Judiciary, Subcommittee to Investigate the Administration of the Internal Security Act and Other Internal Security Laws, *Part 5: Hostage Defense Measures,* Hearings, 94th Congress, July 25, 1975. Washington, D.C.: Government Printing Office, 1975.

———, Senate, Committee on the Judiciary, Subcommittee on Security and Terrorism, *Committee on the Judiciary, U. S. Senate,* 97th Congress, February 4, 1982. Washington, D.C.: Government Printing Office, 1982.

United States Department of State, *Patterns of Global Terrorism: 1984.* Washington, D.C.: Government Printing Office, 1985.

United States Department of State, *Patterns of International Terrorism: 1982.* Washington, D.C.: U.S. Government Printing Office, 1983, Doc. 5.

———, *Terrorist Bombings.* Washington, D.C.: U.S. Government Printing Office, 1983.

United States Department of Transportation, Federal Aviation Administration, Office of Civil Aviation Security, *Explosions Aboard Aircraft.* Washington, D.C.: U. S. Government Printing Office, 1985.

VAN GELDER, ARTHUR P., and HUGO SCHLATTER, *History of the Explosives Industry in America.* New York: Arno Press, 1972.

VENTURI, FRANCO, *Roots of Revolution: A History of the Populist and Socialist Movements in 19th Century Russia.* New York: Knopf, 1960.

VIDAL, GORE, "Now For the Shooting of George Wallace," *New York Review of Books* 20 (December 13, 1973): 17–19.

VON BORCKE, ASTRID, "Violence and Terror in Russian Revolutionary Populism, The Norodnaya Volya, 1879–1883," in *Social Protest, Violence, and Terrorism in 19th and 20th Century Europe.* London: Macmillan, 1982.

Wall Street Journal (New York), December 2, 1983, p. 1.

——— (New York), April 30, 1984, p. 1.

WALTER, EUGENE V., *Terror and Resistance: A Study of Political Violence.* New York: Oxford, 1969.

WARDLAW, GRANT, *Political Terrorism: Theory, Tactics and Countermeasures.* Cambridge: Cambridge University Press, 1982.

Washington Post, May 13, 1975, p. 22.

WATSON, FRANCIS M., *Political Terrorism.* Washington, D.C.: R. B. Luce, 1976.

WIDGERY, LORD, *Report of the Tribunal Appointed to Enquire into the Events on Sunday, 30th January, 1972 in Londonderry.* London: HMSO, 1972.

WILKINSON, PAUL, *Political Terrorism.* London: Macmillan, 1976.

———, *Terrorism and the Liberal State.* London: Macmillan, 1977.

———, "Armenian Terrorism," *The World Today* 39 (September 1983): 336–50.

WILLRICH, MASON, and THEODORE B. TAYLOR, "Nuclear Theft: Risks and Safeguards," *Studies In Nuclear Terrorism,* eds. Augustus R. Norton and Martin H. Greenberg. Boston, Mass.: G. K. Hill, 1979.

WILSON, JAMES Q., "Thinking about Terrorism," *Commentary* 72 (July 1981): 34–39.

———, *The Investigators: Managing F.B.I. and Narcotics Agents.* New York: Basic Books, 1978.

WOLFGANG, MARVIN, and FRANCO FERRACUTI, *The Subculture of Violence.* Beverly Hills: Sage, 1982.

WOODCOCK, GEORGE, *Anarchism: A History of Libertarian Ideas and Movements.* New York: World Publishing, 1962.

WRIGHT, ROBIN, *Sacred Rage: The Wrath of Militant Islam.* New York: Simon & Schuster, 1986.

WYDEN, PETER, *Bay of Pigs: The Untold Story.* New York: Simon & Schuster, 1980.

YALLOP, H. J., *Explosion Investigation.* Edinburgh, Scotland: Scottish Academic Press, 1980.

ZOBEL, HILLER B., *The Boston Massacre.* New York: Norton, 1970.

INDEX

A

AAG, see Avengers of the Armenian Genocide
Air piracy, see skyjacking
Alexander II (tsar of Russia), 30
Alpha 66, 85-87
Amal, 177, 223-224, 226
American Nazi Party (ANP), 28, 70, 88, 95-96, 240
Anarchism, 33-36
Anarcho-syndicalists, 34-35
ANP, see American Nazi Party
Anti-Semitism, 88, 94
ARA, see Armenian Revolutionary Army
Arab-Israeli conflict, 99-104, 107, 220-23
Arab Liberation Front (ALF), 104, 108

Arab Nationalist Movement (ANM), 103
Arafat, Yasir, 57, 102-6, 108, 176
Argentina, 64-65, 135-36
Arizona Patriots, 94
Armed Forces for National Liberation (FALN), 73-76, 156
Armed Forces of Popular Resistance (FARP), 76
Armed Resistance Unit (ARU), 92-93
Armenian Revolutionary Army (ARA), 55, 79
Armenian Secret Army for the Liberation of Armenia (ASALA), 78-80
Artukovic, Andrija, 83
Aryan nations, 70, 94-95
ASALA, see Armenian Secret Army for the Liberation of Armenia

Assassination, 25-27, 35, 165-66
  by terrorists, 166, 172-78
  by the Narodnaya Volya, 30-31
  definition of, 167-68
  in Iran, 176-77
  in the Middle East, 172-78
  in the United States, 168-71, 178-89
  origin of word, 25
  types of, 168-172
Assassins (religious sect), 25-26, 167
Athletes, Israeli, 56, 132
Avengers of the Armenian Genocide (AAG), 79

B

Baader-Meinhoff gang, 54–55
Bakunin, Michael, 34, 158
Balfour Declaration, 100
Begin, Menachem, 25, 106
Belgium, 118-20
Birmingham (Alabama), 28
Black and Tans, 111
Black Legion (BL), 91
Black Liberation Army (BLA), 71-72, 90-93, 240
Black Panther Party (BPP), 58, 70-71, 91-93
Black powder, 145, 147, 151-52
Black September, 46
Black September (terrorist group), 56, 108
BLA, see Black Liberation Army
Blast pressure, 150
Boatlift, Cuban, 87
Bombing:
  in Lebanon, 144, 156-157
  media coverage of, 145
  of aircraft, 160-63
  statistics related to, 144

  use of, by terrorists, 143-45, 153-64
Bombs:
  availability of explosive materials, 145-46
  detection of, 193-94
  history of, 145-46
  types of, 148-49, 153-63
Booth, John Wilkes, 180, 185
Boston Tea Party, 36
Boxer Rebellion, 25
Bremer, Arthur, 186-87
Byck, Samuel, 187

C

California Peace Officers Association, 63
Canada, 2, 205
Carron, Owen, 53
Carter Jimmy, 206-7
Castro, Fidel, 85-87
Censorship, 63-65
China, 25
Churches, identity, 94
CIA, 85, 198, 203-205
Civil rights, 2, 57
Civil Rights Act, 72
Civil rights movement, in Ireland, 113-14
Civil War (U.S.), 37
Cleaver, Eldridge, 91
CO, see May 19 Communist Organization
Colombia, 209
Communist Workers Party, 95-96
Composition 4 (C-4), 146-147, 152-53, 159
Conflict:
  low-intensity, 228
  types of, 229-30
Contagion theory, 45-50
Cooper, D.B., 48

Copycat syndrome, see contagion theory

Covenant, the Sword and the Arm of the Lord, the (CSA), 70, 94, 240

Counterterrorism:
intelligence gathering, 195-99
response measures, 192-95
security measures, 193-94
threat analysis, 198-99
use of covert operatives, 196

Counterterrorists, 111

Criminal justice system, 2

Croatian Liberation Movement, 81-84

Croatian National Resistance (CFF), 45, 81, 84

Croatian Revolutionary Brotherhood (HRB), 84

CRP, see Revolutionary Commandos of the People

CSA, see Covenant, the Sword and the Arm of the Lord

Cuba, 85-88

Czolgosz, Leon, 181-82

D

Delta Force, 70, 206-7

DGI (Cuban Intelligence), 87

Dielectric analysis, 193

Direct Action (AD), 119-20

Disinformation, 4

Document on Terror, 32-33

Dynamite, 30, 146-147, 151-152

E

Egypt, 208

Ejercito Revolucionario del Pueblo (ERP), see People's Revolutionary Army

ERP, see People's Revolutionary Army

Euroterrorism, 119

Explosives, rate of velocity, 151. See also bombs

Extremism:
left-wing, in U.S., 90-93, 95
police support of, 95
right-wing, in U.S., 93-96

F

FALN, see Armed Forces for National Liberation

FARP, see Armed Forces of Popular Resistance

Fatah, 102-5, 107, 108

FBI:
and domestic terrorism, 92-93
and investigation of kidnapping, 126
and investigation of nuclear threats, 235
and investigation of terrorism, 206
and Sara Jane Moore, 188
establishment of, 125

Fenian Brotherhood, 26, 110

Fighters for Free Croatia, see Croatian National Resistance

Films, and contagion theory, 49

Financing of Terror, The, 197

Ford, Gerald, 187-88, 204

Forghan Fighters, 177

Fragmentation, 148-49

France, 118-20

Free Ireland (Saor Eire), 51

Free press, and censorship, 63. See also mass media

Freedom fighters, 6. See also terrorists

Freedom for the Basque Homeland (ETA), 120, 127, 137

Fromme, Lynette "Squeaky," 187-88
Fuerzas Armadas de Liberation Nacional (FALN), see Armed Forces for National Liberation

G

Gaddafi, Moammar, 135, 201
Garfield, James A., 180-81
Guilt transfer, 4
Guiteau, Charles Julius, 180-81
Great Britain:
    colonial rule, 26-27
    role in formation of Israel, 100
    troubles in Northern Ireland, 110-11, 114-115
Guevara, Che, 32, 59, 90
Gush Emunim, 222

H

Habeas Corpus Act, 27
Hearst, Patricia, 59
Hijackers, 48-49. See also sky- jackers
Hill, Joe, 35
Hinckley, John W., 188-89
Hizbollah, 177, 224, 226
Hostages:
    American, in Iran, 131, 140, 206-8
    Israeli athletes, 56, 132-33
    political, 47
    rescue attempts, 206-209
    response of, to hostage-takers, 130-31
    selection of, by terrorists, 135- 37
    surviving hostage situations, 138-41
Hostage-takers, types of, 126-29

Hostage-taking:
    and negotiation, 131-32, 133- 35
    and ransom, 135-38
    as a terrorist tactic, 123, 132
    compared to kidnapping, 137- 38
    factors involved in, 129-32
    history of, 124-25
    in Italy, 141
    in the U.S., 125-28
    selection of hostages, 135-37
    types of, 128

I

India, 26
Indian Wars, 37-38
Industrial Workers of the World (IWW), 34-35
Intelligence gathering, 195-99
IRA, see Irish Republican Army
Iran, 176-77, 206-8, 225-27, 236
IRB, see Irish Republican Brother- hood
Ireland, 65, 110–118
Irgun Zvai Leumi-be-Israel (Na- tional Military Organization of Israel), 24-25
Irish National Liberation Army (INLA), 53-54, 115, 117
Irish National Volunteers, 110-11
Irish Republican Army (IRA), 50- 51, 55, 74, 117
    campaign of assassination, 171-72
    censorship of, by Republic of Ireland, 65
    decline in support, 111
    history of, 27, 110-12
    popularity of, 121
    terrorist activities, 70, 109-11
    terrorist strategy, 110

Irish Republican Brotherhood (IRB), 27, 110-11. See also Irish Republican Army
Islamic Jihad, 127, 225-226
   attraction of media attention, 224
   connection to Khomeini, 177
   suicide truck bombings, 224
Israel, 6, 88–89
   acquisition of nuclear weapons, 232
   Arab-Israeli conflict, 90-107
   censorship in, 65
   conflict with Palestine, 220-23
   counterterrorist operations, 208-9
   formation of, 99-100
   invasion of Lebanon, 106
   response to terrorists, 199-200, 202-3, 210
Italy, 118-20

J

JCAG, see Justice Commandos for the Armenian Genocide
JDL, see Jewish Defense League
Jewish Defenders (JD), 89
Jewish Defense League (JDL), 88-89, 240
Jewish Panthers, see Jewish Defense League
Justice Commandos for the Armenian Genocide (JCAG), 78-80

K

Kach, 88
Kahane, Meir, 88-89
Kennedy, John F., 183-84, 204
Kennedy, Robert F., 185-86
Khaalis, Hamaas Abdul, 60

Khomeini, Ayatollah, 176-77, 225-226
Kidnapping, see hostage-taking
King Alexander (of Yugoslavia), 81-82
King, Martin Luther, 184-85
Ku Klux Klan, 27-29, 40, 169, 240
   acts of anti-Semitism, 88
   origin of, 27
   use of terrorism, 93, 95-96

L

Lebanon, 64, 106, 174-75
Libya, 201-3
Lincoln, Abraham, 180
Lindbergh Law, 125-126

M

MacCumhaill, Finn, 26
Macheteros, 74, 76
MacNaughton Rule, 170
McKeague, John, 116
McKinley, William, 181
Malcolm X, 90-91
Manson, Charles, 188
Marighella, Carlos, 32, 114
   Mini-Manual of Urban Guerrilla Warfare, 32, 65, 90
Marx, Karl, 29
Mass media:
   and terminology used to define terrorists, 195
   and the Palestine issue, 46-47
   as a source of information about terrorism, 195
   censorship of, 63-67
   guidelines for coverage of terrorist events, 63, 65-67
   interference of, with police operations, 61-62, 133
   use of, by terrorists, 44-61, 145

May 19 Communist Organization, (CO), 90, 92-93
Microtagging, 193
Middle East, 172-78, 223-27
Military response, to terrorism, 205-210
Mini-Manual of Urban Guerrilla Warfare, 32, 65, 90
Minutemen, 37
MLN, see National Liberation Movement
Molly Maguires, the, 38
Montoneros, 64, 136
Moore, Sara Jane, 187-88
Moro, Aldo, 57, 137
Moslem, Hanafi, see Muslims, Hanafi
Mossad, 105
Mujahideen, 177
Muslims, Hanafi, 60, 62

N

Narodnaya Volya (People's Will), 29-31, 33
National Liberation Movement (MLN), 76
Nazi party, 28
Nechayev, 31-32
    Revolutionary Catechism, 31
Nidal, Abu, 105, 107-108
Nitroglycerine, 145-46
Nixon, Richard, 187
Nobel, Alfred, 146
Northern Ireland, 2, 6, 51-54, 154-55, 214-215
    violence in, 24, 72, 109-118
Nuclear Emergency Search Team (NEST), 235

O

O'Connell, David, 52
Official IRA (OIRA), 115

"Old Man of the Mountains," 25
Olympic Games, Munich, 56, 132-33
O'Mahony, John, 27
Omega 7, 86-87
Order of Bruder Schweigen, the, 70, 94-95, 240
Organization of Volunteers for the Puerto Rican Resolution (OVRP), 76
Oswald, Lee Harvey, 183-84
OVRP, see Organization of Volunteers for the Puerto-Rican Resolution

P

Palestine, 99, 107, 175-76, 220
Palestine Liberation Army (PLA), 108
Palestine Liberation Front, 104, 108
Palestine Liberation Organization, 104-107, 176, 202
    formation of, 102
    future of, 223
    introduction of skyjacking, 103
    recognition by U.N., 57, 104, 121
    role in international terrorism, 220
    terrorist activities, 221-22
Palestine National Front, 108
Palestine Resistance Movement, 78, 99, 220-23
Paramilitary groups, Protestant, 115-17
Pavelic, Ante, 82-83
People's Liberation Army (PLA), 51
People's Revolutionary Army (ERP), 64, 135-36

People's Will, see Narodnaya Volya

PETN, 146, 152

PFLP, see Popular Front for the Liberation of Palestine

PLO, see Palestine Liberation Organization

Popular Democratic Front for the Liberation of Palestine (DPFLP), 103, 107-108

Popular Front for the Liberation of Palestine (PFLP), 107-108
   introduction of hijacking, 103-4
   terrorist activities, 46-47, 74, 138, 208-9

Popular Front of the Liberation of Palestine–General Command (PFLP–GC), 107-108

Posse Comitatus, 70

Product tampering, 49

Propaganda, 50-61

Propaganda by the deed, 18, 34-36, 169, 171

Provisional Irish Repulican Army (PIRA), 116, 212
   objectives, 51-54
   origin of, 24
   terrorist activities, 110, 115
   use of vehicle bombs, 154-56

Provos, see Provisional Irish Republican Army

Puerto Rico, 72-76

R

Racism, 94

RATF, see Revolutionary Armed Task Force

Ray, James Earl, 184-85

Reagan, Ronald, 188-89, 200-1, 204, 227

Real Terror Network, The, 7-8

Red Army Faction (RAF), 74, 119-120, 127, 138, 166, 236

Red Brigades (RB), 57-58, 74, 119-120, 127, 137

Red Hand Commandos (RHC), 51, 116

Refugee camps, in Palestine, 102

Religious extremism, 223-26

Republic of New Africa (RNA), 90-93

Resistance, passive, 24

Revolutionary Armed Task Force (RATF), 89-90, 92-93

Revolutionary Catechism, 31-32

Revolutionary Commandos of the People (CRP), 76

Revolutionary groups, in U.S., 90

Revolutionary War, 36-37

RHC, see Red Hand Commandos

Riots:
   and National Guard, 40, 42
   in the U.S., 185
   race, 40-41
   urban, and creation of modern police system, 40, 42

RNA, see Republic of New Africa

Roosevelt, Franklin D., 182-3

Roosevelt, Theodore, 182

S

Sacco, Nicola, 35

Sadat, Anwar, 172, 175, 223

Saiqa, 107, 108

Sands, Bobby, 53

Saor Eire, see Free Ireland

Scalawags, 28

Schrank, John, 182

Schwarz, Berthold, 145

SDS, see Students for a Democratic Society

Secret societies:
   Assassins, 25-26, 29, 167
   Fenian Brotherhood, 26-27, 29

Narodnaya Volya, 29-31, 33
in Russia, 29-33
in the U.S., 27-29
Islamic Jihad, 25-26
Thugs, 26, 29
Security, airport, 193-94
Self-sacrifice, see suicide
Sheriff's Posse Comitatus (SPC), 94
Shi'ite Muslims, 224-25
Sicarii, 23
Sinn Fein, 65, 111-12
Sirhan, Sirhan, 185-86
Skyjacking:
as terrorist strategy, 46-49, 83, 85
introduction of, 103-4
rate of occurence, 193
Sons of Liberty, 36
South Africa, 65
South Korea, 2
Soviet Union, 2, 7, 227-29, 231, 233-34
Spain, 118-20
Special Operations Force, 203, 205
SPETNAZ, 229-230
Stockholm Syndrome, 124, 129-32, 140
Strikes:
hunger, 53-54
labor, 15-16, 38-40
Students for a Democratic Society (SDS), 71-72, 91-92
Suicide, as terrorist strategy, 26, 54-55
Sweden, assassination in, 165-66
Symbionese Liberation Army (SLA), 58-59

T

Television, and relationship to violence, 45-46
Terror Network, The, 7

Terror, state, 8, 227-228
Terrorism:
affect on community, 238-240
and bombing, 143-145, 153-64
and low-intensity conflict, 228-29
and role of media, 43
and terrorist atrocities, 16-18
and theory of expressive symbolism, 74-75
as a technique for inducing fear, 10, 18
as distinct from other crimes, 10
as law enforcement problem, 210
biological, 231, 236
chemical, 231, 236
comparison of terrorism from below and official state terrorism, 20
definitions of, 2-11
during war, 16
finances, in *The Financing of Terror,* 197
future of, 219-241
history of, 23-43
importance of, to revolution, 228
indiscriminate nature of, 14-15
in Guernica, Spain, 16
insurgent, 20
international, 2, 99, 138, 228-229, 241
international response to, 210-16
in the U.S., 36, 69-96
affect on society, 238-240
supported by government, 8
in Latin America, 71, 136-37
in Turkey, 76-80
in Uraguay, 2
in western Europe, 118-19
in Yugoslavia, 81-85
morality of, 5-8

Terrorism (*cont.*)
　nuclear, 231-36
　objectives of, 171-72
　problems of definition, 9, 11,
　　241
　purpose of, 18-19
　state-sponsored, 20, 227-228
　super, 231-38
　transnational, 2, 15
　typologies of, 11-16
　use of, for political goals, 20,
　　56-57
Terrorists:
　and advanced weapons tech-
　　nology, 42
　and mass media, 44-61
　and nuclear weapons, 197
　Armenian, 55-56, 76-80
　confrontation with U.S. gov-
　　ernment, 36
　Croatian, 81-85
　in Argentina, 135-36
　in Cuba, 85-88
　international, 192, 199, 203
　international guidelines for
　　handling, 211-15
　Iranian, 225-27
　Islamic, 223-27
　modern, compared to Narod-
　　naya Volya, 31
　national, 2
　organization of, 196
　Palestinian, 56-57, 132, 208-
　　209
　　attack on El Al ticket
　　　counter, 105
　　success of, 99, 103-4
　Puerto Rican, 72-76
　strategies of, 74, 114-15, 138,
　　195, 219, 231
　use of aliases, 93
　use of chemical substances,
　　236-37
　use of fear, 36

Thatcher, Margaret, 52-53
Thugs, 25
Thunder of Zion, 89
TNT, 146-147, 149, 152
Truman, Harry S., 73, 183, 189
Tupamaros, 2, 70, 214
Turner, Nat, 40
Tylenol, and product tampering, 49

U

UDBA, see Yugoslav Security Ser-
　vice
UFF, see Ulster Freedom Fighters
Ulster Defense Association (UDA),
　51, 65, 115
Ulster Freedom Fighters (UFF), 51,
　116
Ulster Volunteer Force (UVF), 51,
　110-11, 115-116
United Croats of West Germany,
　84
United Freedom Fighters, 240
United Freedom Front (UFF), 92-
　93
United Klans of America, 94
United Nations, 57, 80, 211-12
　and formation of Israel, 100
　and observer status of PLO,
　　104, 106
　and Palestine refugee camps,
　　102
United Racist Front, 29
United States:
　affect of terrorism in, 238-40
　and Northern Ireland, 111
　and nuclear weapons, 233-36
　and Puerto Rican terrorists,
　　72-76
　antiterrorist policy, 226-27
　antiterrorist specialists, 87
　arrestof KKK members, 28
　assassination in, 168-171, 178-
　　89

civil rights in, 72
conflict with Iran, 224-27
covert operations, 203-5
criminal justice system, 71
expedition of terrorists, 212
intelligence gathering in, 197
legislation concerning terrorists, 215-16
military response to terrorism,
  206-8, 210
response to terrorists, 199
retaliation against Libyan terrorists, 201-3
sponsorship of Cuban guerrillas, 85
terrorism in, 69-96
U.S. Congress:
  and day to remember Arme-
    nian dead, 55-56
  and law to bar foreign anarch-
    ists, 35
U.S. military, in Puerto Rico, 74
Uruguay, 2, 64-65, 214
Ustasa, 82-84, 166
UVF, see Ulster Volunteer Force

V

Vanzetti, Bartolomeo, 35
Vietnam War, and anti-war protests, 91
Violence:
  and labor history in U.S., 38-
    40
  and Native Americans, 37-38
  and serial killers, 41-42

and urban riots in U.S., 40-41
as justified by Revolutionary
  War, 37
between Catholics and Protestants in Northern Ireland,
  113-16
history of, in U.S., 37-43

W

Wallace, George, 186
War Measures Act, 2, 205
Warren Commission, 184
Washington, D.C., 157
Weathermen, see Weather Under-
  ground Organization
Weather Underground Organiza-
  tion (WUO), 70-72, 91-93
West Germany, 118-20, 209, 214
White Patriot Party, 94
White People's Supreme Party, 28-
  29
Wounded Knee, 38
WUO, see Weather Underground
  Organization

Y

Yippies, 71-72
Yugoslavia, 81-85
Yugoslav Security Service, 83-84

Z

Zangara, Guiseppe, 182-83
Zionism, 99-100, 102